'Olivier Masclet and his team of expert researchers have produced an exemplary account of those in the middle tier of the working class today: those who are not so poor and insecure as to be the subject of moral panic and political censure but not so affluent and privileged as to be on the edge of the middle class. They are getting by, struggling on, trying to be "like everyone else", with hopes, dreams, struggles, failures and fears for the future. Embedding rich, detailed case studies of individuals and couples within rigorous reviews of the changes sweeping France as much as any other Western social order, the team skilfully manage to unpick the effects of declining working class solidarity, precarisation and feminisation of employment, changing gender relations and the race for credentials on the everyday experiences, biographies, self-perceptions and self-evaluations of workers and families in the 21st century. This is a must-read for anyone interested in working-class life in contemporary Europe'.

Will Atkinson, *Professor of Sociology, University of Bristol, author of* The Class Structure of Capitalist Societies *and* Beyond Bourdieu

SUBALTERN WORKERS IN CONTEMPORARY FRANCE

This volume explores the lives and work of those who are kept out of poverty by their employment, but who occupy tenuous social positions and subaltern jobs.

Presenting a score of household portraits – urban, suburban, and rural – the authors examine what it means to 'get by' in France today, considering the material and symbolic resources that these households can muster, and the practices that give meaning to their lives. With attention to their aspirations and disappointments – and their desire to be 'like everyone else' in a supposedly egalitarian society that nonetheless gives them little credit for their effort – this book offers a sociological interpretation of their situations, offering new insights into what it means to be 'working class' in a 21st-century post-industrial society. Combining statistical analyses with ethnographically based examinations of how changes in the structure of the employment market relate to plans for upward mobility, *Subaltern Workers in Contemporary France* sheds light on the ways in which class identity – along with all its associated practices, tastes, and aspirations – has changed since the sociological classics on the working classes were published over half a century ago.

As such, this book will appeal to sociologists with interests in the sociology of the family, social class, and the sociology of work.

Olivier Masclet is a Professor of Sociology at the Université de Limoges and co-director of the GRESCO Research Centre, France.

Thomas Amossé is a researcher at the Conservatoire National des Arts et Métiers, Lise-CEET Research Centre, Paris, France.

Lise Bernard is a researcher at CNRS and a member of the Centre Maurice Halbwachs, Paris, France.

Marie Cartier is a Professor of Sociology at Nantes University, France.

Marie-Hélène Lechien is a Lecturer in the Department of Sociology at the Université de Limoges, France.

Olivier Schwartz is a Professor of Sociology at the Université Paris Cité, France.

Yasmine Siblot is a Professor of Sociology at the Université Paris 8, CRESPPA-CSU Research Centre, France.

Routledge Advances in Sociology

This series presents cutting-edge developments and debates within the field of sociology. It provides a broad range of case studies and the latest theoretical perspectives while covering a variety of topics, theories, and issues from around the world. It is not confined to any particular school of thought.

Debates Around Abortion in the Global North
Europe, North America, Russia and Asia
Fabienne Portier-Le Cocq

Class Boundaries in Europe
The Bourdieusian Approach in Perspective
Johs Hjellbrekke, Cédric Hugrée, Étienne Penissat, Alexis Spire

Covid-19 Responses of Local Communities around the World
Exploring Trust in the Context of Risk and Fear
Khun Eng Kuah, Gilles Guiheux, and Francis K.G. Lim

Space, Mobility, and Crisis in Mega-Event Organisation
Tokyo Olympics 2020's Atmospheric Irradiations
Rodanthi Tzanelli

Subaltern Workers in Contemporary France
To Be Like Everyone Else
Edited by Olivier Masclet, Thomas Amossé, Lise Bernard, Marie Cartier, Marie-Hélène Lechien, Olivier Schwartz and Yasmine Siblot

For more information about this series, please visit: https://www.routledge.com/Routledge-Advances-in-Sociology/book-series/SE0511

SUBALTERN WORKERS IN CONTEMPORARY FRANCE

To Be Like Everyone Else

Edited by
Olivier Masclet, Thomas Amossé, Lise Bernard, Marie Cartier, Marie-Hélène Lechien, Olivier Schwartz and Yasmine Siblot

Translated by Juliette R. Rogers

Routledge
Taylor & Francis Group
LONDON AND NEW YORK

Translated by Juliette R. Rogers
Designed cover image: Getty Images.

First published in English 2023
by Routledge
4 Park Square, Milton Park, Abingdon, Oxon OX14 4RN

and by Routledge
605 Third Avenue, New York, NY 10158

Routledge is an imprint of the Taylor & Francis Group, an informa business

Published in French by Raisons d'Agir 2020.

British Library Cataloguing-in-Publication Data
A catalogue record for this book is available from the British Library

Library of Congress Cataloging-in-Publication Data
Names: Masclet, Olivier, editor. | Amossé, Thomas, editor. | Bernard, Lise, editor. | Cartier, Marie, editor. | Lechien, Marie-Hélène, editor. | Schwartz, Olivier, 1951– editor. | Siblot, Yasmine, editor. | Rogers, Juliette (Translator), translator.
Title: Subaltern workers in contemporary France : to be like everyone else / edited by Olivier Masclet, Thomas Amossé, Lise Bernard, Marie Cartier, Marie-Hélène Lechien, Olivier Schwartz and Yasmine Siblot ; translated by Juliette R. Rogers. Other titles: Être comme tout le monde. English
Description: New York : Routledge, 2023. |
Series: Routledge advances in sociology | Includes bibliographical references and index. |
Identifiers: LCCN 2022037154 (print) | LCCN 2022037155 (ebook) | ISBN 9781032360560 (hardback) | ISBN 9781032360577 (paperback) | ISBN 9781003330073 (ebook)
Subjects: LCSH: Working class—France—History—21st century. | Working class—France—Economic conditions—21st century. | Employees—France—Social conditions—21st century. | Employees—France—Economic conditions—21st century.
Classification: LCC HD8431 .E7713 2023 (print) | LCC HD8431 (ebook) | DDC 331.0944—dc23/eng/20220823
LC record available at https://lccn.loc.gov/2022037154
LC ebook record available at https://lccn.loc.gov/2022037155

ISBN: 978-1-032-36056-0 (hbk)
ISBN: 978-1-032-36057-7 (pbk)
ISBN: 978-1-003-33007-3 (ebk)

DOI: 10.4324/9781003330073

Typeset in Bembo
by codeMantra

CONTENTS

FIGURES

TABLES

CONTRIBUTORS

Thomas Amossé, Conservatoire National des Arts et Métiers, France

Anne-Marie Arborio, Aix-Marseille Université, France

Angel Baraud, Université Paris 8 Vincennes-Saint-Denis, France

Lise Bernard, Centre National de la Recherche Scientifique (CNRS), France

Anya Bouamama, INSEE des Hauts de France, France

Marie Cartier, Nantes University, France

Clément Degout, Université Paris 8 Vincennes-Saint-Denis, France

Henri Eckert, Université de Poitiers, France

Violaine Girard, Université de Rouen, France

Marie-Hélène Lechien, Université de Limoges, France

Muriel Letrait, Université Paris Cité, France

Olivier Masclet, Université de Limoges, France

Gérard Mauger, Centre National de la Recherche Scientifique (CNRS), France

Séverine Misset, Nantes University, France

Marie-Pierre Pouly, Université de Limoges, France

Tristan Poullaouec, Nantes University, France

Jean-Noël Retière, Nantes University, France

Cyrille Rougier, Université de Limoges, France

Olivier Schwartz, Université Paris Cité, France

Yasmine Siblot, Université Paris 8 Vincennes-Saint-Denis, France

Matéo Sorin, Institut Supérieur de l'Electronique et du Numérique Yncréa Ouest France

Vanessa Stettinger, Université de Lille, France

Marjorie Tilleul, Université Paris Cité, France

Lucas Tranchant, Université Paris 8 Vincennes-Saint-Denis, France

Maulde Urbain-Mathis, Université Paris I Panthéon-Sorbonne, France

Antoine Younsi, Université Libre de Bruxelles, Belgium

1

INTRODUCTION

Subalterns in a 'society of the similar': A study of the lifestyles of the stable-modest fractions of the contemporary working classes

Olivier Masclet[1]

This book sets out to identify key elements of the everyday lives of the working classes in contemporary French society. At its heart is a collection of portraits of households of 'basic employees' and 'labourers' who aspire to at least get by, if not succeed, by successfully balancing the family budget without the need for social assistance.[2] These portraits retrace their paths to such stable social positions and explore how these women and men relate to each other on the domestic scene, to their own social group(s), and to other social groups. They describe the itineraries, ordinary practices, and choices – always personal, but never reducible to an individual – of the people we interviewed, who all bear signs of the lifestyles of workers with modest incomes.

These portraits attest to the continuity of a condition of subaltern employment – a large proportion of actively employed people are destined to such poorly paid and unrecognised jobs, without hope of improving their situation – and the persistence of similar ways of living, seeing others, and seeing themselves. However, any assessment of their circumstances must also take account of deep transformations that have affected French society, including the 'undoing' of the working class (Mauger 2006), and acknowledge the differences between the categories of people in executant positions. The working classes of today are not a homogeneous social class with well-demarcated boundaries. Instead, this book shows that they are scattered in a constellation of heterogeneous and ranked positions that may be sheltered from poverty or on its cusp, working in jobs approaching the more comfortable 'intermediary professions' (which includes technicians and nurses) or far below them.

The first aim is descriptive: providing an account of life outside of work and the social trajectories of a selection of what we term 'stable-modest' households.[3] We characterise this fraction of the working classes as follows: on the

DOI: 10.4324/9781003330073-1

one hand, their positions and living conditions are clearly lower than those of the middle classes and the better-off fractions of the working classes, such as police officers or administrative workers[4]; on the other hand, they are not in the most insecure and impoverished situations of the working classes, either. They are in a more delicate economic and social situation than higher fractions but at the same time distinguish themselves from the most insecure fractions by the fact that they 'more or less get by'.[5] Statistically, most basic employee and labourer households come under this middle fraction of the working classes, but they are overlooked by sociologists and journalists, who are more interested in poverty and downclassing from the middle class.

Our second aim is to study the constraints and aspirations of this middle fraction of the working classes. How are subaltern workers' daily lives configured today? What remains of the traditional working-class traits described in labourers of the past? What are their hopes and dreams? What does it mean to be at the bottom of the employment ladder in a society where the emphasis for over 50 years has been on moving labourers to the middle classes?

This book is the fruit of a four-year collective research programme that brought together sociologists from a variety of backgrounds to re-examine what it means to speak of 'the working class' today.[6] The label is mainly used to measure social, economic, and scholastic inequalities in access to cultural practices, consumption, health care, and so on. This statistical identification of economic and cultural gaps makes it possible to objectify the proximity of basic employees and labourers 'on paper', but it is inadequate for figuring out how they actually think, act, or do things, and thus their lifestyles.[7] But at the same time, there is a lack of recent empirical research describing the forms of culture particular to various social groups.[8] In fact, the sociology of social classes is falling to the wayside with the increasing specialisation of the discipline, which is less and less concerned with the configurations and relations of power and domination in which the studied individuals and processes are caught up.

Even if they are no longer as socially and politically visible as they were from the 1950s through the 1970s, basic employees and labourers are still quite present in French society: they represent about half the working population. While they still exist, at least on paper, the working classes no longer have the political clout or the sociological obviousness that 'blue collars' once had. The end of working-class prominence is related to several well-known processes. One is the transformation of work and the rise of what Robert Castel calls 'mass vulnerability' (2003b, 140). Subaltern workers are no longer predominantly industrial labourers and now include a great many female basic employees, often consigned to unskilled jobs, and many of them are subject to unemployment, insecurity, and poverty. These transformations have obviously contributed to the dismantling of the labouring world, in terms of its political clout and union participation.

Merely noting the crumbling of working-class havens – neighbourhoods, factories, unions, and so on – is only part of the work to describe the lifestyles of today's employees and labourers. The 1970s economic crisis is often interpreted as the moment of a great shift, when a once-cohesive working class bound by internal solidarity is said to have transformed into the 'undone' working classes, deprived of the support from work and activism that had made it possible to assert the existence of both an in-group ('Us') and the individuals composing it. From this perspective, the individuals ('Me') who express themselves today are described as fragile, isolated, and alienated.

This grand narrative is a reminder of the processes that politically and socially weakening subaltern workers. Fifty years ago, such basic employees and labourers would not have needed to occupy roundabouts or wear yellow vests to make themselves visible and testify to their difficult living conditions.[9] This narrative forgets that working-class environments were transformed well before the crisis.

We mustn't forget that the dawn of the 'wage-earning society' made subaltern workers 'similar' (Castel 2003a, b).[10] If it did not reduce the gaps between classes, it did make social positions comparable by allowing labourers and basic employees to aspire 'to be like everyone else', living according to the consumption, housing, health, educational, and other norms common to many social groups.[11]

The integration of labourers into the wage-earning society deeply reshaped the lifestyles of subaltern workers: by the 1950s–1970s, they had already begun to break with Richard Hoggart's classic model (1957), in which they were kept far from the dominant segments of society and found their own cultural forms as a way to protect themselves from this exclusion. Since then, working-class worlds have changed in three ways:

1 The realm of the common has expanded: The 1950s–1970s favoured or accelerated access to material comforts (housing, appliances, cars, etc.) and symbolic goods and services that used to be monopolised by middle and upper social categories – things like education, leisure pursuits, and health care.
2 The realm of judgement has expanded: Access to things that are now common inflicts a higher risk of stigmatisation of working-class social categories.
3 The realm of aspirations has expanded: The domination of labour culture is waning. The relationship between 'Us' and 'Me' is shifting in favour of 'Me', as seen in the assertion of lifestyles that are less defined by community (neighbourhood or working group) norms, the formulation of plans for upward mobility through education, and a growing desire for independence, among men and women alike (the younger generation of women rejecting the housewife model, for example).

For one thing, today's subaltern wage earners' social and economic foundations have been weakened by unemployment and the precarisation of employment.

This amplification of inequalities contrasts with the previous period, when such gaps narrowed. New occupational inequalities have appeared with the greater importance accorded to possessing formal educational attainments, which are now all but necessary for rising professionally or even keeping steady employment. At the same time, cultural boundaries are blurring. Education has made its way into the lowest categories of the social space, even if school has yet to be fully democratised, which is a point we will discuss later. Likewise, televisual and digital media are now quite present in the everyday life of the working classes, where they seem to be 'permanent guests' (Masclet 2018, Pasquier 2018). Among other things, they contribute to making the physical, grooming, and child-rearing norms of the middle and more highly educated social categories more common across social groups.

This means that over the past 40 years, the world of working-class social categories has been affected by processes leading them to venture farther from their enclaves and open themselves more to the outside world, while being much more vulnerable to unemployment and insecurity. They are consequently subjected to opposing forces, one pulling upward – the expansion of the realms of the common and aspirations – and the other pulling downward – heightened risks of economic marginalisation and negative social judgement.[12]

This book thus sets out to explore how these developments have caught men and women holding the lower positions on the employment ladder in a sort of pincer movement and to show how they handle it, alone or with a partner. What does it mean to be a basic employee or labourer in a society that marginalises them more than it used to, while being more inclusive in other ways? How can subaltern workers in contemporary French society assert their 'similarity'?

The 'working classes' still exist

According to the definition given by INSEE, the French national statistical agency, there were slightly over 5.3 million active workers in the 'labourer' category in 2016, which is 18% of all employed persons. In that year, there were about 7.2 million people in the category of 'basic employees', in sales, services, public services, and health care (including home-based health care, child care, cleaning workers, auxiliary nurses, service agents, cashiers, sales clerks, waiters, office workers, security guards), amounting to 28% of the labour force.

'At the bottom of the ladder': half of the labour force

Three common characteristics suggest that all these categories of basic employees should be bundled together with labourers (Schwartz 2011). The first common characteristic is how low their occupational status is: basic employees have little social recognition or autonomy at work. Eighty per cent have their working hours imposed by their employer (the case for only 20% of those working in *cadre* positions). They are moreover more likely to work nights or start very early in the morning: one-third of the working hours of labourers and unskilled employees fall before 9 in the morning or after 6 o'clock at night (as opposed to 20% of *cadre* working hours) (Brousse 2015). The second is how low their economic resources are. The incomes of basic employees and labourers are on average a third of those of *cadres*. Inequalities in net worth are even more striking: the top 10% of the wealthiest social categories accumulate 50% of gross net worth, while the lower 50% of social categories possess only 8% (Cazenave-Lacrouts et al. 2018). The third characteristic is how little cultural capital they possess. Basic employees and labourers still have significantly lower educational attainments than intermediary professions and *cadres*. Success in *collège* (early secondary school) is highly variable according to social background: while nearly eight out of ten students reach the point of being able to sit for the *baccalauréat* today, only one in ten has a parent who is a labourer.[13]

Furthermore, the nature of work is evolving in a way that moves basic employees closer to labourers. There is an evident trend in labouring jobs shifting toward the tertiary sector, as seen in the development of transportation and logistics jobs, and a portion of the jobs done by basic employees have industrialised: clerks in small shops have been replaced by jobs in self-service shops and large retail chains. Basic employees and labourers also have similar social backgrounds: half of the people in both groups have at least one parent who is a labourer (Amossé 2015).

This situation thus hardly represents a model of society where subaltern workers' continued existence is a legacy of industrial history.[14] Not only do they remain numerous, but also the increase in low-skill jobs in the tertiary sector has largely made up for the significant reduction of positions for unskilled industrial labourers since the 1970s.[15] Moreover, the majority of people who are not active in the labour force (due to retirement or other reasons) are former subaltern workers.

The land of the lost 'Blue Collars'

Although executant employees represent nearly half the labour force, 'blue collars' have vanished from collective perception. The crumbling of the ramparts of labour, mass layoffs of industrial labourers between 1975 and 1985, the automation of production, and the offshoring of manufacturing to countries where production is cheaper all contributed to the erasure of labourers in the public space.

Labourers are very scattered today, most of them working for small construction companies or food manufacturers, for tradesmen, or alone as lorry or cab drivers. Home care service providers, childminders, and housekeepers work for private individuals. These men and women are even less publicly visible because they go to work earlier and later than middle- and upper-class workers, and a greater proportion of them live in towns and smaller cities, urban peripheries, and rural areas. Although labourers had less free time than higher categories in the 1950s–1970s, today they have the most free time of all active members of the labour force: on average, *cadres* work seven hours a week more than labourers (Chenu and Herpin 2002). These changes lead many executant workers to close in on the domestic scene, which is another factor hiding them from view.

Although the French Communist Party and the left-leaning CGT labour union managed to give body and voice to industrial labourers, not to mention a large share of other subaltern workers, they began to crumble in the 1980s. In addition to the disqualification of 'real socialism' and the hopes associated with it, mass unemployment and management harassment of union delegates dissuaded engagement. Additionally, new ways of organising work based on individualising bonuses and careers favoured the dispersal of collective labour groups.

The result of all this is the deterioration of the 'labour centrality' (Vigna 2012, 181) that peaked in the 1950s–1970s. The working class was a dominated group at the time, supported by intellectuals and artists, but a point of great concern among the dominant classes. Collective resistance in major factories was organised around the figure of the delegate and line workers managed to make their antipathy felt through daily transgressions. Layoffs proliferated in the 1980s onward, and the management of shop floors changed, with more flexible hiring practices and the introduction of new working relations, thus weakening everyday practices of resistance (Beaud and Pialoux 2012). Labour issues – wages, working conditions, the future of the class, the labour movement's hope of offering an alternative to capitalism – faded, even in organisations that had previously been defined by their rootedness in the labouring world (Mischi 2014, Béroud et al. 2016). Today, labourers with a job are the lucky ones, compared to those who are deprived of work. Poverty is the latest emergency for experts and political administrations, not to mention the leadership of the Socialist Party, which relegated income and working condition issues to the background (Pialoux and Weber 2002, Lefebvre and Sawicki 2006).

A major transformation of working-class lifestyles

One must keep in mind the working-class condition as it was before the *Trente Glorieuses*, the 30 years of prosperity that followed World War II: dependency on wages, material mediocrity, harsh working conditions, exclusion from secondary school, difficulties in getting vocational training, and marginalisation from legitimate culture. From the 1920s to the 1950s, the labourer's condition developed into a 'labour lifestyle' in which neighbourhood sociability played a major role in the community's self-image and a 'specific labour experience' characterised by feelings of exploitation and exclusion from the dominant cultural forms (Dewerpe 1989, 137–167). According to Hoggart, the boundary between 'Us' (the labourers) and 'Them' (the well-off) appeared unbreachable at the time, so deeply was it ingrained in body and spirit. The labouring class was uncontestably central until the late 1950s and was not an intellectual construction. The labouring class was an everyday, living reality, visible through its particular cultural traces, which were markers of independence from domination (Noiriel 2012). At the same time, and more hidden from view, other entirely necessary but rarely mentioned processes were underway; while the labouring class represented a numerically significant and symbolically charged group, it nonetheless moved ever closer to other social groups.

The analysis of Robert Castel (2003b) is based on a longer timeframe than that of labour historians; he asserts that employment transformations in the 1930s through the 1970s are responsible for labour losing its sociological centrality and becoming more integrated into society at large. In so doing, he highlights some developments that are central to this book's objective – trying to understand what it means to 'belong to the working classes' in a society where they have long been caught up in processes opening them to other social groups – that deserve a deeper look.

For one thing, transformations in work and pay and the rise of women in the labour force deprived labourers of their character as a group apart. They increasingly resemble basic employees; their work is no longer exclusively in production. This process of task diversification began in the 1930s but accelerated after World War II. The jobs of labourers came to include more tasks like shipping, handling, delivery, and guarding. Labourers became more numerous in the tertiary sector and the boundary with basic employees grew fuzzier, since their work was also transformed with the mechanisation and standardisation of office tasks. Once 'the boss's colleague', the 'white collar' morphed into a subaltern worker facing challenges similar to those of industrial workers: drudgery, employment insecurity, and low income (Chenu 2005). This process melding low-ranking workers was confirmed when monthly pay became generalised in the 1970s, extending the advantages of basic employees (who enjoyed a monthly pay schedule) to labourers, including vacation time, sick pay, and retirement. Lastly, many subaltern workers are women. Apart from a period from the early 1950s to 1968 when many women stayed in the home (Maruani and Méron 2012), the number of women on the job market has risen steadily (even as early as 1954, half of all basic employees were women). The great frequency of marriages between basic employees and labourers could only bring the categories closer.

For another thing, the number of people working for an employer (as opposed to being a business owner or self-employed) grew considerably. Such employees represented less than half of the labour force (49%) in 1931 and consisted primarily of labourers (both men and women); by 1975, it was nearly 83%. In 40 years, basic employees caught up with labourers in this group, but not as much as the middle and upper classes, who joined the ranks of employees at a rate even faster than subaltern workers. The latter would henceforth be the base of the employee pyramid: they are in the lowest positions on the increasingly differentiated scale of employees.

Despite their dominated position, these subaltern workers are still part of what Castel termed the 'wage-earning society' (2003b, 304–305). They enjoy the same benefits as other wage-earning employees (paid by the hour or on salary), the first benefits created with the first legislated social programmes and new ones added with the creation of the French Social Security programme in 1945. As the same rights were extended to all persons working for an employer and became consolidated, the resultant wage-earning society came to form a common social safety net that made the 'society of the similar' possible (Castel 2003b, 34). Castel's society of the similar coalesced around the economic growth of the 1950s–1970s (when the GDP grew an average of 5–6% annually), sharp wage increases related to increased productivity, and the continual rise in the living conditions of all social categories. Trends that deproletarianised labour likewise contributed (Castel 2003b, 316–324): a decline in poverty, improvement of housing conditions, access to secondary education for the children of labourers and basic employees, an increase in vacation travel, and the expansion of consumption.

A 'society of the similar', yes, but not one of equals. Society did not become uniform from the extension of identical social rights to all employees, the constant improvement of living conditions, and the circulation of goods and services spurred by the growth of the 1950s–1970s, and the situation of basic employees and labourers remains characterised by strong inequalities. But if the 'wage-earning society' did not make living conditions equal, it did make them comparable: being part of a continuum of positions makes inequalities both more visible (people are more conscious of them[16]) and less acceptable. They are all seen as unfair. In this configuration, the members of each social category think of themselves relative to the category below them, to take their distance, and the category above, to which they aspire to move closer. One consequence of the comparability of positions is that union and political party demands intensified under the relatively prosperous economic conditions of the 1950s–1970s, as the fight for a better position and higher rank spread to subaltern workers. Castel discerns a new form of social conflict specific to the wage-earning society – competition among the ranks of employees – that replaced the confrontation of two antagonistic blocs: labourers versus the bourgeois or work versus capital.

Has the labouring class really lost?

Dissolution of the revolutionary alternative and redistribution of social conflict according to a model other than that of a class society (the 'wage-earning society'): these are the reasons Robert Castel gives for why 'the labouring class lost' (2009).

This theory has raised several objections. For Mauger (2012), the loss was primarily over ideas: changing schemes of perception in the intellectual field, with the decline of Marxism and the development of an individualist view of the social world, meant the denial of social class. Transformations in the political field also factor in: the ebb of union struggles and labour politics and the near elimination of political party representation by the French Communist Party explain the current political invisibility of the working classes. Mauger also questions the purportedly appealing role reserved for *cadres* and the middle class in general. While he acknowledges that 'the deepening division of labour and specialisation has added complexity to the bi-polar antagonism between owner-bosses and proletarians overseen by a few foremen', he does not think that these developments have led to the disappearance of 'the primary relationship of domination' between the dominant and dominated classes that finds itself 'diffracted' in a 'myriad of secondary relationships of domination' (95).

The authors of *En Quête des classes populaires* (Béroud et al. 2016) also refuse to see all as lost. Like Mauger, they stress that although the morphology of the labour force has changed, the wage ratio is still characterised by a deeply inegalitarian structure. They call for the definition of the contemporary working classes' potential for rebellion and challenging the capitalist social order and for the political rearmament of the notion of the working classes, whose descriptive finality, the authors say, would be 'to erase the major political connotation of the expression "labouring class"' (24). The authors are in line with Castel, however, in highlighting the importance of the wage-earning society insofar as the integration of dominated groups in the first two decades after World War II is concerned:

> The wage-earning society does not produce egalitarianism, but it does make a degree of social integration previously unknown in France possible [...] A new dynamic of social struggles is established. The theme of equality between categories of employees and citizens henceforth occupies a central position, which had been impossible so long as social inequalities were primarily related to the opposition between owner and employee.
>
> (64)

Working to be 'similar'

These processes do not involve the erasure of specific lifestyles – labourers' habituses – but they do have significant cultural repercussions. Over the first two decades after World War II, they contributed to expanding the horizons of the working classes, making them more porous to middle-class lifestyles and awakening aspirations to live by standards other than those of the classic working classes (Schwartz 1998). The wage-earning society appealed to the subordinate categories of the labour force by feeding their desire 'to be like everyone else', not necessarily like the bourgeois but enough like others to escape the stigmatisation of the lower classes.

This 'conquest of norms' (Verret 1979, 30) in terms of housing, consumption, and attitude toward their children's future has not led to undifferentiated conditions. In the wage-earning society, every advance by the dominated social categories is followed by a new gap created by the categories just above them – that is, when they hadn't already moved on in anticipation (Bourdieu 1984).[17] However, the cultural alterity of subaltern groups no longer seems to be 'a static reality or like they are trapped in separation, but [*more*] like a dissimilarity' (Schwartz 1998, 89). The period beginning in the 1950s changed the condition of labourers and their lifestyle: cultural alterity no longer ruled out processes of assimilation.

As attempts to catch up became widespread, they largely replaced the renunciation of higher ambitions, the 'choice of the necessary', and the 'principle of conformity' (Bourdieu 1984, 372, 280). The comparability of positions led the working classes to partly or entirely reshape how they do things and how they situate themselves in relation to other social groups. They set out to make themselves 'similar', both as a response to the threat of the stigmatisation of working-class traits and to free themselves from traditional working-class culture. Basic employees and labourers are also transformed by participation in ever-broader segments of the dominant culture (school, leisure, consumption, health care, etc.), but since these developments do not close the gaps between social classes, they do not lead to the 'middling' of French society, either. They do, however, come with effects on the practices and representations of the working classes, who are engaged in a process of acculturation to middle-class norms, values, and lifestyles. The cultural alterity of the working classes has become 'flexible and relative' (Schwartz 1998, 72–73). Three clusters of transformation highlight the reality of this acculturation process that the labouring world was going through during the post-war economic boom.

A three-part transformation

In traditional labour milieus, labourers have a specific relationship to work: simultaneously esteemed and hated, it gave rise to intense investment. Miners in the north of France were pressed into forms of sacrifice by 'necessity' (the requirement that they produce a given amount to earn their full wage, the pressure of foremen, the absolute necessity of keeping their job) and by belief in the values of virility (pride, honour). Miners internalised the 'model of exertion' (Schwartz 1990, 288–307). Their feeling of personal legitimacy depended on physical exertion in and out of work, which explains the importance of 'work on the side' (gardening, tinkering, working under the table) (Weber 1989), a preference for the outdoors, and engagement in antagonistic behaviours (fighting, interpersonal disputes, fights at work) allowing them to expend energy and earn the recognition of other men.[18]

This traditional labourer model of virility and honour did not disappear in the following years, but it is no longer dominant. Labourers in northern France born after World War II enjoyed access to mass consumption, modern comforts, and (in some cases) property ownership, and have followed another model that is more hedonistic and focused on the family space.

> With entry into the world of goods, the lightening of certain frustrations, and the possibility of imagining a future (especially for the children), the entire family system ended up being reconfigured around this new space that authorised novel experiences of appropriation and previously unrecognised forms of gratification and investment. A social 'opening' gradually appeared on the path to building up the family. Constructing a private sphere far from the factory, in a 'cosseted' apartment or in an entry-level housing development, is to tear oneself away from the terraced miners houses, the neighbourhood, the mine; it is to sneak away from places that carried a high degree of a certain form of proletarian markedness and enclosure.
>
> *(Schwartz 1990, 308)*

Men of this new generation invested in this family sphere by heightening the importance they accorded to leisure activities, the interest they showed in their children's education, and the attention they paid to interior decoration and vacation plans.[19] These investments changed the relationship between the personal and work-related poles: they are now also fathers, husbands, and school parents.

The second cluster of transformations relates to the radical challenge to women's biographical destinies. In the late 1960s, in labouring circles, the most likely fate for women was to stop school early, marry young, and give birth to many children (Schwartz 1990, 203–223). In 1982, half of such women were not in the labour force and were married to labourers (Bernard and Giraud 2018). But greater numbers of younger women began to pursue school longer and join the labour force for the long term. The paid employment of women took off in 1968 (Maruani and Méron 2012). As a result, the division of roles between spouses is less clear-cut than in previous periods: women rely less on husbands and new aspirations for personal independence emerge (Campagnac and Tabary-Taveau 1979).

Lastly, the third cluster of transformations concerns how labouring families relate to education. With the school system reforms between 1959 and 1975 that created a single *collège* (early secondary) system for all children, school came to be seen as a way to obtain higher qualifications and reach the new middling ranks of employees (Terrail 1984). Economic growth and public policies favoured new job growth in the tertiary sector. The daughters of labourers, who used to spend the least time in school, caught up to the boys. This growing demand for education had several consequences. Starting in 1964, the fertility rate of labouring women began to drop. 'What changed in the 1960s–1970s is the significant increase of the proportion of households in the labouring class adopting the fewer children/greater success in school model' (Terrail 1984, 430). Control over the future presupposed 'conferring it with a meaning more related to the self than to the vagaries of existence', meaning a relationship very different from the traditional labour experience that, 'far from inciting the self-affirmation of the individual subject, teaches, to the contrary, that it only has value if it is part of a collective' (432). This new belief in the possibility of an individual destiny is rooted in several structural transformations, the development of social welfare, the greater openness of the institution of education, and fewer economic limitations, with the increase in wages chief among them. These are all transformations of the living conditions and modes of reproduction of labour as a group that has broadened labouring families' temporal horizons and shaped new aspirations, unburdened by the group culture. Labouring parents born in the period when schooling opened up in the 1950s–1970s stress the 'child's will', the only thing that they think should decide career choice for the future (Poullaouec 2004). As with the parents of other social groups, 'free choice' should prevail.[20]

An expansion of lived experience

Without a doubt, the attention (rightly) given to the heavy subjugation to which subaltern workers were still subjected during the period of great growth of the 1950s–1970s led to an underestimation of the effects of the period's changes on their lifestyles and aspirations. And yet their impact proved to be decisive: the working classes saw their traditional characteristics – testaments to the cultural alterity inherited from industrial society that doomed them to an insurmountable subordinate position – fade as a result of changes in their living conditions, their perception of their children's future, gender relations in the marriage, and so on. These changes are not without effect on the lived experience of basic employees and labourers, who find themselves reshaped by the consequences of three realms of expansion.

The first is the expansion of the realm of the common. As we saw earlier, the 1950s–1970s favoured access to goods (housing, appliances, cars, etc.) and services (such as school, leisure activities, health care) that had largely been monopolised by the middle and upper classes. For instance, while more than half of labouring households lived in insalubrious housing in 1955, by 1975, 97% of them had normal lodgings. At the same time, the proportion of spending on furniture and bedding, household appliances, linens, hardware, and housewares became very close across social categories (Enquête INSEE, 1972, in Verret 1979, 28):

> By reducing the gap of its housing conditions to those of the average, the labouring class also leaves the situation of relegation and exclusion. It takes spatial contact not only with the closest classes or elements close to other classes (small businesses and trades, always present in all working-class neighbourhoods), but with the middle strata (technicians, lower and middle *cadres*), previously drawn to bourgeois housing.
>
> *(Verret 1979, 134)*

Secondly, the realm of judgement expanded. The influx of more socially diverse students into secondary education up through *lycée* (later secondary school), the widespread proliferation of consumer goods, and the superior comfort of housing made possible by the construction of housing estates impose a higher risk of stigmatisation on the lower categories of the pay scale. Now children have a duty to succeed in a school system that claims to be the same for everyone. The threshold over which working-class families run the risk of being downclassed or judged unfavourably is even higher when the boundaries between categories of schoolchildren are institutionally removed. Likewise, greater access to consumer goods meant they actually had to be consumed, and in the right way, raising the spectre of symbolic and economic sanctions in situations of 'bad' or non-consumption. Many observations from the 1950s through the 1970s make sense in light of this threat, since the lower-earning categories were far from being able to provide themselves with the economic and cultural resources to guarantee an irreproachable relationship to consumption. The importance accorded to consumption and the frequent recourse to credit to satisfy desires attest as much to the new needs engendered by mass production/consumption as to labouring families' hopes of joining the norm and being considered 'normal'. The acquisition of goods becomes the new standard for measuring respectability, but there was also the risk of its opposite – the indignity of not being able to assert oneself as a full-fledged member of modern society (Bourdieu 1966, 120).

Likewise, occupation of the new housing estate flats called not only for filling them with modern comforts (television, refrigerator, a living room set, and so on) but also for living in them according to middle-class cultural standards (Flamand 1989, Magri 1991). Being re-housed in these new estate neighbourhoods exposed labouring families to the denigration of their life and behavioural styles and created deep divisions according to their ability to live up to the demands of their new housing. While skilled categories tried to conform to the lifestyle of the middle-class households around them, the unskilled and less secure fractions were designated as 'deviant' 'incapable' families 'to be excluded or re-educated' (Pialoux and Théret 2019). The old solidarity that had bound them together in traditional labouring neighbourhoods unravelled (Coing 1966, Chamboredon and Lemaire 1970). By reducing the freedom that people in working-class categories once had to protect themselves from domination – building a bubble around a locally and family-based cultural world, constant reminders to conform to the group, the culture of necessity – the processes of cultural desegregation made them much more vulnerable to judgement by the dominant. Large immigrant families from North Africa and the most economically and culturally impoverished French-born labouring families are considered 'welfare cases' (Pialoux and Theret 2019).

Thirdly, the realm of individual aspirations expanded. The shift toward the 'Me' in the 'Us'/'Me' balance was a transformation arising from a variety of causes that add up to a system. Labourers' access to consumerism at least temporarily put an end to forced asceticism and created the possibility of asserting personal taste in the acquisition of consumer goods, standardised though they might be. If rehousing people in new estate developments undid the solidarity that had grown out of common material living and working conditions, it also opened the field of experience: the social diversity of neighbours prompted working-class households to adopt new lifestyles that were no longer defined by the community norm that prevailed in the old labour neighbourhoods (Coing 1966, Young and Willmott 2011). Likewise, the extension of early secondary schooling (*collège*) to all made it possible to plan for a future not limited to their present situation (Terrail 1990); it became possible for individuals to break away.

Working-class aspirations are not limited to the will to deepen the divide between the individual and their background conditions and group culture. In the time around May–June 1968, characterised by intense union and political activity, basic employees and labourers challenged traditional authority roles: young basic employees and labourers opposed power-drunk supervisors as students opposed all-powerful professors (Terrail 1990, Pudal and Retière 2008). Although the social and cultural distance between young people remained, they all questioned familial and sexual norms (Mauger and Fossé 1977). Likewise, although the feminist view, spread by the ferment of May–June 1968, did not radically affect gender relations in the family, it did nurture the right to defend dignity at work among working-class women (Zancarini-Fournel 2008, Gallot and Meuret-Campfort 2015).

Where are we now?

What forms do the realms of the common, judgement, and aspiration take in working-class worlds today? The current period has its own specificities. While basic employees and labourers seem more vulnerable to the accumulated risks of unemployment, more recent transformations nonetheless favour their inclusion in a 'society of the similar'.

A more subordinate position

There is one major thing that must be kept in mind about work and employment: basic employees and labourers' subordinate position in the employment structure has grown increasingly marked over the last 30 years. In 1982, 59% of the labour force consisted of labourers and basic employees. In 2016, they added up to only 46%. The growth in the number of basic employees over the past 30 years (+32% from 1982 to 2012) has certainly made up for the decline of industrial jobs, but it was slower than that of intermediate categories (+60%) and cadres (+159%), which together represent 44% of the labour force today. Improvements in productivity, the closing of the last major factories, offshoring, and the reduction in the number of workers in the public service as well as in the sales and services sector due to digital technologies will certainly further reduce the number of basic employees and labourers.

Moreover, among subaltern employees, the skilled categories are in decline while the lower categories are growing. The percentage of skilled labourers in the labour force dropped by a quarter between 2000 and 2012. Likewise, 'business administrative employees', which used to be the leading category of skilled workers among basic employees, has declined in the same proportion since 2002 (Chenu 2005). The ranks of cleaning workers, security guards, home care service providers, childminders, deliverers, warehouse workers, and the like are burgeoning – jobs that are classified as 'unskilled', hard to move offshore, at the bottom of the income and working conditions hierarchy, disproportionately held by immigrant workers. The polarisation of qualifications – a situation where the highest and lowest employment categories are growing apace – is getting stronger and is especially marked in France, where the lowest-level jobs are characterised by low wages and high part-time employment when full-time is desired (Peugny 2018).

Growth in economic inequalities is another trait of the contemporary period. Of course, the wage-earning society of the *Trente Glorieuses* was not egalitarian, nor did it fully integrate everyone, but it did set out to limit inequalities and did so successfully to a point. When this model was challenged, these inequalities took an upward turn, especially in employment, which lost its status of 'great integrator'. Unemployment returned as a major reality: today, it concerns 3 million jobseekers, or nearly 5 million counting the unemployed who declared they have stopped looking for work. This level has held for over 30 years now and concerned 10–12% of the labour force. According to INSEE, in 2016, 3.5% of *cadres* and 5% of people in intermediary professions were unemployed, but so were 11% of basic employees and 15% of labourers. In addition to unemployment, employment contracts are increasingly for less secure forms of work:

limited-term (CDD), temporary, part-time, and assisted jobs. Open-ended employment contracts are still the most common, but the precarisation of employment statuses seems irreversible. Most new hires are contracted as insecure positions, most of which go to young workers, but many to labourers and basic employees as well. These categories are more likely to work part-time and be under-employed.

The lower strata of employees are not the only ones hit by these inequalities – the middle is hurt, too. The 'destabilisation of the stable' (Castel 2003b, 387) designates precisely this return to the 'mass vulnerability' that had been curbed by the wage-earning society. Today,

> a segment of the integrated working class and the wage earners of the lower middle classes threatens to collapse. Whereas the consolidation of the wage-earning society continuously enlarged the employment base of secure jobs and eased the pathways to social mobility, the inverse movement now prevails.
>
> *(Castel 2003b, 287)*

Professional qualifications and the assurances of public-sector employment are protective resources allowing working-class social categories to manage the risk of precarity, but they are less accessible than they used to be because they now require higher levels of educational qualifications.[21] The 'qualification norm' has risen across occupational sectors (except in construction), even in low-skill Grade-C civil service jobs, which currently attract overqualified young people fearful of the insecurity of employment in the private sector (Kopel 2005).[22] While basic employees and labourers under age 30 are more likely to have a vocational *baccalauréat*, the vast majority of those over 50 only have a now-devalued CAP (a secondary-level vocational degree). These workers were qualified and steadily employed in the previous employment market but are vulnerable today because the retirement age is being pushed later and later.

A new expansion of the 'common'

More vulnerable today than during the period of great growth, the subaltern categories of the labour force are also affected by other processes that open them even further to the world around them. The rising level of basic employee and labourers' formal educational attainments is one indicator of the extension of the realm of the common since the 1980s.

While 90% of the labour force had no formal educational qualifications or at best a primary school diploma (CEP) in 1955, by 1982, this was so for only 43% of the labour force, and 21% of them had a *baccalauréat*. In 2014, the 'educational pyramid' was inversed: 16% of the labour force had no formal educational attainments or only the CEP and 54% had the *baccalauréat* or higher. People without qualifications and those only possessing a CEP became a minority among labourers (35%) and even fewer among basic employees. The most common qualifications among labourers are still the secondary-level vocational CAP and BEP, but higher-level vocational *baccalauréats* are on the rise. In 2014, 43% of skilled industrial labourers and 42% of skilled labourers in warehousing, handling, and transportation under the age of 40 had a *baccalauréat*. Among basic employees the rising level of formal qualifications is even more striking: only 27% of personal service providers have a *baccalauréat*, in contrast to business administrative employees, 29% of whom did not get as far as a *baccalauréat* but a strong proportion of whom have post-secondary qualifications, most often a (vocational) BTS (41%) (Poullaouec 2010). Their academic resources place them in the upper fraction of executant workers, if not in the middle classes.

Despite such progress, 'educational democratisation' is still socially segregating (Merle 2012). The educational qualifications that are accessible to most children of basic employees and labourers only rarely give them access to dominant positions. At the end of *collège*, they are often guided to vocational tracks for the remainder of their secondary education (Palheta 2012), and many young people from housing estates who enrol in university are doomed to failure by the gap between their academic resources and the implicitly required knowledge and skills (Beaud 2003).

However, the persistence of strong academic inequalities does not prevent many young people from finishing their studies with a *baccalauréat*-level degree that they can put to use on the employment market. Schooling has indeed filtered into the lives of young people and families of the working classes, a tangible reality that expands their educational and professional resources and lessens the weight of social reproduction.[23] Attesting to this is the fact that the majority of labouring families aspire to post-secondary studies for their children (Poullaouec 2010).[24] Another sign is the boom in continuing education offerings and employees' interest in pursuing them – employees' continuing education participation rate doubled between 1974 and 2004, and a strong majority of labourers and basic employees say that they want further training in the next five years.[25] This is due as much to a desire to resume studies that had been cut short prematurely as a need to conform to the qualification norms of a society in which qualifications have become commonplace but still offer assurances of access to employment and even higher qualifications (Millet and Moreau 2011). Although there are still inequalities in education, examination of the gaps between social groups over the long term reveals that they are no longer of the same magnitude.

This observation also applies to other social fields, such as housing and health care. As a result of programmes supporting property ownership that began to develop in the late 1970s, more basic employees and labourers are homeowners today than in the late 1960s: in 2012, 52% of basic employees and 48% of labourers were homeowners or buyers, as opposed to 22% and 24% in

1967 (Durif 1969). Likewise, although there are still significant disparities in health care (especially in access to specialists and preventative care), all social groups – including the working classes – show increased use of health institutions and doctors (Jusot 2013). This development might explain the increase in life expectancy since 1980, which has benefitted women and men of all social categories, although gaps between them persisted over the whole period (Blanpain 2011). Labourers and basic employees can no longer be described as being generally out of step with health care, dietary, and personal hygiene norms. On the contrary, these norms promulgated by doctors and passed along by middle and upper social categories have filtered into humbler milieu, especially the more secure and those who have stopped seeing food as a way to compensate for the challenges of everyday life. In stable-modest working-class families, food is more associated with health and dietary norms as they are taught in magazines, television programmes, and interactions with health professionals (Régnier and Masullo 2009, Le Pape and Plessz 2017, Arborio and Lechien 2019).

The study of household budgets also demonstrates the opening of working-class worlds. Household spending among basic employees and labourers is less marked by meeting primary needs than it was in the 1960s. They generally spend most of their incomes on food, housing, and transportation, since petrol and automotive expenses put a particular strain on working-class households. Such necessary expenses do not prevent them from saving or spending on pleasure, however. One recent study concluded that, 'when they have the means, working-class households aim to not only have the same goods, but also enjoy the same services, especially in vacation and leisure, as the middle and upper classes' (Amossé and Cartier 2019).

Portraits of 'ordinary' households

This book is about women and men, basic employees, and labourers, who aspire to 'be like everyone else': steadily employed, making a living off their work, and managing to escape the risk of poverty, or at least not succumb to it. The portraits in this book depict a working-class France that is often described as tangential, far from major cities and their influence. But these workers represent a populous social group that interacts with members of the middle and upper classes more than it ever has since the transition from a production economy to a service-based economy, because these higher classes are consumers of services ensured by basic employees or labourers while also offering their professional services (in education, health care, and the like) to the working classes. The portraits depict many familiar figures: childminder, supermarket cashier, cleaning woman, foster-care provider, lorry driver, tradesman, hairdresser, auxiliary nurse, industrial labourer, shop clerk, civil servant, security guard, administrative worker, postal worker, and metre reader. Their standard of living places most of them above the poverty line, but below the median[26] – higher than insecure populations, but below the categories of basic employees that are closer to being to intermediary professions, such as police officers or secretaries with the *baccalauréat* or higher. We refer to them here as 'stable-modest' working-class households, or the middle fractions of the working classes.[27] This book consists of 21 portraits of labourer and basic employee households that reveal 'ordinary' lives: many own their own homes, regularly practice sport in a club, value time for themselves taken from family time, think extracurricular activities are important, have a taste for interior decoration, are attentive to personal appearances, and make carefully considered choices as consumers that leave room for pleasure. A quick visit to some of these households provides a sampling of these contemporary lifestyle traits.[28]

Cécilia and Éric Dufar, a married couple of 41 and 42 years old, have a ten-year-old daughter. They live in the centre of a small city in the region of Nouvelle Aquitaine. He possesses a CAP and works full-time as caretaker of a library, a local-level grade-C civil service job. She has a BEP in secretarial work that she earned later in life and works as a part-time supermarket cashier on an open-ended employment contract. The household's monthly income is around 2,500 euros (for an estimated living standard of 1,413 euros). They have use of an apartment that comes with Eric's job, which explains how their consumption margin is higher than that of other low-skill basic employees. They have two cars, including a sedan that was practically new when they bought it. They take a two-week vacation at the seaside every year at a rental property found online. Cécilia and Éric also manage to go away for the weekend and eat out from time to time. Part of their budget is spent on clothing; being well dressed is very important to Cécilia, for herself and her daughter but also for her husband, who she encourages to look after his image. She goes to the hair salon monthly and buys several fashion and gossip magazines every week. Eric also looks after himself by regularly practicing sports (running, lifting weights, basketball) and seeing an osteopath several times a year. He also volunteers to train his basketball club's women's team every Wednesday.

Jean and Manou Audouin are 55 and 41, have a 14-year-old daughter, and live in a house they own in a town in the department of Deux-Sèvres. The household income is 2,500 euros, with an estimated living standard of 1,172 euros. He delivers trucks for a living and regularly teaches training sessions on the side. She is a foster-care provider employed by the administrative department. She earned a *baccalauréat* in the tertiary sector in Martinique, where she is from, and then tried studying English at university for a year. Jean cut his studies short in *collège* (around age 14) and then obtained professional qualifications by earning a CAP and other certifications in transportation. Although he is not particularly interested in politics, Jean was a municipal counsellor for a time and, a regular swimmer, is on the swim club board. Manou was a long-time volunteer at the town social centre and is now involved in the school parents' association.

Cécile and Jean-Marc Pilier are both 30: she is a hairdresser and he is a security guard. They have a three-year-old son. Their household income is 2,700 euros (estimated living standard of 1,425 euros). Originally from the region of Haute-Normandie, they recently bought an old house in a suburban town near her parents and are in the process of renovating it in their spare time, with the help of her father and DIY advice on the Internet. Cécile's mother babysits their son, and such parental help allows them to keep expenses down and save up for improving the house. The couple regularly goes out to eat on Saturday nights; Cécile likes having evenings free of domestic and parental labour and says she enjoys being served. Jean-Marc plays badminton regularly.

Régine and Hervé Leblanc are both 46. Both of their daughters are adults, and although they no longer live in their natal home, their parents still have financial responsibility for them. Both are working on earning BTS degrees, one in greater Paris and the other in a regional capital in western France, close to the parents. They own a house in a residential town dominated by the middle classes. Their income is around 3,000 euros (including bonuses and pay for a 13th month), bringing their estimated living standard to 1,500 euros. Régine works full-time as a childminder, and Hervé drives busses for the public transportation company, which they say pays well (he earns 1,600 euros/month). They each practice sports in clubs: he is a competitive boules player, and she does archery, also competitively. She recently took a trip to Rome with her daughter, and he bought a Peugeot convertible on credit. They are careful about their budget, however – Régine keeps a close eye on the household's finances and devotes time to seeking out good deals online and posting advice on prudent, moderate, and environmentally aware consumption practices on a website.

Myriam and Nicolino Sanatanazefi are 36 and 39 and have two children, aged seven and ten. Nicolino has a CAP and a BEP and works full-time as a lorry driver, earning about 1,500 euros/month. Myriam left school without any qualifications, but earned a CAP as an adult and currently works part-time as a cleaning woman. She earns 300 euros a month. The household's estimated living standard is 872 euros, making home ownership impossible. The family lives in a public housing estate in a mid-sized town in the Nouvelle-Aquitaine region. Television fills a significant share of the household's free time. Myriam is active in an association organising fêtes at her children's school, which is located in a neighbourhood where the tone is set by middle and upper classes, and in the football club, which she helps with fundraising. She also does Zumba and Latin-American dances like salsa and bachata twice a week. Their children are also active in club activities: the eldest swims in a free municipal programme and dances in an association, and the youngest plays football on Wednesdays and Saturdays.

By all appearances, this relatively socially stable slice of the French working classes seems close to the middle classes. However, for several reasons that will be developed in the portraits and further discussed in the conclusion, we do not refer to them with the commonly used terms 'lower middle classes' or 'impoverished middle classes'.

The first two reasons are evident. The first is material living conditions. Although the corpus includes households of diverse social characteristics, these men and women are generally not in the same position as intermediary professions and *cadres* who are public employees, usually put together into 'the middle classes': interviewees' incomes are below the median and their formal educational qualifications are lower than the general *baccalauréat*. They do not enjoy the same job security, either. They have known periods of unemployment and poverty, and some may well experience them again. Lastly, their work is not only poorly paid with little social recognition but also lacks opportunities to grow. This indeed makes them subaltern workers.

In addition, the households we studied are far from reproducing the behaviours of social categories possessing notable academic, cultural, and/or economic resources, in how they raise their children, organise their domestic lives, or manage their money, or in their cultural practices, leisure-time activities, or relationship to the school system or the future. Television is still a significant source of diversion in these households, and although the desire to see the children 'go as far as possible' in school is quite present, it is not backed up by the daily schoolwork support provided in more highly educated social categories.[29] While some households are inspired by academic and professional ambitions, overall these ambitions appear to be modest and heavily dependent on the limited resources that they are able to mobilise.

That is not to say, however, that they act in ways that only reproduce the traditional working-class model. One of the main strengths of the portraits presented in this book is showing how they differ from this model, especially in terms of domestic relations and how they relate to other social groups. Today's working classes can no longer be described according to the same traits that were long its hallmarks: strong division of gender roles, housework almost exclusively the responsibility of women, women's removal from paid employment, sticking to the neighbourhood and family fold against the outside world, assertion of a strong class identification, defiance of the child-rearing and grooming norms of dominant categories. For those who still think in terms of the traditional working-class traits found in sociological descriptions of the 1960s, these portraits attest to a major transformation. As a result of the expansion of the common, judgements, and aspirations, working-class lifestyles have lost many of their specificities – but they have not become 'middle', either.

There is a third reason that dissuades us from describing today's working class as the 'poor working classes'. Analyses that do so (such as Lazarus 2006) postulate that a cultural 'middling' has taken place: although basic employees and labourers do have economic limitations, they want to live in step with the rest of society. But simply pointing out that basic employees and labourers have lost traditional working-class cultural specificities or aspire to modal forms of schooling, consumption of goods and services, or relating to time does not go far enough; sociology must also describe the practices, morality, and ethos that they need to have a chance of turning these aspirations into reality, and take account of the high economic and cultural limitations typifying executant workers. The practices and morality of the households studied here, as well as their concrete living and working conditions, justify the choice to consider them part of the working classes: they illustrate a 'conquest of norms' more than a process of 'middling'. This desire for conquest is amplified in a context of weakening social and economic foundations for the subaltern labour force. Stable-modest basic employees and labourers are working to 'be like everyone else' so they can avoid being relegated to the poor and claim full-fledged membership in the 'society of the similar'.

Notes

1 This text is based on numerous discussions in the research team over the four years of research (see note 3). It also benefitted from conversations I had with Olivier Schwartz over the same period. I thank him for reading successive versions of the text, his suggestions, and his unflagging support. I would also like to express my debt to Marie-Hélène Lechien, a constant interlocutor and demanding reader. Many warm thanks also to Stéphane Beaud, Gérard Mauger, and Tristan Poullaouec, for their attentive re-reading of this text and their suggestions for improvement.

2 The employment categories used for statistical purposes in France do not entirely correspond to those used in the United Kingdom or the United States. See the appendix (Socio-professional Categories) for a detailed description of the French system and explanations of how its categories are defined – especially those most relevant to the book, 'basic employee' and 'labourer' (the former primarily low-skill jobs in the service sector, the latter historically low-skill manual jobs in industrial production), and those to which we compare them: 'intermediate professions' and '*cadres*'.

3 This notion was suggested by Olivier Schwartz and presented in Bernard, Masclet, and Schwartz (2019).

4 There is no consensus on the exact boundary between the middle classes. Goux and Maurin (2012) think of them as the 'combination of a solid core of well-established social categories at the core of society and more distant and shifting peripheries [...] with traditional small business owners on one side and a vast middle of the salaried workers that INSEE designates as intermediate professions on the other' (p. 10), to which could be added some salaried employees that INSEE and job classification grids designate as *cadres*, such as secondary school teachers and civil servants. Far from being in decline, the central importance of these middle classes has only been confirmed over the past 30 years: in a competitive educational and employment context, they have managed to maintain their position and play a key role in the development and dissemination of norms concerning the body, education, and the family.

5 Chapter 2 contains a more precise statistical description of these households in the median fractions of the working classes.

6 This research programme, which I directed, was headed by a steering committee composed of Thomas Amossé, Stéphane Beaud, Lise Bernard, Marie Cartier, Violaine Girard, Marie-Hélène Lechien, Olivier Schwartz, Yasmine Siblot, and myself. It was titled 'Le "populaire" aujourd'hui. Les recompositions sociales

et culturelles des mondes ouvriers et employés contemporains' (The 'working class' today: The social and cultural reconstitution of the worlds of contemporary labourers and basic employees). It brought together 27 researchers from four research centres: the Centre de Recherche sur les Liens Sociaux (UMR 8070), the Centre Nantais de Sociologie (UMR 6025), the Centre Maurice Halbwachs, and the Groupe de Recherches Sociologiques sur les Sociétés Contemporaines (EA 3815). It enjoyed the financial support of the Agence nationale de la recherche (ANR, National Research Agency).

7 Pierre Bourdieu (1985) distinguishes between 'class on paper', built by sociologists, and 'mobilised class', which is built by political actors ('class for itself'). 'Class on paper' consists of 'sets of agents who occupy similar positions and who, being placed in similar conditions and subjected to similar conditionings, have every likelihood of having similar dispositions and interests and therefore of producing similar practices and adopting similar stances' (198). Our research (see Chapter 2) shows that basic employees and labourers do indeed form a 'class on paper', but it is far from homogeneous since there can be significant differences between the positions of various categories of labourers and basic employees. This heterogeneity of positions explains the diversity of their practices and positions: the stable-modest households whose portraits we present in this book differ considerably from those of the insecure and unskilled fractions described in other publications (Pigot et al. 2009, Roche 2016).

8 Although there is less of such work today than there was in the 1960s–1980s, it does still exist. It is presented in several books providing an overview of research, notably Alonzo and Hugrée (2010), Siblot et al. (2015), and Béroud et al. (2016).

9 The French 'Yellow Vests' (*Gilets Jaunes*) movement that began in the fall of 2018 against an increase in taxes on gasoline and for improved purchasing power made the increasingly visible yellow vests into a symbol. The first obstacle it had to overcome was the very social and political invisibility of the population that was the most active in the movement.

10 Castel defines the 'wage-earning society' as 'a continuum of positions that all share the characteristics of the wage-labour condition, especially the right to employment and social welfare' (Castel 2009, 365).

11 We use the expression 'to be like everyone else' in the same way as Claude and Christiane Grignon (1980). Their study of labourers' eating practices indicates working-class concern with catching up with the norm. 'Labourers make an effort to overcome the contradiction between their limited resources and the need to reduce the gap between their quality of life and the average quality of life – in short, to normalise their consumption'. They go on to add, 'One could almost say that working-class families consume first of all so as to not distinguish themselves'. The portraits in this book demonstrate this in how these basic employees and labourers in the stabilised fractions of the working classes aim to overcome the contradiction between their economic and cultural resources and the norms of society in many aspects of life. In the conclusion, we will come back to the 'goodwill as necessity' that characterises them, by which we mean the work that stable-modest households do to 'normalise' themselves and make themselves part of the 'society of the similar', Robert Castel's term according here with Claude and Christiane Grignon's conclusions.

12 This picks up on a hypothesis formulated by Schwartz (1998, 2011).

13 The *baccalauréat* ('the *bac*') is a rigorous examination marking the end of secondary studies and allowing progression into university. For an explanation of the French educational system and its attainments, see Appendix.

14 Mike Savage and his colleagues come to a similar conclusion concerning changes in employment in England (2015).

15 There is more on this point in the next chapter.

16 As examples of societies where disparities can be great without individuals seeing themselves as unequal, Castel cites slaveholding societies and the society of orders under the Ancien Régime: in such societies, the difference between conditions is not seen as inequality or injustice, but as an unbridgeable distance. The slave could no more compare himself to the master than a Third Estate peasant could to a noble.
17 Working-class families' access to new lodgings in housing estates in the 1960s did not turn out to be an opportunity to get closer to families of the petit-bourgeoisie: the distance was re-established in child-rearing practices. The families of unskilled labourers that (still) have more children were often accused of 'letting them loiter' outside, or even being failures as parents (Coing 1966, Chamboredon and Lemaire 1970).
18 Florence Weber demonstrates that productive leisure-time activities are less present in the working classes today because the old family survival strategies and power relations between labourers and bosses changed with the arrival of mass unemployment. The loss of paid employment and difficulties balancing the budget fuel more under-the-table work. Tightening economic constraints undermine the importance of non-commercial activities and exchanges as well as the moral gratifications associated with them. It is now a matter of surviving by finding the money at any cost. Additionally, the spread of unemployment reduces the free spaces that labourers had built for themselves: the unemployed are caught up in logics of closure and unable to do 'work on the side'. On top of that, the excess of available labour, just-in-time practices, and automated stock management techniques have led employers to grow intolerant of semi-deviant practices associated with 'work on the side' (using machines for personal ends, salvaging scrap materials or even stealing from new stocks), while new management approaches are more concerned with cost-reduction than fostering worker loyalty. 'Work on the side' can no longer be an opportunity for the same tacit accommodations with the factory. When it is preserved, it takes the form of pastimes for retirees, who in the 1990s gradually became more numerous than the actively employed (Weber 2008).
19 In the 1950s, Young and Willmott observed similar transformations in labourers of London's East End. The rising quality of life and improvement of housing conditions set off a number of cultural changes, especially among men. They said they wanted to limit the number of children they had. Visits to the pub declined and family time became the norm; the arrival of television in homes coincided with this homeward turn. Beyond that, new ways of being a man and a father took shape. Men no longer held on to their income as they used to, only giving their wives allowances that were often too little for food and child-related expenses. Money came to belong to the couple and be invested in the children's education. Men were seen with their children more often, doing parental activities previously reserved for women. As one of them said in an interview, 'It used to be thought very undignified for men to have anything to do with children. You'd never see a man wheeling a pram or holding a baby. Of course all that's changing now' (Young and Willmott 2011, 13).
20 This process of individualisation of the child also emerges in Young and Willmott's study (2011). The first names given to children are less often those of the parents or grandparents, as tradition would have it: 'Custom is being replaced by fashion' (11). And fashion comes from Hollywood, not the neighbourhood.
21 Comparison with other European countries demonstrates how protective the French public sector still is for basic employees and labourers. It employs 16–26% of the working classes (depending on the definition), which is more than in the United Kingdom (15–22%) and much more than in Germany or Spain (7–12%). However, the protections associated with public-sector jobs are less accessible

today: the reduction in the number of positions and hikes in the level of civil service examinations compromise the possibility of becoming a civil servant and enjoying its job security. For more on these points, see Hugrée, Penissat, and Spire (2020).

22 The 'qualification norm' is the level of formal educational qualifications corresponding to those most commonly held by workers at a given employment level.

23 A recent INSEE study of the social mobility of people born in the 1970s and 1980s (Poncelet, Trigano, and Sagot 2016) reveals an increase in the likelihood that the children of labourers and basic employees could become *cadre* or hold an intermediary profession. Even if they are less likely to reach these higher positions (even less likely if they live outside of greater Paris), they nonetheless benefit from the prolongation of education and occupational opportunities due to the increase in intermediary profession and *cadre* jobs. The analysis of social mobility conducted by Vallet (2014) from 1977 to 2003 also reveals an increase in social fluidity, meaning a lesser statistical association between background and position. In a way, the future is less statistically predictable, which is expressed both in more cases of upward mobility and in more cases of downward mobility for the children of all social categories.

24 Based on his analysis of INSEE's 2003 survey Éducation et famille, T. Poullaouec shows that 71% of labouring families with children in secondary school would like their children to pursue post-secondary education (Poullaouec 2010).

25 This is according to studies by J. Dubois and E. Melnik-Olive, cited in Poullaouec (2019).

26 According to INSEE, the 2014 poverty line for a person living alone (60% of the median standard of living) was estimated to be an income of 1,008 euros per month. That year the median standard of living in mainland France was 1679 euros a month. The standard of living corresponds to the available revenue divided by the number of consumer units.

27 See the following chapter on statistics and methods.

28 All names of research participants and the cities and towns where they live have been changed in order to respect their privacy.

29 This stands out in Sandrine Garcia's interview-based study (2018) of the parents of schoolchildren of the working, middle, and upper classes. Her research shows the considerable daily investment well-off families make in helping their children with schoolwork, and their constant pressure on children to improve their marks. The recognition and love granted to children depend heavily on their respect of educational norms. Working-class parents are less equipped to be good school 'coaches' and less available to help their children because of their working hours, and they are even less likely to see their children succeed in school if they subscribe to a child-rearing model stressing children's independence, a model vaunted by middle-class parents under an earlier educational system that has since been largely abandoned for a much more coercive model.

References

Alonzo, Philippe, and Cédric Hugrée. 2010. *Sociologie des classes populaires*. Paris: Colin.

Amossé, Thomas. 2015. 'Portraits statistiques des classes populaires contemporaines.' *Savoir/agir* 34: 13–20.

Amossé, Thomas, and Marie Cartier. 2019. '"*Si je travaille, c'est pas pour acheter du premier prix*". Modes de consommation des classes populaires depuis leurs ménages stabilisés.' *Sociétés contemporaines* 114, no. 2: 89–122.

Arborio, Anne-Marie, and Marie-Hélène Lechien. 2019. 'La bonne volonté sanitaire des classes populaires. Les ménages ouvriers et employés stables face aux médecins et aux normes de santé.' *Sociologie* 10, no. 1: 91–110.

Beaud, Stéphane. 2003. *80% au bac… et après? Les enfants de la démocratisation scolaire.* Paris: La Découverte.

Beaud, Stéphane, and Michel Pialoux. (1999) 2012. *Retour sur la condition ouvrière. Enquête aux usines Peugeot de Sochaux-Montbéliard.* Paris: La Découverte.

Bernard, Lise, and Christophe Giraud. 2018. 'Avec qui les ouvrières et les employées vivent-elles en couple?' *Travail, genre et sociétés* 39: 41–61.

Bernard, Lise, Olivier Masclet, and Olivier Schwartz, eds. 2019. 'Classes populaires d'aujourd'hui. Questions de morphologie et de styles de vie.' Special issue, *Sociétés contemporaines* 114: 5–21.

Béroud, Sophie, Paul Bouffartigue, Henri Eckert, and Denis Merklen. 2016. *En Quête de classes populaires. Un essai politique.* Paris: La Dispute.

Blanpain, Nathalie. 2011. 'L'espérance de vie s'accroît, les inégalités sociales face à la mort demeurent.' *INSEE Première* 1372.

Bourdieu, Pierre. 1966. 'Différences et distinctions.' In *Le partage des bénéfices. Expansion et inégalités en France*, edited by Darras. Paris: Les Éditions de Minuit, 117–129.

Bourdieu, Pierre. (1979) 1984. *Distinction: A Social Critique of the Judgment of Taste.* Translated by Richard Nice. Cambridge, MA: Harvard University Press.

Bourdieu, Pierre. (1984) 1985. 'The Social Space and Genesis of Groups.' *Social Science Information* 24, no. 2: 195–220.

Brousse, Cécile. 2015. 'Travail professionnel, tâches domestiques, temps 'libre' : quelques déterminants sociaux de la vie quotidienne.' Économie et Statistique 478–480: 119–154.

Campagnac, Élisabeth, and Lydia Tabary-Taveau. 1979. *Nouveaux Quotidiens ouvriers.* Paris: Éditions Cru.

Castel, Robert. 2003a. *L'Insécurité sociale. Qu'est-ce qu'être protégé?* Paris: Seuil.

Castel, Robert. (1995) 2003b. *From Manual Workers to Wage Laborers: Transformation of the Social Question.* Translated and edited by Richard Boyd. Piscataway, NJ: Transaction Publishers.

Castel, Robert. 2009. *La Montée des incertitudes : travail, protections, statut de l'individu.* Paris: Le Seuil.

Cazenave-Lacrouts, Marie-Cécile, David Guillas, and Guillaume Lebrault. 2018. 'Le patrimoine des ménages en 2018.' *INSEE Première* 1722.

Chamboredon, Jean-Claude, and Madeleine Lemaire. 1970. 'Proximité spatiale et distance sociale. Les grands ensembles et leur peuplement.' *Revue française de sociologie* 11, no. 1: 3–33.

Chenu, Alain. 2005. *Sociologie des employés.* Paris: La Découverte.

Chenu, Alain, and Nicolas Herpin. 2002. 'Une pause dans la marche vers la civilisation des loisirs?' Économie et statistique 352–353: 15–37.

Coing, Henri. 1966. *Rénovation urbaine et changement social (l'îlot n°4, Paris 13e).* Paris: Éditions ouvrières.

Dewerpe, Alain. 1989. *Le Monde du travail en France, 1800–1950.* Paris: Armand Colin.

Durif, Pierre. 1969. 'Propriétaires et locataires en 1967.' Économie et statistique 3: 41–56.

Flamand, Jean-Paul. 1989. *Loger le peuple. Essai sur l'histoire du logement social.* Paris: La Découverte.

Gallot, Fanny, and Ève Meuret-Campfort. 2015. 'Des ouvrières en lutte dans l'après 68. Rapports au féminisme et subversions de genre.' *Politix* 109: 21–43.

Garcia, Sandrine. 2018. *Le Goût de l'effort. La construction familiale des dispositions scolaires.* Paris: Presses Universitaires de France.

Goux, Dominique, and Éric Maurin. 2012. *Les Nouvelles classes moyennes.* Paris: Seuil.

Grignon, Claude, and Christiane Grignon. 1980. 'Styles d'alimentation et goûts populaires.' *Revue française de sociologie* 21, no. 4: 531–569.

Hoggart, Richard. 1957. *The Uses of Literacy: Aspects of Working Class Life*. London: Chatto and Windus.

Hugrée, Cédric, Étienne Penissat, and Alexis Spire. 2020. *Social Class in Europe: New Inequalities in the Old World*. London: Verso.

Jusot, Florence. 2013. 'Les inégalités de recours aux soins. Bilan et évolutions.' *Revue d'épidémiologie et de santé publique* 61: 163–169.

Kopel, Sandrine. 2005. 'Les surdiplômés de la fonction publique.' *Revue française de gestion* 155: 17–34.

Lazarus, Jeanne. 2006. 'Les pauvres et la consommation.' *Vingtième siècle* 91: 137–152.

Lefebvre, Rémi, and Frédéric Sawicki. 2006. *La Société des socialistes*. Bellecombe-en-Bauges: Éditions du Croquant.

Le Pape, Marie-Clémence, and Marie Plessz. 2017. 'C'est l'heure du petit-déjeuner? Rythme des repas, incorporation et classe sociale.' *L'Année sociologique* 67: 73–105.

Magri, Susanna. 1991. 'Des "ouvriers" aux "citoyens modestes". Naissance d'une catégorie : les bénéficiaires des habitations à bon marché au tournant du XXe siècle.' *Genèses* 5: 35–53.

Maruani, Margaret, and Monique Méron. 2012. *Un Siècle de travail des femmes en France, 1901–2011*. Paris: La Découverte.

Masclet, Olivier. 2018. *L'Invité permanent. La réception de la télévision dans les familles populaires*. Paris: Armand Colin.

Mauger, Gérard. 2006. 'Les transformations des classes populaires en France depuis 30 ans.' In *Nouvelles luttes de classes*, edited by Jean Lojkine, Pierre Cours-Salies, and Michel Vakaloulis, 29–42. Paris: Presses Universitaires de France.

Mauger, Gérard. 2012. 'Les classes populaires ont-elles vraiment perdu la partie? Sept questions à Robert Castel.' In *Changements et pensées du changement*, edited by Robert Castel and Claude Martin, 90–99. Paris: La Découverte.

Mauger, Gérard, and Claude Fossé. 1977. *La Vie buissonnière. Marginalité petite-bourgeoise et marginalité populaire*. Paris: Maspéro.

Merle, Pierre. 2012. *La Ségrégation scolaire*. Paris: La Découverte.

Millet, Mathias, and Gilles Moreau, eds. 2011. *La Société des diplômes*. Paris: La Dispute.

Mischi, Julian. 2014. *Le Communisme désarmé. Le PCF et les classes populaires depuis les années 1970*. Paris: Agone.

Noiriel, Gérard. (1986) 2012. *Les Ouvriers dans la société française*. Paris: Le Seuil.

Palheta, Ugo. 2012. *La Domination scolaire. Sociologie de l'enseignement professionnel et de son public*. Paris: Presses Universitaires de France.

Pasquier, Dominique. 2018. *L'Internet des familles modestes. Enquête dans la France rurale*. Paris: Presses des Mines.

Peugny, Camille. 2018. 'L'évolution de la structure sociale dans quinze pays européens (1993–2013) : quelle polarisation de l'emploi?' *Sociologie* 9, no. 4: 399–416.

Pialoux, Michel, and Bruno Théret. 2019. 'État, classe ouvrière et logement social.' In *Le Temps d'écouter. Enquêtes sur les métamorphoses de la classe ouvrière*, edited by Michel Pialoux, 43–109. Paris: Raisons d'Agir.

Pialoux, Michel, and Florence Weber. 2002. 'La gauche et les classes populaires. Réflexions sur un divorce.' *Mouvements* 23: 9–21.

Pigot, Nathalie, Christophe Delay, Arnaud Frauenfelder, and Franz Schultheis, eds. 2009. *Les Classes populaires aujourd'hui. Portraits de familles, cadres sociologiques*. Paris: L'Harmattan.

Poncelet, Thomas, Lauren Trigano, and Mariette Sagot. 2016. 'Gravir l'échelle sociale est plus aisé en Ile-de-France qu'en province.' *INSEE Analyses - Ile de France* 50.
Poullaouec, Tristan. 2004. 'Les familles ouvrières face au devenir de leurs enfants.' *Économie et statistiques* 371: 3–22.
Poullaouec, Tristan. 2010. *Le Diplôme, arme des faibles. Les familles ouvrières et l'école.* Paris: La Dispute.
Poullaouec, Tristan. 2019. 'Regrets d'école. Le report des aspirations scolaires dans les familles populaires.' *Sociétés contemporaines* 114: 123–150.
Pudal, Bernard, and Jean-Noël Retière. 2008. 'Les grèves ouvrières de 68, un mouvement social sans lendemain mémoriel.' In *Mai-juin 68*, edited by Dominique Dammame, Boris Gobille, Frédérique Matonti, and Bernard Pudal, 207–221. Paris: Éditions de l'Atelier.
Régnier, Faustine, and Ana Masullo. 2009. 'Obésité, goût et consommation. Intégration des normes d'alimentation et appartenance sociale.' *Revue française de sociologie* 50: 747–773.
Roche, Agnès. 2016. *Des Vies de pauvres.* Rennes: Presses Universitaires de Rennes.
Savage, Mike. 2015. *Social Class in the 21st Century.* London: Pelican.
Schwartz, Olivier. 1990. *Le Monde privé des ouvriers. Hommes et femmes du Nord.* Paris: Presses Universitaires de France.
Schwartz, Olivier. 1998. 'La Notion de classes populaires.' HDR thesis, Université de Saint-Quentin en Yvelines.
Schwartz, Olivier. 2011. 'Peut-on parler de classes populaires?' *La Vie des idées*, 13 September 2011. https://laviedesidees.fr/Peut-on-parler-des-classes.html.
Siblot, Yasmine, Marie Cartier, Isabelle Coutant, Olivier Masclet, and Nicolas Renahy. 2015. *Sociologie des classes populaires contemporaines.* Paris: Colin.
Terrail, Jean-Pierre. 1984. 'Familles ouvrières, école, destin social (1880–1980).' *Revue française de sociologie* 25, no. 3: 421–436.
Terrail, Jean-Pierre. 1990. *Destins ouvriers. La fin d'une classe ?* Paris: Presses Universitaires de France.
Vallet, Louis-André. 2014. 'Mobilité observée et fluidité sociale en France de 1977 à 2003.' *Idées économiques et sociales* 175: 6–17.
Verret, Michel. 1979. *L'Espace ouvrier.* Paris: Armand Colin.
Vigna, Xavier. 2012. *Histoire des ouvriers en France au XXème siècle.* Paris: Perrin.
Weber, Florence. 1989. *Le Travail à-côté, Étude d'ethnographie ouvrière.* Paris: INRA.
Weber, Florence. 2008. 'Une enquête dans l'histoire.' In *Observer le travail. Histoire, ethnographie, approches combinées*, edited by Anne-Marie Arborio, Yves Cohen, Pierre Fournier, Nicolas Hatfeld, Cédric Lomba, and Séverin Muller, 201–214. Paris: La Découverte.
Young, Michael, and Peter Willmott. (1957) 2011. *Family and Kinship in East London.* Oxon: Routledge.
Zancarini-Fournel, Michelle. 2008. *Le Moment 68. Une histoire contestée.* Paris: Seuil.

2

AN EXPLORATION OF THE WORKING CLASSES STARTING WITH THEIR MIDDLE FRACTIONS

A two-pronged approach, through statistics and case studies

Thomas Amossé, Lise Bernard, Marie Cartier, Marie-Hélène Lechien and Yasmine Siblot

Although the term 'the working classes' is commonly used in sociology, the media, and some political discourse, its imprecision is obvious as soon as one tries to determine its perimeter, internal variations, or schisms. Both in and outside of the academic world, this vagueness fuels numerous debates over its boundaries and structure as well as the nature and intensity of the relations of social domination that are the basis of the economic, cultural, and symbolic demarcations between social classes, not to mention within them.

The research presented in this book was intended to tackle these issues head-on. In 2013, the collective research programme that was the basis for this book set out with one central objective, a few preliminary hypotheses, and an intuition about how we might set about finding answers. Starting with the observations that inequalities are increasing, the least privileged social categories are falling, and 'the people' is resurging as a political issue, we set out to analyse the social reconfigurations and actual living conditions of working-class people. Their lifestyles, cultural practices, and conceptions of the social world have changed considerably, and we wanted to describe them in a way that let us rethink the working classes without comprehending them solely on the basis of where their boundaries with other social groups may be or splitting analysis into multiple approaches, each corresponding to a specialised research domain. This was our objective. The hypotheses emerged from our readings and experience as sociologists, which highlighted three traits traditionally associated with the working classes – the gendered division of roles, hedonism, and the importance of in-group sociability – that we wanted to subject to new scrutiny.[1] Lastly, the intuition was to take the novel approach of focussing on an under-studied but probably large fraction of the working classes: the middle.

DOI: 10.4324/9781003330073-2

This imprecise term designated an agenda more than a proper object of research and is implicitly rooted in the idea that this middle fraction was distinguishable from both a lower fraction composed of the households with the lowest levels of economic resources, social protection, and cultural capital and an upper fraction approaching the middle classes due to its job security, elevated degree of wellbeing, and participation in socially selective activities.

This produced an outline of this midsection of the working classes that was more of a sketch than a portrait, and inadequate for defining the criteria for which households should be studied. At the outset of the programme, in line with experiments trying to understand ordinary social categorisation (Boltanski and Thévenot 1983), we committed as a group to developing an explicit list of the characteristics that are implicitly associated with these middle fractions of the working classes, and all participating researchers indicated their conception of the relevant socio-professional categories and their typical social properties. An initial series of statistical analyses (some presented later in this chapter) then helped us to deepen the discussion of this preliminary list, which reflected our combined knowledge and conceptions of society. This summary of the experiment provides a behind-the-scenes glimpse of the process. Now that the programme has drawn to a close, reconstructing the insights that emerged from these initial steps seems particularly relevant because the points of (dis)agreement that arose and the questions raised in the process led to the first milestones for situating ourselves in the working-class space. Retrospectively, these early steps also foster better understanding of the statistical studies and household portraits and what they have to teach us.

Among the convergences, the socio-professional aspect of the middle fraction of the working classes took shape around a core of occupations held by skilled 'labourers' and 'basic employees' (especially in the public sector), and for the most part excluding 'intermediary professions' (with higher educational attainments) and lower 'independents' (self-employed people and small business owners with higher income and net worth).[2] The research team imagined typical households as being composed of couples who either held such occupations or owed their middling social position the fact that one member of the couple had a job associated with the upper middle classes and the other a job associated with the lower, such as a couple consisting of an accounting secretary and a low-skilled labourer, thus averaging each other out. Lastly, in addition to the median level expected of labourers and basic employees' economic resources, this fraction was predominantly defined by excluding the households with high cultural capital (a *baccalauréat* or post-secondary degree, for example) above them and households in less secure employment situations below them. Most of the sociologists in the programme thus agreed on the objective of conducting research on a little-known type of working-class household that is relatively distant from educational and social institutions, which are the channels sociologists tend to favour for researching the educated or the impoverished fractions of the working classes on either side of this central core.

Defining what we call the working classes on paper, or at least certain fractions of them, was easier said than done. Conscious of the fact that these social categories do not exist in and of themselves and that their boundaries and very existence are subjects of social struggle (Bourdieu 1984) (as the *Gilets Jaunes* [Yellow Vest] movement launched in late 2018 in France reminded us), several researchers in the team stressed the dangers of a reading consisting of three stratified layers of households that are otherwise seen as much more diverse than the 'labouring class' was in the 1960s and 1970s: the job held by the 'head of the household' used to be enough to define a household's social position, or at least that was the common belief at the time.[3] Another voiced concern was the risk of using these middle fractions to essentialise what the 'real' working classes might be, their core group, which would marginalise the 'excluded' to one side and the 'lower middle classes' to the other. There is indeed a real risk of wanting to describe 'the working class' this way, as a smaller but unified entity: awareness of this risk convinced us to always analyse the working classes in the plural, showing how their diversity is hierarchically organised around their middle section.

These preliminary thoughts made it possible to at least hypothetically identify a key trait of such households: stability. Not that their situations should be seen as immutable, but we posited that the social position held by the middle fractions of the working classes was characterised by the acquisition of some form of stability, if only temporary. Neither fully drawn into social ascension nor haunted by social regression but lacking notable professional or social mobility, they were able to accumulate a little net worth, such as becoming property owners (even moving away from urban centres to be able to do so). This stability is thus social, residential, and familial as well, ensured by a relative economic security that, reading between the lines, exposes the precarity of single-parent households. When two people form a couple they may share expenses and be ensured of two incomes (even if they are low) in case of difficulty, so it seemed necessary to take account of working-class households' family configurations and activities in order to understand their social position. This presumed multifaceted stability of the middle fraction was moreover seen as liable to facilitate a form of cultural autonomy, by which we mean the potential for having their own norms, or at least not relating to the norms of other classes in a purely dominated way.[4] Lastly, we hypothesised that this stable middle fraction of the working classes especially incarnated 'triangular social consciousness' (Collovald and Schwartz 2006, Schwartz 2011) in how it relates to the middle and upper classes and the insecure working classes on either side.

Our discussions led to a preliminary outline of the middle of the working classes that we were trying to know and understand better, akin to the outline Luc Boltanski established for *cadres* (1987, 37 onward). This outline was then fleshed out and largely confirmed by the statistical objectification presented in the rest of this chapter, which informed the organisation of the research around household case studies that appear as portraits in this volume.

Research through case studies and statistics

Exploring the working classes through their middle fractions presupposed that our attention not be focused on the 'little-middles' of the Parisian suburbs (Cartier et al. 2016), the 'modest households of urban peripheries' (Girard 2017), or the 'rural petite bourgeoisie' (Bruneau et al. 2018), to cite a few recent studies. It also means not approaching our research through the indebted households of 'urban renewal zones' (Perrin-Heredia 2013), 'young people in rural areas' (Coquard 2019), or 'the other working-class world' of home-based service workers (Avril 2014). We did encounter many people in each of these situations over the course of the study because we took a relational approach, meaning that we focused on the middle fractions of the working classes but also included working-class people in small social ascension (closer to the middle classes) as well as poorer and more insecure households in the analysis. The case studies and statistical data show heavy interactions between fractions, and the positions people hold can be vague and change. Unlike many studies conducted in other countries, and some in France, we have always favoured the hypothesis of continuity within the working classes. We understand them as a cluster of groups with common traits beyond their differences and inequalities, not marked by strong discontinuity between, for example, 'stable' and 'insecure', or 'traditional working class' and 'precariat' to cite the distinction made in the massive Great British Class Survey, directed by Mike Savage and Fiona Divine in partnership with the BBC (see Savage 2015).

In order to take account of the ties between the middle fractions and those close to them but slightly better or worse off as well as how they relate to other social class groups, we quickly agreed that we would all gather ethnographic-type materials. We designed a research plan revolving around situated household case studies rather than decontextualised individual interviews as a means to reveal families' lifestyles, living conditions, and relationships to other social groups.

At the same time, we thought it essential to test the hypothesis that the working classes are structured around the middle, so we tried to objectively define the characteristics of these middle fractions using statistical data on labourers and basic employees. Although there is no lack of quantitative analysis of social class and inequality, there are few recent empirically oriented publications that statistically describe the working classes: there are rich publications on the 1980s (especially Herpin et al. 1987, Chenu 1990), but it is difficult to find anything presenting detailed data on all labourers and basic employees in the 1990s, 2000s, and 2010s, especially at the household level. Furthermore, books presenting an overview or broad analysis of the working classes (Alonzo and Hugrée 2010, Siblot et al. 2015, Béroud et al. 2016) stress how rare such data is. The statistical part of our study (summarised below) was thus conceived to respond to three needs: making up for the absence of recent empirical publications on the working classes in terms of the socio-professional categories used in public statistics; exploring the internal structure of the working classes by studying what characterises its middle section; and situating the households featured in our in-depth case studies within this working-class space.

Box 2.1: Presentation of the statistical analyses used in this book

Statistical analyses

The analyses summarised in this chapter are based on an original treatment of a long series of *Emploi* (Labour Force) surveys from 1982 to 2012 conducted by Paul Hobeika and Claire-Lise Dubost (under the supervision of Thomas Amossé, Lise Bernard, Violaine Girard, and Yasmine Siblot). It was then expanded and supplemented by Thomas Amossé (*Emploi* and *Formation et qualification professionnelle* [Training and Professional Qualifications] surveys from 1993 and 2014 to 2015 and the *Revenus fiscaux et sociaux* [Tax and Social Revenues] survey from 2013), Lise Bernard and Christophe Giraud (*Emploi* surveys), Claire-Lise Dubost (*Emploi* surveys), and Lucas Tranchant (the *Formation et qualification professionnelle* survey from 2014 to 2015).

Some of the statistical findings were read and further analysed by several sociologists in the programme, in addition to those already cited: Anne-Marie Arborio, Marie Cartier, Muriel Letrait, Olivier Masclet, Séverine Misset, and Tristan Poullaouec (for the kinds of *baccalauréat* obtained, Figure 2.2). They were also discussed more generally in seminars.

The programme made other uses and analyses of the data that are not presented in this chapter: on time use (Thomas Amossé and Cécile Brousse, using the *Emploi du temps* [Time Use] surveys 1974–2010), the division of domestic labour and family relations (Muriel Letrait, using the 2010 *Emploi du temps* survey and the 2011 *Erfi* [Family and Intergenerational Relations] survey), cultural practices and use of new telecom technologies (Francis Marchan, using the 2008 *Pratiques culturelles des français* [Cultural Practices of the French] survey and the 2013 *Technologies de l'information et de la communication TIC* [Information and Communication Technologies] survey), sociability (Christelle Avril, in collaboration with Violaine Girard and Yasmine Siblot, using the *SRCV* [Resources and Living Conditions] survey, 2006–2011), consumption practices (Rémi Sinthon and Thomas Amossé, using the *Budgets de famille* [Family Budgets] survey, 1985–2010), and the spatial distribution of working-class households in several regions and geographical scales (Thomas Sigaud, using the *Recensement de la population* [Population Census] of 1968 and 2013).

For statistical analyses and case studies alike, we chose to study working-class living conditions and lifestyles through households rather than individuals.[5] Indeed, although the position of individuals in the world of remunerated work (long the primary classificatory principle in the sociology of social class) is still structuring, we have known since Halbwachs that lifestyles are formed in the setting of the household and its domestic activities, often ensured by women: like other classes, the working classes 'walk on two legs' – their male and female members (Baudelot and Establet 2005, 40). Basing our research on households rather than individuals makes it possible to study the full range of practices, resources, and representations that define a social condition and lifestyle, without presupposing or over-estimating their uniformity. This approach seems all the more important today because more working-class women have paid employment than in the past and, whether they are basic employee or labourer, their occupations often differ from those of their spouses due to the strongly gendered division of subaltern occupations and asymmetry of social position within couples (Siblot et al. 2015). Working on households thus prompts us to re-examine the boundaries of the working classes in relation to the occupations of the people within them and to examine the 'entanglement of gender and class' (Hamel and Siméant 2006), since women's employment tends to multiply their interactions with other social groups through the service jobs that many of them have (in shops, healthcare, early childhood, and so on). Such experience can transform how these working-class households share domestic work, agree or disagree on child-rearing norms, and situate themselves in the social space, especially in the 'Us/Them' split.

Using the available statistical data, the next section provides an empirical and cartographic presentation of the contemporary working classes, beginning with a review of their defining criteria and main characteristics at the individual level and then detailing their variants at the household level.

The reconfiguration of the working classes: a drop in blue-collars, a rise in clerical, sales, and services employees

It is never easy to put a social group into statistics. The term 'working class' as we use it, following Olivier Schwartz and a variety of recent publications, only partly aligns with the logic behind INSEE's socio-professional classification, which is the primary instrument for identifying socio-economic positions for use in producing public statistics. The official classification is more occupational than social or cultural, since its main groups are based on categories inherited from the civil service grades and the 'Parodi conventions' (the collective bargaining agreements first established under Minister of Labour Alexander Parodi following WWII), resulting in boundaries that are arguably artificial. It is also imprecise in describing the social position of 'independents' (people working for themselves), a vast category including the sub-groups 'tradesmen, shopkeepers, and company heads' and 'farm operators', which taken together seem particularly heterogeneous in terms of income and net worth. Despite these limitations, we retained the socio-professional groups 'basic employees' and 'labourers' for defining the working classes, in line with common research practice.

This choice has two main consequences that should be signalled, although they do not invalidate the following findings.[6] Firstly, it excludes 'independents' because the groups 'labourers' and 'basic employee' are specifically designed to include only people employed by someone else, while the groups 'intermediary professions' and '*cadres* and higher intellectual professions' include both people working in the professions (lawyers, doctors, etc.) and the self-employed. Among 'independents', however, a share of farm operators, tradesmen, and shopkeepers could be considered being in the working classes (Bessière and Gollac 2014), along with some of the small but growing number of people working as an '*auto-entrepreneur*' (Abdelnour and Lambert 2014).[7] Unfortunately, these self-employed workers cannot be identified using the socio-professional groups, although we would have a better understanding of their condition if we could count them among the working classes.

The second consequence of our choice of definition works in the opposite direction: among the job categories listed under the 'basic employee' group, 'business administrative employees', whose educational attainments and income are very close to those of 'intermediary professions', and 'civilian public service employees', whose employment status affords them security, could be excluded from the ranks of the working classes. Indeed, this choice was made in a study of social class in Europe (Hugrée, Penissat, and Spire 2020), because the divide is even wider between them and other, less-skilled basic employees and labourers on the European Union scale. In France, where such discontinuity is less striking, we hypothesised that these skilled basic employees hold the most advantaged position in the working-class space.

One more point should be made clear: we focused on all members of the 'labour force' (meaning anyone either currently employed or unemployed and seeking work) and did not include people who are not in the labour force, which includes retired persons (with the exception of some analyses concerning couples).

The description proposed here is thus centred on labourers and basic employees as a whole, groups that still include the majority of jobs found lower in the social space and for which statistical data are most widely available. Provided that we bear in mind how it was developed and is used, the socio-professional classification system is still a precious tool for understanding social class, especially the shifting boundaries and internal variations of working classes.

According to this definition, then, the working classes included more than 14 million members of the labour force in 2012, 52% of the total.[8] This proportion had been slipping over the previous 30 years (it was 59% in 1982), while the proportion of '*cadres*' and 'intermediary professions' surged (from 26% to 41%) and the decline of 'farm operators' and non-farming 'independents' seems to have stabilised by this period (around 8%).

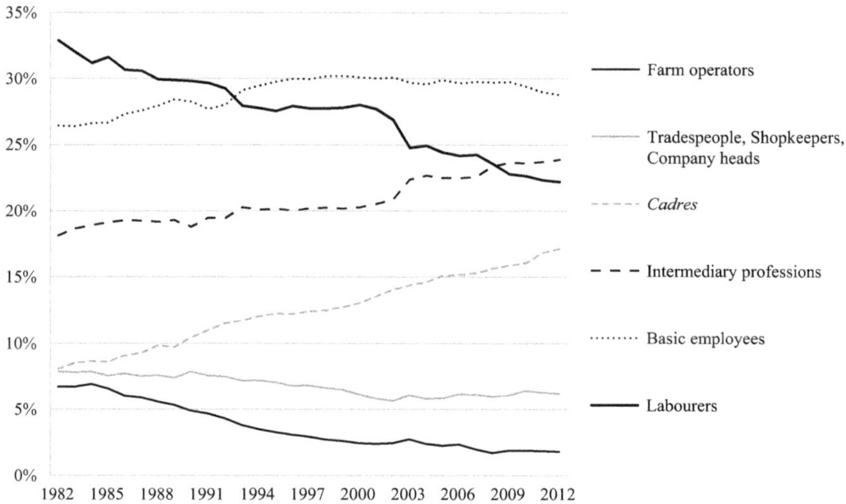

FIGURE 2.1 The evolution of each socio-professional group

Expressed in percentage of the labour force (1982–2012).

Field: Members of the labour force (actively employed or seeking work), by socio-professional category (see 'Appendix, 'Socio-professional Categories' for definitions of these categories). *Source*: The *Emploi* (Labour Force) surveys, 1982–2012 (INSEE).

Defined in this way, the working classes will soon cease to represent the majority of the labour force, despite the considerable dynamism of basic employees as a group (due to the creation of many jobs in the service sector that are held by women), which has more than made up for the decline in blue-collar jobs. This trend confirms the relative but symbolically important decline in working-class clout in French society and comes with a profound reconstruction of their occupational and social worlds.

In the first place, the labouring and industrial world has been steadily losing its position. Assembly-line work has certainly not vanished, but the image of the factory worker as part of a group structured around work and unionism is now far from being the norm, and the proportion of low-skilled labourers has dropped in the industry (over 800,000 jobs of this kind were lost in 30 years). Industrial workers are increasingly skilled, supervising teams or operating heavy installations. More importantly, most labourers now work in small working groups in other sectors such as the trades, in mid-sized companies in the construction or food industry, or as bus drivers.

The development of distribution jobs to the detriment of production has affected more than the labouring world. It contributed to the redistribution of working-class jobs by supporting the strong growth of jobs in sales (500,000 jobs added in 30 years), which numerically compensated for the decline in office jobs related to computerisation and administrative rationalisation. A similar trend has been observed in the public sector, which experienced parallel dynamism in skilled (auxiliary nurse) and low-skilled (service agent) jobs alike. The most significant progression, however, was in personal services and care jobs (particularly childcare and elder care), which added a million jobs in 30 years. The early 2000s marked a turning point in the social morphology of

TABLE 2.1 The occupational world of the working classes, then and now

Field: Number of people (employed or seeking work) in the socio-professional groups 'basic employee' and 'labourer' (see Appendix: 'Socio-professional Categories' for definitions of these categories).

Socio-professional categories	*Main occupations*	*Number (in thousands)*	
		2012	*Change since 1982*
Basic employees		8,050	+1,900
Public service employees and service agents	Agent and administrative assistant, auxiliary nurse, service agent	2,340	+630
Police and military	Police officer, *gendarme*, member of the military, firefighter, security guard	510	+120
Business administrative employees	Secretary, accountant, receptionist, transportation agent	1,720	−530
Sales employees	Stocker, cashier, salesperson, telemarketer	1,330	+530
Personal services employees	Hotel or restaurant employee, hairdresser, childminder, home care service provider, housecleaner, building superintendent	2,150	+1,150
Labourers		6,290	−940
Skilled industrial workers	Foreman, skilled public works worker, skilled operator and assembler, plant operator	1,240	−390
Skilled workers in the trades	Construction worker, automobile mechanic, cook or food preparation worker, arts worker	1,560	+180
Drivers	Lorry driver, messenger, taxi driver, public transportation driver	710	+130
Skilled shipping, handling, and transportation workers	Forklift-truck driver, transportation workers, train conductor, longshoreman	500	+20
Low-skilled industrial workers	Low-skilled worker in public works or industry, warehouse worker, mover, recycling worker	1,130	−820
Low-skilled worker in the trades	Low-skilled worker in construction or food preparation, cleaning agent	850	−70
Agricultural labourers	Farm worker, seaman-fisherman	300	+10
Total		14,340	+960

Source: The *Emploi* surveys of 1982 and 2012 (INSEE).

basic employees, when the proportion of low-skilled and often part-time basic employees rose to the detriment of the proportion of those with higher educational attainments, close to intermediary professions.

The differences between labourers and basic employees should be seen as somewhat flexible, since the definitions of these two socio-professional groups are mainly based on conventions developed from occupational classification grids and decisions made by public statisticians. For instance, cleaning workers are counted in the clerical, sales, and services employee group when they work in private homes or schools, but as labourers when they clean offices, means of transportation, or industrial sites. Additionally, the way that many jobs have evolved tends to make these groups more similar, as some labourer jobs have shifted to the tertiary sector (like forklift-truck operators for Internet businesses) and manual labour has risen in some jobs held by tertiary employees (such as supermarket cashiers or stockers). The fact remains that there was a fundamental reconfiguration of subaltern jobs over the past 30 years, partly related to their gender composition.

A wide range of social attributes, a common economic condition

'Basic employees' and 'labourers' are by far the most gendered groups of the socio-professional classification system. The percentage of women in each has remained stable over the past 30 years – 80% in the former and 20% in the latter – while the proportion of women has risen steadily in the 'intermediary professions' and '*cadres*' groups. In addition to averages, it is striking how greatly the feminisation rates vary according to the type of occupation. The range is tremendous in the working classes, from one in ten drivers, skilled workers in the trades, and members of the police and military being women to the reverse for personal services employees. This heightened gender segregation in employment fields has direct implications on the composition of working-class couples and households, as will be seen later in this chapter.

Furthermore, the working classes are still, on average, younger than other social groups. But this age difference is less marked than before, because of the decline in the number of low-skill factory jobs, usually held by young people, and the development of service jobs, which offer the possibility of career change or return to the employment market mid-career.

Another specificity that remains constant is the presence of foreigners, which is still more marked that in other social classes: it averaged 8% in the labourer and basic employee groups in 2012, twice the percentage observed among *cadres* and intermediary professionals. It is practically the same level as 30 years earlier, but this apparent continuity is partly misleading because it results from a convergence between labourers (where it is in decline) and basic employees, where they are increasing, especially in certain occupations (security guards, salespeople). As with gender and age, strong differences between categories stand out: foreign-born workers are still massively concentrated in the trades, both low-skilled jobs (22%, heavily in cleaning) and skilled jobs (13%), and among personal services employees (13%) and agricultural labourers (10%). In contrast, only 3% of public sector employees are foreigners, and only 5–7% of other categories of labourers and basic employees.

Unsurprisingly, the level of formal educational attainment strongly distinguishes the working classes from other social classes: in 2012, 24% of labourers and basic employees had, in addition to a primary school diploma, a *brevet des collèges* (10%) or a CAP or BEP (34%).[9] Only 34% of people in the working classes had the *baccalauréat*, as compared to 75% in the intermediary professions and 91% of *cadres*. But they have experienced degree inflation like other social categories. The proportion of labourers and basic employees having no more than a primary school diploma has plummeted over 30 years: from 66% to 33% for labourers and 45% to 19% for basic employees, due largely to demographic renewal. The largest number now has a CAP, BEP, or equivalent, as is the case for 39% of labourers and 30% of basic employees. It is still only a minority to possess a *baccalauréat*, but the percentage has risen from 11% to 24% for basic employees and from 2% to 15% for labourers. Likewise for post-secondary degrees, which went from 3% to 17% for basic employees and from less than 1% to 5% for labourers.

The two groups have changed at roughly the same pace, but there is a noteworthy disparity in educational levels, as basic employees have always had a distinctly higher average educational attainment than labourers. Differences in the educational tracks also highlight the gap between the two groups: as Figure 2.2 shows, basic employees were much more likely than labourers to have a more academically oriented General *baccalauréat* in 2012. Among basic employees, the (considerable) differences between categories were maintained or even increased, with business administrative employees possessing increasingly higher educational attainments and personal services employees having far fewer. The percentage of sales employees with post-secondary degrees has risen particularly sharply, from 2% to 19%, which in many instances is a reflection of downclassing. Among labourers, there is a very clear distinction between the skilled and the low-skilled. The dramatic rise in educational attainment levels over the 30-year period has thus only slightly reduced the gaps between categories of the working classes, despite the fact, demonstrated in countless publications in the sociology of education and social groups (Poullaouec 2010, for instance), that the massive opening of the educational system deeply altered how the working classes relate to schooling.

Diverse in gender, age, nationality, and educational attainments, the working classes share a similar economic condition, due to their position in the employment market and in occupational hierarchies. In 2012, 12% of people in the working classes were looking for work, 15% were seasonal workers or on government-subsidised, limited-term, or temporary employment contracts,

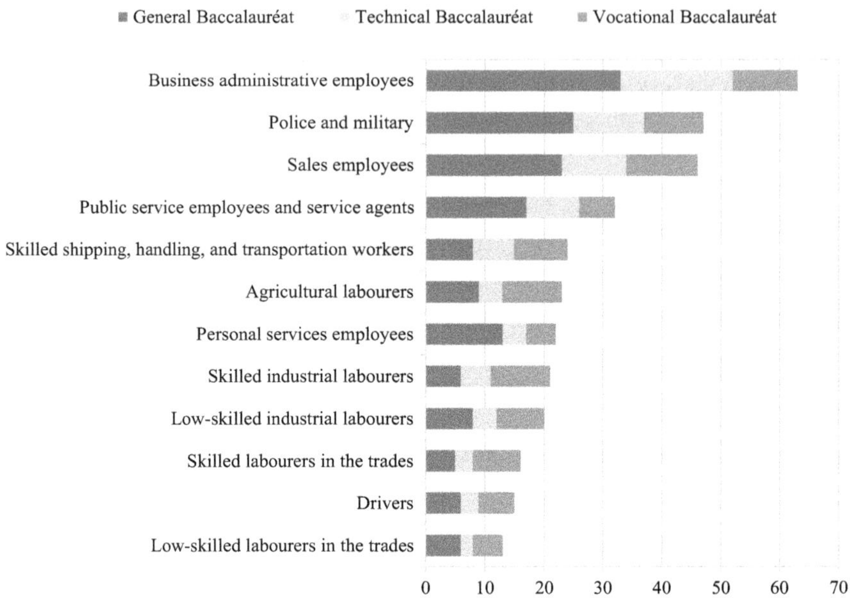

FIGURE 2.2 A very strong dispersal of the percentage of *baccalauréat* holders (General, Technical, and Vocational)

By percentage of each category of basic employee and labourer in 2012.

Note: This figure indicates the highest formal educational attainment obtained in secondary education, be it generalist (university-track), technical, or vocational. It thus does not represent the highest degree obtained, which could be a post-secondary degree.

Field: Members of the labour force (employed or seeking work) in the socio-professional groups 'basic employee' and 'labourer'.
Source: The 2012 *Emploi* survey (INSEE).

and 39% had a steady employment contract (open-ended contract or civil service), but with a monthly income under 1.4 times the minimum wage (that is, 1,560 euros net). These characteristics have nothing in common with the situations observed in the middle and upper classes, where the percentage of those working on a steady employment contract earning less than 1.4 times the minimum wage is no more than 14% for intermediary professions and 3% for *cadres*. Additionally, employment conditions have deteriorated over the decades, with the marked rise in unemployment and insecurity, specifically among the working classes, taking forms that affect labourers and basic employees differently: labourers are slightly more subject to limited-term contracts (19% in 2012) than basic employees (16%), but basic employees are by far the most subject to part-time jobs (32% in 2012, as compared to only 11% of labourers).

The economic situation of the working classes thus varies according to the kind of job, with low-skill labourers being distinctly more exposed to unemployment and insecurity (in 2012, nearly half of them were either unemployed or had a limited-term contract), and many low-skill sales and services employees having very low monthly incomes (especially due to the high proportion of part-time work among them). This divide is re-enforced by the opposition between employees who run the risk of long-term unemployment and those who keep their jobs (Dubost and Tranchant 2019): an examination of occupational 'immobility' (staying in the same job) reveals a stabilised group of the working classes, two-thirds of which consisting of basic employees and skilled labourers, which is strongly distinguished from an unstable, insecure group where low-skilled and/or routine employees are over-represented. The employment of less-skilled, younger, and less-educated employees is thus observably stalling. But as we shall see, the fault line between the skilled and low-skilled is not the only one running through the working classes.

The permanence of working-class backgrounds, the diversification of alliances

As we have seen, a job-based examination of the working classes attests to the persistence of the gap separating them from the middle and upper classes, and sharp internal differences as well. Analysis of their social backgrounds and conjugal alliances confirms this reality and allows us to identify the various fractions composing them.

Indeed, the social backgrounds of people in the working classes set them distinctly apart from other social groups: the father of 46% of labourers and basic employees is/was a labourer, a proportion three times higher than for *cadres*. Labouring roots are less significant for basic employees (41%) than for labourers (52%), and there are important differences between categories, since business administrative employees and sales employees come from higher social backgrounds. These labouring backgrounds constitute an important line demarcating the working classes from the middle and upper classes, and a widely shared trait among them. Moreover, this specificity persists: the percentage of labouring backgrounds has remained practically unchanged for 30 years, since the slight progression of the proportion of children of *cadres* and intermediary professions in the working classes (16% in 2012, up from 10% in 1982) is mainly balanced by the decline in farming backgrounds (which dropped from 14% to 7%).

Concerning household composition, the working classes are distinguished by a high proportion of people living alone (37%, as compared to 29% of intermediary professions and 25% of *cadres*). Over the studied period, conjugal life has certainly become less attainable for a large share of actively working people in France, but it seems to be especially marked in the working classes, differing by gender in the form it takes.[10] There is an over-representation of one-person households (single adult or separated/widowed parent not living with the child) among men over 30 working as a labourer or basic employee (18% of labourers and 22% of basic employees, compared to 16% of men in intermediary professions and 14% of *cadres*). Working-class women are more concerned by single parenthood than women of other social classes: in 2012, 14% of female labourers and 13% of female basic employees were in this situation, along with 23% of unemployed women who had never worked (compared to 8% of female *cadres* and 9% of women in intermediary professions).

The composition of couples has also changed over the period, especially in the working classes. In 1982, the model of conjugal specialisation (a man working outside the home and a woman homemaker) was dominant in the households of male labourers active in the labour force: 43% of them lived in a couple with a woman not in the labour force, 32% with a basic employee, and 18% with a female labourer. This conjugal configuration was dominant in all social milieus at the time, but it has become specific to the working classes as it lost ground in society at large. By 2012, the proportion of households corresponding to this model had dropped to 23% in homes where the primary male adult was a labourer, which is indeed higher than other social groups (15% in homes of male *cadres* and higher intellectual professions, 13% of homes where the man is in the intermediary professions, and 18% of those where the man is a basic employee).

Between 1982 and 2012, in a context of declining homogamy (defined in the strict sense of a conjugal alliance within the same socio-professional group) that could be attributed to mass education, the share of male labourers in a couple with a female basic employee rose significantly (from 32% in 1982 to 46% in 2012), reflecting the progression of female employment and the decline of the housewife model. An analogous progression occurred for male labourers in a couple with a woman in an intermediary profession (5–13%). Likewise, men who are basic employees are even more likely to be in a couple with a female basic employee (43–47%) or a woman in an intermediary profession (11–20%). Symmetrically, the percentage of female labourers living in a couple with a male labourer may still be the majority, but it has declined (from 68% to 54%). The share of female basic employees whose partner is a male labourer or basic employee has declined (from 44% to 37% and from 16% to 13%, respectively), the opposite of female basic employees living with a male partner working in an intermediary profession (steady at 22%) or as a *cadre* (from 3% to 10%).[11]

So the formation of working-class households is influenced by opposing dynamics, pulling them into and out of the groups. Between their labouring roots and homogamy, and the persistence of the couple composed of an actively employed man and a stay-at-home woman, people in the 'labourer' and 'basic employee' groups tend to form their families at a remove from other social groups. At the same time, they are less homogamous than before, especially skilled basic employees (who usually partner with *cadres*, intermediary professions, tradespeople, shopkeepers, or heads of a company[12]) and skilled labourers, many of whom are with women in intermediary professions. Most strikingly, the working classes have the highest proportion of single men and women raising children by themselves at a time when the family tends to serve as an economic refuge from the crumbling wage-labour system, which accentuates their internal differences in terms of skill levels.

The tripartite social space of contemporary working-class households

In order to identify the dividing lines in the working classes, we conducted statistical analyses to better identify their internal diversity, using factorial analyses and ascending hierarchical clustering. This is in continuity with recent studies deepening statistical analysis of social structure by mapping contemporary social space (Amossé 2011, Bernard 2017, Robette and Roueff 2017, Caveng et al. 2018) and starting to explore the diversity of the working classes (Cayouette-Remblière 2015, Peugny 2015).

The resulting figures show two divisions, one between insecure households and those having acquired some form of stability in their residential and economic situations, and another between households with higher and lower educational attainments and social backgrounds. These two poles of tension structuring the working-class space partly confirm the intuitions that fuelled our early research plans as well as the description that we had drafted of the situations and socio-professional characteristics of the middle classes.

Several clusters emerge within the working classes. One of them, near the top of the diagram, features business administrative employees and police and military, who in most cases accumulate possession of a *baccalauréat*, comfortable social backgrounds, and a certain degree of economic and residential stability.[13] In the opposite position, to the right of the diagram, personal services employees and low-skilled workers in the trades (half of whom office or industrial cleaning workers) stand out due to their less secure situations and more limited resources. Between them is a vast array associating a degree of (economic and residential) stability with working-class roots (from a working-class background, more rural) and low-level vocational educational attainments. This array, mainly composed of skilled labourers and basic employees in the civil service, more specifically corresponds to the kind of household the programme set out to study.

To deepen the understanding of these first elements, we used a variety of statistical studies to develop a series of classifications, varying the populations we analysed and giving more direct consideration to how individuals' situations interconnect in order to define household social positions.[14] As we have mentioned, one thing that makes our approach distinctive is our decision to be attentive to the household as a unit, but it was hardly a foregone conclusion. Since the socio-professional groups and categories are a nomenclature applying to individuals, most research using this statistical system concerns individuals

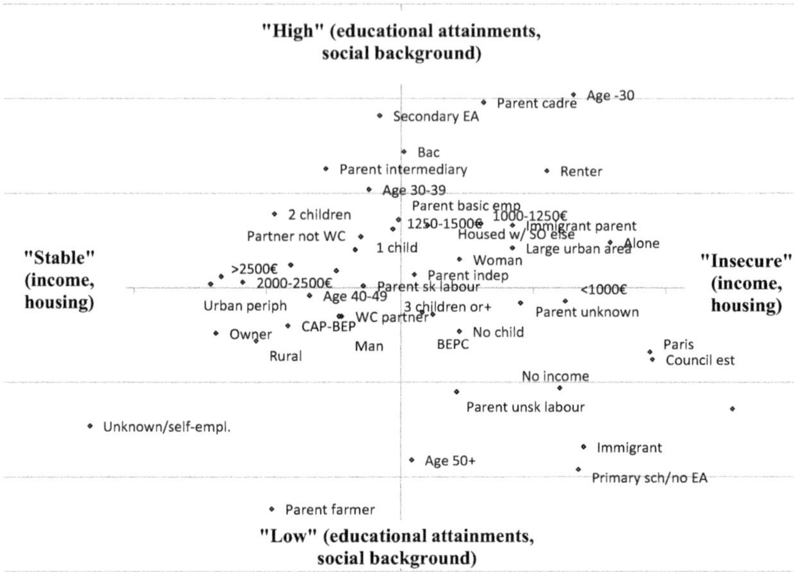

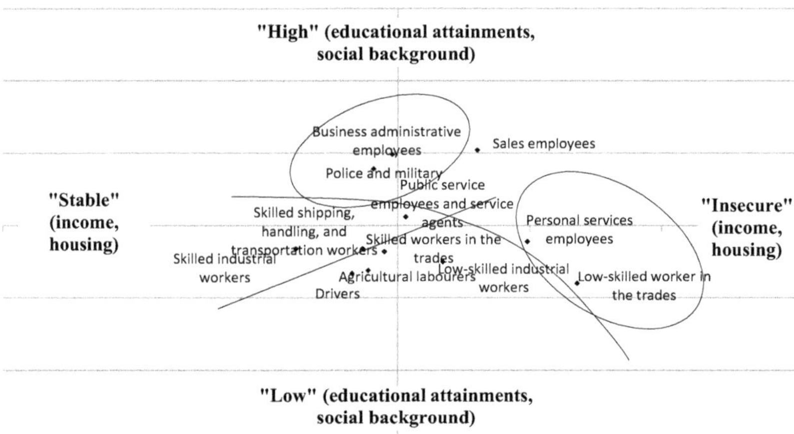

FIGURES 2.3 AND 2.4 Factor maps of the working classes

Method: First factorial plane from multiple correspondence analysis of data from the *Emploi* survey (variables: gender, age, number of children, partner's social position [when applicable], income, educational attainment, social background, residential situation; modalities of Table 2.2).

To read: Figure 2.3 presents the modalities of the variables taken into account (the active variables of the analysis), and Figure 2.4 presents the socio-professional categories of the corresponding individuals (the supplementary variables of the analysis).

Field: Households containing at least one active member of the labour force and one male or female labourer or basic employee (actively working or unemployed).

Source: The 2014 *Emploi* survey (INSEE).

rather than households, or defines households according to their 'person of reference'. But defining the social position of a household solely based on the socio-professional category of the 'person of reference' (who in 99% of couples is a man, according to the definition retained by INSEE's *Emploi* survey) is even more limiting as women have now largely joined the employment market. Consequently, we set out to conduct statistical analyses that accounted for the occupational position of both members of the couple.

The typologies we obtained provided supplementary information about the diversity of working-class couples. Although they were built on different fields, data, variables, and degrees of precision in the socio-professional nomenclature, they led to convergent results that were anything but obvious before the fact: they confirm that the working classes are indeed organised in a relatively stratified manner into 'upper', 'middle', and 'lower' fractions, based on the employment status and occupational positions of both members of the couple.

The analyses reveal concentrations that, while designed to have no specific ranking, do largely form a hierarchical continuum from the least secure and most impoverished in resources to the best off and closest to the middle classes. The 'upper' categories are characterised by economic, cultural, social, and conjugal proximity with the middle classes: they are especially composed of women and men with the highest educational attainments, incomes, and social backgrounds. They mainly include couples with a woman working as a business administrative employee or a man in the police or military.[15] Households on the 'lower' end are characterised by low levels of economic, educational, social, occupational, geographical, and familial resources. Their occupational situations are particularly marked by precarity, unemployment, or non-participation in the labour force. Low-skilled labourers (especially in the trades) and personal services employees (home care service providers, domestic workers, childminders), positions most frequently held by immigrant workers, are over-represented in this group.

Distinguishable from these two is the middle tier, which contains households in which both members of the couple have middling resource levels (in income, education, etc.) and somewhat socially asymmetrical couples in which one is more solidly established in the labour market than the other. It seems that the extent to which both members of the couple are established in the labour market is central to the couple's social position. In fact, 'being a couple' is a decisive resource for the social position of labourers and basic employees. Households consisting of a man or woman who is single or a single parent and employed as a labourer or basic employee are indeed in a distinctly less secure position than couples in the same social groups due to their weaker resources (economic in particular). This point is all the more important because the equivalent gap is smaller in households of one man or woman working as *cadre*, intermediary profession, or small business owner.

Our analyses moreover allow for a more precise characterisation of this middle tier. There are actually two kinds of middle fraction in the working classes, distinguished mainly by households' occupational worlds and geographical locations. One fraction is denoted by the world of big companies (skilled industrial workers are found in this fraction) and is particularly present in rural, sparsely populated, or urban peripheral areas; the other fraction assembles households that are more likely than not to live in large urban centres and work for small businesses (personal services workers are particularly concentrated in this group). This differentiation reflects two typical forms taken by labourers' and basic employees' occupational trajectories (Dubost and Tranchant 2019). The first form is regionally rooted and predominated by workers in industry and the civil service and is characterised by internal promotion (for at least one member of the household) in a major organisation's internal labour market. The second group is predominated by the trades, commerce, and personal services and characterised by trajectories where people set themselves up in business, strongly tied to the world of small business.

These analyses thus suggest the existence of a high, a low, and also a middle fraction in the space of working-class households, revealing divisions that are less known and less visible than the opposition between 'labourers' and 'basic employees' and that add complexity to the opposition between 'skilled' and 'low skilled' (Amossé and Chardon 2006), recalling the working-class diversity that Joanie Cayouette-Remblière (2015) demonstrated in her study of a city in the suburbs of Paris.

Case studies for exploring the middle fractions of working-class households

In addition to the statistical analyses, between 2014 and 2017 we conducted targeted household case studies that led to the portraits in this book, all in pursuit of our goal to study the working classes without focussing on their lower fractions or the lower middle classes. Our approach combining quantitative and qualitative methods made it possible to situate the resulting corpus of field studies within the social structure and achieve levels and forms of observation unreachable by statistics alone. The case studies were designed to collect information on the full range of economic, residential, familial, political, and occupational dimensions composing household lifestyles. The procedure followed by the programme's field researchers was inspired by ethnographic methods. Case studies were based on a minimum of three in-depth interviews (usually well spread out over time), observations of material living conditions, and contextualisation of households according to the characteristics of their residential space. Most case studies were of heterosexual couples; partners were usually interviewed separately and then together, and some children were also interviewed. The interview guide was prepared collectively and designed thematically (rather than through specific questions) to explore social trajectories and everyday practices as best as they can be reconstructed through interviews: leisure activities (of parents and children), distribution of domestic and familial labour, relationships to school, work, vacations, budgeting, dietary practices, the body, health care and use of health institutions, and how household members are embedded in the local social space (sociability, involvement in community groups, voting practices).

These case studies were developed as a tool for developing a more general picture that could take us farther than either individual documentation of the social condition or splitting the 'working class' into a multitude of specialised topics and delimited ethnographic field sites. They make it possible to analyse households as domestic groups where power relations as well as solidarity and socialisation between men and women and between generations are in play, and as places where transformations affecting the condition of the working classes are refracted – especially the opening of cultural enclaves and the rising economic domination evoked in Chapter 1. Another major change has been the inversion of time spent working, since labourers and basic employees currently work fewer hours than *cadres*, which makes analysis of private life outside of work even more necessary in working-class households.

The parameters of the household corpus were defined dynamically, apace with the statistical analysis to describe the socio-economic positions of various fractions of working-class households. Thus, during the first series of case studies conducted in 2014, the primary objective was couples composed of men and women actively working as basic employees or labourers with at least one school-aged child, probably not in possession of a post-secondary degree, and working for a small business if possible. Relative to the portrait of the working classes generated by statistical analysis of the *Emploi* survey, this first body of field research was characterised by an over-representation of labourers and basic employees in the public sector living in large or mid-sized urban areas. This bias was corrected in the next series of case studies, collection of which began in 2015, chosen to strengthen the diversity of the corpus and favour interviewees living in rural and suburban areas and working more in the private sector (security guards, sales employees, lorry drivers) or unemployed, as well as men living alone.

Our research methods combined ethnographic methods and qualitative interviews, so the materials we collected go well beyond the recorded word. We made observations of households (such as interior decoration, the meals to which sociologists were invited) and public places like school fêtes and sport clubs and took photographs (of the neighbourhood and housing, sometimes of work and/or leisure activities). We also consulted private documents (like letters to and from a primary school teacher deploring the behaviour of an interviewee's son) and used our e-mail exchanges and elements from websites used by research participants (Facebook, the French social networking site *Copains d'Avant*, sporting associations, consumer forums, and patient forums).

The wide-reaching character of research and the private dimension of some themes led to the choice of people who had been previously identified as being 'disposed to talking' (Mauger 1991), supposing that they would have a reflexive disposition and adequate linguistic resources, and who would be accustomed to interacting with members of other social classes and/or have a previously established relationship of confidence with the sociologist interviewing them. The households were largely found by activating our direct or indirect social networks: interpersonal relationships through families, friendships, or colleagues, or forged by frequenting the same school for those with school-aged children. In some cases, sociologists and research participants were brought closer by geographical proximity: metropolitan Paris, other major urban areas, smaller cities, urban peripheries, or rural areas. In the latter, relations between social groups are not necessarily more convivial or systematic, but places like nursery and primary schools, sporting associations, and school parents' associations can be more socially diverse than in urban settings.

Some research participants were approached because they had been informants in a previous study. Participants and researchers were somewhat generationally matched: sociologists established in their careers generally met with older households, while undergraduate and graduate students usually met with younger ones. If we had used more official channels to contact households, we might have missed some of them. The contextualisation and confidence intrinsic to ethnographic research are thus present in our research plan, since most case studies developed out of relatively close relations between the households and the sociologists, some going back many years. These accumulated past relations fostered a kind of moral obligation in participants, especially women, that favoured their agreement to participate in the study. Manifesting little cultural goodwill despite expressing (unequally distributed) forms of educational goodwill (Bourdieu 1984, 318), many of them did have talkative dispositions related to their occupations (many of which are relational), their sense of legitimacy stemming from their capital of autochthony (Retière 2003) and/or their experience in therapy with a mental health professional of some kind (men and women alike). One other factor, the very setting of the interviews: the private setting tends to favour speaking because it is 'relatively sheltered from relations of domination and confrontation between social classes' (Gilbert 2016) – even if the sociological interview activates a form of cultural domination, and women may be more comfortable than men with questions about the everyday creation of a lifestyle.[16]

The variety of ways in which we reached the households studied in this book ultimately produced a diverse corpus of case studies. As Table 2.2, presenting a summary of these households, demonstrates, guidelines for the social properties qualifying households for inclusion in the study did not end up imposing criteria strictly excluding any particular situation. There is an over-representation of couples composed of a female basic employee and a male labourer, both from working-class families, possessing a CAP or BEP, owning their own home in a rural area or urban periphery, but the corpus also includes other family situations (women living alone with their children, a single man, a couple of men), employment situations (retired, housewives, unemployed, technicians and associate professionals, tradespeople), cultural situations (no educational attainments, possession of a post-secondary degree), and residential situations (renters in low-income housing, living in greater Paris or another major urban area).

In order to better objectify and verify the specificities of the people we studied, we overlaid their households onto the social space resulting from the previously presented factor analysis (Figures 2.3 and 2.4). This confirmed that the corpus of studied households is indeed for the most part situated in the middle swath of the working classes, which is generally characterised by lower educational attainment and social background levels but a degree of economic and residential stability. They are households that 'more or less get by', to use Lise Bernard, Olivier Masclet, and Olivier Schwartz's expression (2019). However, the corpus is not statistically representative – the diversity of case studies is not a faithful representation of the working classes as a whole, or even of its middle fraction. Under a statistically representative logic, there should have been more households composed of a single man, more in greater Paris, more with at least one immigrant adult, and more composed of male and female labourers. The corpus nonetheless accounts for a wide range of gender, residence, occupation, and household structure situations within the middle fractions of the working classes, while offering a secondary counterpoint with some poorer households and some closer to the middle classes. Households with the lowest incomes are those of women living alone with their children and couples where the women are either homemakers or hold poorly paid part-time jobs. Households closest to the middle classes follow two scenarios: relatively older couples that have gradually accumulated the resources of stability (even if their trajectories were not linear) and younger couples with higher educational attainments. The corpus thus proves to be diverse enough to bring out certain consistencies in the middle-working-class lifestyle as compared to other fractions, but also certain principles of internal variation in terms of social stabilisation processes, domestic gender relations, and the forms taken by 'Us/Them' relations.

The diversity of stages in the life cycle found among the studied households is a result of how they were contacted, a consequence of the researchers' ages as described earlier. It ultimately ended up being a strength in analysing new lifestyle developments and the conditions for reaching social stability. Indeed, research on the working classes has yet to adequately account for the variable of life cycle position. While young couples are present in our corpus (as well as in the work of Isabelle Clair [2011] and Benoît Coquard [2019]), they are for the

TABLE 2.2 Social characteristics of the 21 households

First and last name (age)	*Family situation*	*Occupation and employment situation*	*Monthly income*	*Educational attainment (social background)*	*Residential situation*
Chantal Monlouis (52) and Robert Joseph (58)	Unmarried couple, two children	Laundry worker; Transporter at a public hospital	Both between 1,250 and 1,500 euros	No EA (basic employee background); No EA (background unknown)	Renters in low-income housing, greater Paris area
Régine (46) and Hervé (46) Leblanc	Married, two children	Childminder; Bus driver	1,000–1,250 euros; 1,500–2,000 euros	CAP-BEP (farm labour background); CAP-BEP (labour background)	Homeowners, periphery of a major urban area
Cécilia (41) and Eric (42) Dufar	Married, one child	Cashier (part-time); Caretaker of the municipal library	900–1,000 euros; 1,500–1,700 euros	No EA (labour background); CAP-BEP (basic employee background)	Apartment provided with job, centre of a small city
Mina (55) and Michel (55) Carry	Married, two children	Auxiliary nurse (public hospital); Hairdresser (owns his business)	1,500–2,000 euros; comfortable income (exact amount unknown)	CAP-BEP (labour background); *baccalauréat* (labour background)	Homeowners, centre of a small city
Sylvie Barderon (44)	Separated, two children	Cleaning woman (part-time, on limited-term employment contract)	Under 1,000 euros	CAP-BEP (intermediary profession background)	Renter in low-income housing, periphery of major urban area
Véronique Delage (39)	Divorced, two children	Childminder (part-time)	Under 1,000 euros	CAP-BEP (labour and basic employee background)	Renter in low-income housing, small city
Nathalie (51) and Alain (49) Rigaux	Married, three children	Homemaker; Tourist bus driver	2,000–2,500 euros	No EA (labour background); CAP-BEP (basic employee background)	Renters, rural area

Manou (41) and Jean (55) Audouin	Married, one child	Foster care provider; Lorry deliveryman	Under 1,000 euros; 1,250–1,500 euros	Both CAP-BEP (farming backgrounds)	Homeowners, rural area
Myriam (36) and Nicolino (39) Sanatanazefi	Married, two children	Cleaning woman (part-time); Heavy goods vehicle driver	Both 1,250–1,500 euros	CAP-BEP (labour background); CAP-BEP (labour and basic employee background)	Renters in low-income housing, small city
Laurent Douillard (37) and Thomas Guillet (24)	Unmarried couple, no children	Machine maintenance worker; Funeral and burial service employee	1,250–1,500 euros; 1,000–1,250 euros	CAP-BEP (labour background); Brevet de *collège* (comfortable background)	Homeowners, rural area
Mireille (74) and Roger (79) Monteil	Married, one child	A variety of jobs ending with agent at the unemployment office; Skilled mechanic (both retired)	Live comfortably, no specific indications of their pensions	No EA (farming background); CAP-BEP (farming background)	Homeowners, periphery of a small city
Cécile (30) and Jean-Marc (30) Pilier	Married, one child	Hairdresser employee; Security guard	1,000–1,250 euros; 1,250–1,500 euros	Both CAP-BEP (labour and basic employee backgrounds)	Homeowners, periphery of a city
Romain Boyer (32)	Single, no children	Electric metre reader for a private subcontractor	1,000–1,250 euros	*baccalauréat* (basic employee background)	Renter, periphery of a city
Vanessa Le Coz (35) and Samuel Bidaud (35)	Unmarried couple, two children	Supply technician (part-time); Turner and milling machine operator	1,250–1,500 euros; 1,500–2,000 euros	*baccalauréat* (labour background); *baccalauréat* (farming background)	Homeowners, rural area

(Continued)

First and last name (age)	*Family situation*	*Occupation and employment situation*	*Monthly income*	*Educational attainment (social background)*	*Residential situation*
Laeticia Kergal (27) and Valentin Dufour (27)	Unmarried couple, one child	Shipping and handling worker (unemployed); Delivery driver	Under 1,000 euros (benefits); 1,500–2,000 euros	No EA ('independent' background); Two years post-secondary education after the *baccalauréat* (basic employee background)	Renters, periphery of a city
Stéphanie (39) and Nicolas (36) Fontaine	Married, three children	Manager at the Social Security office (on maternity leave); Associate maintenance technician	Under 1,000 euros (leave pay); 1,500–2,000 euros	Two years post-secondary education after the *baccalauréat* (labour and basic employee background); No EA (intermediary profession and basic employee background)	Homeowners, periphery of a city
Elodie Paillé (27) and Clément Jacquet (35)	Unmarried couple, no children	Sales assistant (limited-term contract); Postman	1,000–1,250 euros; 1,250–1,500 euros	CAP-BEP (basic employee background); *baccalauréat* (background unknown)	Homeowners, periphery of a city
Michou (61) and Yvon (64) Ratelier	Married, one child	Preschool classroom assistant; plumbing and heating specialist (both retired)	Live comfortably, no specific indications of their pensions	CAP-BEP (farming background), CAP-BEP (small business owner background)	Homeowners, periphery of a city

Marianne (50) and Philippe (52) Chapalain	Married, two children	Auxiliary nurse; System operator	1,500–2,000 euros; 2,000–2,500 euros	CAP-BEP (background unknown); *baccalauréat* (labour background)	Homeowners, periphery of a city
Nadège (39) and Patrick (45) Lancel	Married, two children	Homemaker; Heavy goods vehicle driver	1,500–2,000 euros	CAP-BEP (intermediary profession and basic employee background); CAP-BEP (background unknown)	Renter in low-income housing, periphery of a city
Yamina (30) and Souleymane (36) Diallo	Married, three children	Medical secretary; Sales employee	Both 1,000–1,250 euros	*baccalauréat* (labour background); BTS (basic employee and labour, then small business owner background)	Renters in low-income housing, greater Paris area

Source: The 'Le 'populaire' aujourd'hui' study.

Employment status is only indicated in the Occupation column when it differs from the most common situation in the corpus: a wage-earning full-time job on an open-ended employment contract, or civil service job.

most part slightly older couples with children, which allows a more systematic analysis of exposure to educational and healthcare institutional norms (which are strengthened with the arrival of children) and residential strategies building new patterns of sociability (intended to get away from neighbours seen as negative social influences on children). Likewise, the presence of households where members are late in their careers or retired, with adult children, allows us to study a period when domestic constraints are lifting and the role of women is redefined, as they have an easier time finding leisure activities outside the home at this time of life. Just as spacing out interviews over the relatively short case-study timeframe allows us to assess the amplitude of the effects of occupational, economic, and/or conjugal vagaries on working-class lifestyles, comparing the trajectories of households of different generations allows us to historicise our analysis of the social conditions of working-class stability: it seems more difficult to succeed today, with the crumbling of the wage-earning society, the

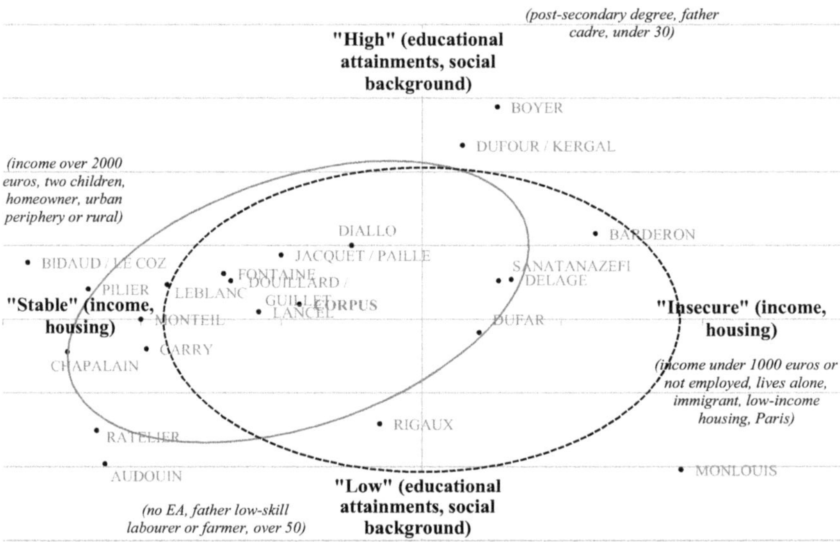

FIGURE 2.5 A factor map of corpus households

Method: Households from our corpus were projected onto the factor analysis map presented in Figures 2.3 and 2.4, according to the average of the coordinates of its adult members.

To read: The ellipses represent the dispersion of the clouds of points from the *Emploi* survey (dotted line) and the corpus (solid line).

Field: Households with at least one active member of the labour force and at least one labourer or basic employee (actively working or unemployed).

Source: The 2014 *Emploi* survey (INSEE) and the corpus of case studies from the research programme 'Le "populaire" aujourd'hui'.

rising bar for educational attainments, and the decline in occupational advancement in subaltern jobs.

Portraits presented in three thematic sections

This book contains portraits of 21 households. While case studies have been common practice in anthropology and in history since the early 1980s (Lewis 1961, Ginzburg 1992, to name but two well-known examples), such in-depth study of a single family and/or individual is more rare in sociology, a discipline that tends to favour a statistical approach to social phenomena. Recently, Bernard Lahire's work has helped to spread the use of 'sociological portraits' in France, with the intention of showing 'the same individuals in a plurality of scenes' (Lahire 2002, 1). This method renews the spirit of the anthropological origins of ethnography and prevents research from being too narrowly focussed by including a variety of scenes of informants' lives, allowing us to contextualise their speech and observed behaviour (Beaud and Weber 1997).

> The portrait, as a scientific genre freely inspired by the literary genre, has two fundamental requirements: one, based on 'data' and attentive to critique of the contexts of its production, is the painting of a particular model that, unlike literary discourse, really exists; and the other, it must clearly reveal the specific manner of the painter, the viewpoint from which he observes and explains the world.
>
> *(Lahire 1995, 15)*

This book presents neither portraits of individuals nor of families but rather portraits of households, meaning portraits of people living in the same housing in a particular residential context. Because it gives access to configurations of conjugal and filial relationships as well as residential and local positions, the household appeared to be the most relevant level of analysis for researching working-class living conditions and lifestyles. The decision to present portraits comes from the overall intention of our research: comprehend the ways in which the working classes live without falling into scholarly or 'common sense' reductionism. Like those of other social classes, working-class lifestyles cannot be summed up by only one property or a single kind of social relationship, nor can they be divorced from the contexts in which they develop; just like the lifestyles of other social classes, they form complex and singular groupings that can be more or less unified and sometimes contradictory. There are also internal variations in the lifestyles of the stable middle fractions of the working classes that can only be addressed if we allow ourselves the flexibility to adapt our writing to their circumstances, rather than obliging ourselves to favour one element to the exclusion of others and isolate it in contexts where it is in interaction with other elements. Although the portraits are carefully written to reproduce the singular complexity and dynamic of household configurations, they are not purely idiographic accounts: they lead the reader to discover general processes that are central to the recrafting of working-class lifestyles. Although they could be read as literary portraits, they were nonetheless written from a sociological perspective, and we included many of them to allow comparison. This book's general introduction, section introductions, and conclusion take this more distinctly sociological approach and give readers the analytical ties for reading them in relation to each other.

Portraits were clustered into three thematic sections corresponding to different analytical themes, and section introductions highlight the traits in the portraits that are relevant to these themes. In fact, each household case study could have figured in any of the three sections because they all explore all of the retained analytical angles, but each household has some traits particularly salient to one of these themes that have been emphasised in its portrait.

The first section studies the modalities for access to social stability in the working-class milieu, with particular insistence on the stabilising resources stemming from being in a couple, a decisive factor driven home by the statistical description earlier in this chapter. These portraits are grouped to work as variations and counter-examples, with two examples of unstable households. This grouping reveals the complexity of the social stabilisation process, which is never due to one sole explanatory factor but to a combination of individual biographical properties, contextual effects, and configurations of conjugal and familial relations.

The second section focuses on the gendered division of domestic organisation and gender relations in the home. It provides a broad array of family situations that are connected to the degree of women's decisive but tenuous participation in the labour market. Pulled between overcoming and perpetuating gendered routines, between resignation and demands for more sharing between partners, the portraits reveal numerous ways of functioning on the working-class domestic scene that are strongly related to the households' occupational constraints.

The third section focuses on practices of sociability, relations with other social groups, and how households position themselves in the social space. The opposition between 'Us' and 'Them' is reconstructed into a triangular social consciousness that is no longer dichotomous: in addition to feeling a distance from 'Them', the dominants, there is a new rejection of the figure of the 'benefits scrounger'. The portraits shed light on the highly variable forms of goodwill towards institutions, especially those concerning health, education, and employment. Lastly, they suggest that these middle fractions of the working classes are significantly involved in the community.

Notes

1 Sometimes reformulated, they resulted in several special thematic journal issues (Amossé and Cartier 2018, Bernard, Masclet, and Schwartz 2019, Lechien and Siblot 2019).
2 See 'Appendix A: Socio-professional categories', for a description and definition of the French occupational categories and corresponding social positions that are found in this chapter and throughout the book.
3 The lack of a statistical definition of social position other than that based on the occupation of the (male) head of the family has yet to prompt the adoption of an alternative approach, although some authors, including P. Bourdieu in *Distinction* (1984), have already indicated the necessity.
4 We will return to the issue of cultural autonomy later in the book, especially through the role of women, their occupations, and how they relate to institutions (and the norms they promote).

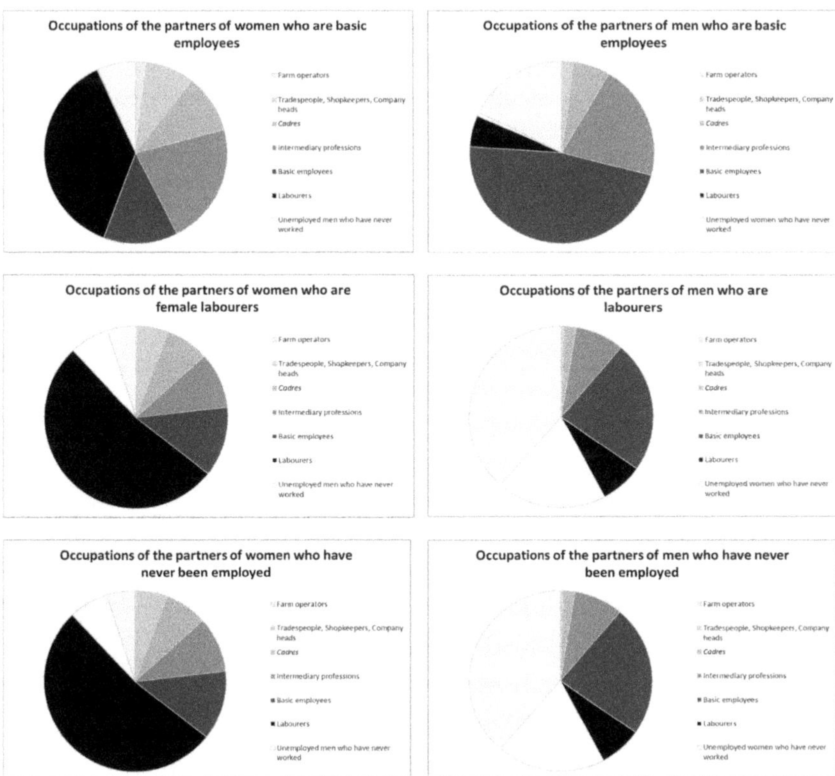

Field: Female basic employees, labourers, or unemployed who have never worked who are in a couple
Source: *Emploi* survey (INSEE, 2012).

Field: Male basic employees, labourers, or unemployed who have never worked who are in a couple
Source: *Emploi* survey (INSEE, 2012)

FIGURE 2.6 The socio-professional groups of the domestic partners of basic employees, labourers, and unemployed people who have never worked, in 2012
Source: *Emploi* survey (INSEE, 2012).

5 INSEE defines a household ('*ménage*') as all the persons living in the same lodgings, regardless of how they are connected.
6 For more on this, see Amossé (2019b).
7 This is a recently created formal employment status for self-employment with simplified accounting and fiscal advantages but an earnings cap of around 33,000 euros.
8 Meaning either actively employed or actively seeking work (for those who have already worked), and excluding retired people, people with home-based activities (e.g., family care work), and others who are not on the labour market (non-working and not looking for work).
9 For a full explanation of the educational attainments mentioned here, see the Appendix.
10 For more on this point, see Bernard and Giraud (2018).
11 A more detailed presentation of this data is provided in Figure 2.6.
12 This is the case for 34% of them, as compared to only 10% of low-skilled male labourers. For more detail on conjugal alliances, see Figure 2.6.
13 The singular position of sales employees is notable; many younger people in sales are in a situation of downclassing or work in sales while waiting for a job in their field. They are near the least secure in terms of residential and economic stability, although they have significantly higher educations.
14 One of the first typologies (Bernard and Giraud 2018) concerns couples consisting of a woman who is under 60 and does not work or who is a labourer or basic employee (actively employed or unemployed) and a man working as a labourer or basic employee. A second typology concerning couples composed of at least one labourer or basic employee (male or female) uses the occupational positions of six close family members (the couple and their parents) to highlight the diversity of working-class social structures (Amossé 2019a). A third analysis (Amossé 2019b) was conducted of all households and of heterosexual households in which both members come under one of the following groups: labourer, basic employee, and non-worker (excluding retired persons). It outlines their diverse social positions and shows how the variety of resources they possess (income, educational attainment, social background, type of protections they have related to their job, geographical trajectory, where they live, and residential status) all interact.
15 One of the analyses used the socio-professional nomenclature at a finer level than the other two (Bernard and Giraud 2018). It highlighted the fact that women employed as skilled civil service employees also come under the upper fraction of the working classes (a point supported by earlier findings, based on individual data, by Guillaume Burnod and Alain Chenu [2001] and Olivier Chardon [2002]) and also placed female wage-earning salespeople, hairdressers, and manicurists/beauticians in the 'upper' fraction of the women studied.
16 On all of these points, see the article by Gérard Mauger and Marie-Pierre Pouly (2019) analysing the research relationship as 'a particular situation of face-to-face relations between socially ranked individuals' and thus a 'situation that lends itself to the study of symbolic exchanges between social classes', which are in turn influenced by societal transformations such as the prolongation of education, the spread of 'psychological culture', and the proliferation of service jobs held by people from the working classes as well as from the middle and upper classes, which makes some kinds of interactions between distant social groups commonplace. In this book, we chose to not emphasise the research relationship in the portraits unless it shed important light on the material and analysis. The aim was to get straight to the portrait, which was made long enough to respect the logic of an ethnographic case study without losing sight of the bigger sociological picture of all stable fractions of the contemporary working classes.

References

Abdelnour, Sarah, and Anne Lambert. 2014. "L'entreprise de soi." Un nouveau mode de gestion politique des classes populaires? Analyse croisée de l'accession à la propriété et de l'auto-emploi (1977–2012).' *Genèses* 95: 27–48.

Alonzo, Philippe, and Cédric Hugrée. 2010. *Sociologie des classes populaires.* Paris: Colin.

Amossé, Thomas. 2011. 'Cadres/non cadres: une frontière toujours persistante.' In *Cadres, classes moyennes : vers l'éclatement?*, edited by Paul Bouffartigue, Charles Gadéa, and Sophie Pochic, 32–45. Paris: Armand Colin.

Amossé, Thomas. 2019a. 'Diversité et dynamique des couples populaires au regard de leur milieu social familial. Une analyse statistique à partir des enquêtes *Emploi* (2011–2014) et *Formation et qualification professionnelle* (1993 et 2014/2015).' *Sociologie* 10, no. 1: 17–36.

Amossé, Thomas. 2019b. 'Quelle définition statistique des classes populaires? Propositions d'agrégation classification des situations socio-professionnelles des ménages.' *Sociétés contemporaines* 114 23–57.

Amossé, Thomas, and Marie Cartier, eds. 2018. 'Ménages populaires.' Special issue, *Travail, genre et sociétés* 39.

Amossé, Thomas, and Olivier Chardon. 2006. "Les travailleurs non qualifiés : une nouvelle classe sociale?" Économie et statistique 393–394: 203–229.

Avril, Christelle. 2014. *Les Aides à domicile: un autre monde populaire.* Paris: La Dispute.

Baudelot, Christian, and Roger Establet. 2005. 'Classes en tous genre.' In *Femmes, genre et sociétés*, edited by Margaret Maruani, 38–47. Paris: La Découverte.

Beaud, Stéphane, and Florence Weber. 1997. *Guide de l'enquête de terrain.* Paris: La Découverte.

Bernard, Lise. 2017. *La Précarité en col blanc. Une enquête sur les agents immobiliers.* Paris: Presses Universitaires de France.

Bernard, Lise, and Christophe Giraud. 2018. 'Avec qui les ouvrières et les employées vivent-elles en couple?' *Travail, genre et sociétés* 39: 41–61.

Bernard, Lise, Olivier Masclet, and Olivier Schwartz, eds. 2019. 'Classes populaires d'aujourd'hui. Questions de morphologie et de styles de vie.' Special issue, *Sociétés contemporaines* 2, no. 14.

Béroud, Sophie, Paul Bouffartigue, Henri Eckert, and Denis Merklen. 2016. *En Quête de classes populaires. Un essai politique.* Paris: La Dispute.

Bessière, Céline, and Sibylle Gollac. 2014. 'Travailleur indépendant.' In *Dictionnaire sociologique de l'entrepreneuriat*, edited by Pierre-Marie Chauvin, Michel Grossetti, and Pierre-Paul Zalio, 537–550. Paris: Presses de Science Po.

Boltanski, Luc. (1982) 1987. *The Making of a Class: Cadres in French Society.* Translated by Arthur Goldhammer. Cambridge: Cambridge University Press.

Boltanski, Luc, and Laurent Thévenot. 1983. 'Finding One's Way in Social Space; A Study Based on Games.' *Social Sciences Information* 22, no. 4/5: 631–679.

Bourdieu, Pierre. (1979) 1984. *Distinction: A Social Critique of the Judgment of Taste.* Translated by Richard Nice. Cambridge, MA: Harvard University Press.

Bruneau, Ivan, Gilles Laferté, Julian Mischi, and Nicolas Renahy, eds. 2018. *Mondes ruraux et classes sociales.* Paris: Editions EHESS.

Burnod, Guillaume, and Alain Chenu. 2001. 'Employés qualifiés et non qualifiés : une proposition d'aménagement de la nomenclature des catégories socioprofessionnelles.' *Travail et emploi* 86: 87–105.

Cartier, Marie, Isabelle Coutant, Olivier Masclet, and Yasmine Siblot. (2008) 2016. *The France of the Little-Middles: A Suburban Housing Development in Greater Paris*. Translated by Juliette Rogers. New York: Berghahn Books.

Caveng, Rémy, Fanny Darbus, François Denord, Delphine Serre, and Sylvain Thine. 2018. 'Des morales de classe? Dispositions éthiques et positions sociales dans la France contemporaine.' *Actes de la recherche en sciences sociales* 224: 76–101.

Cayouette-Remblière, Joanie. 2015. 'De l'hétérogénéité des classes populaires (et de ce que l'on peut en faire).' *Sociologie* 6, no. 4: 377–400.

Chardon, Olivier. 2002. *La Qualification des employés*, Document de travail Insee no. F0202.

Chenu, Alain. 1990. *L'Archipel des employés*. Paris: Insee.

Clair, Isabelle. 2011. 'La découverte de l'ennui conjugal. Les manifestations contrariées de l'idéal conjugal et de l'ethos égalitaire dans la vie quotidienne de jeunes de milieux populaires.' *Sociétés contemporaines* 83: 59–81.

Collovald, Annie, and Olivier Schwartz. 2006. 'Haut, bas, fragile: sociologies du populaire.' *Vacarme* 37: 50–55.

Coquard, Benoît. 2019. *Ceux qui restent. Faire sa vie dans les campagnes en déclin*. Paris: La Découverte.

Dubost, Claire-Lise, and Lucas Tranchant. 2019. 'Changer d'emploi, est-ce changer de position sociale? La structure des classes populaires au prisme des mobilités professionnelles des ouvriers et des employés.' *Sociétés contemporaines* 14: 59–88.

Gilbert, Pierre. 2016. 'Classes, genre et styles de vie dans l'espace domestique.' *Actes de la recherche en sciences sociales* 215: 4–15.

Ginzburg, Carlo. 1992. *The Cheese and the Worms: The Cosmos of a Sixteenth-Century Miller*. Translated by John Tedeschi and Ann Tedeschi. Baltimore, MD: Johns Hopkins University Press.

Girard, Violaine. 2017. *Le Vote FN au village. Trajectoires de ménages populaires du périurbain*. Paris: Editions du Croquant.

Hamel, Christelle, and Johanna Siméant. 2006. 'Genre et classes populaires.' *Genèses* 64: 2–4.

Herpin, Nicolas, Olivier Choquer, Liliane Kasparian, and Daniel Verger. 1987. 'Les conditions de vie des ouvriers.' *Les collections de l'Insee, Série M* 126.

Hugrée, Cédric, Étienne Penissat, and Alexis Spire. 2020. *Social Class in Europe: New Inequalities in the Old World*. London: Verso.

Lahire, Bernard. 1995. *Tableaux de familles. Heurs et malheurs scolaires en milieux populaires*. Paris: Seuil/Gallimard.

Lahire, Bernard. 2002. *Portraits sociologiques. Dispositions et variations individuelles*. Paris: Nathan.

Lechien, Marie-Hélène, and Yasmine Siblot, eds. 2019. ''Eux/nous/ils'? Sociabilités et contacts sociaux en milieu populaire.' Special issue, *Sociologie* 10, no. 1.

Lewis, Oscar. 1961. *The Children of Sanchez: Autobiography of a Mexican Family*. New York: Random House.

Mauger, Gérard. 1991. 'Enquêter en milieu populaire.' *Genèses* 6: 125–143.

Mauger, Gérard, and Marie-Pierre Pouly. 2019. 'Enquêter en milieu populaire. Une **étude** des **échanges** symboliques entre classes sociales.' *Sociologie* 10, no. 1: 37–54.

Perrin-Heredia, Ana. 2013. 'Le 'choix' en économie. Le cas des consommateurs pauvres.' *Actes de la recherche en sciences sociales* 199: 46–67.

Peugny, Camille. 2015. 'Pour une prise en compte des clivages au sein des classes populaires. La participation politique des ouvriers et des employés.' *Revue française de science politique* 65: 735–759.
Poullaouec, Tristan. 2010. *Le Diplôme, arme des faibles. Les familles ouvrières et l'école.* Paris: La Dispute.
Retière, Jean-Noël. 2003. 'Autour de l'autochtonie. Réflexions sur la notion de capital social populaire.' *Politix* 63: 121–143.
Robette, Nicolas, and Olivier Roueff. 2017. 'L'espace contemporain des goûts culturels. Homologies structurales entre domaines de pratiques et entre classes sociales.' *Sociologie* 8, no. 4: 369–394.
Savage, Mike. 2015. *Social Class in the 21st Century.* London: Pelican.
Schwartz, Olivier. 2011. 'Peut-on parler de classes populaires?' *La Vie des idées*, 13 September 2011. https://laviedesidees.fr/Peut-on-parler-des-classes.html.
Siblot, Yasmine, Marie Cartier, Isabelle Coutant, Olivier Masclet, and Nicolas Renahy. 2015. *Sociologie des classes populaires contemporaines.* Paris: Colin.

PART I

Stories of stabilisation

3

INTRODUCTION TO PART 1

Stories of stabilisation

Lise Bernard and Olivier Masclet

The trajectories of the following grouping of households, for the most part in the middle fractions of the working classes, shed light on the social conditions of stability. This section of this book deals with stabilisation processes, which it details through eight portraits. Speaking of 'stabilisation' by no means signifies that it is a permanent acquisition: the positions of these households can still be somewhat fragile, and many have been destabilised at one time or another. Several elements contribute to this relative stability. After showing that employment, being in a couple, and housing can be significant factors of stabilisation, we will demonstrate that each of the life courses studied here has its singularities, especially regarding household members' resources, experiences of family life, age, and generation.

Factors of stability

Position in the employment market, household morphology, and residential situation are determinants of social position that may also be factors of stabilisation.

We'll start with work. Although the vast majority of research participants hold subaltern positions, the incomes of many are higher than those of basic employees and labourers working the most insecure jobs and people who struggle the most to find and keep work. In addition to income level, having a job (even a humble one) with a future or the possibility of growth was a precious resource for many interviewees in establishing their social position. Possession of qualifications, educational attainments (especially for the younger generations), and passing a competitive examination may have facilitated access to this kind of job. The same is true for some working in a large company or a civil

DOI: 10.4324/9781003330073-4

service job, as the following examples attest. Yvon Ratelier, a retired plumbing and heating specialist, had a valuable qualification.[1] Possessing recognised skills let him voluntarily work as a temp for most of his career; this qualification sheltered him from the fear of not finding work that plagues most temporary workers, and he could allow himself to turn down job offers while his wife was on vacation from her pre-school classroom assistant job, so he could enjoy the time with his family. As to Mireille Monteil, who only has a certificate of completion of primary school, a competitive examination made it possible for her to stabilise her professional path: after working on her parents' farm, she moved to the city and worked as a housekeeper, sales assistant, bookkeeper for the tax service, and secretary in a marriage agency.[2] Left unemployed after it closed, she passed a competitive hiring examination at the national unemployment office that gave her access to a humble job ('accounts worker'), but one with an assured future that she kept until she retired. Lastly, Mina Carry's case shows just how stabilising a job in the civil service can be.[3] The child of immigrants, she left school during her last year in *lycée* (upper secondary school) without any educational attainments and initially worked in exhausting unskilled industrial and food service jobs.[4] Getting into a public hospital job allowed her to become an auxiliary nurse at nearly 40 years old and thus have a better income, greater job stability, and previously unattainable prospects for career development.

Living in a couple is the second stabilising factor. As we have already stressed, being in a couple is a determinant resource for labourers and basic employees: with or without children, households composed of a single labourer or basic employee (male or female) are in a more delicate position than those of couples of labourers and/or basic employees – especially in economic terms. It is even more significant for male labourers and basic employees over 30 years old, who are over-represented among one-person households, and women from working-class milieus, who are more likely than women in other social milieus to be head of a single-parent household (Bernard and Giraud 2018). In a context of rising female employment, especially in the working classes, being in a couple often means that they can count on two incomes: it allows easier access to expensive goods (like housing or a car) and costly leisure-time pursuits (like going away on holiday) and may serve as a buffer when one of them experiences a drop in income. Moreover, the case studies highlight the importance of a pact between partners to 'make it' and improve their lives: many of the interviewed partners were bound by a common desire for ascension or to escape instability, and this mutual solidarity seems to be a decisive resource for 'improving' or managing to maintain the household's position. A good example of this is found with Yamina and Souleymane Diallo, both children of immigrants, who have three children.[5] Yamina (age 30) is a medical secretary and Souleymane (36) works nights at a gas station. Two years ago they went back to school to study sociology at university. They have common aspirations (hoping to become teachers) and work together to raise their social standing. Major effort and conjugal solidarity made it possible for them to resume their studies. This solidarity allows them to endure their very tight schedules combining paid work (each works 30 hours a week), shared care of their two pre-school-aged children (taking the oldest back and forth to school), and attending university courses (by sharing their notes).

Thirdly, housing may be a factor of stabilisation. Access to homeownership is (or was) a strong aspiration for most of the people we interviewed. Being a homeowner may be a way to attain a single-family home or to build net worth with retirement in mind. Many of them also see it as a significant element in social advancement. Additionally, place of residence is seen as a decisive element in their status: many of them are committed to keeping their distance from the more insecure fractions of the working classes through their choice of neighbourhood.

In the stories of many of the studied households, all three of these factors of stabilisation – work, couple, and housing – are closely intertwined. Professional and conjugal stabilisation can, for example, favour residential stabilisation by making homeownership possible. It was when Mireille Monteil got an open-ended employment contract that she and her husband Roger, a skilled labourer with a stable job in a large company, were able to buy their first house. Moreover, residential destabilisation can result from professional destabilisation: this is notably illustrated by the case of Elodie Paillé and Clément Jacquet, who became homeowners at ages 24 and 31, when they were both working (she as a sales assistant, he as a postman).[6] Three years after their purchase, they were forced to put their house up for sale; Elodie was unemployed and Clément's income was not enough to cover the monthly payments. For that matter, conjugal destabilisation may engender residential or professional destabilisation, as Véronique Delage's story makes clear.[7] After leaving her husband, this childminder living alone with her children had to move several times. As she fell in love with new men, she abandoned childcare work, first moving in with a cook in a small rural town, and then living with a farmer, who she helped on the farm (unofficially and unpaid) while working at a factory.

Singular trajectories

One strength of this study is that it opens the black box of the social fate of working-class households to reveal a number of ways that their life courses may achieve stability (meaning improving strength and security), but also how unpredictable and fragile they can be. Upon closer examination, which we did through household case studies, each trajectory seems to have its own unique elements. We tried to reconstruct their specificities in the *stories of stabilisation* that we outline here.

These stories first of all differ in terms of the resources that could (or could not) be accumulated relative to the previous generation (in the form of economic worth in families of tradesmen or farmers, for example, or a little cultural capital derived from vocational qualifications or union experience), and in terms of interviewees' parents' professional situations, which could give them a stable footing from the start or, to the contrary, enduringly mark them with insecurity. These stories also differ in terms of employment opportunities and the possibilities for calling on allies for guidance in seeking a job and over the course of professional life. Lastly, they differ according to educational paths. Some members of studied households left school without a secondary-level diploma (Mina Carry, Véronique Delage, Thomas Guillet, Élodie Paillé, Mireille Monteil, and Roger Monteil), while others were able to earn vocational qualifications (Michel Carry, Laurent Douillard, Michou Ratelier, and Yvon Ratelier) and others still went as far as the *baccalauréat* or beyond (Romain Boyer, Yamina Diallo, and Souleymane Diallo).

All these initial economic and cultural divisions between the studied households and between the members of those households explain the heterogeneity of paths of stability. This is what sets Mireille Monteil so far apart from other interviewees who grew up in families that could not financially support them: as the only child of a property-owning farming family, she could receive economic help from her parents at key moments in life, especially when she set out to buy a house in a more socially selective neighbourhood. In the portraits examined in this first part of this book, half of the 14 adults mention a background of economic destitution, even though it is hard to share memories of poverty. When surveyed by INSEE, one in four labourers and basic employees living as a couple said that they experienced 'major money problems' in the family of their childhood, which is ten points higher than intermediary professions and cadres in couples, but half the percentage of our interviewees.[8] We were able to touch on this subject during our interviews because our interviewees had been able to acquire a stable position and put space between themselves and the difficult years. Stabilising one's situation represents a victory over poverty and also feeds the self-esteem of those having grown up in a poor family.

There is also a generational opposition among the studied households. On one side are those who benefitted from the major economic growth of the 1950s–1970s, when living conditions and incomes rose significantly, and workers could enter the working world young, with low levels of educational attainments and vocational qualifications. The Monteils, who were around 30 years old in 1968, and the Rateliers, born in the early 1950s, were able to find steady jobs and support themselves over the long term, despite periods of unemployment. On the other end, households whose members grew up in later periods managed to find stability through life courses that were often dotted with pitfalls and are still threatened by a return to insecurity.

Indeed, the once-common option of early entry into employment and obtaining vocational qualifications on the job crumbled in the mid-1970s, with the rise of mass unemployment, the weakening security of employment contracts, and growing competition between subaltern workers that gave a clear advantage to the most highly educated. This break with the old career path not only makes it harder for a swathe of young people to get jobs, not to mention independence, but it also means that they are the first to be hit by economic crises and have more difficulty obtaining the main attributes of adulthood: work, housing, and life partner (Mauger 2015, Galland 2017). This inequality particularly affects working-class men, significant numbers of whom live alone today. Romain Boyer's situation attests specifically to the risk of prolonging the youthful phase of life indefinitely: he has a *baccalauréat* and an open-ended employment contract for a job that he knows is likely to become obsolete; he is 32 and single and living with an old school friend in a house bought by his parents, who he reimburses with a modest rent.[9]

Stabilising oneself represents an even greater challenge today as the efforts expended to acquire a skilled job are far from being rewarded. In the previous period, minimal ambitions to promotion were met with a promise of minimal success (Baudelot and Establet 2005). The creation of many jobs in the industrial and tertiary sectors favoured structural mobility that came with the possibility of climbing within the company. The current period is, to the contrary, typified by less structural mobility and a heavy inflation of managerial demands on the labour market, where supply outstrips demand. These processes explain why there are so few ascendant careers among labourers and basic employees. This is demonstrated very well in the statistical analyses of Claire-Lise Dubost and Lucas Tranchant (2019): although people working as basic employees and labourers experience professional mobility as frequently as those in intermediary, *cadre*, and higher intellectual professions, five years of observation found this mobility to be significantly less towards better-paying and higher-ranking jobs and much more frequently towards joblessness or horizontal mobility (equivalent positions). Today, candidates for promotion are required to demonstrate a considerable effort for quite uncertain results: skilled positions are still frequently inaccessible to people without educational attainments. Elodie Paillé's story illustrates the difficulty that subaltern workers run up against as they try to rise today, even when, like Elodie, they manifest professional goodwill: although her superiors exploited her desire to occupy a skilled position in the sales sector (a way for her to make up for her failure in school), they never formally rewarded it. Such logics denying recognition of personal engagement in work can be sources of discouragement. Elodie ultimately gave up.

Curbing family misfortune

There are other elements that differentiate life courses and should be taken into account. Lived experience of family life is one. Members of the studied households describe their childhood families as highly variable in the 'affective support' they provided, meaning that they gave a sense of recognition simply by being part of it (Mauger 2015).

In some cases, their families were able to help them pursue education or, as we have already mentioned, acquire real estate. Most of all, the security they provided favoured the interiorisation of a degree of social assurance amounting to a sort of self-confidence in difficult situations. Mireille Monteil benefitted from this kind of affective resource, and it had a strong influence on her desire for social advancement. Likewise, Souleymane Diallo got enough support from his parental family to pursue an education, leading him to a vocational post-secondary BTS degree rather than drifting into delinquency while growing up in a housing estate on the outskirts of Paris.

Other households speak to family misfortune, however. Of the 14 adult members of the households in this section, eight went through painful ordeals in their childhood or youth: early loss of a parent (Mina Carry, Yamina Diallo, Clément Jacquet, Michou Ratelier, and Yvon Ratelier), divorced parents (Thomas Guillet, Élodie Paillé), alcoholic father and family shame (Véronique Delage), and retaliation towards girls (Mina Carry). In the previously cited INSEE *'Emploi du temps'* survey, around 12% of labourers and 9% of basic employees living in a couple say that before the age of 18 they had experienced 'problems of violence in the family where they grew up' (compared to 6% of *cadres* and intermediary professions in a couple). Approximately one-quarter of them declare having experienced the illness, disability, or a serious accident involving one of their parents (the case for 17% of *cadres* and 19% of intermediary professions in a couple). While these figures are a warning to avoid exaggerating family misfortune in working-class milieus, it is still more present there than elsewhere. It is thus likely to have more significant consequences on the futures of the children of basic employees and labourers. The accounts gathered in this study prompt us to think so: they suggest the existence of a rather clear connection between the early death of a parent and early departure from school and between certain behaviours by fathers and children's early departure from the childhood home, especially for girls.

Twice widowed, Yvon Ratelier's mother raised five children alone, placing them in apprenticeships young. Yvon thus learned about plumbing and heating work 'randomly' at age 14. He was lucky that he was able to appropriate it for himself and turn it to his advantage: the trade allowed him to obtain high vocational qualifications and maintain independence his whole working life. Thomas Guillet, whose mother had committed suicide two years before our study, did not speak of the consequences that his parents' divorce had on him when he was an adolescent.[10] His mother was a factory worker and his father a *cadre* in sales. Their separation plunged her into depression. His mother raised their two children alone, but she was not really able to help them with their schoolwork because she lacked adequate educational resources and was hindered by her illness. Thomas twice failed the examination for a CAP, the lowest-level vocational diploma. His relationship with Laurent, 13 years his senior, helped him to reach a stable position. Mina Carry and Véronique Delage, who both describe themselves as good students in *collège* (lower secondary school), sacrificed their educations in *lycée* (upper secondary school) in order to preserve their integrity from their fathers' moral impositions and denial of freedom. They had to flee the parental home. Like Thomas, not to mention Yamina Diallo (orphaned at age 14), they found a refuge in the couple, 'a lifesaver' in Véronique Delage's words, that let them leave an unacceptable family life. They, too, found stability by entering into a relationship with older men while they were young: Yamina was 18 when she met Souleyman, ten years her senior; Mina met Michel (four years older) shortly after leaving the family home, the year when she was to have taken the *baccalauréat* exam; Véronique Delage was 16 when she got together with the boy who would become her first husband, and would move in with him two years later, determined to never again suffer from her father's alcoholism. After 18 years together, Véronique divorced him and went on to raise their two children alone, supplementing her income as a childminder with RSA benefits.[11] Her divorce made her a member of the working poor, but at the same time, it freed her of a man who she said 'dragged her down' by not acknowledging her efforts to 'grow' professionally and demanding that she satisfy only his desires. If she lost the economic security that her household enjoyed thanks to her ex-husband's status as a civil servant and income as caretaker, the separation allowed her to live a life that she thinks is closer to a 'normal' life: today, she regularly practices a sport, goes out with friends, and asserts her self-worth.

The effects of age and lifestyles

It is difficult to sum up the lifestyles of these stable-modest households of the working classes in a few unifying traits. The diversity of ways in which they achieve stability engenders a variety of ways of living it. It is even more difficult because these households not only belong to different generations but are also situated at different stages of the life cycle. Some, like the Monteils and Rateliers, are retired and have thus gotten past the age of challenges like educating their children, remaining actively employed, preserving their relationship, and buying their own home. Other, younger households – like those of Véronique Delage, Souleymane and Yamina Diallo, and Clément Jacquet and Élodie Paillé – are actively facing these challenges. Still others are between these two ages: these challenges are largely behind them but they are not free of worry over their children's ability to achieve stability in turn, as is seen in the portrait of Mina and Michel Carry.

Although we were unable to find indicators for identifying a unifying lifestyle, accounting for the effects of age at least allows us to avoid overly melodramatic analyses of the middle fractions of the working classes that would inevitably result if analyses were limited to younger households. In fact, the living conditions of the middle fractions of the working classes are subject to biographical cycles: according to age (phase of the life cycle), these households are more or less sheltered from precarity and thus present rather different moralities. One of the strengths of this first part of this book is the light it sheds on the effects that age has on lifestyle.

Among the households in our study, we were thus able to identify a voluntarist morality driven by the objective of remaining stable (Véronique Delage) or climbing socially (Clément Jacquet and Elodie Paillé, Souleymane and Yamina Diallo) and a more hedonistic morality that was more common among the older and more established couples in the study. The latter allows us to see the importance of life outside of work as a space for symbolic requalification, which can be glimpsed in all of the studied households. Upon retirement, the older couples built upon a lifestyle that they had tirelessly vaunted during their working years, expressing tastes and desires that marked a break with the dominated or subaltern condition. This occurred for the Monteils through the purchase of a new single-family home in a relatively well-off residential area, bringing them closer to the middle classes. For Mireille, this house indicates a desire for social reclassification as much as an assertion of her personal worth, after a career of unskilled jobs following her need to leave school at the secondary level, despite having been a good student and admitted to a good *lycée*. In a different vein, the Rateliers manifested this by turning their back on mass consumption and pursuing a lifestyle borrowing much from the cultural pole of the middle classes (reading, love of travel and meeting people). The younger households exhibit practices of requalification that align them with one of these two poles. Through their investment in decoration, for example, Thomas Guillet and Laurent Douillard make their home into a nest to shelter themselves from devaluing professional lives, while Souleymane and Yamina Diallo invest in legitimate culture by resuming their studies and reading widely. There is a quest for private happiness in opposition to low-skill and subaltern jobs that we could call restorative subjectivity.

Notes

1. See 'Making a virtue of simplicity: The hedonistic choices of a working couple' by Jean-Noël Retière.
2. See 'A story of social reclassification: A couple from rural backgrounds gone to the city' by Henri Eckert.
3. See '"You've got to fight": Work as a resource for a fragile success' by Anne-Marie Arborio.
4. See Appendix, 'Equivalency chart of the primary and secondary educational systems in France, the UK, and the US'.
5. See '"Getting it right this time": Aspiring to join the world of intellectuals' by Clément Degout.

6 See '"We went too high": A household destabilised by its residential and professional aspirations' by Lucas Tranchant.
7 See 'Holding on: Sparing no effort to stabilise an unstable position' by Marie-Hélène Lechien and Marie-Pierre Pouly.
8 The figures presented here were developed by Muriel Letrait, based on the 2010 *'Emploi du temps'* survey (INSEE).
9 See '"A mellow job" and living with a friend: A young, single male worker's adjustment to a subaltern condition' by Cyrille Rougier.
10 See 'Arranging life: A strong investment in activities other than work' by Matéo Sorin.
11 RSA: *Revenu de solidarité active* (active solidarity income), a social welfare programme supplementing the incomes of workers earning less than the official living wage.

References

Baudelot, Christian, and Roger Establet. 2005. 'Classes en tous genre.' In *Femmes, genre et sociétés*, edited by Margaret Maruani, 38–47. Paris: La Découverte.

Bernard, Lise, and Christophe Giraud. 2018. 'Avec qui les ouvrières et les employées vivent-elles en couple?' *Travail, genre et sociétés* 39: 41–61.

Dubost, Claire-Lise, and Lucas Tranchant. 2019. 'Changer d'emploi, est-ce changer de position sociale? La structure des classes populaires au prisme des mobilités professionnelles des ouvriers et des employés.' *Sociétés contemporaines* 114: 59–88.

Galland, Olivier. 2017. *Sociologie de la jeunesse*. Paris: Armand Colin.

Mauger, Gérard. 2015. *Âges et générations*. Paris: La Découverte.

4

'WE AIMED TOO HIGH'

A household destabilised by its residential and professional aspirations – Élodie Paillé and Clément Jacquet

Lucas Tranchant

When I first met Élodie and Clément at their house in Villy, an outer suburb of Paris, in October 2015, they were going through a rough patch.[1] Élodie was starting a training programme in sales after a period of unemployment, and Clément was thinking of quitting his job as a driving postman. They were preparing to put their house up for sale because they could no longer make the monthly payments on one income. This was why they were letting one of the rooms, where I would live for six months, until they sold the house, moved to the Centre region, and had their baby, Ange. This immersion in their everyday life at a critical moment in their lives, along with two recorded semi-structured interviews in 2016 and regular contact to catch up on their news, shed light on the mechanisms of destabilisation likely to affect the middle fractions of the working classes. Their case reveals the challenges, pitfalls, and fragility of social promotions occurring in the lower tiers of the social space.

The path taken by Clément and Élodie as a couple expresses a desire for social ascension that was undermined by professional and residential destabilisation. A bad real-estate deal, Élodie's employment insecurity, and Clément's growing sick of his job all combined to shatter the couple's dreams of embourgeoisement. They give the impression that they had poor control over their professional and residential investments, that they lost their gamble, as if their aspiration to rise ultimately turned against them. This is why Élodie and Clément have the feeling that they might have 'aimed too high' when the house that was once 'the dream of a lifetime' became a 'nightmare'. This social drop probably also reflects some consequences of the major economic recession that began in 2009, since rising unemployment and the burst real-estate bubble particularly affected the working classes. Clément and Élodie preferred to drop everything and go live in the country, rebuilding themselves away from the city and everything they lost.

DOI: 10.4324/9781003330073-5

Growing up working class in Greater Paris

Clément does not like talking about his childhood. He was born in Villy in 1981 and grew up in a working-class neighbourhood of an adjacent town. His father died when he was still a child, and neither of his parents ever worked; he refers to them as 'welfare cases'. Clément has a sister who is a bank teller in a neighbouring region and a brother who is a nursing student in the Grand Est region of France after having been an emergency medical technician. He sums up his relationship to his parents this way: 'Our parents never worked, but us, all three of us work. We don't owe them a thing'.

He says he was an 'average' student at the local *collège*, where he had to repeat the last year, but was able to enrol in the technical track of the 'generalist' *lycée* in the same town and earn a *baccalauréat* STT (Sciences et Technologies Tertiaires, preparing for office and administrative work).[2] The following year he began working through a temporary employment agency, like so many young people in the area. His assignments reflect the range of possibilities for employment offered locally, where a heavy presence of warehouses means a lot of logistics work: he was a warehouse worker and a delivery driver. After a year he got an open-ended employment contract as a stocker at a hardware chain store, where he stayed for three years. For a few months, he also had a limited-term employment contract to be a clerk in a produce shop. He remembers this was a 'difficult' time but he 'earned a good living'. He 'wanted to change', though, so he 'applied everywhere' and was hired as a postbus-driving postman on an open-ended employment contract.

Élodie was born in the inner suburbs of Paris in 1988 but grew up in a working-class neighbourhood of Villy. Her mother first went to work the line at a perfume factory at age 16 and is now a classroom assistant (ATSEM) in a school in Villy, where she lives. Separated from Élodie's father since Élodie was a child, she is currently in a relationship with a computer technician who works for a maintenance company in Paris. Élodie is the third of four children. One of her older brothers is a cook in an overseas region of France, and the other lives in central France, without steady employment. Her younger sister is still in *lycée*, on the general studies track.

Élodie's *collège* was a designated ZEP (Zone d'Éducation Prioritaire, education action zone) in Villy. Her marks led her to consider pursuing higher education, so she shunned the closest *lycée* in favour of Villy's 'prestigious' *lycée*, and chose Russian as an elective her first year. Her entry into *lycée* went so badly that she did not even finish the year. She reoriented to studying hospitality at an apprenticeship-training centre (CFA), but once again quit after six months. She is still quite frustrated by her academic failure: 'When, basically, you want to pursue higher studies and in the end you find yourself in a vocational thing, you think, "shit"'.

She then went through a difficult period during which she was neither in school nor old enough to work. For three years she went through a string of limited-term job contracts and temp jobs and then, at age 20, began training at the postal service, where she met Clément. She finished the training programme but did not have a driving licence, a prerequisite for being hired on an open-ended contract by the postal service. She finally found a sales job at a shoe store, ShoesIt, where she had a limited-term contract before landing an open-ended one. She worked full-time and said she was 'paid well' because she worked Sundays.

Making a home far from 'welfare cases'

Shortly after getting together, Clément and Élodie moved into a small house adjacent to Élodie's mother and stepfather's home. They stayed there two years, paying a rent well below the going rate, which made it possible for them to set money aside. This saving allowed them to decide to buy a house in 2012, when they were only 24 and 31. The couple vigorously rejects the idea of living in public housing ('We don't like housing estates, we don't like that') and raising their children there: 'That's not right. It's not like we're welfare cases!' They looked in Villy, where they both worked, and near public transportation, since Élodie still could not drive. They did not have long to find a place but felt 'love at first sight' for one house in particular. In order to pay the 200,000 euros it cost, they had to take out a 30-year fixed-interest loan to cover costs beyond their down payment.

The house was a single-family home built in the 1970s in a residential housing development on the outskirts of Villy. It had an area of about 120 m^2 on two levels, with a little yard, garage, and workshop. It was of mediocre quality, with thin walls and a tarpaper shingle roof that was cheap, degraded quickly, and provided poor insulation. Most houses in the neighbourhood are identical, gathered in clusters of five or six around a shared parking area. The residential neighbourhood is between the city estates and the forest, and home to many retired people.

Élodie and Clément's daily lives were closely focused on the domestic sphere and their desire to create a comfortable existence for themselves in their home. They rushed home after work. Since neither had many hobbies of their own, they did most domestic and consumer activities together. After ten years as a member of an Ultra supporter group for the Paris Saint-Germain football team, Clément quit. Few people visited, and most of their contacts were with family. Clément only saw his family for special occasions, since his mother lives in eastern France with his brother, while Élodie had a stronger relationship with her family, seeing her mother and sister almost weekly.

Their quest for domestic comfort was most manifest around dinnertime. After walking their Labrador retriever, they would eat in front of the television, usually a dish Élodie had made, sometimes takeout like McDonald's or a 'cheese naan'. Food was one of their domestic pleasures, and so they rarely ate out. Élodie tried to provide a balanced diet and would regularly prepare vegetables in an electric steamer because she wanted Clément to eat them, and although their consumption practices were marked by financial constraints, they claimed to pay attention to food quality. As Clément said, 'If I work it's not to buy the cheap stuff'. So Élodie bought some organic foods, and they sometimes got their meat from the butcher shop at the shopping centre. Reconciling the purchase of name brands with a tight budget required the serious work of identifying what was on sale in supermarket fliers.

It was also quite rare for them to go out. The television was on whenever they were home, and it was a central fixture in their free time. In addition to entertainment programmes, he frequently watches sport and she religiously follows reality television programmes featuring 'extreme cases' of households facing serious family problems, 'not couples like me and Clément'. They also like to watch DVDs in their bedroom, and he sometimes plays video games on his afternoons off. Their free time is really a time to relax and contributes to building a domestic bubble impermeable to the frustrations of their working lives.

Élodie, from stymied promotion to professional instability

Élodie's working career is marked by frustrated aspirations of promotion and great instability. With neither experience nor training, she became a sales assistant in a shoe store belonging to a national chain in 2011. In the beginning, she only stocked the shelves and occasionally helped customers, but after the company changed its sales methods she had to do 'assisted sales', meaning approaching clients to help them, which she did not like. Over the months her dynamism and motivation led her to assume responsibilities to the point of standing in for the store manager, but without changing her job status. In 2013, she accepted an offer to transfer to another store and become assistant manager, an opportunity presented as a chance to grow. She worked two unpaid hours every morning to train herself for her new position. Psychologically weakened by an ambiguous intermediary position and physically drained by long working hours, Élodie quit after several months, ending her open-ended employment contract after three years. She thinks that she 'gave a lot to ShoesIt' and is still bitter about her unmet aspiration for promotion.

Her ambition to rise out of executant positions and her inability to do so both appear in how Élodie presents what she liked the most in her various jobs:

> Well, the management side, that they could give me a chance, yeah, I really liked that part. Even if, well, it didn't go all the way – I didn't get the pay, I didn't get all that. But anyway. But the management side of things, where you've got to manage a team, where you're a little higher, yeah, I really liked that. Because I, like I told you before, I loved school

> and all that. Actually, when I was there, I wasn't frustrated anymore. I thought, they've given me a chance. Even if things worked out so I couldn't stay in school, well, there I could land on my feet. Because for me, to find myself kinda at the bottom, doing really shit work, well, I find it frustrating when you know that you've got other abilities, actually. As far as that goes, I liked it a lot, the management side, classes, the whole training thing, that part, all that.

Her experience as assistant manager at ShoesIt expresses the gap between her aspirations and the demands of these mid-level supervisory positions. Faced with pressure from both her superiors and her subordinates, she quickly realised that she had neither the status, nor the training, nor the dispositions allowing her to garner respect from the employees as assistant manager – and they had no compunctions about letting her see it. When one employee told her she had 'no manners' and was 'not polite', it was indeed a criticism of her working-class *hexis*, which prevented her from incarnating a position of authority relative to other young women from similar social backgrounds. It is as if she wanted to leave their ranks and was called to order. There was also a bodily aspect to this gap: at the end of her next job as assistant manager at a discount clothing store (on a limited-term contract), Élodie's superior made several critiques: 'I wasn't the right profile, I dressed badly, I did my hair badly, I did my makeup badly. There was no problem with my work, but…'.

After quitting the shoe store, Élodie had difficulty finding another steady job. She first got a limited-term contract working in another chain shoe store, where she opened and did 'assisted sales', and then went through a string of limited-term contracts with a discount clothing chain and another in a paint store. In late 2005, she started training to be store manager for a discount chain that was newly arrived in France and expanding rapidly. She saw it as a 'tantalising' offer, because she was assured that in the medium term she would have a store manager position with a salary of 2,500 euros, plus bonuses. She started with unpaid 'theoretical' training and then did hands-on internships that were supposed to lead to a permanent job. She was quickly disenchanted when she began the internship phase because her income was only 1,350 euros, very low considering the long hours and stresses of responsibility. Because her position was classified as management (*cadre*), she was paid a fixed salary and thus not compensated for overtime like wageworkers in the store. She was further disillusioned when she got her first real job in the company but had to share her assistant manager position with another employee. Constantly wondering just where her place was, she quit the programme after three months.

After this latest defeat, she decided to look for a job, any job, so they could pay their homeowners loan. She interviewed for many sales positions and finally got a renewable one-month job contract at a bakery in a neighbouring town. Shortly thereafter, she found out that she was pregnant. She did not like her job, especially because the owner did not pay for the half-hour it took her to open and close the shop. During an argument towards the end of her second month on the job, Élodie told her employer that she was pregnant. Her contract was not renewed, effective the following week.

Clément, stability with few prospects

Clément started working as a postman in 2006, doing 'mixed' postbus deliveries, meaning he brought the post to both private and business addresses. He began the rounds in his van after sorting the post for about two hours at the Villy sorting facility. He alternated between one week working mornings (5 am to 1 pm, Monday–Friday) and one week working afternoons (11 am–1 pm, 3 pm–7 pm, Monday–Saturday). He did not find anything particularly interesting in his work and hurried home when his shift ended. Although he was alone in the van most of the time, his independence at work was curtailed by his obligation to deliver mail to business clients on a set schedule according to specific time slots. He regularly complained about his new boss, who he said was only there to correct and discipline everyone. He thought that the 'policing' was getting heavier and felt that the work was getting more intense.

Clément held the same position since he began working for the postal service ten years earlier and was deeply weary with his job, which he often virulently criticised. In addition to the loss of independence and the intensification of the work, and despite what he admitted were rather comfortable working hours, he feels like he lost ten years of his life in the company. He has not advanced in the company job classification chart and has barely gained in seniority points, which brought his earnings up to 1,300 euros a month in 2016. To this was added an annual bonus of 300 euros, from the sale of calendars at the end of the year and the overtime he earned when the opportunity presented itself. It is possible that the household's increasing financial difficulties after the purchase of the house and Élodie's departure from her first job accentuated Clément's feelings about his income stagnation and limited prospects for promotion. He thought that he was stonewalled by his direct superiors, who do not like him, although he felt he had 'killed it in interviews with HR'. There was an internal examination to become a counter clerk, but he was not interested. Early in 2016, he sat for an internal examination to become customer service representative in Paris, drawn to the position's management-level (*cadre*) status, but he was eliminated in the first step, the written tests.

Clément's frustration seems to have been equal to the hopes for internal promotion that he may have nurtured when he entered the postal service. Convinced that career change was the only way he would be able to earn more money, over 2016 he spoke more and more frequently of his desire to quit. He was attracted to sales work because of the way income is calculated according to a set income plus a commission. He could easily imagine himself in such a job, to the encouragement of Élodie, who told him he has a 'mind for sales'. He wanted to be a real-estate agent because selling high-value goods earns bigger commissions. Although he admitted it would be difficult in the beginning, he thought it was a risk worth taking and, regardless, he had nothing left to lose given how tired he was of the postal service. He expressed his desire to work around the obstacles to his social promotion and put himself on an entirely new path.

The uncomfortable position of being 'in the middle'

Élodie and Clément's wish to rise socially through work is rooted in a great respect for work and virulent moral condemnation of social welfare and those who receive it. As Élodie said,

> well, nah, I say we've got to stop giving too much money to people who don't work. It's not all that anymore. Why are you going to tax someone who works, who has an occupation, who's going to look for a real job? And in the end, they live better than you do.

This opinion comes along with esteem for family legacies accumulated through work; together, they define what Clément and Élodie call their 'right-leaning side'. Although such a political orientation certainly comes from conservative upbringings – especially in Élodie's case, as she was raised in a practicing Catholic family – it also expresses their uncomfortable social position by stressing their distance from the bottom of the social scale, an impulse arising from their indirect recognition of how close they are to it themselves. This tension is expressed in a tripartite view of society, as Clément explains:

CLÉMENT: In France, you're either too poor and they give you a ton of stuff, on assistance, or you're too rich and they take a bunch of stuff away. And in the middle there's nothing.

ÉLODIE: In the middle there's us, who slog away.

CLÉMENT: Right. So us, we want it to be balanced – either there's assistance for everyone, or there isn't any.

Finding oneself in the middle, between the 'too poor' and the 'too rich' above all means being adjacent to the most weakened fractions of the working classes while being at an unbridgeable distance from the higher classes. Despite Clément's job security, their working lives constantly remind them of their subaltern positions in the organisation of labour. Both had multiple experiences of being exploited at work, arbitrary bosses, and even workplace mobbing. They explicitly attribute this situation to a dominated position in social relations, and one day they described it to me as follows:

CLÉMENT: Nothing but shit! If you haven't gone to school, honestly, you're in deep shit. You do shitty work and people treat you like shit! [...] So really stay in school, unless you want to find yourself at the grocer's [they both laugh].

ÉLODIE: That's a good one! [...] Nah, it's realistic, it's true.

CLÉMENT: You're gonna work for blokes that'll only exploit you.

ÉLODIE: When you see the bosses, how comfortable their lives are, you think, what the fuck. Yeah, it's too much.

This practical experience of exploitation comes with a feeling that they are replaceable in their jobs, which hinders recourse to legal or collective action. According to Élodie, 'There are so many people looking for work that [companies] don't care, they play it to their advantage', which Clément laconically summed up as 'You're unhappy, get out'. The high unemployment rate at the time of the study and the low level of their qualifications put them in a segment of the labour market where having a stable job is divorced from possibilities of promotion. Clément has stability without promotion while Élodie's attempts to climb ultimately destabilise her.

Property ownership, a lost gamble

Their home ownership plans, concretised by the purchase of their house, were the residential manifestation of this will for social promotion, but they were jeopardised when Élodie left her job in 2013. As the household alternated between working, unemployment, and training, its household income plummeted and Élodie and Clément had to tighten their belts. This only made access to higher-ranking and better paying jobs more desirable, and their failure more frustrating. The indirect cost of time spent in training rose and became untenable in face of their need for income. This is how to read Élodie's resignation to seeking unqualified sales jobs. Loan payments were over 1,000 euros a month, and Clément and Élodie tried to reduce expenses to a minimum to stay afloat. They put off big expenses in equipment and repairs, sold one of their cars, and only took five days of vacation in a modest vacation village. To trim unnecessary spending, Clément unsubscribed from the premium cable chains Canal+ and Bein Sport.

Their situation became untenable in 2015, and they decided to put their house up for sale. In the time it took to find buyers, their need for money led them to let one of their rooms for a supplementary income of 400 euros a month. I was their third lodger since they began letting at the beginning of the year. They asked to be paid in cash and put the money in a tin into which they dipped when needed.

They advertised the room on several websites for roommates and demonstrated great solicitude when I came to see it. Letting a room marked a break in their family plans, as the room destined for a future child was instead rented out to someone from outside the family. There was also a broader process of subjective disinvestment in the house manifest in lagging maintenance and improvement work: the garden was left to run wild, and the dining area of the open living area served only to store things that piled up on the table.

In May 2015, they found buyers, but for a price lower than what they had paid. Unfortunately, the would-be buyers left them in the lurch when the time came to close the sale, unable to get a loan. Élodie and Clément had prepared everything, planning to buy a new house with a big yard in the Centre region for about 100,000 euros. Clément had even already begun the procedure for a transfer within the postal service, and he had informed his co-workers they were leaving.

The cancellation of the sale was a bitter pill for them to swallow. They thought that the winter months could work to their disadvantage, so they did not put the house back on the market immediately. And indeed, the poorly insulated and rather dark house was not very inviting on a drizzly day. They put it back on the market in March, through an agency but without an exclusive contract. The next two months were filled with great expectations. There were few interested in the house, and they prepared assiduously for each visit, one of them taking a day off to clean the house from top to bottom. They finally found buyers in May. Up to the closing, they lived in fear that the sale might fall through again.

The sale went through this time and had considerable consequences on their financial situation. Élodie and Clément sold at a loss, not receiving enough to pay off their mortgage loan, so they had to take out another loan (with payments of 300 euros a month for several years) to finish paying it off. Home ownership went from a 'dream' to a 'nightmare'. In the end, the closing was a 'relief', but one considerably tarnished by feelings of failure. As Élodie described it:

> We sort of had butterflies in our stomachs. Well, I was happy, y'know, the day of the closing, because I thought it was a relief. You see, even if I was happy when we signed in March, I wasn't doing well, because I thought to myself, well, I was still a property owner. It's the dream of a lifetime, you see? And plus, I'm young. Well, I thought, we invested every month. The thought makes you sick when you think, he put his sweat, he put his time, he put his money into it, and to say in the end, you lost. It's a hell of a hit to your morale at first. And then, actually, the day we signed, I was relieved. I thought well, actually, we aimed too high, and then, with life and all... We'll land on our feet, but we're going to give ourselves a little more time [...] After, I didn't even say goodbye to my house because it was a nightmare for us, both of us. When you can't manage living there anymore, you're happy to get rid of it.

Dropping everything and starting over

The sale of their house marked the end of a residential sequence, but also a complete change in their lives. Six months earlier, in December 2016, they had learned that Élodie was pregnant. They had been trying for three years, and the impending birth crystallised their plan to start over by leaving metropolitan Paris for the country. They had fleshed out the plan for several months since the first sale fell through. Having to empty the house, they urgently sought a rental and finally found a small raised one-story house in Arnosoy, a small, very rural town in the Centre. They were aware that they were losing in comfort and space, but they saw their situation as temporary, for as long as it takes to 'bounce back'. It is a case of residential downclassing, perhaps made easier to accept because of their departure for the country. Indeed, their rejection of the city also has to be understood as their rejection of the alternative, subsidised housing, since it had always been out of the question for them to request a place in a public housing estate in order to stay near Villy, which would have brought them closer to the insecure and immigrant working classes.

Their move to Arnosoy also had the positive attribute of going back to their 'roots': 'We're fed up with the stresses of the [Paris] region, we want lots of air. Unpolluted air, fields, all that – the country. We want to be country people. Back to our roots', as Élodie put it. After their move, they said they were happy with their new living environment. They vaunted the quality of the landscape and relations with the people there. Significantly, the move came with changes in their consumption practices. Élodie and Clément saw their move to the country as an opportunity to provision themselves with good products from local farmers: they began buying milk directly from the farm and plan to do the same for meat. Élodie subscribed to a weekly veg box and planted tomatoes in the yard. This change in consumption also nourishes feelings of a more 'comfortable life' and improved 'buying power'.

Their separation from the house only partly lightens their financial burdens, however. The combination of their rent (800 euros) and the loan reimbursement (300 euros) adds up to monthly expenses equal to what they paid before. At the same time, their income has dropped. When they moved, Clément quit the postal service without asking for a transfer or unpaid leave, thus acting on his desire for change. They both went on unemployment. She got 1,100 euros a month, and he got 1,200. They wanted to take a few months to 'land on [their] feet' and devote themselves to the baby, who was born in August. Élodie would love to have '7 or 8 children' but she thinks that would be 'selfish' because 'these days [...] you can't, life's too expensive'. They want to give the best to their child before thinking about having a second one. The choice of an uncommon name for their son, Ange, might moreover be understood as a rejection of the ordinary, a desire to escape social determinants ('We don't want to be ordinary. [...] Then the child will have a story'), at the risk of exposing themselves to mockery ('I hope they won't make too much fun of him').

Élodie resumed work shortly after the birth of Ange. She began to work in a bakery in the village in September 2017 and then got an open-ended contract as a part-time cashier at a discount grocery store in the neighbouring town. Clément is looking for work. He has applied for several sales jobs, but they do not call back after the interview and he does not understand why, which throws him into turmoil: 'It's harder than I thought to find a job'. He turned down a minimum-wage job at a local supermarket because it would not earn him any more than his unemployment benefits. If he does not manage to find anything, he will 'stay at home like the welfare cases' he said with a laugh tinged with resignation. Clément is aware they are walking a tightrope, because 'it's tight with only [minimum wage]'. Their low incomes oblige them to make sacrifices. They had to cancel their 2017 summer vacation to pay for car repairs. Their destabilisation puts them in a highly vulnerable situation relative to the vagaries of life. They see their situation as only temporary, as long as it takes to put things back together, and are thus planning on buying a house in the country as soon as they both have jobs.

This household's trajectory is that of a social drop. It illustrates the fragility of households in the middle fractions of the working classes, for which making the slightest false move could lead to major difficulties. This portrait also demonstrates that the capitals accumulated during small social moves are quite volatile: Élodie and Clément's professional and residential investments evaporated in two years. They think that they have to start all over again, but taking another approach, and indeed their inclination to hold the lower fractions of the working classes at arms' length, prevents them from being satisfied with their new situation. Young, full of energy, and optimistic, new parenthood gives Élodie and Clément a new reason to work it out.

Notes

1 The names of the cities, Arnosoy and Villy, are pseudonyms to help preserve informants' anonymity.
2 For an explanation of the French educational system, see the Appendix.

5

PLANNING LIFE

A strong investment in activities other than work – Laurent Douillard and Thomas Guillet

Matéo Sorin

Thomas and Laurent just moved into a custom-build house in a development in a town of 1,500 residents in the Vendée, in west-central France. The couple's activities and plans attest to a search for stability that is hampered by their low incomes, lack of options for professional development, chronic illness, and one of them having been fired from his job. Together and individually, they *plan their lives*. The process of planning their lives has three dimensions. The first, residential planning, takes place through the concretisation of their plan to become homeowners and the attention they devote to crafting their living space (decoration and growing their own food). Secondly, their planning of time and leisure activities can be seen in how involved they are in activities other than work (consumption, decoration, sociability around food) while being little invested in their professional activities. Lastly, as men holding subaltern jobs and with a sexual orientation that sets them apart locally, their plans for a cocoon for themselves are seen in their efforts to foster a comforting inner circle that nourishes their self-worth. The strength of their relationship, their mutual solidarity, and their closeness to their friends and family are precious resources in their quest for stability.

Discreetly becoming an ordinary household

In 2011, when Thomas was 20, he left his parents' home to move into a small house that Laurent had rented in Arrouix.[1] Laurent was 33 at the time and had already been in a long relationship with another man, but it was Thomas's first lasting homosexual relationship. Arrouix is a rural town on the northern coast of the Vendée, where the economy is heavily dependent

DOI: 10.4324/9781003330073-6

on agriculture and oyster farming. Political parties of the right and extreme right get better election results here than in Nantes (the major city nearby) or nationally. Like other rural towns in the area, Arrouix was historically more influenced by the political right and the clergy than by socially and culturally liberal ideas.

Although the geographical setting and its historical context are relatively conservative, which might lead one to expect it to be propitious for open expressions of intolerance of homosexuals, Laurent and Thomas report having had few homophobic experiences, only citing two. One was an altercation at a music festival, but the other took place in a more private setting. Laurent recounted that at a female friend's party several years earlier, a 'young person' 'threw a fit because he didn't want me to stay because I was gay'. The hostess intervened, retorting '"If you're unhappy, get outta here! That's it". And after, he kept his mouth shut'. Generally speaking, their encounters with homophobia are usually indirect. Case in point, they felt targeted by certain aggressive declarations that proponents of the 'Manif pour tous' made on television in 2013, as Laurent related[2]:

> There aren't many, but some don't like that [homosexuals]. And then, it's the same, when we go to Gay Pride and all, it was 'Mariage pour tous' and… and then it went badly [referring to demonstrations against same-sex marriage]. And at the same time, I almost didn't go because I thought, 'What if there'll be opponents and all that'll show up, or maybe bombs, you never know these days…' And so yeah, I almost didn't go, and actually it went really well. […] I think it still hurt me, though, yes, because I was afraid to go to Gay Pride.

Homophobia is rarely aimed directly at them, however, and they have good relations with their neighbours. For example, they are close to the owner of their previous house, 'an old lady who spends all her time in the street' and shares 'all Arrouix's gossip' with them. When they moved, she told them how disappointed she was at the idea that she would not see them anymore. Likewise, they regularly see their new neighbours in the development, having drinks at each other's homes and actively participating in the annual neighbourhood party.

Their perception of a gap between their sexual orientation and the dominant norm has no impact on most of their everyday practices in public, but in some situations, it does make them cautious about what they reveal of their relationship. This may be to avoid possible aggression from a stranger, but most often it is to avoid making their relationship a topic of conversation. So although Laurent has never heard a homophobic comment in the factory where he works, he has only shared this aspect of his private life with a handful of co-workers. Even if his homosexuality is hardly a secret in the company, he prefers to keep it quiet. Besides, he supposes that there are unpleasant things said about him:

> It was the company lottery, I'd told Thomas, 'Now you stay discreet!' And the idiot won first prize! [...] And I was so ashamed, I mean, like, out for all to see! [...] Well, not everyone knew that we came together, or [they thought that] he was just a friend. But you don't normally have the right [to bring friends], so I heard at work: 'yeah, that's not right...'
>
> MATÉO: What about?
>
> LAURENT: That some come with friends like that. Yeah, I heard people say it! Some even repeated it to me, some I like a lot. At the same time I'm not gonna say, 'hey, we're shagging!' See, I don't like Christmas parties, things like that, that much, because you hear about it for three months afterwards at the factory.

By making sure to cloak their homosexuality in discretion and controlling the image they give of their relationship, Laurent and Thomas work to avoid potentially conflictual situations. It is probably also to sidestep interactions where mention of their intimate life might cause embarrassment for themselves or others. Their homosexuality is no secret to their families, although explicit references may sometimes be avoided with them, as well.

Local working-class life courses

Laurent was born in 1978. When he was a child, his father was a cook and his mother a waitress in different restaurants in a town of 7,000 near Nantes. They moved to Arrouix before he started secondary school, and his father became a butcher in a small grocery and his mother a childminder. His elder brother quit his studies in architecture and became a tradesman in the same town. After *collège* Laurent passed his second attempt at the examination earning him a CAP in Hospitality and Food Service.[3] His younger sister has a BEP in Accounting and works in a store in the same administrative department. She also lives in Arrouix and has been raising two children alone since the departure of their father. Her financial situation declined after the separation and she was put on the national list of persons banned from opening a bank account.

Thomas was born in 1991. His father is from the Vendée and was the commercial director of a food factory, and his mother was a waitress north of Paris before she moved to Arrouix and got a job as an industrial worker. When his parents separated in the mid-2000s, Thomas left the educational system without a degree after twice failing the written examination for a CAP degree in Baking and Pastry. His younger sister earned a CAP in Early Childhood Development a few years later. During their teenage years, their mother suffered from depression and then committed suicide in 2013. Thomas does not speak much of this difficult time.

Laurent and Thomas' families accepted their homosexuality with ease. After Laurent told his mother of his sexual orientation, she cried and then said with a smile, 'I'll have another son-in-law!' They are integral parts of each other's families. They frequently go to lunch together with their parents, and Thomas sometimes goes shopping alone with Laurent's sister. When summing up their families' reactions to their relationship, Laurent says 'We were very lucky'.

But in certain circumstances the subject is left unspoken. When Thomas attends Christmas dinner with Laurent's extended family, which he has done for years, he is 'a friend'. Laurent presents this choice as a way of protecting his grandmother, but it is probably also to protect himself from the negative moral judgements she might express: 'My grandmother is super-nice, but my parents are afraid that … that she'll be disappointed'. Although the term 'friend' can be used to describe a life partner, in this case, it is used to hide the conjugal dimension of their relationship by allowing them to avoid making the nature of their relationship explicit.

Thomas and Laurent rarely speak of their homosexuality with their older family members. Thomas has never spoken with his father about it: 'I was more anxious about my father, but in the end everything's fine. [...] My mother told him and we've never spoken about it'. This discretion at the prospect of talking explicitly about his relationship with Laurent with his father does not seem to be a manifestation of a taboo specific to the homosexual nature of their relationship; the thing that father and son 'never speak of' is the intimacy of a relationship (feelings, sexuality), which are aspects of private life that children rarely share with their elders, regardless of their sexual orientation.

At the same time, some of their attitudes do seem specifically connected to their sexual identity. They each mention how uncomfortable they are at the thought of kissing each other in front of their parents should they marry. Thomas would like to get married, but Laurent reminds him that the cost makes it impossible for the time being.

Laurent and Thomas want to continue living near Arrouix because they have strong family and friendship ties there. Contrary to what one might think, this rural area's social environment and conservatism do not condemn them to being ostracised for their homosexuality, so they can live there like any other couple. But for all that, their practices show that they have adopted a degree of secretiveness. Making a discreet couple seems to be a necessary precaution in order to live their relationship in peace and thus become an ordinary household.[4]

Low investment in professional activities

Thomas and Laurent both work in sectors unrelated to their initial training. They are not very invested in their work and make the best of subaltern jobs that encroach moderately on their private lives. After working for two years on his first employment contract as a cashier near his family's home, Thomas turned to the funeral sector. He did an internship and a short training programme and got an open-ended employment contract at a funeral and burial service near Arrouix. In 2014, he was the sole salaried worker. Without the oversight of his superiors, he could close the agency for a half-day if he so wished, and some days not a single client came to the door. Apart from a few constraints, Thomas worked fewer than 30 hours a week for a full-time job paid 1,050 euros after taxes:

> Other than my income, I'd hate to leave because I'm really free. I'm all alone, I've got no-one bothering me. If I want to take a day off, I take it. I mean, I do what I want [...] There's no one on my back saying, "Do this, do that". I'm the one that manages my thing. I manage the files, I manage my follow-up, I manage everything.

Thomas was not looking to change employers, saying he'd earn just as little but would definitely see his working conditions decline. He could not hope for a promotion (lacking a degree) nor could he imagine finding another, more advantageous position, since he already has experience in most jobs in the funeral sector. Thomas was unfulfilled in his job, but he made the best of it. He stressed the appeal of not having a boss on site as an advantage.

Despite the reservations of his parents, who had trouble with the working conditions of the restaurant business (low wages and odd working hours), Laurent still pursued studies in the sector. He worked several seasonal jobs but could not get used to the work pace and poor relations with his employers. As a result, he accepted an offer for an open-ended employment contract at a metal assembly factory where he had been employed as a temporary worker. Although he had said 'I will never work in a factory' when he was younger, Laurent has worked as a machine technician for over 15 years in this company of 300 employees, located 15 km from Arrouix.

His job is to maintain ten or so machines upon which women assemble metal and rubber parts. Laurent is free to move around and his work pace is not dictated by an assembly line. He appreciates having weekends off and the 'good ambiance' at work and finds the working conditions better than in food service. Laurent said that prior to holding this position, he was 'allergic to tools', and even today he does not think of himself as handy, entrusting home improvement work to his father. His monthly income after taxes is 1,390 euros. He thinks that he has no chance of being promoted because that would mean taking the position of his boss, whose mechanical, electrical, and all-around tinkering skills are on another order of magnitude. He adds, 'My boss is the one in charge, but I'm the one who manages it all'. Three other employees do exactly the same job, which allows the service to keep operating normally even when he cannot work. And indeed, Laurent suffers from a rare chronic illness that comes with episodes of extremely sharp and debilitating pain that regularly prevent him from doing anything for a period lasting from half an hour to several days.

Laurent and Thomas say that their jobs are not very satisfying (which is why they are so little invested in them), but they do offer a good compromise between the need to earn a living and tolerable working condition. If they have resigned themselves to their jobs, it is also because they have experienced tougher working conditions and can readily see their parents and friends working in more challenging conditions than theirs. Additionally, the difficulties they had in absorbing knowledge at school (repeating years and failing examinations) and their low educational levels limit their chances of rising professionally. For Laurent this lack of potential for promotion is compounded by his limited interest in the technical aspects of his job, so he keeps it apart from his private life, and they rarely even talk about it between themselves. This distance from professional activities is paired with a significant investment in gratifying activities outside of work.

Finding 'good deals', decorating, and inviting friends

Laurent and Thomas' non-work-related practices are typical of the ordinary investment in secondary activities commonly observed when someone's professional activities are not very rewarding. Although leisure activities often figure large in such investments, they take distinctive forms in this household. The three activities to which they devote considerable time and money are consumption, decoration, and socialising around food. They are far from the activities associated with physical strength and virility historically valued by working-class men, and closer to those usually connected with women (food, decoration). These tastes make Thomas and Laurent consistent with a prominent image in the collective imagination (literature, film, television) associating homosexual men with a particular disposition for the aesthetic. These three activities, which are often combined, hold a central position in their lives. In contrast to their professional activities, they procure them great satisfaction and contribute to shaping a positive social identity for them as a couple among their friends.

Consumption takes two main forms: shopping as an end unto itself in search of what they call 'good deals', and consumption in order to draw satisfaction from the social use of their purchases. Laurent ensures the food shopping, for which the monthly budget is over 500 euros.

THOMAS: It annoys me and we argue, so, each of us goes on his own. He [Laurent] does the food shopping and that's that.

LAURENT: I look at the prices and dates, Thomas is like, 'WOW! That's great!' The other day he did the shopping and he took too many [marked down] goods nearing the expiration date so we couldn't eat it all. So that time, I hollered.[5]

They flip through the weekly advertising fliers from area supermarkets, which are often left on the living-room coffee table. Laurent looks for sales and uses them to prepare the grocery list, which he often forgets. His quest for discounts continues in the aisles, where he looks at the aisle end-caps because 'that's where they put sale items'. The intent is not to reduce food expenses, but rather to raise its quality: 'That way we can buy brand-names at the price of generic'. He indicates, however, that he is careful not to study the advertisements too much because knowing about the 'good sales' ultimately leads him to spend more.

Buying decorations is also a major part of their consumption practices because they both love dinnerware, candleholders, table linens, garlands, and holiday decorations (Christmas, Easter, Halloween). As with their food shopping, they devote considerable time to hunting out good deals. On the trail of cut prices of all kinds, they once spent 500 euros in a month on decorations from a store that was going out of business. They comb flea markets and consult classified advertisement websites for 'good deals'. They joke about their behaviour, which they liken to a mental illness:

LAURENT: I have a serious disease. It's candleholders! [...]

THOMAS: We go to buy things cheaply, but when we get to a store like that [going out of business], we go crazy, actually. We buy everything and then afterward we say, 'No, we're not going to use that, and we put it back. But actually it's... I dunno, once it's seventy per cent off everything, we take everything!

MATEO: But only in decorations.

THOMAS: Yes. But there are things we will never use! There's things, we've had them for two years, they've still got the labels on! Candleholders, for example: 'Oh, we had one here!'

Their quest for deals is a source of satisfaction that is at least as important as the possession and use of these objects. Some of them are never taken out of the package. This pastime means that they possess 17 dinnerware sets (services of 6–12) and a 9 x 9 m garden shed filled exclusively with Christmas decorations.

In addition to their interest in digging up good deals, they like decorating their home with their purchases. Thomas is the one who most enjoys putting them in harmonious arrangements and stresses how important the activity is for him: 'It's for me and me alone'.

Decorating is also a way of boosting their esteem in the eyes of friends and family, who they frequently invite over to eat; their sisters are their most frequent guests. Laurent's mother passed along her love of setting a nice table, and so he is particularly attentive to table decorations when she is invited to dine. They plan big dinners for Easter and Halloween every year, decorating the table and living room according to theme. At Easter, the interior is enlivened with figurines of chicks and bunnies, and at Christmas, the outside of the house is festooned with 50-some strings of lights and the yard dotted with 15 artificial pine trees, and the interior is decorated as well. Some friends come to their house expressly to see the decoration, including one of Laurent's co-workers who brings his son every year. These decorative activities give Laurent and Thomas an activity in common and garner symbolic gratification from their near and dear.

Likewise, Laurent often cooks in quantity so that they can invite friends over or give some away. One night, for example, he cooked 20-odd endives with ham so he could give some to his sister. Thomas and Laurent say 'We love it when there's people over to eat', which is at least once a week. Their food-related activities are not limited to cooking, however, as they also produce some ingredients themselves. They have 13 chickens and ten quail, and Laurent keeps a vegetable garden. Amidst the rows of tomatoes, beans, potatoes, strawberries, and raspberries, he has a ten-metre row of garlic, part of which will be distributed to friends and family. A significant proportion of the food they grow serves as a sort of currency in frequent swaps of food with friends.

Their non-work activities contribute to maintaining a social network focused on a core of friends and family members. A majority of their friends are women: a cook in a retirement home (with a vocational *baccalauréat*), an accountant (BTS), a hairstylist (vocational *baccalauréat*), a master's degree student in psychology, and a house painter. Two of them are lesbian. Laurent and Thomas have built themselves a social cocoon within which they feel valued and self-confident, because in their company they can relax their usual control over the public image that they convey as a male couple. With their closest friends they have no fear of upsetting or hostile reactions. This cocoon also boosts their self-esteem, through their loved one's appreciation for the activities they enjoy: dinner invitations, admiration of the decorations, and exchange of food. Ultimately one of the prime functions of their non-work activities and social life is building and maintaining this in-group that fosters senses of security and self-worth.

A delicate stability

After living in a one-bedroom house of 50 m^2 for two years, in 2013 Thomas and Laurent set out to become homeowners. At the time they both had open-ended employment contracts and their economic situation was stable, which made it possible for them to consider taking out a real-estate loan. They had no prior savings, but they had a contribution of 10,000 euros that Thomas had inherited after the death of his mother earlier that year. They officialised their relationship in a civil union (delaying the party for a year) and acquired a loan of about 180,000 euros so they could have a house built. In order to stay in their budget, they had to have it built 15 km from Arrouix, limit the floor space to 80 m^2, and have only two bedrooms. In-kind family contributions also helped them to reduce the final cost of the house, as Laurent's brother laid the tile. Thomas' inheritance, the low-interest rates at the time, and the reduction of the cost of the lot by 20,000 euros indicate that this project was made possible by a convergence of particularly favourable circumstances.[6]

Their remaining financial resources dropped dramatically after this move, however. Their old rent of 320 euros a month was replaced by 750 euros a month for their homeowner's loan and 210 euros to reimburse their kitchen. Laurent admitted outright in 2015 that, 'Financially, it's tight...' They saw their fixed expenses increase, further straining their budget, since they usually spent their incomes in the month. Two events occurred in this period that further worsened their economic situation. In 2014, a year before the move, Laurent suffered from a number of acute flare-ups from his chronic illness. He tried to stop his treatment to reduce its side effects, and for weeks he suffered from up to five attacks per day, effectively incapacitating him for work for several months. After three months of sick leave, his sick pay went from full to partial, so he lost 500 euros a month in income in late 2014. He was even thinking about quitting, his attacks being so frequent and severe that work was periodically unbearable. But despite the secondary effects of his medication, Laurent resumed his treatment and his job on a regular schedule. The illness is a source of vulnerability whose effects are even more significant because his partner's employment was also destabilised. Two months after moving, Thomas was fired for something he denies. He is still working in funeral services, but now as a temporary worker, as a paid pallbearer. He works part-time most of the time, and some months his income is 500 euros lower than what he earned before. But Thomas remains optimistic and hopes to get an open-ended employment contract at a funeral service agency where he temps often.

The fact that these events came on the heels of acquiring property highlights the fragility of their trajectory and the stabilisation process they have begun. When domestic partners with low incomes experience a simultaneous decline in revenues at the same time that their fixed expenses increase, the couple is hard-pressed to serve as a buffer to the vagaries of life. Their friends and families are quite present and certainly provide them with symbolic and affective security, but they cannot help them financially due to the limitations of their own resources. But Thomas and Laurent are a resilient couple, which allows them to confront their frailties in health and employment. The strength of their relationship is an indispensable resource for avoiding insecurity ... and for pursuing their quest for lasting stability. This is what they are working on when they plan their life together.

Notes

1 The names of people and the town where they live have been changed to preserve confidentiality.
2 The 'Manif' pour tous' (Protest for All) was a conservative social movement that arose in opposition to the French state's plan to allow same-sex couples to marry, commonly called 'Mariage pour tous' (Marriage for All), which became law in 2013.
3 For an explanation of the French school system, see the Appendix.
4 Colin Giraud (2016) also emphasises the fact that male homosexuality in rural and working-class settings is kept quiet, but without being kept a secret. His work and the story of Thomas and Laurent challenge the theory of particularly high hostility toward homosexuals in rural areas.
5 Thomas and Laurent pepper their conversation with teasing. In front of another person, their little disagreements are played out in exchanges alternating sarcastic retorts with mocking barbs and feigned outrage.
6 It was the last plot in a development, and the developer was in a hurry to sell so it could start work on the next development.

Reference

Giraud, Colin. 2016. 'La vie homosexuelle à l'écart de la visibilité urbaine. Ethnographie d'une minorité sexuelle masculine dans la Drôme.' *Tracés. Revue de Sciences humaines* 30: 79–102.

6

'A MELLOW JOB' AND LIVING WITH A FRIEND

A young, single male worker's adjustment to a subaltern condition – Romain Boyer

Cyrille Rougier

At the time of research, Romain Boyer was 32 years old and roommates with a co-worker, an old friend since *lycée*. They are both electric metre readers on open-ended employment contracts with a private sub-contractor. They live in a new house in a rather residential town near a mid-sized city in the Limousin, a region in southwest-central France. The situation of these single men, both relatively well-educated and in a job classifying them as 'administrative employees', is characterised by two kinds of social suspension: between the working and middle classes and between two phases in the life cycle. They have not entirely left the state of being 'young people' but have not entirely reached that of 'adults', generally associated with attaining occupational stability, forming a lasting relationship in a couple, the arrival of children, and becoming property owner. Their representations and practices seem to be governed by an effort to hold the truth of their situation at bay: their progress towards the state of adulthood has broken down, and the expectations formed over the course of their educations are dropping. The first part of this portrait presents the refuge that they have created between friends and their shared leisure practices, which reveal their particular version of the working-class condition. In the second part, we will see that the friendly hominess between roommates does not prevent Romain from having leisure activities away from home, especially in sport and associative engagements, in a geographical area in which he is even more symbolically invested because of his 'capital of autochthony' (Renahy 2010, Retière 2003). Lastly, Romain's relationship to work – his professional trajectory, how he describes his job and company, the supervisory experience that he put to an end – will reveal how he is adjusting to a relatively comfortable but dominated social condition.

DOI: 10.4324/9781003330073-7

Being roommates as a friendly refuge

In many ways, Romain and Ludovic's joint living situation seems to be a space that grew out of their friendship and protects them from the outside world. Friends since *lycée* (where each earned a *bac* ES) and now working at the same company, this is not the first time they have lived together.[1] Their first was not while they were in school, as is often the case, but after they started working. This choice stemmed from a desire to leave the city they knew from their years at school and move to the country. At university, Romain had to repeat his first year of sport studies (STAPS), while Ludovic passed the first two years of a *licence* in Economics in a regional capital in central France, but he failed the final year at another university, this time in western France. Upon leaving school, Romain and two friends from *lycée* (one being Ludovic) realised that by living together they could move into a large renovated house in a rural town near where they live today. When the third went into a relationship and moved out a year later, Romain and Ludovic sought another house. They lived together for a few months, until Romain left to work in southern France, where he rented his own apartment. When he returned to the Limousin region (specifically, the administrative department of Haute-Vienne), Romain convinced his father to go in on buying a house with him in a recent development, where he and Ludovic have lived ever since.

The roommates both come from relatively working-class backgrounds, although Romain's parents did experience some professional and social ascension. His father, now retired, spent most of his working life as a prison guard. He had initially hoped to take over the family farm in the neighbouring department of Charente, but the farm was in financial difficulty, so he decided to take the civil service examination for penitentiary administration. He was first posted to greater Paris, but he wanted to move closer to his home region and managed to get transferred to the Limousin. He has a relatively comfortable pension today, since he was promoted to Supervisor in the last couple years of his career (the very years that are taken as the basis for calculating the pension). At the time of the study, Romain's mother was still working as a secretary in an agricultural accounting firm. He has one sister who is a nurse in the Creuse, another department in the Limousin. Ludovic has a stronger farming background, through his grandparents and parents. His father was long a family worker on his parents' farm, until he left to join his wife as a factory worker. After their company closed and they were laid off, they tried to resume farming on a small piece of land inherited from the father's family and a few purchased cows. His father had a heart attack, and his health problems forced them to give up their plans to live off farming. So, Ludovic's father went to work part-time as a school bus driver, and his mother went to work for a non-profit organisation as a home care provider. Ludovic also has a younger sister who is a worker in a rural porcelain factory and lives with another metre reader at the same company.

Although they mention in interviews that they regularly get vegetables grown by their parents, who live an hour away, they seem to get little financial assistance. Attesting to this is the fact that Romain's parents only paid for one year of his studies, and Ludovic's parents live in marked insecurity. But more significant than regular help, Romain's parents' financial assistance was decisive in the purchase of the house where the friends live today. Indeed, Romain 'convinced' his father to invest in the house, which they 'bought together' – although his father was the main (perhaps sole) contributor at the beginning, since Romain sends him 275 euros a month. Ludovic also pays Romain's father the same sum in rent, bringing it to a total of 550 euros, although the rent should be about 800 euros given the current local real-estate market. It thus seems that the father's investment in the house is more a favour to his son than a genuine real-estate investment.

Romain and Ludovic live in this single-family house located in a development dating to 2010, near the town centre. The house looks relatively new both inside and out and seems to be very well maintained, perhaps in part because it is a family investment. The basement, which is as big as the house and serves mainly as a garage, is the only part that is less cared for. The housemates have set up a coffee table and a few armchairs for use mainly as a smoking room, since they do not smoke in the rest of the house.[2] It opens to a yard of a little over 50 m^2.

The fact that their house is well kept is a strong confirmation that they are not 'partying student' roommates. This can also be seen in the fact that Romain and Ludovic are gradually dropping some of their former favourite pastimes, most notably video games (especially one involving football that they played frequently in their first house) and evenings in the bars of the department's largest city. Now they mostly see friends at each other's homes, theirs included ('We really like having people over'), and it seems to usually be the same people – the co-worker and friend that got them their current jobs, and their former roommate. They do not go out every weekend, though, which amuses Romain: 'We stay home like hermits'. The friends' refuge is also built on shared domestic tasks and the attention they pay to their evening meal, which they eat together. Ludovic takes care of the cooking and says he likes it; he sometimes buys meat from 'the good butcher' in town, and often makes homemade lasagne, pizza, and croque-monsieurs, along with elaborate deserts and a hot pepper oil using peppers grown in the garden of his last house. They eat together at the dinner table, unlike many temporary or student cohabitation situations where roommates plan own their food and meal times according to their own schedules, eating in front of the television.

The roommates' everyday life outside of work is marked by certain rites: the 'after-work beer' together at home, the Sunday-night football match and the preceding programme dedicated to the championship. When asked about their leisure activities in an interview, they replied spontaneously, 'Well, a little of everything – gardening, tinkering … reading, films – we're well equipped so we take advantage of that'. They invest in these activities, buying a big-screen television and subscribing to cable sport channels.

Romain has also tried his hand at online gambling, betting on the Africa Cup of Nations, the American NBA championship, and tennis matches. He has won significant sums three times, and once put his winnings in his account to put back into betting, losing it all. He has since reined in his gambling. Ludovic sometimes goes hiking or mountain biking nearby, usually alone or with his dog (when he had one). They have a vegetable garden of about ten square feet where they grow tomatoes, courgettes, and lettuce.

They enjoy reading graphic novels and fiction. Their old roommate is also a fan of graphic novels and regularly loans them his, many of which have more or less explicitly activist content. This friend also made their bookcase, which occupies a significant portion of the living-dining area: located beside the imposing television, it contains history books (especially about the Resistance in the Limousin) and popular young-adult books (such as Harry Potter) alongside their graphic novels.

They watch television regularly, but only for specific things: football matches (up to three a week, since they subscribe to two premium channels that broadcast the French Championship and the League of Nations) and films downloaded from the internet. Other than that, they watch little television; as Romain sarcastically remarked, 'We don't watch *The Voice* on Saturday night…' If they go to the cinema relatively often, it is because they have access to reduced-price tickets through the works council of a friend from *lycée*, the partner of the friend that got them their current jobs. They go most frequently during promotional weeks like 'Printemps du cinéma' (Cinema Springtime) or 'La Fête du cinéma' (Festival of Cinema). They stress the cost of going out to see a film and their preference for 'big openings – blockbusters'. They have a taste for the spectacular that the big screen can offer, which they connect to the fact that they are 'well equipped' for watching more ordinary films or old favourites at home. Most of the films they watch have been downloaded illegally online, despite their rather large collection of DVDs. The cases that can be seen in the living room (*Friends*, for example) show, however, that they date to a time when downloading was more difficult. They go out to see films at a recent multiplex in an industrial area that is close to home, has ample parking, and schedules lots of blockbusters. The fact that they do not go to the multiplex located in the city centre seems to indicate that these movie nights do not include dinner out or going to bars in town. It is actually rather rare for them to eat out at a restaurant.

The decision to share housing over the long term is in part explained by material arguments, since splitting the rent opens access to higher quality lodgings, and in part in affective terms, as a consequence (and likely explanation) of their celibacy. For all that, their living together can also be interpreted in terms of the pleasure they derive from a relatively comfortable lifestyle enhanced by routine activities with a friend. Their shared home thus seems like a protective and rather happy place. This form of masculine intimacy illustrates the state of dual social suspension of class and age mentioned in the introduction. Their social backgrounds, past experience as temporary workers, modest incomes (1,149 euros a month with very few bonuses), and passion for football make Romain and Ludovic resemble the working classes. At the same time, their having attended university for a time and their friendships and leisure activities (reading politically oriented graphic novels and the satirical press) bring them closer to the middle class or cultural petite bourgeoisie. In terms of social age, they are gradually leaving the state of youth, without accumulating markers of the state of adulthood: establishment of a conjugal relationship, children, property ownership, and possible career advancement – although Romain distinguishes himself from Ludovic in the last two respects.

Attachment to a place without localism

Their enclosure in a private sphere of friendship includes external sociabilities, and both manifest an almost political attachment to the area where they live, being among the most politicised interviewees and positioning themselves distinctly to the left. Romain has played football in a club for several years. Although he took up football relatively late, when he was 17, he had been in clubs for basketball, swimming, and track and field as a child. He said that he finally focused on football to stay active and because he likes team sports. There were two rationales behind his enrolment in this club – the pleasure of playing and its affordable cost: 'I play in the town where I live because football is a hobby for me, and I don't want to put a lot of money into it. So, cheap membership, short trip'. He is uncomfortable with his current teammates in the club, who he thinks do not share his vision of football as fun.

> It's true that I like the sport a lot, I really like physical effort, so I kept that, yeah, in a team sport. Because depending on the team, you can find a great atmosphere. And the reason that I keep with it is because I had good atmosphere in the beginning, which I have trouble finding now, a lot of trouble. [...] [My current teammates] are morons. I mean, these blokes don't get that football is a game, that football is a sport, you do it for fun, and that [smiling] there's no point in pounding on each other every match.

The gap between Romain and his teammates is even wider because the club president asked him to be coach-player of the reserve team, meaning that he plays and is responsible for composing and directing the team. Unlike the first team, expectations of the reserve team's results are generally few to non-existent, and it does not hold practice. As a result, he has to deal with players not showing up for matches, which regularly forces him to negotiate with the opposing team to loan him players to avoid having to forfeit the match and pay a fine. The way that other players' define football in competitive terms and reserve-team players' limited engagement leave him feeling rather dissatisfied. If he sarcastically says that he does not understand 'why [he hasn't] been fired yet' as coach, due to the team's poor results, he announced that he did not want to continue once the season was over. Other than coaching, he helps to organise club events, including a 'Creole night' and a pétanque tournament, although with some detachment: 'There, I've done my good deed'.

Romain's dissatisfaction is partly derived from how club recruitment has changed in terms of generations, social backgrounds, and geographical origins. When he began in the club, Romain played alongside older players (35–40 years old), often workers in local companies who lived in town with whom he got along well, in a configuration reminiscent of those described in classic studies of rural football clubs (Faure 1989, Renahy 2001). The older players gradually withdrew from the club, often after an injury: 'When you sprain your cruciate ligaments in the knee at age 35, you've gotta be strong to try to resume playing'. These players were gradually replaced by younger ones who live and work in the larger town nearby. Some are from the French Antilles, and they are more often basic employees than labourers. Romain feels that this new group of players, of which there are at least eight, has changed the ambiance of the club and its matches. Likewise, although most of the younger members of the club are from the town and environs, the better players tend to go play in more ambitious teams, which further weakens the club's local rootedness.

As someone who is originally from the Creuse (in the northwest Limousin), has experienced some residential mobility, and is engaged in his town's football club, Romain manifests an attachment to the territory that can be partly attributed to his tight circle of friends and partly to more symbolic or even political motivations based on having been born there and having his networks there. Romain and Ludovic seem to be proud to live in a region identified with the left, due to its long history of left-leaning elected officials, the strength of the Resistance during World War II, and the current-day clout of the leftist movements Front de Gauche and France Insoumise (which made a joint list, 'Limousin, terre de gauche' [Limousin: Land of the Left] for the 2010 regional elections). Both keep up on political news by listening to the radio (mostly France Info, the public news station, while driving all day for their jobs) and regularly reading print media, especially the daily regional paper and the satirical weeklies *Charlie Hebdo* and *Le Canard enchaîné*. Their home offers some indications of this politicisation, including many of the titles in the bookcase and the poster of the anti-nuclear 'Sortir du nucléaire' collective hanging in the water closet, identifying all the nuclear sites in France and their potential dangers (Romain 'picked up' the poster someplace, but he does not remember where). They have voted 'for the left or far left' in every election since they came of age. During an informal conversation, they had a disagreement over the composition of a list for which they had both voted: Romain was certain that it was the Front de Gauche ('I think I know who I voted for!'), while Ludovic was insistent that it was the Partie Socialiste. The list – which won the election by a high margin – was in fact a joint list composed mainly of members of the Socialiste and Front de Gauche parties, an unusual configuration that is nonetheless found in many towns in their department.

Although neither has ever belonged to a political party or union, Romain stressed that he supported Sud-Etudiant (a student union in which his former roommate held a leadership position) while at university and participated in some student movements, even if most of them did not concern his discipline. Romain's family tends to lean to the right, so he has made his own path. This political vision of the world can be observed in his view of how his company operates.

Making do with a job for 'morons' to avoid the factory?

Romain reads electric metres for a private sub-contractor, subsidiary of an industrial group claiming 7,000 employees. His company seeks a variety of contracts, especially for reading metres, and has 12 employees in the Haute-Vienne. Romain started working there seven years before our interviews, thanks to the help of a friend who was a supervisor. After a two-month employment contract, he signed an open-ended contract for 35 hours a week. Romain and Ludovic were both approached to work there, and they jumped at the opportunity as a way out of unemployment for Ludovic and the uncertainty of a string of short temporary jobs for Romain. After his failure in STAPS, Romain had temped for a few years in manual jobs, sometimes spending long periods in a single company. In one of them, a food processing plant where he worked for about a year, he said that the working conditions were gruelling due to the cold working conditions and particularly physical and repetitive character of the work. Romain was offered a full-time job there, but these conditions made it hard for him to imagine working there over the long term and he turned it down. He then worked for six months in a company manufacturing automobile parts, then granted himself a few months of unemployment. He then went back to intensive temporary work– 'sixty bosses in three months' – before he was approached to work for his current employer.

A degree of wear and tear might explain his decision to accept this new offer of an open-ended employment contract: his temping and manual labour experiences prompted him to seize this opportunity for professional and social stability. In fact, the striking thing in interviews with Romain and Ludovic is the deep ambivalence with which they described their work. Romain spoke of it as 'profoundly brainless' and a 'thing for morons'. This tendency to debase his job is probably related to the interview situation, as he may have anticipated a negative view on the part of the researcher, who has a much higher education. When put in the context of his lifestyle and the expectations he developed over the course of his education, being a metre reader might seem like – and be experienced as – downclassing. For all that, we can also make out how Romain adapts to it: he has considerable independence (there is little oversight and he can organise his work as he sees fit), enjoys a pace that is less intense, repetitive, and limited than factory work, 'meets people' in his job through short interactions with the clientele, uses a company vehicle in which he spends a significant percentage of his time, and travels a lot, bringing him through lovely landscapes.

> It's a mellow job, a job that's... [...] If you want to compare it to the factory, our rhythm is a lot less... heavy. Let's just say that reading meters is profoundly brainless, I mean, you enter five numbers into a machine. But the pleasant part is meeting people, and also the pretty areas. There, that's it, every day you're in a different area, in a different place, different people, and that's what's pleasant.

When Romain makes comparisons with other occupational groups (postmen and refuse collectors), they are far from negative and made to emphasise the advantages the jobs supposedly share with his own – the postman doing his rounds, the refuse collector calling it a day once the work is done. Such comparisons suggest that Romain has a taste for calm, which he himself stresses: 'It's a good deal, yeah. You aren't paid thousands, but the working conditions are such that you're not going to complain'.

Well-informed and precise on union issues and how the company operates, he applies a political and above all moral template in interpreting professional relations. Romain first criticised the former union representative of the CGT, who he thought never got anything from management, never reached out to employees, and 'made a bundle' off his shockingly high expenses, and then proceeded to rail against the management and bosses in general.[3] He identified two phases in the recent history of the company – before and after the early 2010s, when the company joined a bigger group. For example, he assessed the advantages that were lost when EDF delegated work to a sub-contractor, citing the example of workers' daily trip from home to the first metre of the day, which is no longer counted as work-related travel and thus no longer paid. Although he and Ludovic described a relatively utilitarian relationship to unionism and voted for the CFDT (Confédération française démocratique du travail, a labour union historically close to the centre-left Parti Socialiste) by default in the last professional elections, one can imagine that they hope their company develops along the lines of bigger companies, which have works committees and policies generally more favourable to employees (bonuses, higher wages, a thirteenth month's pay, etc.). This is how Romain described the halting progress:

ROMAIN: Lately, let's just say that they are starting to give a bit more, but it's not bonuses – we still don't have a thirteenth month, for example. We're fighting, that's why we voted, but... [smiling] we're still waiting.

LUDOVIC: Yeah, the results of the elections for the works council are [coming soon], but the thirteenth month, that's in April.

ROMAIN: Yeah, the one that came to give us his speech, he said so [tapping fist on tale in ironic emphasis].

LUDOVIC: Yeah, he sold us on it, he promised us that.

CYRILLE: And who promised you that?

ROMAIN: The CFDT

LUDOVIC: Oh yes, because we had the CGT for three years and the only progress we made was getting a water bottle for 1.50€.

ROMAIN: We'll show it to you if you want [laughing]

LUDOVIC: He made a bundle and he never came. [...] So we changed [...]

ROMAIN: So I think that now, we ought to be seeing the CFDT representative again after the results of the elections, I think that he'll have to come see us again. At least I hope so [...].

LUDOVIC: So anyway, if you want to situate the company, we've got an annual revenue of 14 million euros every year. [...] When I learned [that it was] 14 million, I was like 'Oh, the bloody bastards'. [Smiling] They are making a bundle.

Despite the characteristically dark sense of humour with which he describes the planned obsolescence of his job, Romain seems to be fairly confident about the future because he is relatively sheltered by his employment contract, although his fate depends on his company being able to get new contracts:

> We've got an expiration date. [...] What makes me laugh every time, it's that we've got to install the [automated 'smart'] meters that are destroying our job. [...] But replacing meters is going to take 10 years, so if we get the contract, we still have 10 years of work.

For the time being he refuses to move, having had a brief experience as a supervisor in a mountainous region in southern France that he cut short after a year, requesting to return to his metre-reader position. There are two dimensions to his explanations for this failure: the first is related to the isolation in which he found himself in an unfamiliar region and the second is related to his difficulties in managing a team. He thus describes himself as uncomfortable in higher positions in the hierarchy:

ROMAIN: But it was the job, I didn't choose [to go] to the deepest depths of the mountains… The job they offered me was located there.

CYRILLE: And there, so, it was also in a rural area?

ROMAIN: Not so much, because I lived in a town about the size of Guéret [largest town in the Creuse]. And let's just say that Guéret, where I went to *lycée*, you like it when you know people. That was the problem…[smiling] I didn't know anyone. […] The work team wasn't… well, and then you've got to accept being a boss, y'know, [smiling] being a pretty whore. No, really, it's that I had some readers who were serious cases, who were hard to manage. You see, I had a team of 11; out of the 11, before I left, I had three that got themselves fired – no, two, and one who preferred to be cashier, which I still don't understand, for that matter. And the two that got themselves fired – one because he was stealing from clients and the other because he was stealing gas from the company. So there, that's roughly the mindset I was up against, and then, the southern mindset, it's like they say, it really isn't the same […], it's true that it's pretty odd.

CYRILLE: Yeah, so it wasn't an experience you liked that much?

ROMAIN: Yes, it was a learning experience, but besides that, did I like it? No.

CYRILLE: And so you asked to come back here?

ROMAIN: The possibility of coming back was one of the conditions for my agreeing to go […].

CYRILLE: And as team supervisor, was there a significant income difference?

ROMAIN: No, the income difference was 150€ a month, for a lot more work. So no, no, it wasn't big at all.

Was Romain's renunciation of this promotion related to the isolation in which he found himself, deprived of the resources of his network of friends by his transfer to another part of the country? Is he in the process of justifying refusal of all positions of authority after this experience? Did he prefer to keep a sort of moral peace, even if it meant a modest social status? It is also plausible that he might feel a structural distance from certain employees: indeed, he seems not to share their virile definition of work, especially when he spoke in relatively neutral terms of the company's recent policy to reduce metre-reader accidents by sanctioning risky driving practices. He does not seem to feel concerned by the new policy, no more than he was moved by the management's line, since implementation of this 'vigilance' bonus was largely dictated by the cost of insurance. He is more offended by the lack of political and moral consciousness of employees who take advantage of their jobs to steal. A string of little differences and strategies of distinction indeed separate him from other metre readers and more broadly from other working-class men; twice using the term 'moron', in speaking of his job and the football players he coached, he keeps his distance from a certain way of being a wage-earning man.

This relationship to the working-class condition or 'working-class bohemia' (Mauger 2006) is not new, but in this instance, it seems to be updated by their educational experience, as young men who are among 'the dominated with longer educations' (Schwartz 1998). Their educational trajectories (*baccalauréat général* and some university, even if, as Romain says, it ended in failure[4]) have indeed favoured the acquisition of a vocabulary that is both more formal and more 'youthful' and free than that of many other interviewees, as suggested by the use of words such as 'pleasant', 'hermit', and 'academic failure' (*plaisant, ermite, échec scolaire*). Romain and Ludovic provide us with a case study showing the condition of young, single, childless men with a fair level of education and political awareness, working as temporary workers and then subaltern employees, who are making a virtue of necessity. Despite the differences in their social trajectories, these childhood friends with abbreviated university experience are working to stay loyal to one another.

Notes

1 For an explanation of the French educational system, see the Appendix.
2 Romain smokes tobacco and occasionally marijuana.
3 The CGT (Confédération générale du travail) was long the leading labour union of France and is still widely seen as the main union of contestation (as opposed to the CFDT, which is more reformist). The CGT has historic ties to the French Communist Party.
4 'Both academic failures led us to the factory', he indicated, speaking of both his and Ludovic's trajectories.

References

Faure, Jean-Michel. 1989. 'Les 'fouteux' de Vitré,' *Actes de la recherche en sciences sociales* 80: 68–73.

Mauger, Gérard. 2006. *Les Bandes, le milieu et la bohème populaire. Étude de sociologie de la déviance des jeunes des classes populaires (1975–2005)*. Paris: Belin.

Renahy, Nicolas. 2001. 'Football et représentation territoriale. Un club amateur dans un village ouvrier.' *Ethnologie française* 31, no. 4: 707–715.

Renahy, Nicolas. 2010. 'Classes populaires et capital d'autochtonie. Genèse et usages d'une notion.' *Regards sociologiques* 40: 9–26.

Retière, Jean-Noël. 2003. 'Autour de l'autochtonie. Réflexions sur la notion de capital social populaire.' *Politix* 63: 121–143.

Schwartz, Olivier. 1998. 'La Notion de classes populaires.' HDR thesis, Université de Saint-Quentin en Yvelines.

7

HOLDING ON

Sparing no effort to stabilise an unstable position – Véronique Delage

Marie-Hélène Lechien and Marie-Pierre Pouly

At the time of the initial study, Véronique Delage was a 39-year-old childminder living with her two children; four years later, she and her children were living with someone and she had become a factory worker. Her trajectory illustrates a variety of forms of instability that primarily affect working-class women, shedding light on ways of relating to this unstable social position, some strategies for making it secure, and how she and her children have worked to contain destabilising factors. Véronique Delage manifests dissatisfaction with her situation and is not in a hedonistic relationship with the present: she demonstrates a will for professional ascension that is both strong and 'realistic', but this tension regarding the future does not exclude affirming her value in the present. In order to hold on, keep it together, and remain stable when faced with destabilising situations, she first of all fosters aspirations of development, hoping for and working towards a stable future by investing herself and her children in education and by keeping a tight budget. It also means maintaining her rank, preserving the respectability of her family, avoiding social notoriety, and making sure to set herself apart in word and deed from what Max Weber called 'negatively privileged' groups. Véronique thus works to avoid the most stigmatised fractions of the working classes ('welfare cases', immigrants, black and 'Arab' youths) and distinguish herself from them. Conversely, she tries to get closer to the middle classes with cultural capital, through the mothers who employ her as childminder. 'Holding on' means knowing how to find support, sometimes by opening up about yourself and 'letting loose', but also by doing what it takes to benefit from the help of family and friends while nurturing relationships useful to maintaining your position. More generally speaking, 'holding on' is an incorporated disposition to defending oneself that is usually associated with how working-class men relate to the world – 'values of

DOI: 10.4324/9781003330073-8

virility' – but in this case interiorised by a woman: hold your head high, don't let others walk all over you, spare no effort, hang on, and keep it together in times of exhaustion and sadness.

Destabilisation

Véronique Delage's professional, marital, and residential trajectories have been deeply marked by the possibility of downclassing, which she attributes partly to the failures of the male figures (father, husband, partners) whose protection she has sought (activating gendered class dispositions in the process), although she has often gone without such figures throughout her life. Frequent changes to her relationship, occupational, and residential status reveal how closely these three dimensions are connected and combine to destabilise her social position. Her children are her primary anchor, and everything she does is to make their futures more stable than hers.

Her first confrontation with instability was in childhood, when her family was economically weakened and shamed by the alcoholism of her father, who was a printing worker and for many years no longer able to work. Mother and daughter held the family together: after doing seasonal farm work and informal childcare when Véronique was a child, her mother resumed full-time work, getting a job contract with the *Inspection académique* (the governmental body in charge of overseeing public education regionally) and, 'one thing leading to another', ending up with a stable secretarial job in a university library. Véronique and her mother also tried their utmost to honour the household's debts.

> When... I mean, you see the car arrive on the tow truck in the morning and all that, and the whole neighbourhood is watching, and when you get to *lycée*: 'Wow, this morning we saw your father in handcuffs!' - 'Well yeah, he was drunk, what am I supposed to do about it?' [...] Sometimes they'd find him on the sidewalk, not knowing where he'd left the car. So we'd do [the whole town] to find out where he'd been the night before, where he went drinking. [...] So one morning there was no electricity. What do you do? Well you empty the piggy banks, you look around to see what you can give, how to handle it... Actually, whenever he was in rehab, my mother and I got by twice as well as when he was with us.

Véronique associates this period with two biographical breaking points, concerning schooling and family. She was on the literary track in *lycée* and would have liked to become an English teacher, but she left home to marry quite young.[1] She met her husband when she was 16, 'We went for it and too bad for the rest'. In retrospect she thinks of her husband as a 'life preserver': 'I repeated the final year [of *lycée*], and the last year, since my father drank, hit me and all that, I wanted to leave home with my husband. So I started looking for a job'.

Her husband had a CAP in pork butchering and held a string of jobs, most notably as a temporary worker in the food industry, and after a few years got a job as library caretaker, initially on a limited-term and then an open-ended contract. For a decade Véronique also worked in sales in a variety of stores (a bakery chain, fast food, hardware store, supermarket), with several sick leaves (one after five months of pregnancy, following two work-related miscarriages) and maternity leave. After the birth of her first child when she was 25 – a daughter who was 14 at the time of the study – she ranked jobs according to the working hours and their compatibility with the intensifying domestic work accompanying the arrival of children (her husband seems to have been little invested in such things). She became a childminder in 2005 (practicing for 10 years) specifically so she could be present for her children during 'normal hours', a condition that the variable and non-standard working hours in supermarkets could not meet. The work 'bored' her quickly, however: she describes it as isolating and shutting her in, further consigning her to domestic tasks. So, after a few years in childcare, she put herself in a frame of mind to move up and out of child care and the supposedly traditional feminine condition. She wanted to change jobs because working from home made her 'everyone's maid' – the children she minded, her own children, and above all, her husband. She earned a CAP in Early Childhood Development and sat the examination for preschool classroom assistant (ATSEM) several times. Throughout her attempts to leave childminding, Véronique felt like her husband constantly 'put [her] down' and was not very supportive while she was working on her CAP:

> And so... being always treated like shit and put down, like 'Well, that way, she won't go looking at what it's like elsewhere. Anyway, she's an idiot and she'll always be an idiot'. When actually, even culturally, I'm more cultivated than him, more intelligent, so... [...] And then, being acknowledged as a woman, not acknowledged as an object. I'm not a broom and I'm not a... a stuffed toy to put in bed and do what you want with.

So, in 2010, she began separation proceedings, which exposed her to instability once again. Leaving her husband was in effect leaving the apartment that came free of charge with his job and losing the second income, when that of child-minder is not very high. But she did not seek out new clients so that she could keep her RSA (Active Solidarity Income) benefits and still have time to take care of her own children's schooling and extracurricular activities. She moved several times after the separation (living first in privately owned housing, then in social housing) and was looking for a new romantic relationship while living on her own with her children. First, she had a periodic relationship with a man who worked for the police, then she met a much older man, a cook, and quit childminding to move in with him in his small rural town. Lastly, in 2016, she moved in with a farmer, just when she finally passed the ATSEM examination. But the lack of open positions in the region deprived her of any benefit from her success, and she became a worker in a factory that operates two eight-hour shifts a day while working on the farm without pay or any formal position in the business. The path to stability and occupational advancement that opened when she passed the ATSEM examination (a path taken by many working-class women) was blocked from the outset. Her instability comes with a form of social anxiety that is expressed in her relationship with her body and fear of getting fat and falling ill. Véronique thus fears getting early-onset Alzheimer's disease like her father and his mother ('I have the memory of a goldfish'). Always working jobs that are physically exhausting and nerve-wracking (supermarket, assembly line, farm labour, and childminding – carrying children, strollers, and other equipment, bending down to their level, gathering everything they drop), she suffers from regular backaches, which sometimes force her to stop work, leading to a drop in income. She also expressed another fear: being unable to sleep, handle the accumulating fatigue, and hold up to the stress. Her sleep quality has been declining for several years, and so she takes Stilnox regularly, although it is only intended for severe insomnia (treatment should be for the shortest possible time, 'from a few days up to four weeks', according to the package insert). 'I toss and turn', she says, adding half seriously that she fears it is another hereditary trait, because 'in my family, they [parents, uncles and aunts, cousins] all take pills to sleep, [...] maybe it's genetic?'

Educational salvation

Faced with the threat of family and occupational destabilisation from a rather early age, Véronique spontaneously gave a detailed description of what appears to be a series of interconnected strategies for remaining stable, a coherent collection of ethical attitudes and systematic actions to help her hold on and keep her head high. If investing in education and budgetary control are the themes she developed most prolifically, occupying her thoughts whether sociologists asked about them or not, it is because they are the fundamental economic and cultural (or material and spiritual, in Weber's terms) bases of social salvation. Aspiring to social salvation requires ascetic dispositions such as self-control, careful management of economic resources, and academic assiduity that must be passed along to the children by making the stakes the whole family's business.

Educational salvation is on Véronique's own horizon. She often thinks about changing careers, discussing it with acquaintances and encouraged by her children. She knows which degrees are required for getting specific jobs, stays informed on the possibilities for obtaining equivalencies through the validation of experience or being promoted to a permanent position, and manifests a realistic and explicit vision of what she would gain or lose in other jobs. 'I take any examination I can', she says: CAP in Early Childhood Development, the ATSEM exam, and next, the *baccalauréat*, which for a while she was thinking of obtaining through equivalency. But this aspiration went dormant when her conjugal situation stabilised. Two years after getting together with the farmer, she relativises the benefits of being an ATSEM, which pays less than her new job as factory worker.

Her personal educational endeavour also extends to her children. For her, raising children well means doing what it takes so they will be polite and obliging, and above all diligent at school. She collectivises the stakes of education (which she discusses frequently with them) so her children will interiorise a sense of obligation to succeed in school, rather than repeating the rules for behaviour every day (as far as that goes, one senses that she does not have the strength to enforce bed- and screen-time). Véronique attentively follows her children's education, and her educational goodwill is particularly manifest in her precise knowledge of their schedules and grades, her help with maths and English, her investment as a member of the primary school parents' association, her requesting appointments to speak with teachers, her participation in school meetings, and the telephone calls she made to *collège* teachers while trying to get her daughter put in a 'better class'. Having been very active in the primary school, she continued her investment in the *collège* parents' association. Having weathered the statistical probability of being eliminated from the running, her investment in a politically neutral stance (which other parents might see as the pragmatic behaviour of a consumer) allows her to orient her children toward the 'good classes'. Speaking of her eldest daughter, who was in *troisième* (midway through secondary schooling) at the time of the interview:

> So it was really helpful for her to do Latin as the other two languages. And then, after that, she said, 'Did you see my schedule? Next year they're adding yet another language. [...] I don't really want to take it'. And so she wanted to stop there [at the end of the previous school year].... She landed in a class, my word... I thought I was in the wrong class, at the first class council meeting. I looked around, I thought, 'No, the music teacher is indeed the main teacher'. I heard nothing but negative remarks about the children. Not about mine, but the class in general. I thought, 'But how does she manage to work?' And they were saying, 'We congratulate the children at the head of the class for their... assiduity, because honestly, working well in a class like that, they deserve it'. And so all those kids – there were six of them – were rewarded by putting them in other classes. The parents had written letters to put them in a class of better students so they could listen better and work harder... and give everything they've got. [...] But actually, her main teacher, regardless ... he took care of it on his own. When they created the classes, he called me that very night, himself, telling me he'd done what had to be done,

that I would be super-happy with the class. He said, 'I am very happy, you'll see, she's going to be good in this class, I think it's really where she belongs. You'll see, it'll be great'.

Véronique also got involved quickly when she realised her son was having trouble in primary school.

MARIE-HÉLÈNE: And it was the teacher who told you that he was dysorthographic and that he had to go see a…?

VÉRONIQUE: No, it was the speech-language therapist who said he was, when she did a screening. But they only figured out that he had problems when he was in CM1. And I'd been saying it all along, I said, 'This child…' I said, 'My son, I think he's got problems'. He'd been in basic tutoring in French when he was in CP because he held his pencil wrong. […] But I said, 'Given how many mistakes he makes […] And when you talk to him, he confuses his p's and b's, his m's and n's'. 'But no, you think that because you're always comparing with your daughter' […] I always got [comments back from the teachers]. And in CM1, the teacher did a screening of all the children as a matter of course and she told me, 'I think he should see a speech-language therapist, because actually, he needs it'. […] There was one teacher I didn't like and who had him in CM2. She'd tell me that I didn't know anything, that I was only a nanny, that I was not an educator and that it was none of my …

Holding to her budget

This engagement in education goes hand in hand with several strategies making it possible to stick to a tight budget. Véronique cannot afford to be indifferent to money, but she does have regular resources. Keeping to a limited budget demands an assortment of consistent practices that involve everyone in the family. It involves spending less, mobilising relational resources to save money, and obtaining additional income alongside formal employment, and the three are often closely connected. Spending less means, for example, giving the children a sense of responsibility by making them aware of family expenses, counting on gifts for secondary consumption (clothes, jewellery, beauty products), belonging to the employee's association of the university where her mother works to get discounted cinema tickets, and buying clothes cheaply on sale and at markets when on vacation. Using her relational network to get a better price on services like car repair and haircuts, participating in home-sales networks like Tupperware, and asking advice from a cousin who works in a bank (who encouraged her to save by opening accounts for her children and can intervene in case of overdraft, notably by making the penalties disappear): these are all strategies that allow her to save money by relying on friends, acquaintances, and family. Lastly, Véronique spends uncounted hours making money to supplement her formal income. This money is considered to be special and often earmarked for pleasure (vacations, gifts). She organises flea markets, which are economically advantageous in that they force them to sort their possessions to give them money for summer vacations and Christmas gifts, but less profitable if the preparation time and rental of a garage to store the objects to be sold are taken into account. She also does undeclared work: house cleaning (part of this income goes towards the garage rental, thus towards gifts and vacations), some 'extra' hours at a caterer, and occasional childcare to help out old clients in a pinch.

Véronique treasures the economic solidarity uniting her and her children, which she opposes to the attitude of her ex-husband, who she describes as economically and emotionally calculating and 'stingy' and focused only on his own pleasure. She presents her children as very 'reasonable'. Her daughter, for instance, is planning to babysit to buy her own clothes and build her savings, so as to not drain the family budget. Véronique speaks openly and often with them of budgeting, alimony, overdrawn accounts, and the like. Her omnipresent references to the cost of activities and things are coupled with the explicit description of strategies for sticking to a limited budget and making do with the limitations it imposes while transforming the solidarity it demands of the family into a virtue.

MARIE-HÉLÈNE: Continuing with the budget, you also have specific budgets for food, for leisure, you've budgeted everything?

VÉRONIQUE: [without hesitation] Oh gosh, everything is budgeted. It's easy, 1,193 euros go out every month. [...]

MARIE-HÉLÈNE: And you show them the budget, I mean, you talk about it to... If your daughter is reasonable, it's also because you talk about it, you make it all clear?

VÉRONIQUE: Always. I tell them, 'OK, this month we have an overdraft, again [...] How are we going to handle it? We can't be overdrawn all the time, because it will be difficult to get out of it'...'OK then, this month we don't do any extras. We're not going to eat at Quick [a burger chain], we won't do anything – to go out, we'll go to the movies, but going through the [university personnel] association, that doesn't cost much. [...] We limit ourselves as much as possible. That way, I say, the money we don't spend on that will go toward it [the deficit] next month'. I show them all the time, they always know what I have to pay, they know it well, and so they are reasonable.

In this treatment of the budget as a collective affair, there is an evident early apprenticeship in a sense of limits: money is an ever-present theme, in opposition to its avoidance in families of the cultural petite bourgeoisie, for example.

There is also a discernable on-going negotiation within the family to work around certain economic limitations, restraining spending one month to be able to pay for something in particular the next.

'Effort' is still one way to work around a tight budget. The ethos of activity is distinctive to the working classes (the middle and upper classes are identified with other forms of activity, such as the educational activity of the cultural petite bourgeoisie), and in Véronique's case is manifest in practices like doing flea markets and having multiple declared and undeclared paid activities, including Tupperware parties. Véronique hosts at least one per year and attends one or even two a month. They are another practical example of how economic calculations have integrated an ethos of activity and fit into sociability with family and friends. She gets gifts of Tupperware for hosting parties and reaching sales figures far above average: 'Because, since there's a lot of people, still, who like me, well, when they come to my place… last time it went to 1400 euros'. The revenue is immediately interpreted as an indication of the affection that members of her social network have for her. She keeps some host rewards (like components to a steamer that she is collecting gradually), and others are sold half-price at flea markets.

Keeping a distance from 'welfare cases' and being respected

While engagement in educational salvation and sticking to her budget are ways that Véronique invests in the future, the assertion of her self-worth also plays out in the present, in everyday interactions. At issue are preserving family respectability, setting herself apart from the most stigmatised fractions of the working classes, and finding support from women in the petite bourgeoisie without exposing herself to social scorn. In many dimensions of her practices, and in the anecdotes she enjoys telling, she demonstrates several forms of a fighting spirit – standing up to others, holding up under stress – that are usually analysed as 'virile' (thus specifically masculine) in the working classes.

First of all, Véronique manifests a distinct will to set herself apart from a disqualified working-class condition and to attain a more respectable one, whether it be moving up and out of her job as childminder (work seen as invisible and downclassing) or the rejection of her ex-husband, 'a lump in his couch in front of the telly'. Being associated with him by marriage consigned her to a 'working-class' style from which she wants to distinguish herself.

More generally, she fights for respectability by asserting that she is in the right camp. Firstly, she distinguishes herself from supposedly 'bad' childminders, who she says do it 'for the cash' or take poor care of children by ready use of physical punishment without the knowledge of parents or the child development specialists who supervise them. She next rejects the 'bad' working classes: rather than seeing them as part of the working classes, she sees them as a 'minority of the worst', to use Norbert Elias's expression, 'chavs' composed of immigrants and young people from council estates. With her strategies for avoiding the 'bad' classes in *collège*, she expresses her fear that immigrant children disrupt her own children's educations by obstructing a climate conducive to work in the classroom and imposing violent relations among the pupils. Speaking freely in a rather indignant tone, she recounted several anecdotes presenting immigrant families as 'benefit scroungers', denying them any sense of effort or restraint, expressing a resentment of those who she imagines chose unemployment, welfare, and the easy way. She thus mentioned the case of a 'Maghrebian' man who supposedly obtained child benefits for all of his children despite being 'polygamous' (she called him out on it, 'It's not allowed in France, polygamy!'), and the case of a child in primary school who had allegedly stabbed his teacher; she does not understand how parents could have let him leave for school without checking to see what he carried with him, and that they did not come immediately when the school called, claiming they were at work when, according to Véronique, they definitely do not work. Unlike those she denounces, she says she has a 'clear conscience'. The expression crops up regularly, notably when saying she wants to sit for a competitive examination even if she thinks she will fail ('I'll do it. After, I've got a clear conscience that way, I know I did it, you've gotta do it'). Beyond a strategy of demarcation with the working classes 'on benefits', she expresses a more general relationship to the social order and the future: she tries to improve her condition and play by the rules (even though she wonders what the possibilities for winning actually are), thus exposing herself to sanctions of the social order – trying for the CAP in Early Childhood Development despite doubting her merit and having long deserted school, trying five times for the ATSEM examination, having multiple revenue streams both declared and under the table – as if her only way out was to believe without believing in the possibility of social promotion.

Avoiding being confused with the stigmatised working classes and their behaviour or being seen as one of the 'bad' or 'fake' poor is probably even more important to Véronique because her own unstable trajectory and her economic calculations expose her to disrepute as well. Indeed, she restricted the number of children she minded so that she could escape the extensive hours worked by so many childminders and have time for her own children while also continuing to be eligible for the RSA, which could draw criticism from certain quarters.

At the other end of the social space she inhabits, Véronique seems to seek confirmation of her social dignity by frequenting women with higher cultural and economic resources than her own while nurturing relationships useful for maintaining or improving her position. She thus seems interested in opportunities to talk about herself and verbalise and compose her emotions (interviewing with sociologists is but one example; at the end of an interview, she jokingly asked how much she owed us). Conversations in which she opens up about herself and where other women speak of themselves offer her a glimpse of other lives and allow her to think that another way is possible. In the past, she has used certain work-related interactions to talk about herself and find the strength to leave her husband, particularly with a childhood development specialist who came to see her for the renewal of her childminder licence.

The ethic that allows her to withstand the strains and harder blows of life resembles a female version of the masculine working-class values of virility (Avril 2014, 137–141). Or, we might call it a working-class fighting spirit with male and female versions, since these values of virility concern several aspects of life, from work (being respected; demonstrating endurance and hiding her fatigue, first as a cashier working off hours, then as a childminder, and now as a factory worker helping her partner with farm work), to family (running a household and managing a budget, watching over her children, encouraging them to work, suggesting activities for them, and here again hiding her fatigue and worry from time to time) and all other social interactions. The feminine version is manifest in Véronique's taste for a 'heavy-handed' approach and a disposition to not let people 'walk all over' her. Generally speaking, she likes things that are direct, efficient, or may require an intense effort but have clear results (Boltanski 1971): cleaning products that smell nice and make things shine rather than a drop of an unscented environmentally sound product, a potent shot against gastro-enteritis rather than traditional or holistic treatments, Zumba over yoga, 'a good cry' when she is down rather than psychotherapy, and so on.[2] Another aspect of it is appearing to be in a good mood and full of energy. She revels in how her friends, family, and colleagues appreciate her for it, as was the case when she worked in the supermarket:

> My co-workers, I got along well with them. When I came back [from maternity leave], they said "We're really happy you're back because at least we'll have fun, we'll laugh. You arrive at six in the morning, even if you slept badly, you're always bright-eyed and bushy-tailed".

Lastly, although she willingly does favours, she wants the service to be fully recognised for what it is worth, being careful to not be 'treated like shit'. She likes to tell stories that put her up against some kind of social disdain where she regains the upper hand. For example, when she was a childminder and curiosity or suspicion led parents to ask what she did during nap time (some of them were even ready to deduct nap time from her pay or bring ironing for her to do for nothing), she would mock them, replying 'Either I watch them sleep, or I take off – they're sleeping, after all!'. She likewise told us how she had refused to mind one little girl during school vacations, although she had cared for her for many years. The girl's parents had high incomes, but a comment by the child made her realise that the mother thought the daily rate was too high, so she responded to every subsequent request by letting it be understood that she would be on vacation herself. Faced with these annoyances from parent-employers who do not consider childminding to be a real job, she demonstrates that she will not let them walk all over her and that it is more important to her to assert her worth than it is to make money. Véronique recounts the episode, starting with the phone call from the mother:

> 'I'm checking in for your news – I suppose you're on vacation those two months'. I say, 'Yeah, that's it, exactly'. It would have made some money, but I didn't like the way… Plus, they own a business so they earn a good living, it comes rolling in. [She explains that they own two Mercedes cars and let several apartments whose exact rents she knew]. My salary is a drop in the bucket for them, and, I mean, you don't make remarks like that. She bent over backwards to have me and no one else for nanny because she heard about me from a woman at the university. So it's not nice, I didn't appreciate it, so I said, 'OK toots, you'll have to figure it out for yourself now!' [laughs].

Notes

1 For an explanation of the French educational system, see the Appendix.
2 This combativeness is partly related to the 'somatic culture' of the working classes identified by Luc Boltanski in his analysis of 'social uses of the body' (1971).

References

Avril, Christelle. 2014. *Les Aides à domicile : un autre monde populaire.* Paris: La Dispute.
Boltanski, Luc. 1971. 'Les usages sociaux du corps. *Annales ESC* 26, no. 1: 205–233.

8

'GETTING IT RIGHT THIS TIME'

Aspiring to join the world of intellectuals – Yamina and Souleymane Diallo

Clément Degout

Yamina Diallo was born in 1986, child of parents who migrated to France from Algeria in the 1970s. Her mother, a housewife, died in 1994. Her father began as a construction worker and went on to work in a tire factory for 25 years. He died in 2000. Yamina was 14 at the time and continued to live with her step-mother and four siblings in the family's house. In 2004, she met Souleymane, six years her senior, who worked with his parents as a market vendor in Sarcelles, a working-class suburb north of Paris where he was born and grew up. Souleyman's mother started the business after having worked as a care assistant in a retirement home in the Val-d'Oise and as a receptionist in a Parisian hotel. Souleymane's father had migrated from Senegal as a professional footballer in 1974, but he did not make a career of it. He was a labourer at Alstom until he quit to join his wife at the market. She had joined him in France six years after his migration, leaving the Dakar area where she had been helping her mother, who was divorced and did not work.

Today, Yamina works as an administrative assistant in a network of private radiology centres. She started at the reception desk of a centre in the outer suburbs of Paris but now works in nice neighbourhoods in Paris's 7th and 17th arrondissements. Souleymane works the night shift at a motorway service area near their home, selling petrol and goods in the shop. They live with their three preschool-aged children in a low-income housing estate near the centre of a town in the Val-d'Oise, not far from their families. This portrait of Yamina and Souleymane Diallo was made at a particular moment in their social trajectories marked by a process of social requalification. At 30 and 36 years old, they had been studying for *licence* degrees in sociology for two years in a university in the Paris metropolitan area, with great expectations. As Souleymane put it, 'We're hoping to break through in our studies, we thought it was the best way

DOI: 10.4324/9781003330073-9

for us to change our lives, even intellectually'. By resuming their studies later in life, they intend to 'make up for lost time' and 'get it right this time' relative to their earlier educational experiences. With this determination to close the gap with the most highly educated, they formulate their hope of reaching more highly paid and interesting jobs. They describe shifting their positions in the employment market as a secondary motivation, following their desire to acquire academic knowledge and culture and develop their understanding of the world. The choice of the social sciences, rather than other courses of study with the potential to offer greater and more rapid employment opportunities, makes sense when it is contextualised in their account of their return to education. More than money, Yamina and Souleymane value having cultural capital, erudition, and the ability to pass them on. Drawn to the cultural branch of the middle classes, they are trying to prove to themselves that they are worthy of the academic world by practicing an everyday asceticism that reveals as much of their material living conditions as it does of their aspiration to join the world of 'intellectuals'.

Finally becoming intellectuals

Yamina and Souleymane have bitter memories of their years in *collège* and *lycée*.[1] Souleymane recalls being 'unmotivated' throughout his school years, 'I didn't really go all out, I just did the bare minimum'. School was not the focus of his interests and ambitions, which he analyses today as relating to his socialisation as a teenager in a working-class neighbourhood of the Parisian periphery. And indeed, although he stuck it out through a *baccalauréat technologique* and a BTS in sales, many of his friends from *collège* quickly 'left school' to take unskilled jobs or join the local illicit economy. Since he did not see the point of 'losing years' studying at a university, which was unimaginable to everyone he knew and neither parents nor educational professionals ever suggested, he planned a shorter education and rapid entry onto the employment market.

Yamina went to predominantly white middle-class schools in the Val-d'Oise, the outer suburbs of Paris, and describes herself as having been a gifted and engaged student. She does recall having felt 'class shame' at school in this town of housing developments, especially citing her lies to save face as a way of dealing with other students' tales of ski vacations and extracurricular activities. She now sees that she went to a vocational *lycée* as a result of the racist and classist discrimination present in the school guidance system. She remembers that her main teacher in *seconde*, for example, 'sold her' on the vocational path and discouraged her from continuing in a general *lycée* the following year, despite her fairly good grade average of 12/20. The few 'immigrant' students in her class, all from post-colonial migrations, were the only ones shunted away from the general *lycée* and towards a vocational one, a truth it 'took [her] time to understand' and that she now talks about with the university students she frequents today. Despite the praise she got from her teachers who prepared her to sit for the *baccalauréat* in STT (*sciences et technologies du tertiaire*), which is usually prepared for in a general *lycée*, she did not transfer schools, which she regrets today. Regardless, after getting her *bac* she took the advice of a teacher and enrolled for a *licence* in law at the university closest to home. She soon quit, feeling 'lost at the university' and lacking any clearly identified career goals. Like Yamina, Souleymane also analyses his initial 'lack of motivation' in light of his going to school in an education action zone *(Zone d'éducation prioritaire)* and discrimination rooted in geography and the school system.

At the time they met, Souleymane was working the markets of his hometown with his parents and Yamina was working occasionally as a cleaner and camp counsellor, which she had been doing since she was 14. At age 26, Souleymane was thinking over his school years and felt dissatisfied with his social and occupational situation. He developed the desire to 'get some distance', travel, and learn Arabic and English. He decided to follow in the footsteps of a childhood friend, who had gone to study in several European countries and then Egypt. Since Yamina did not want to continue their relationship long distance, she went with him to Cairo, where they lived for four years. Souleymane enrolled in a prestigious university in Cairo that took a lot of foreign students. They both learned literary Arabic at the university and from private teachers, and Yamina gave French classes to college students.

They present this trip and overall experience as their first biographical disruption, one that particularly allowed them to develop what they call a 'more intellectual' relationship to Islam as a faith. Religion is important in their daily lives, although they keep away from spaces of group practice. They lament that the tradition of 'great [Muslim] intellectuals' and a Muslim 'elite' has been forgotten and that their social ambitions do not strike a chord with this tradition. They think that attending mosque did little to encourage them 'to culturally integrate', in Souleymane's words, meaning that they had not been 'encouraged to be teachers, business owners, doctors, engineers' there. Referring to their knowledge of literary Arabic and the possibility it affords them to read the text of the Koran, they define religion as a healthy 'way of life', which they oppose to a system of guidelines and prohibitions censuring their aspirations 'to become somebody in the national arena' and shutting them into systems of inter- and intra-community assignation that cannot be undone. With that they are also emphasising one of the stakes in promoting the cultural heritage of their parents, which could not be converted into educational capital.

Souleymane puts particular emphasis on one of the functions of their resumption of studies since they returned to France: they want to restore their self-esteem and stop feeling the 'embarrassment' that their vocational degrees cast over their friendships by pursuing the intellectualisation they began in Egypt. This led them to enrol in a university in sociology, a discipline in which Yamina's brother was working on a Master's degree. In addition to the way already being paved, the humanities and social sciences represent an opening to the intellectual world to them. Sociology facilitates a dispassionate relationship to knowledge and nurtures curiosity about the world, in language sometimes borrowed from the lexicon of personal development. The idea of studying for themselves – out of a taste for knowledge over any strategic or career considerations – is also a way for them to see and prove themselves as worthy of university, for Souleymane and Yamina alike:

SOULEYMANE: We're trying to sort of correct what we've done, basically. And even if it should lead to nothing, because there is no certainty where the future's concerned, at least it lets us avoid coming home and going stupid in front of the telly. [...] Even if it's a degree that'd be useless for me, I know that socially I can be with anyone, I know that he's got nothing more than me, basically. He's got a Master's, I've got a Master's. If he's got a doctorate, I've got a doctorate. I won't feel weak, actually. So already, for self-esteem, it's already not bad. And if there's an opportunity... if it opens a door for us, that will be good; otherwise, we'll see, y'know. But at any rate, it keeps us young, let's say. The fact of going off to study. And it's interesting, too, it's another approach. We don't go to learn because we have to – if we go it's really for us, it's not the same thing anymore.

YAMINA: There's no question that, since we resumed our studies, it's still so we can completely change jobs. But it's not... it's mostly with an intellectual objective, I mean. Mostly so we'll be enriched. But we think that afterward, we might be able to change lines of work, maybe earn a slightly more normal living.

Both intend to continue through a Master's degree, and despite their stated lack of ulterior motives when they portray their relationship to knowledge, they also frequently discuss the new occupational possibilities that they anticipate. They are planning on becoming primary or secondary school teachers. While there are material advantages that make the occupation so appealing (especially the pay and holiday leave), they are most of all fond of describing it as a 'noble occupation'. For instance, Yamina opposes teachers to the doctors she knows from work, 'interested in the money' and not practicing 'out of love for the job'.

These assessments are conditioned by the restriction of the careers that are available to them, they also shed light on the ethical way in which they relate to the world that goes far beyond a simple question of degrees and jobs. From this perspective, they situate their studies in sociology – as an exercise in decentring and 'opening to the world' – into a logical continuity with their return from Cairo. Yamina in particular realises that 'discovering another culture' was the basis for her critique of the consumption styles of Western societies and her esteem for simpler lifestyles.

Everyday asceticism borne of conjugal and family solidarity

The deference they express towards academia and the rigour they exhibit in how seriously they take their studies to manifest their aspirations to reach the space occupied by intellectuals. The down-to-the-second planning of their weekly schedules and rarity of free time are signs of asceticism, as is the sobriety of their domestic space: in their clean and uncluttered apartment, the living-room furniture is populated only by their computers and a pile of sociology books from the library. All their efforts are made possible by a strong solidarity, within the couple and with their extended families.

Their decision to go back to the lecture hall together, when they were 28 and 34, was rooted in shared plans and ambitions that Yamina and Souleymane discuss frequently. Together they work for social recognition, which they see as a family and conjugal project. They seem bound together in how they see and talk about themselves, so that they never interrupt each other and always agree with what one says of the other, or of him- or herself. This agreement in their accounts of their life course and the formulation of shared ambitions is also based on good everyday relations that make their accumulated engagements in their jobs, at the university, and in their domestic space tenable. They regret they have little time for themselves as a couple and have made the televised 8 o'clock news a sacred moment just for the two of them, after the children have gone to bed. In this context, they describe a spontaneously balanced division of domestic labour, taking turns doing the shopping and cooking and putting the children to bed together, 'like an assembly line'.

For the past two years, their resumed studies have significantly influenced how their time is organised and justifies their remaining in subaltern jobs that they do not like very much. Weekly, Yamina works 30 hours in the day, Souleymane 30 hours at night, mostly on weekends; they only 'break even' thanks to the disjointed hours of their jobs with open-ended employment contracts. These working conditions make it possible for them to ensure care for their children, take the eldest to school, and take a university course while jointly earning about 2,200 euros a month, supplemented by 750 euros from the child benefits office. An array of marital and organisational arrangements thus allows them to pursue all these activities. They share daytime care for their pre-school aged children, and they chose their university because it was close and readily accessible from home. Classes are chosen according to their work schedules, and they share their notes, especially when Yamina cannot attend class. Souleymane sometimes studies his notes or works on assignments in the middle of the night, when the petrol station is not busy. Unable to explore elsewhere, they have both already used their workplaces as field sites for observation exercises assigned by their professors. This organisation and these strategies have allowed them to earn credit for the first two years of their three-year *licence* programme without needing to repeat.

In view of their social ascension, Yamina and Souleymane also rely on the solidarity of their extended families. They regularly attend family reunions and religious holidays, since their respective families live nearby. Most significantly, they also benefit from material help from their siblings when their weekly organisational machine gets jammed, such as when unexpected extra working hours or illness disrupts their childcare routine, or when an unforeseen expense demands occasional financial help at the end of the month.

In these family relationships, Yamina and Souleymane stress the role of the eldest siblings (including Souleymane) in the educational and professional careers of their brothers and sisters. Their educational goodwill made Souleymane and Yamina's oldest brother highly attentive to their siblings' choices and opportunities, strongly encouraging them to pursue their educations and resume studies that had been cut short or interrupted for several of them. Yamina moreover recalls her older brother's disappointment and resentment when she went into a vocational *lycée* rather than a general one. In addition to that, the youngest are urged to study and educate themselves. The couple thus also notes that their own enrolment in university had been inspired by one of Yamina's brothers' working on a Master's degree in sociology and that their return to school had 'given ideas' to others. While another of Yamina's brothers, a 35-year-old lorry mechanic with a *bac pro*, is thinking about going back to school in hopes of realising his old dream of working in architecture, Souleymane's youngest brother is 'tempted' to go after a Master's degree on top of his BEP, *bac pro*, and BTS. This attention and the effect of being carried along by their siblings thus lead them to think about their own plans for social ascension that involve further studies. It is also a way to 'regain control' over a family history that their own children will be part of in turn.

Resisting social judgement through scholastic and academic culture

> [Our children] will grow up seeing their parents going to school, so it's like it's a message to tell them that you've got to do your studies right, or you run the risk of growing up bitter, not having done what should have been done.

As Souleymane's statement makes clear, this resumption of studies is also a way to make themselves a model for their children. As parents, they intend to pass along the tools for succeeding in school to their children. Although they are still young (the eldest is five), their parents anticipate their future activities and socialisation. They make a particular distinction between outside activities (which they prefer) and inside activities. The former are associated with legitimate cultural practices, meeting other children, and training them to be 'open-minded' and develop 'curiosity'. They oppose this to an excess of television or video games, synonymous with closing in and becoming stupid. Both value the inclusion of children in housework and teaching them politeness and respect for adults, which was evident whenever the researcher came by and the children were asked to greet him and put their toys away. Yamina and Souleymane see these everyday ways of disciplining mind and body as the conditions for scholastic and social success. They do rule out an overly strict approach to childrearing that could lead to frustration in their future social interactions. They are allowed to watch television, but the time and programmes are limited to cartoons in the morning, after breakfast, giving their parents time to get ready. Yamina explained,

> The eldest has a tablet, he got a tablet for Christmas, a gift from one of his uncles. I was against it at the beginning, because, well, I know that screens can be dangerous for children. But we try to put educational things on it for him. But then, it's true that we don't want to be too strict, either, because later he'll probably be frustrated in relation to his friends. So sometimes we allow him to watch some videos. He likes The Avengers a lot, so we let him watch some Avengers videos, or cartoons, of course. But it's true that we don't want him to play on a Playstation, either. We'd rather he take his scooter, we go for a walk, we go to the park, he meets other kids.

> SOULEYMANE: We try to make it so our children will be a lot more curious than we were, basically. Much more open to the world, curious. Whether it's... going to a museum, seeing shows, going to the zoo... Being interested in lots of things, y'know, to be rather open-minded.

They thus use a collection of childrearing strategies directly oriented to the future. Yamina, for example, would like to teach her children to read before they start CP. Every night she devotes time to the eldest to read him books from the children's publisher *L'École des loisirs* or *Tralalire*, a children's magazine to which they subscribe. She is also interested in pedagogical theory, including the Montessori method, and refers to the weekly visits to the library imposed by her father when she was a child, which she credits with favouring her taste for literature. Yamina is also attentive to her children's expressions and signs of creativity, noting for instance one son's talent for drawing and artistic activities. Souleymane was the one to describe their residential strategies, closely tied to the prospect of their children's education. Referring to his own childhood in the council estates of the northern suburbs of Paris, he explained that their main criterion for accepting low-income housing is that it be located outside the working-class council-estate neighbourhoods. The neighbourhood schools and their population were also subjected to close scrutiny.

The couple's characteristic mobilisation on many fronts attests to their self-discipline, which is also a basis for distinguishing themselves from other groups with which they could be confused. During this period, which they see as a time of transition in their social trajectories, their positions are uncertain. They thus hope that their status as subaltern employees is only temporary, but this distancing does not prevent them from expressing solidarity. They share their co-workers' professional and income demands and also criticise their employers for the working conditions reserved for workers in low-skill jobs. In this regard, they consider themselves to the political left because they were raised that way and as a logical consequence of their social positions, since they are both from post-colonial immigrant backgrounds and children of the working class. Concerned with escaping certain forms of workplace subordination, Yamina prefers duties like transcribing dictated medical reports, 'off quiet by [her]self' to working the desk, which exposes her to view and the mixed dictates of patients and doctors. She does take part in forms of professional sociability and solidarity with the other medical administrative assistants and x-ray technicians. She occasionally swaps working hours with a co-worker as a favour (and vice versa), and she attends birthday and goodbye parties for co-workers of the same hierarchical position.

In the ambivalent relationship they have towards the social groups closest to them, the appropriation of sociological language acquired at university signals a distance. They shape their discourse by using concepts and categories from the social sciences, and sometimes introduce their memories with the formula, 'with sociological hindsight…'. The ability to anticipate the researcher's categories and control their personal accounts is also, by the same gesture, an ability to objectivise the groups from which they are extracting themselves. Because he did not have the time to explore another place for a class assignment, Souleymane described, counted, classified, and sketched his workplace and the movements of customers in the petrol station. The shop being closed at night, they go to the window to place an order or pay for petrol. He noted the young people who have 'just left the night clubs', those 'who loiter' and hurl insults at each other; he described the activities of drug dealers and comings and goings between the station and nearby council housing estates. His position as sociologist in training, observing from behind the locked door of the cashier's booth, confirms this perspective and distance. He got the best mark in the class for this assignment.

So for now, being sociology students allows them to restore their self-esteem by raising their social status and expanding their professional opportunities in the future. Yamina and Souleymane further signal their distance from the working classes by manifesting concern for the place of 'intellectuals' in social mobilisations, using an erudite lexical field in interviews, and criticising news chains targeting a general viewership, which they find too sensationalistic. They oppose them to the 'independent' and 'intellectual' media. Souleymane is a regular reader of *Mediapart* (an investigative news website) and *Métropolitiques* (an online journal of public scholarship on urban issues), and Yamina regrets that deeper news coverage 'stays within a very intellectual milieu' and is not 'spread across the whole population'.

Nevertheless, Yamina and Souleymane want to 'rehabilitate' the working classes through reading and the practice of sociology. Although their life courses and plans for social ascension distance them from the working classes today, they have also developed a discourse of solidarity with them, evidenced by their decrying discrimination in the school system or health care as causes of inequality. Accordingly, Yamina says that she is 'disgusted' by the medical world, which she finds disrespectful of the working classes. She cites as proof the differential treatment of patients that she has observed in two of the offices where she has worked: the doctors in the centre located in a working-class neighbourhood systematically spent less time on patient cases than those in the centre in a posh Parisian neighbourhood.

These opposing tendencies towards distanciation from and defence of the working classes can also be seen in Yamina's research topic. For her Master's degree, she is planning on conducting a study on the upper classes rather than the working classes, which are much more common objects of sociological research and recommended by faculty for their Master's theses. At the same time, she wants to unpack the miserable image of working-class people conveyed by certain television programmes. She cites programmes like Super Nanny or Baby Boom, which she says obey 'marketing objectives' instead of serving knowledge and hold up a distorted mirror to working-class families, offering them a degrading and false image of themselves. In both cases, by clearly articulating her potential research topics and the social trajectory from which she approaches them, Yamina places sociological work in a progressive epistemology and a dynamic of social justice. So, while Yamina and Souleymane are taking a marked distance from their social backgrounds, they have no intention of breaking with it, either. They situate their plans in the migratory and labouring histories of their respective families. Yamina's quest for a new social status is symbolically associated with the memory of her father, who was frustrated by his distance from legitimate culture and equally concerned with his children's success in school and passing along a delegitimised cultural and spiritual heritage.

Notes

1 For an explanation of the French educational system, see the Appendix.

9

'YOU'VE GOT TO FIGHT'

Work as a resource for a fragile success – Mina and Michel Carry

Anne-Marie Arborio

Mina and Michel Carry form a working-class couple that seems to have been somewhat successful, already planning for retirement although it is still a few years off. Mina, 55 years old, is an auxiliary nurse for a home hospitalisation service in the small town where she lives that is run by a university hospital in the nearby prefectural capital. Her husband Michel, aged 59, is a hairdresser who was once an employee and now owns his own salon. They have been married for over 30 years, have two daughters (Céline [30] and Laeticia [25]), and are even grandparents, since the eldest has two children. They own their apartment as well as a vacation home – a studio by the sea, about 100 km from home – and seem to be fairly comfortable. Their jobs are not especially well paying, but they do allow them to accumulate overtime to earn more money. A heavy investment in work and a simple lifestyle (like swimming in the river and cycling for him, and occasionally going out to eat since the children left home) made it possible for them to become property owners and live in conditions they find satisfactory. Case in point, Mina reports that when she asked Michel, who she describes as 'anti-bling-bling' and 'anti-consumption', what he would do if he won the lottery, he replied 'Why are you asking me that? What more could you possibly want?'

This feeling of success is the fruit of continual effort, however, if we believe the representation that Mina gave of her life in the first interview: 'So, my life hasn't been a picnic. [...] It was very hard, but at the end: success. That's why I say you've got to fight'. More than making an effort, it's a battle. If Mina seems to be the main actor in the story, it is partly due to research conditions, since she is the only one that I could interview: she kept her husband away from the study, presenting him as someone who 'works all the time' and is 'a loner', little inclined to open up the way she does. It is also related to her life

DOI: 10.4324/9781003330073-10

course: the daughter of immigrants without educational qualifications, she had to stand up to the authority of her family, which consigned her to the domestic space, and find her place in the working world by accumulating unskilled work experience until she became an auxiliary nurse. For her, 'success' refers to the victorious outcome of this struggle in face of threats to her freedom, affective relationships, and material comfort. In these battles, engagement in work appears as a decisive resource, as is the stability of her relationship with Michel, who is a fundamental source of support. For all that, the success is fragile.

A child of immigrants fighting her foreign roots

Mina's first battle was against her parental family, and it lasted until her marriage to Michel. Mina describes herself as someone 'attracted to French culture' who rejected the imposition of any religion or practice from her parents' home country, Algeria, which she does not perceive as being hers. She makes this story the linchpin of her entire life: in the first interview, after speaking of her job as auxiliary nurse for the home hospitalisation service, I asked her how she got a job at the hospital, and she responded: 'You want my employment history? Well in that case I've got to tell you my life's story. So, my parents are Maghrebian…' We understand from this that she has already had the opportunity to give this narrative and think about what has to be said so that she will have a hope of being understood. She mentioned having spoken about it with friends who concluded that she should 'write a book about [her] life'.

Her long tale begins with the arrival of her Algerian father in France, at age 17. He came to work as a miner and made of career of it. He got married in Algeria, to a divorced woman with three children from her first marriage. He brought them to France, and the couple had two daughters of their own, Mina and her sister, who is five years younger. Her parents divorced when Mina was 7, and her mother returned to Algeria with her first three children; Mina would never see her again. Her father placed his daughters in a boarding school 'with the nuns', charging Mina with learning to 'get by and take care of her sister': this is the condition he sets for them to return to the family home, and Mina's first challenge. She was 12 when their father took them back. Shortly thereafter he remarried a woman that Mina refers to as her 'mother', and she calls the three children her father had in this second marriage her 'brothers' and 'sisters'. She is grateful to this woman for having raised her and her sister as if they were her own children. But their smooth relationship became rocky when Mina was a teenager and 'generational and cultural conflict arrived'.

Over the course of the interviews, Mina forcefully asserted a conviction: she says she is 'atheist' because she has 'suffered too much from religion'. She has been an atheist since adolescence, a period that was marked by being raised 'between two religions'. In fact, the details in her account show that her Roman Catholic schooling is what first made her hostile to religion: the 'meanness of the nuns', the 'blows' they used as punishment, and the 'racism' of which she felt she and her sister (who were not Catholic) were victim. She was not particularly familiar with any religion other than that of the boarding-school nuns until the arrival of her second mother, who she describes as 'illiterate' and believing in 'rubbish'. Mina had noticed that her father did not eat pork before his remarriage, but he had no reservations about placing his daughters in a Catholic boarding school and he did not inform the school of any dietary restrictions: 'He just wanted his children to be raised well, that's all'. Islam as a religion was brusquely imposed on Mina as an adolescent, in the form of rules and injunctions imposed by her new mother and adopted by her father. Today these precepts lead her to describe the religion as doing everything it can to 'take away everything that is good', and as a young person made her oppose her parents vehemently. In addition to Ramadan being imposed, she was subjected to rules for her clothing: although she was not required to wear a veil (her stepmother did not wear one at that time, either), she was forbidden to wear makeup and miniskirts, which prevented her from being able to continue being a majorette, an activity she really enjoyed. Hardest of all, it included control over her going out: no bars, no nightclubs, no going out at night at all, when Mina 'wanted to live her life to the fullest'. She resisted a little and tried to talk about it, but could not soften her parents' position, so she ultimately chose to avoid conflict by lying: she changed clothes and put on makeup after leaving home and pretended to follow Ramadan 'even if it meant eating four times more'. Dissimulation became difficult and conflict inevitable when it came to marriage, however.

When her parents began to talk about 'someone who was going to ask her to marry him', Mina initially protested but gave in to the 'pressure' and agreed to see him. She met a man she found 'old' (30, when she was 19) and ugly – 'an ogre, like, someone scary'; worse yet, he was 'an Algerian from there' whereas she is 'drawn to French culture'. She felt trapped. Her engagement was planned for the following Saturday. She fell into a sort of depression that contrasted with her parents' joy: 'I thought, "Well, that's it. That's life, it's all over…" I gave up'. She described how she was taken 'like a robot' to buy an outfit for her engagement. But once engaged, Mina recovered, thinking that the marriage would not take place for another two years and she still had time to act:

> I told my sister, 'I'm going to tell them I can't'. I was caught in a cycle where they pressured me and I thought, 'All this has got to stop'. […] When I told them that!!! They were happy – they'd gotten their daughter engaged. Everyone was happy but me, but no one could see it. Oh, the blow-ups that happened! … They said, 'How's that possible? The engagement happened!' I told them, 'But you're the ones that wanted it'.

The battle thus resumed, and the string of punishments and privations had no effect. Mina asked her parents to break off the engagement before her intended's next visit, but when she realised that they hadn't, she informed him herself that he should never come to her home again unless it is to ask to be reimbursed for her engagement outfit, for which he had paid. She had not entirely put the subject to rest, however. The following summer she went to Algeria with her parents, haunted by the fear of being married there and having her 'papers taken away'. Her parents subjected her to a variety of rituals because they thought she was 'bewitched', but the last marabout they consulted ended up confessing his impotence over the matter, informing them that 'her thing, it's that she wants to marry a Frenchman'.

When she speaks of this past Mina develops a kind of spontaneous sociology that makes her understanding of her parents. She says their upbringing justifies their behaviour: 'I managed to say to my father, "But if you wanted me to be like that [...], you should've had me down there [in Algeria], so I wouldn't see all that"'. 'All that' is what she refers to as 'French culture', meaning the lifestyle she projects for herself. In this regard she did not feel split between two cultures; she simply felt French, and she did not want to renounce it for her parents. The dilemma was even worse because she loved them and did not want to break off relations with them.

She finally resolved to arrange to run away from home. She quit *lycée*, found work in the nearest prefectural capital 45 minutes away, got her driver's licence (which her father paid for, as with all his children), and bought a car. She rented an apartment unbeknownst to her parents and left one morning for work without intending to return. She left a letter for her parents and siblings in which she said she loved them and understood them but could not stay because they did not understand her. She took care to call them from time to time so as not to cut off all ties, but was not sure she would ever see them again. A few weeks later, she noticed that her father was following her and waiting for hours in his car to catch a glimpse of her, so she invited him into her apartment and they reconciled. Gradually she went back to seeing her family on Saturdays while keeping her own apartment near her workplace. She sums it up with the declaration, 'I won! Huge victory!'

It seems as though her parents had still not fully accepted the idea that she would choose her own husband, because conflict resurged when Mina announced her intention to marry Michel. The battle was twice as hard because Michel's parents, with deep local roots, also expressed hostility: 'They didn't want an Arab in the family'. Mina thinks that her foreign origins were only a pretext, however, since they had not been more welcoming to Michel's previous girlfriend, with whom he had lived for five years. Mina and Michel thought they might get married without their respective parents in attendance. Mina's father finally ended up calling her, though, and offered to pay for her dress, and the celebration ultimately took place with members of both families. 'And so, I won, another victory', Mina remarked. The relationship with Michel's family is still tense to this day.

The couple thus built itself in opposition to both of their families, but for Mina this challenge was only the last step in a battle to assert her independence from her parents and their religion.

Earning her place in the working world

Mina and Michel were initially a couple of young labourers. Michel has a vocational degree, a CAP in hairdressing that he earned when he was 16, and has enjoyed job security since he was hired in their hometown's hair salon.[1] Things were more difficult for Mina. Although she did not experience the failures or symbolic wounds that some research participants reported in their accounts of school, she did leave *lycée* during the final year, without a diploma, since leaving school early for work was a necessary precondition for leaving her embattled family home. She managed to get hired as a labourer in a variety of factories in the region. Working conditions were hard; of a glove factory where breaks were limited, she recounted: 'We had five minutes to drink our coffee, go to the bathroom, and smoke a cigarette, so we'd do all three at once'. She moved on to the restaurant business in a small town with a hot spring and even became manager of a restaurant there. She kept working after her marriage and the birth of their first child, but with the arrival of the second one she took two years of parental leave. She found a new job as a factory worker once Laeticia started school, but the hard work convinced her to look at other sectors: 'One thing was sure, I didn't want to work in a factory'. She applied for work in several medical institutions and got a positive answer from the university hospital, where she was hired as 'acting' auxiliary nurse at age 33.

The decision to work in a public hospital was not taken at random, since Mina had heard about it from Michel's older sister (a psychiatric nurse) and brother-in-law (a hospital service worker). Although this might make them seem like role models, they are actually counter-examples in many respects. For one thing, this sister seems to be the parents' favourite and Mina suspects she had a hand in the poor relationship with her in-laws. For another thing, Mina criticises them for boasting of their relative privilege – higher incomes, a 13th month of pay, etc. – when she and Michel were in financial straits. She thus got her revenge, in a way, when she got a job with the same employer. Finally, she thinks they are both 'lazy' because they accepted early retirement: the sister at age 45, the legal minimum, after having three children and thus putting in 15 years of actual work, and her husband for permanent disability after a few long sick leaves, 'tired from a job that consists of lifting the gate, lowering the gate, well… And on top of that, at night, when there's no-one there…', Mina added.

Mina invested herself quite differently in her public hospital job, which provided her with unhoped-for possibilities for career development. The higher income and job security allowed the family to buy its own home with a 20-year loan, after years of renting an apartment in a public housing estate and then a small house in town. The hospital also allowed her to catch up on her unfinished studies, although it took a renewed effort. She expresses no regret over leaving school, because of the circumstances and perhaps because she had already pursued her education further than anyone else in the family had at the time (her mother is illiterate, and she is the eldest), but she still had to put all her energy into acquiring an auxiliary nursing degree (DPAS[2]) when she was nearly 40. She took courses to get her French and mathematics skills up to level in order to apply for the training programme just at the moment when she would have the seniority to have her educational costs and salary covered by her employer. She got her DPAS in 1998 and became a full-fledged auxiliary nurse, thus benefitting from the symbolic advantage of the title along with the better pay.

The satisfaction she derives from her job is palpable. She is proud of being an auxiliary nurse and happy that I chose her to talk about the occupation. In fact, our first interview came after a few brief conversations at a regional auxiliary nurses' conference, where Mina was one of the few to speak at the microphone in front of a room of 500 people. She speaks rather passionately about the job and takes pleasure in reporting things doctors have said about the importance of auxiliary nurses, the accuracy of the information they give patients, and the like. She does not try to 'climb' by becoming a nurse, but demonstrates a thirst for learning in the context of her occupation. She regularly takes classes offered by the hospital. She heard about hypnosis in such a class about pain management and plans on taking other classes about it in order to make it a speciality in her home hospitalisation service work. Likewise, as she recounted at the regional auxiliary nurses' conference, she requested and obtained leave to pursue a degree (a *Diplôme Universitaire*; DU) in palliative care after learning about it while working as a replacement. She was initially denied access to the DU programme because she does not have the *baccalauréat*, but she made this quest another of her battles by pursuing all avenues until she was successful. She gave the assembled auxiliary nurses a glowing account of the DU programme and her relationship with the other students, who all held higher-ranking jobs at the hospital. When she explained it to me after the conference, I realised that she had wanted to tout her victory in front of the head of the DU programme that had been reticent about admitting her, who she had spotted in the conference hall. Unlike the DPAS, these subsequent training programmes gave her no career advantages, but they do have symbolic rewards.

Michel is not sheltered from such battles either. Not only does he support Mina in her efforts, but he also had to catch up on his education, which stopped when he was 15, so he could prepare for a professional promotion of another kind. After working in a neighbourhood hair salon for 25 years, his employer passed away and he was offered the chance to buy the salon. His CAP degree had been enough for him to be an employee, but French regulation requires that salon owners have a higher degree, the *brevet professionnel*, and so he resumed his studies. He stumbled over the 'theoretical tests' and only passed on his fourth try, and this with Mina's help. She was on maternity leave at the time and helped him by following the classes with him so she could help him study afterward.

As they reached their fifties, they sought to provide themselves with the conditions necessary to pursuing their wearing occupations for a relatively long time. The unisex salon that Michel had bought had become a little too much for him, especially since the neighbourhood had become 'a problem area', so he decided to sell it and buy a modest salon for men downtown. Mina always seems to have new plans. Before the home hospitalisation service opened in their town, she thought about becoming a 'medical representative', a pharmaceutical industry salesperson for products used by auxiliary nurses in hospitals, but she preferred to work in the same town where she lived 'for the first time' and stop commuting (which added up to an hour and a half round-trip). Her new job was during standard working hours, after working the night shift ten of the past 20 years in her former position. She made up the income lost by working for the home hospitalisation service (she earned 150 euros less each month, since she lost the Sunday and night-shift bonuses) by enrolling with a temporary employment agency and joining the replacement team at the university hospital. Although she was overworked, she appreciated the supplementary income. At the time of our first interview she was already planning for her retirement, with the idea that she could continue to take temporary positions to supplement her pension.

Michel and Mina have both 'succeeded' in the working world: he in a relatively routine manner by staying in the same occupation his whole career and achieving independence by going back to school, and she favouring a path of change and renewal, from factory to hospital, and taking advantage of the possibilities for internal promotion that it offers. Mina insists on the fact that she has never been on unemployment and describes her husband as 'very wonderful', stressing his love for work: 'My husband is not a layabout, he's a hard worker, he's not afraid to work 12 hours a day'. She sees his intense practice of cycling as a confirmation of his ability to commit to strenuous effort. Family seems to be the only justification that moderates this devotion to work, as when she took leave 'to look after the little one' or when she moved to the night shift in order to be more present for their daughters and help them with their homework. They value work a great deal and think they have passed this along to their children. At the same time, this value leads them to block out those who do not share it, like Michel's sister and her husband.

Fighting again, this time to hold on

Despite expressing a sense of a degree of success in our first two interviews, Mina and Michel are still plagued by doubt and the need to keep struggling. The first object of concern was the merely partial success of their daughters. Both followed their mother's example by going to work at the hospital as hospital service workers and are employed, but they still need their parents' support. Unlike Mina, neither of them was able to advance to the next step, auxiliary nurse training, with their employers covering tuition. They are still in insecure positions. Céline is the first member of the family to earn a *baccalauréat* (in literature) and Mina probably hoped that she would have a different professional future. She would not have forbade her to go off to pursue her studies as her own parents did, but she had difficulty imagining her at the university, and so she 'made her go work at the hospital', the university hospital. Céline struggles with relationship and family problems. Her domestic relationship is unstable, and Mina judges her partner harshly: 'He doesn't work and will never work. He has the mental age of a twelve-year-old, and he never saw his parents work'. Céline and her partner had two children that ultimately became a burden for Mina. She arranged her schedule so that she could relieve Céline's childcare burden, either starting at 6 in the morning or wrapping up at 10:30 at night, depending on whether Céline is working a morning or afternoon shift. Mina's support for her daughter includes letting her family live on the ground floor of their house, which explains why she describes domestic chores as ubiquitous. Mina blames Céline's occupational difficulties on her domestic situation and the fact that she 'doesn't get along with the bosses', marking a difference from herself, who always had good relationships with her superiors, who helped her to advance. She nonetheless holds out hope that she may one day see Céline become a nurse.[3]

Laeticia did not have her sister's ambition and preferred preparing for a BEP in health and social work over taking the more general pre-university path. She began to work as a hospital service worker at the local hospital where she had done internships, but without a family to care for she had nothing holding her back from getting qualified for a promotion. Since her employer was making her wait too long for auxiliary nurse training, she decided to take the entrance examination and pay for it all 'herself'. She passed the examination to a school 100 km from home. She was ultimately in the charge of her parents, who also paid for her studies (over 5,000 euros/year). She lived with her partner, who was also in school. Céline and Laeticia's difficulties weigh on Mina and Michel, when their departure from home should have lightened their burden. The daughters have avoided the factory jobs whose harsh working conditions so marked their mother, but they struggle just to try to replicate her professional situation. Their relative dependence obliges their parents to remain overinvested in their work and, in Mina's case, housework.

When Mina and I last met, in 2015, the couple's previously observed success had been reversed. Michel found himself in financial difficulty after setting himself up as a small business owner because he hadn't properly anticipated his social security taxes, so he owed thousands of euros plus the

880 euro monthly payment towards his real estate loan. Mina took this 'step backward' very hard; she did not want to deprive herself any more: 'We hadn't counted like that since the beginning'. She gave the examples of the perfume she cannot buy any more and how happy she is that she still has a few samples so she will not be entirely deprived, and the wardrobe she has not been able to update for a year. They had to live off of her income of 1,450 euros a month, and the rest went towards paying off the debt. Their daughter Laeticia had an inspired possible solution, however. Her situation had worked out well, because upon concluding her auxiliary nurse training, she went to work in Switzerland. This made it possible for her to move closer to her boyfriend, who was enrolled in a Master's degree programme in Lyon. She gave her mother a rosy account of the working conditions of Swiss auxiliary nurses, firstly because the work seems to fit the ideal more closely, allotting more time to each patient, and secondly because she claimed to earn up to 4,000 euros a month.[4] Laeticia lived in a border town in France, and she invited her mother to join her. Mina was already very critical of the increasingly heavy workload in care services in France, and such an income would let her settle the household's financial troubles; she was sorely tempted, although it would mean being far from her loved ones and long commutes. The announcement of changes in the home hospitalisation service where she worked, including new budgetary restrictions further burdening work, ended up convincing her.

In July 2015, Mina was preparing to leave. She made the decision with Michel:

> I say to my husband, 'Well, I'm gonna go', but kind of as a joke. My husband said, 'Well, go, then…' I said, 'but it doesn't bother you, ending up by yourself?' He said, 'No matter what, we're in financial difficulty, so we don't do anything anymore… So we come home at night, we're thinking of only one thing – going to bed'. It's true that we almost fell into depression, like, both of us. And so this is like… a light!

She filed for a six-month leave from the hospital and plans on arranging to work three weeks at a time in Switzerland and coming home for three or four days in between. She also had to ask Céline's approval, since her unflagging help would no longer include watching her children:

> I didn't want Céline to feel abandoned. We talked about it for a long time. We made Céline come upstairs [from her lodgings on the ground floor]. Everyone told me, "go ahead, do what you want." […] Well, it's going to be hard for the little ones, but I'm not their mum, their mother's got to find her place again. And it's not like I'm going to Canada, it's just 4 hours [away].

When I mentioned her elderly parents, who she visits often, she appeared less worried:

> My brothers and sister will be there. And then, sometimes they go to Algeria for six months without asking me about it. And then I think, I'm the oldest – I've given enough, y'know? So, I think I've given enough for everyone. I don't want to do it backwards for my children.

Over the course of the interview Mina made what might seem to be a sacrifice into a godsend for escaping her fate as daughter, mother, and grandmother overloaded in housework:

> When they [the daughters] left home I thought cool, it's going to be just us two, each living our little lives. That lasted two years. Two years, and my daughter came back home, I found myself back in the bath with kids, like when I was young… It's been three years, but I really gave. I gave for three years, so the littlest can start [pre]school and [Céline's] got to get an apartment. And me, I want to breathe. No, there I'm going to work but I'm going to REST. Here I'm up until 11:30 at night, I don't go to bed before… I was the eldest of five, already, so now, enough, I say enough.

Fighting now so they will never have to fight again

Moving closer to higher-ranking social groups is not an issue in Mina and Michel's idea of success. Michel's move to independence occurred because the opportunity presented itself, and, as we said earlier, Mina is proud of her occupation, although she wishes that it was more 'recognised'. Nor do we see any fear of falling in Mina's account, not even in the last instalment when they were suffering from financial difficulties from which they had thought they were protected. If they taught their daughters that 'some day you might find yourself in a hole. You find yourself with something expensive to pay for, what'll you do?', it was mostly to give them a sense of reasonable spending and savings. Mina does not try to make herself look good by stigmatising 'welfare cases' and their presumed abuses, and especially not immigrants, as the child of immigrants herself. Her criticism is not of groups with projected traits, but rather of people she knows like her brother-in-law (lazy, without ambition, dishonest, jealous…), Michel's mother (unloving, ostensibly preferring her daughter to her son), and her son-in-law (also lazy). Work, their main resource, also emerges as a principle for classifying people.

If Mina presents herself as having succeeded, it is in relation to everything she had to fight against and escape: an 'arranged marriage', hard jobs in industry and food service, and her husband's family, where there was little love and with which they finally broke off relations when his father died in 2012. The unexpected financial problems of 2015 might seem to go against this success, but Mina turned it into a new battle in which she thought she would come out victorious once more. As she discussed all these challenges throughout the interviews, she presented herself as both 'relentless' and someone who 'has been lucky'.

Work has always been a way for her to succeed, without her seeing work itself as another constraint to overcome. When she interprets these battles by saying 'ever since I was a little kid I couldn't stand it when something was imposed on me', she makes an exception for the world of work, in which she is wholeheartedly engaged. 'The only person who can impose something on me is my higher-ups, in my job, because they pay me for that'. Her engagement in work is not absolute, however: it is the result of calculations prioritising family relations and adjusting income to need. Mina and Michel slowed down for a while but deepened their engagement once again to address their difficulties, although her departure to Switzerland is also seen as an opportunity for her to rest. This capacity for calculated strategies is seen in how she planned for her retirement as she was leaving for Switzerland: she plans to leave the hospital at 57, with a pension of 900 euros per month, so she intends to keep working: 'To reach 1500, all I have to do is a week of temping, and I could even do two…' Her private retirement pension will start when she is 62. No matter what, they are planning on selling their house and seaside studio to build a little house and put the remaining capital aside for their retirement. Life without work seems like a far horizon.

Notes

1 For an explanation of the French educational system, see the Appendix.
2 This simple certificate had just been named a 'professional degree' and would go on to become a state-recognised degree in 2005. It is a level five qualification delivered by the Ministry of Health following a programme of theoretical and practical training lasting approximately one year.
3 On the website of the DRJSCS (Direction Régionale de la Jeunesse, des Sports, et de la Cohésion Sociale; Regional Directorate for Youth, Sports, and Social Cohesion), we can see that she finally obtained her auxiliary nurse's degree in late 2017.
4 She claimed to earn 20 euros an hour (excluding bonuses) and work 40 hours a week.

10

MAKING A VIRTUE OF SIMPLICITY

The hedonistic choices of a labouring couple – Yvon and Michou Ratelier

Jean-Noël Retière

Yvon is often entrusted with the careful selection of a few good bottles before parties. Not only do his friends recognise his fine palate, but also they know he has a knack for ferreting out the best winemakers nearby. It helps that farmland and vineyards producing muscadet de Sèvre-et-Maine surround Viebert, the town where he and his wife Michou live, which is about 30 km south of Nantes, between the Vendée and the Mauges. Around Viebert's historic town centre are housing developments populated by lower-middle class residents in mid-level jobs, who until recently found work in a specialised hospital. Its distance from Nantes, proximity to Lake Grand-lieu, and the persistent hold of agriculture on the area has limited the encroachment of urbanisation from Nantes and kept the area rather rural. Viebert lacks anything picturesque and thus has no particular appeal, which would explain the low number of vacation homes in a zone where the single-family home has ousted nearly all other forms of housing. There are no signs of luxury or ostentatious wealth to make you think there might be significant social differences.

Yvon, a retired labourer, and Michou, a retired pre-school classroom assistant, are both from Viebert and would not consider moving for all the money in the world. Their family histories are rooted in this area, where they accumulated the right resources for satisfying their common aspiration of 'living well', far from the city, doing their utmost to avoid wearing themselves out at work and to immunise themselves against the pangs of what is commonly referred to as market alienation.

DOI: 10.4324/9781003330073-11

Childhoods marked by challenges

Both were quite young when they lost their fathers. Yvon's mother remarried a tradesman only to be widowed a second time, and she raised her five children alone, guiding them towards early apprenticeships: 'There was no money to send us to school! And everyone around here did apprenticeships – mason, roofer, pork butcher. For me it was plumbing-heating'. His three brothers became a plastics-worker, a mason, and a youth counsellor without formal training who ended his career as a manager in social work, and his sister an auxiliary nurse. Michou's childhood was spent on a very small farm that her ailing father struggled to run ('He had a few cows, a horse he loved a lot…') until his death at age 45. Before finding work at the town's school cafeteria, her mother did piecework boxing candles for a regional company, often with her children's help. Like all seven of her siblings, Michou went to private school 'with the nuns' and earned a secretarial BEP certificate in 1972.[1] Upon the recommendation of the administrators of her *collège*, she was hired by a dairy at age 18, allowing her to pass some of her earnings along to her mother. Her memories of the time are nonetheless tinged with guilt; she remembers being a 'fickle teenager' and thinks she only made minor contributions to family expenses and supporting her elder sister, who raised the younger siblings after the death of their mother and then entered a holy order.

In their youth, Michou and Yvon hung out with the same bunch of friends, and they are still close to some to this day, despite their lives having taken very different directions. These friends were still in *lycée* when he was finishing his apprenticeship with a local plumbing and heating tradesman. Unlike many young rural people from working-class backgrounds who were happy to 'stay in the area' and unmoved by the mood of freedom palpable in the 1970s, they both felt an early urge to travel and defy conventions by distancing themselves from the fates reserved for them locally: compulsory military service, early marriage, a steady job, and buying a house. 'At that time, it wasn't a common habit, people of our age, people in Viebert considered us to be marginalised'. Rejecting the path already laid out for her – *too* laid out for her – with her safe job at the dairy, Michou quit after two years. Taking advantage of the freedom offered by a wide-open job market, she alternated between seasonal work in mountain hotels and working in the hospital as a service worker, sometimes even doing the work of an auxiliary nurse. Other than giving her the opportunity to discover new places, she felt that working in a job for a shorter time had the significant advantage of shielding her from such 'women's environments, where there's so much fuss and rumour'. This cycle also favoured escapades as far as Gabon and Niger to join Yvon, who had fled military conscription and followed his elder brother's footsteps in a five-year voyage in Africa and North and South America. It was during one of these reunion trips, this time in Greece to work the seasonal orange harvest, that Michou learned that she was pregnant. The birth of their son Manuel in 1978 signalled the end of their wandering. Yvon was 26, and Michou was 24. They decided to return home and settle down, renting a house in town for a few months before moving to the house where they live to this day. Michou resumed work sporadically, 'odd-jobs' as she calls them today, 'doing the grape harvest' and 'doing secretarial work' for a friend who was an architect, until she set her sights on a more steady job. The resources of autochthony at her disposal would make it easier for her to find the stability she desired. Her friendship with the son of the mayor at the time, along with the reputation of her family, indeed played a role in her 'getting a town job' in 1984. The town required new employees to work flexible jobs for the first two years, so she worked stints as a cafeteria worker, cleaning worker, and school bus guardian, until she was given a job as a classroom assistant (ATSEM) in 1986. For a while Yvon often took the role of stay-at-home father, tolerating a small job from time to time and taking considerable advantage of '*bien-être*', a term for unemployment that he picked up in Canada signifying 'welfare', but also more commonly meaning 'well-being' in French. Indeed, in hindsight, this period is seen as a golden age of compensation by anyone who, like Yvon, could only conceive of working as much as necessary to give access to unemployment benefits from 'Lady Assedic' (Assedic being the unemployment benefits office at the time). But finally, figuring that 'with a little one [*age 6*], we have to deliver', the couple decided to leave the insecurity it had long accepted in avoidance of the limitations of a regular job.

Domesticating wage-earning subordination

Yvon resumed travel, but this time 'to make money' by going to Algeria for two long stints in petrochemical construction. He then went straight into a string of jobs all over France, while taking care to balance the appeal of travel allowances with his desire to return home weekly. Gradually accumulating experience that expanded on his original skills as a plumber, he specialised in industrial heating installation and worked in this field until his retirement, but resolutely opting to work only temporary, one-off jobs. This choice, like the discourse supporting it, owes much to his acquisition of skills that were recognised and valued by several temporary employment agencies in and around Nantes. He paced his jobs to match Michou's work schedule, which was set by the school calendar. He quickly made a habit of turning down offers that impinged upon his desire to take advantage of the family time that he set aside for the full Christmas, Easter, and All-Saints' holidays and five weeks in the summer.

However, his choice of what today is called annualised flexibility in no way prevented Yvon from working 1,500 hours a year, good year and bad, which is the equivalent of a legal full-time job. This smoothly running system came at the cost of having to put in overtime the weeks when he was working, and, in the beginning, enduring a sometimes chilly reception from fellow workers worried about the impact of businesses' calling on temporary workers (the option was introduced in 1974):

> It wasn't all that easy at the beginning, people had a low opinion of temporary work, the workers saw us arriving: "You're coming to steal our bread!" You really had to prove yourself, it was in your interest to work well. It was never that much of a problem for me.

Sheltered from competition by his skills, Yvon only rarely suffered from the ostracism of his colleagues. Since he was faithful to his temp agency and a few companies that called upon him regularly, he did not need to worry about the uncertainty of work that so often weighs upon temporary employment.

> I ultimately worked for this [temporary employment] agency for 35 years. It changed names but had the same philosophy, the same mind-set, the manager changed but by following the same policy, relations were very good [...]. At the end, I worked when I wanted. All I had to do was tell the agency on Thursday or Friday, "I can start again on Monday of next week" and I'd show up in the company, and often with long spells in the same companies, like at CHAUDAC or UNIGAZ.[2] The final years, I worked in only five companies... Often, even, it's the agency that asked me if I'd like to accept a certain job. I was also solicited many times by these companies' bosses, but I always turned them down, I also wanted to be loyal to the guy at the agency, who I'd known for 20 years.

His aspiration to enjoy retirement, especially by no longer having to suffer 'the ring of the alarm' cutting his sleep short, does nothing to contradict his admission today that he 'liked his job' because, though he always tried to build firewalls against the wear of work and excessive time restrictions, Yvon never misses an opportunity to insist on his satisfaction with a job well done and still enthuses about a perfect pipe installation or soldering job. Thanks to the confidence he had earned, he was asked to plan and execute jobs from beginning to end, quite often single-handedly, and he rarely had to put up with a boss or suffer overly oppressive subordination. He had the autonomy of a specialist jobber, using his manual skills and regulating his meal, coffee, smoke, and other breaks for himself. Recalling his apprenticeship with a particularly benevolent tradesman, he enjoyed teaching tricks of the trade to the clumsy but willing young apprentices that were sometimes confided to him, though not without decrying the failings of professional training and the amateurism of some. One anecdote is revealing of his work ethic, which, much more than a morality of effort, has always included the taste for careful work and pride in the results. A few weeks after he retired, Yvon spontaneously got back in touch with a very young worker who was a Companion of the Tour de France, a very old and traditional system for learning crafts and trades through a series of apprenticeships across the country. Yvon had been impressed by the mastery of the young man's technique, and the young man had rhapsodised about Yvon's handmade tools burnished by decades of use. The call's only purpose was to set a date to offer him the toolbox. They never saw each other again. This gift seems even more emblematic of Yvon's relationship with work when he confided,

> I never had any relations with co-workers ... Because of my temporary status, I changed [jobs] a lot, but more than that, I always separated private and professional life. I liked my work a lot, but I didn't fit the labourer mould, they were two different things: private life, and the rest... Going out for a drink after work, for example, wasn't for me – I'd finish work and I'd go straight home.

And indeed, he has no friends from work. Another sign that he keeps his distance: while never denigrating unionism – far from it – Yvon never joined a union himself. Although he bemoans governmental policies, usually votes for Green or far-left parties, and responds to appeals for donations from UNICEF and Secours Populaire (a secular French charity), he kept clear of any concrete form of professional solidarity such as paying dues, participating in a demonstration, or joining a strike. Unassuming, taciturn, and overly protective of his independence, it is as if Yvon's penchant for withdrawal makes it difficult for him to be part of a group and yield to discipline. Even if he uses his temporary worker status to justify his avoidance of unionism and as an excuse for escaping socialising with colleagues, it all still comes from his admitted desire to close himself off in his private in-group.

Shared moral dispositions

Although neither of them feels any great aversion to his work, both agreed to 'separate private life and professional life'. This distance is based on an understanding in the couple that cannot be entirely unrelated to the balance forged over 40 years of living together. Unlike many wage earners, they say that they never had to endure a harmful environment or an exhausting 'dirty job' that made them suffer. Quite to the contrary. Michou, too, gave a great sigh of relief the day of her last school outing, but she also has happy memories of her old job and the joys of being in contact with small children that come with being a nursery school assistant. She has painstakingly arranged her photo albums in a curio cabinet, including an album specifically for class pictures tracing her 30-year career that served as the basis for a slideshow at her retirement party, which was attended by several generations of parents. Delightful memories are not always enough to make her forget the occasional condescension of parents or teachers that reminded her of the subjugation that came with her low-status job. This is a major factor in her distinction between 'good and bad years', which were particularly determined by the personality of the teacher to whom she was assigned. It was also the source of her inclination to 'want to forget and escape the school', which resulted in her not spending time with her co-workers, other assistants included, outside of work.

Regardless, the couple's active social life makes it impossible to interpret these avoidance behaviours as the result of a preference for solitude. Relatively rich in family and friends, they demonstrate a particular aptitude in maintaining connections that generally go far back, and having friends in common. Many of their friends are of the same generation, turning 20 in the late 1970s. Some have many points in common: rural and relatively working class, limited scholastic careers (some of them cut short prematurely), and all were able to avoid social down-classing. Some even stand out for their social ascension or success, albeit limited. One network of friends, all from the town or nearby, includes a small business-owner in public works who is the son of a tradesman and emigrated to Martinique; a couple of schoolteachers, of which the woman was long one of Michou's co-workers, the eldest of 11 children whose father was a delivery truck driver; another couple composed of an auxiliary nurse and a maître d' who worked for an events organiser; a drawing instructor in an experimental high school; a theatrical technician who is an ingenious handyman. To this circle should be added the 'travellers' that Yvon and his brother met during their wanderings in Africa and the Americas, including a couple of former communications consultants turned cabinetmakers, as well as childhood friends accustomed to alcohol-soaked weekend parties and grape-harvesting sorties spent singing the libertarian repertoire and songs of Brel, Brassens, Ferré, and Béranger rather than listening to the Beatles or the Rolling Stones. In this gang of friends sharing the rebellious spirit of the day, two are from the Viebert area and attended a boarding school for *lycée* in Nantes, but both were expelled for bad behaviour and neither took the *baccalauréat*. They were declared unfit for compulsory military service after simulating psychological problems. One, the son of a cleaning woman, did a training programme at an adult and continuing education centre (AFPA) and then worked for a long time as a solderer for a temp agency before being hired as a landscape maintenance worker in a small town near Saumur. The other is a brother of the previously mentioned female schoolteacher, also a solderer trained at the AFPA who was a member of a construction cooperative in Lyon until, at age 45, he moved to the *departément* of the Ardèche and founded a museum devoted to lavender. A third friend, son of a classroom assistant, became an academic. When all is said and done, although the resources of this array of faithful friends are unequal, there are no affluent friends or chronically poor ones, or even friends that are disaffiliated or in the process of becoming so. Lacking inherited capital and educational attainments, those who are the most independent by necessity have drawn on their sole inheritance – their moral dispositions and the energy indispensable to bouncing back – when a lasting romantic relationship or the birth of a first child makes them decide to end their carefree days. These are the same moral dispositions that, as we saw earlier, were at the root of Yvon and Michou's resolution to put an end to the insecurity marking their early years back in France so they could have the income they needed to improve their living standards. For the 40 years since, the couple has created an existential balance, both and psychological, by taking advantage of their rootedness (in which they are deeply symbolically invested) and carefully planning their domestic economy.

Peaceful comfort

The inaugural act, as it were, was buying the house where they still live on credit in 1989. It was part of a lot of four identical post-war barrack buildings that Yvon's uncle had bought from 'the Americans' at the end of World War II. Altogether the property was a partly wooded lot of one hectare jointly owned and occupied with Yvon's brother and his partner. Each couple had the use of two buildings. Yvon's substantial earnings while he was travelling so much for work made it possible for them to pay off the credit at the Crédit Immobilier de France in nine years, and without excessively burdensome payments.

Although the price the uncle asked of his nephews did not require a heavy loan (it was considered trivial at 330,000 francs in 1989–1990, the equivalent of 50,300 euros today), the shacks' dilapidated condition demanded restoration, which the couple would undertake with care but no urgency, never once calling on a paid tradesman. Be it roofing, exterior cladding, electricity, heating, plumbing, woodwork, painting, door and window frame replacement, or interior layout, Yvon ensured all the work necessary to bringing the house up to safety, comfort, and aesthetic standards, sometimes (albeit rarely) with the help of a manually skilled friend in exchange for his help in return. The major expenses were spaced out and only concerned materials, which were sometimes quite costly ('The solid oak flooring was a real luxury, but we treated ourselves'), used to realise plans that he and Michou had developed together.

The peaceful comfort typifying the couple's living standards is probably less due to their income than it is to their principles for managing their resources. At the end of their careers, Yvon was earning a monthly average of 2,000 euros, and Michou 1,450 euros, and they also received 350 euros in rent for the second house, which has been inhabited by an unmarried childhood friend of their son Manuel for nearly 20 years. This young man, whom they consider practically a second son, is a skilled worker in painting who only works in temporary jobs in order to use the time between paying jobs to do volunteer missions for a non-profit organisation doing humanitarian building projects in Africa. Nothing would justify likening this rental arrangement to a classic lease: Not their relationship with their tenant (they are fond of his unassuming availability: 'sometimes a week or two will go by without seeing him because he can be quite unsociable, sometimes we spend the whole day with him, it depends on his mood, and it's good that way'), not his altruistic engagements ('he lives off of little, he's often on the move, he's a really independent boy, he's generous, too'), and certainly not the rent they receive (considerably lower than the market rate). While the couple is fully aware of the fact that the rent is at an obliging rate, they say it is satisfactory, all the more so because they feel they have everything they need.

Although their retirement income (pension and rent combined) amounts to 2,200 euros, both still feel that they are 'living simply but living well', without any extras but without skimping or particular frustration. It is as if they protected themselves from unbridled spending that could endanger adjusting their purchases to their resources. A recent trip to the French Antilles, for instance, did not challenge their plans to get a new car, but merely put it off for a year. So we should not be misled by the impression of comfort conveyed by their possessions and their preference for quality: this impression is the consequence of a few principles, including how they get their possessions, which are often homemade and always used with great care. Their car, for example, a boxy utilitarian vehicle, was bought new and still looks as if it just left the lot, despite its advanced age for the resale market. The life expectancy of Yvon's tools, which are usually the best quality, is another indication of a buying strategy based on longevity. One need only enter the workshop, where his tools are impeccably arranged, the nails and screws neatly sorted, and each recovered object awaiting reuse, to be convinced that waste has no place here. So it is that clothing has dedicated uses, worn-out jeans and knit hat for working on the home, corduroy pants and felt fedora for going out. Likewise, avoiding mass distribution in favour of buying direct from producers is due as much to a revulsion for supermarkets as it is to attention to flavour, and so they prefer to go directly to local farmers to buy the lamb that goes into their freezer every year and good wines (a prestigious Muscadet at ten euros a bottle, for instance). This keen eye for quality does not prevent them from bargain hunting at flea markets, stopping at used-clothing stores to look for clothes for their three granddaughters, or browsing used bookstores in hopes of finding a 'bargain' for themselves or a gift. They recently consulted a website for classified ads (*Le Bon Coin*) when they wanted a deal on paving stones to make improvements around their house. Having acquired serious organisational skills (if not a real taste for paperwork) from her training for office work with the nuns, Michou is in charge of overseeing the balances of their shared accounts, filing bills (insurance, heat, electric, etc.) and keeping the budget balanced to be able to anticipate major expenses. To improve daily life Yvon sometimes consents to doing work (repairing a heater, installing a bathroom) under the table for friends or friends of friends, but mainly 'on condition that it doesn't take long and I feel like it'. He says that it is not so much about 'making some pin money' as it is 'doing a favour', since he loves nothing more than pruning his trees, cutting and stacking his wood, and gardening between lazy moments, doing the rounds of the market, bi- or tri-weekly visits to his mother Marie-Ange, and trips to see friends, always in the company of Michou.

A taste for time to oneself

Even though the town has a significant array of organised leisure activities and non-profit groups, their participation in local sociability is still limited. As someone whose temperament leads him to balk at deeply virile behaviour, Yvon concedes nothing to masculine conviviality, which is limited to the annual dinner of 'the class' (a dinner for everyone in town born, like him, in 1952). Since she retired, Michou decided to fulfil herself in gratifying volunteer work one day a week at the local library. Despite being interested in the social and political topics discussed at evening 'people's university' (*université populaire*) events, which is organised by a particularly dear cousin who also belongs to the Confedération Paysanne (the left-leaning farmers' union), they do not attend, arguing by way of an excuse that they are unavailable. The amused contentment with which they declare that they have a busy schedule since they retired is the readily apparent expression of a fully assumed hedonism that favours spending time with near and dear and enjoying a peaceful environment. The hours and days that they spend, often together, working on the house, yard, and garden are proof, as is their weekly Wednesday (and other days) devotion to looking after their granddaughters. Likewise for the long summer evenings lingering on the terrace, or winter nights spent listening to the woodstove crackle rather than watching television, turned on rarely and only when *Télérama's* television listings attract Yvon's attention to a geopolitical or world cultures documentary on Arté, the cultural channel. But their deepest aspirations are probably most appreciable in the emotions procured by the 2002 acquisition of a piece of land that they planted with 500 trees of many kinds:

YVON: I used to kind of dream of having... Yes, I can say that I dreamed of a little piece of land in the middle of nature. Because a decade ago I thought, 'I'm going to retire, what'll I do?' And then we had the opportunity to get this land, which belonged to my great-grandfather – I'm the fourth generation. He'd bought the land in 1904, he passed it on to his son, who passed it on to his daughter, so, my aunt, who didn't live there and wanted to get rid of it. So the property has been in the family for four generations ... it's chance that wanted it that way. We bought it in 2002, 750 euros – we didn't borrow a thing. We got a whole bunch of people together, put things on the grill that day, and planted 500 trees – 500 trees! – all together. At an average of 2 euros apiece, that makes about 1000 euros [...] We thought of the children and future generations, it's clear, in hopes that it continues... that they'd be interested, Manuel or our granddaughters. The eldest who has lived the most with us, she loves it… it's true that we bring her there often.

MICHOU: We are also aware of our paradise here [*their house, where the interview took place, which is one kilometre from the wooded property*] when we see where lots of other people live. Here, with birds and everything, it's a real joy. But then, I feel good there because there's no noise… I can't explain it. What we wanted was to build a cabin, something nice we could sleep in without being cold, with a little stove and windows. We really have luxurious tastes! (laughing).

The investment in working on their living space and outdoor activities might lead one to think that the hammer and rake occupy most of their time, but that would be overlooking all the time that Yvon spends coddling his collection of nearly a thousand foreign banknotes, which he started over 30 years ago when he returned from the Americas and has been expanded by gifts from travelling friends. There is also the time he spends reading, a pursuit to which he was introduced quite young by his mother, who only graduated primary school (with a CEP) but who always 'had, even at 87 years old, three-four books underway'. With the advice of his neighbouring brother, who is a big reader, he enjoys settling in by the woodstove to read magazines (*Circus*, *A Suivre*), his favourite comic book authors (including Tardi, Loisel, Bourgeon, Hugo Pratt, and Cabu), and the latest graphic novels. Alongside their granddaughters' dolls in the living room and in the guest room bookshelves, these books mingle with others on gardening and wine, and novels, short stories, and essays by the likes of Jules Verne, Umberto Eco, Mario Vargas Llosa, Mathias Enard, Yasmina Khadra, Amin Maalouf, Cervantès (*Don Quixote*), and Homer (*The Odyssey*).

Making simplicity a virtue rather than a necessity … Ultimately this reformulation of the adage rather suitably sums up the creed that has guided this couple in their existential choices: reduce the constraints of work, seek the pleasures of family life and the good company of friends, build a refuge from the din and atmosphere of the city, take pleasure in consuming quality goods and creating nice everyday things, and protect themselves from media babble.

Notes

1 For an explanation of the French educational system, see the Appendix.
2 Both company names are pseudonyms.

11

A STORY OF SOCIAL RECLASSIFICATION

A couple from rural backgrounds gone to the city – Mireille and Roger Monteil

Henri Eckert

Mireille and Roger's story can be read as one household's gradual accession to the social position into which Mireille was born and might never have left, an ascent Mireille pressed for despite Roger's reservations. If the differences in their ambitions are related to the gap between their respective family and social backgrounds, which were close but unequal, the outcome is more related to the fact that Mireille's family background provided her with resources that Roger lacked, regardless of her initial downclassing (Bourdieu 1978, 1984). I argue here that these resources allowed Mireille to make her desire to restore her initially compromised social position prevail over Roger's more modest aspirations for social ascension. To more precisely account for differences in Mireille and Roger's behaviours and provide a detailed description of their social trajectory as a couple, this portrait starts with their meeting and concludes with their moving into the comfortable single-family home where they still live, in a well-off suburb of a mid-sized city in western France. I will discuss some key moments of their lives while being attentive to the effects of their dissimilar social origins, as well as some aspects of their childhoods, upbringings, professional careers, and relationship as a couple – all the elements factoring into their ascension to their current social position. I will thus demonstrate how their residential path attests to their reclassing, an agenda that is still manifest in Mireille's consumption practices which run counter to Roger's.

Going to the city.... And risking social downclassing

Mireille and Roger were both born into rural farming families in 1940 and 1935, respectively. All similarity between their backgrounds stops there. Mireille is the only child of a comfortably well-off family that owned its house and most of the

DOI: 10.4324/9781003330073-12

surrounding fields that it farmed. When she was born the farm still belonged to her paternal grandfather, and so her parents rented another farm for a few years until Mireille's father, an only child, took over his father's farm and moved the family there. As for Roger, he was the third son of poor farmers who, although they did own some land, mostly worked on land rented from the domain of the town's major landowner. Marrying well, Roger's eldest brother started farming his wife's land, and his other brother was also able to set himself up on a farm with their father's help. Lacking the means to help a third son start farming, his father told him, 'As you make your bed, so you must lie in it!' Roger had to muddle through on his own, which was even more challenging because he had to leave school after primary school (the mandatory minimum at the time), despite his desire to continue, because his father needed his help on the farm.

Roger was a good student and his teacher tried to convince his father to allow him to go to the nearby *collège*. Roger's father refused, even though he had passed the entrance examination.

> I didn't go to sixth class, yeah, yeah… So obviously that kind of upset me 'cause I'd've liked to continue. And then, well, anyway, that's how it was back then. Yeah, yeah… It ended up, time come, I stayed on the farm.

On the farm, he looked after the cows and drove the tractor. He taught himself how the motor worked and became increasingly interested in mechanics. It thus makes perfect sense that, at the end of his military service, he began studies to become a mechanic for agricultural equipment. He was convinced that there was no room for him as a farmer, so he planned to leave the land and take adult education classes to be able to support himself.

ROGER: So I went to register, at the time it wasn't the employment office but there was still a service in Marson, there where the square is, to do intensive training, easily. Yup.

HENRI: What they used to call the *FPA [Formation professionnelle des adultes/* Professional Training for Adults]?

ROGER: Right, the FPA, yeah, yeah. So I waited for a session to go to Rouen, yeah, yeah, as an agricultural equipment repairman. We learned… we began with filing – making parts by filing, all square and everything – doing soldering, doing turning, making parts we didn't have on hand, y'know, to repair things. And then soldering, brazing… so well that after six months we, we got basically an apprenticeship CAP.[1]

Certificate in hand, he solicited employers in the region, but it was his older brother who found him his first job with an equipment dealership where he had bought a new tractor. He only stayed for a year before finding another job, still in farm equipment repair, in a small-town garage in the seat of the canton where Mireille lived.

Mireille also passed the entrance examination to *collège*, and because it was far from home she had to live in a dormitory. Her paternal grandfather ceaselessly encouraged her to pursue her studies, but Mireille had trouble living so far from her family and did not like life as a boarder. She returned home to live with her parents before the year was out, even if it meant giving up school. Ever the good student, she went back to the local school and easily earned her CEP, marking completion of primary school. Her schooling finished, she stayed on the farm and worked with her parents. Alas, she did not really like farming work and dreamed of another fate: 'In my mind I always… I always told myself I wouldn't stay in the country, that I would like to … be a bookkeeper'. More than that, she dreamed of going to the city. While she was still working on her parents' farm, she met a boy, the son of well-off farmers like her parents, and fell in love. A good marriage in the offing: by uniting the properties the couple would have had a significant farm measuring up to the new standards of the day. But the boy's mother wanted a farm wife for her son, and Mireille did not want to stay in the country… Today she admits, 'Yes, yes, I was afraid of those people. […] They were interested because, obviously, I was an only child and my parents had a nice farm, and that interested them a lot. And I could really feel it'. Mireille refused to become a farm wife and thus quashed the possibility of such a good marriage. When she met Roger at a village dance, she immediately told him that she wanted to go to the city, it was a precondition, and that it was out of the question that she move to the town where Roger worked; she wanted to live in the departmental seat, a city of over 100,000 people at the time.

In the city, (more or less) difficulty in finding work

When Mireille and Roger arrived in the city, in the early 1960s, neither of them had a job. Roger had left his job as an agricultural equipment repairman and Mireille stopped working on the farm. Not only was she unemployed, she only had a CEP, with no vocational training and no experience likely to be valued on the job market. Roger could at least make use of his degree in farm equipment repair, which attested to mechanical skills, and his professional experience working for two employers in the country. He first found a job in plumbing and heating that put him at building sites for a few months and then as a mechanic at the city's McCormick dealership. They approached him and he leapt at the offer, preparing tractors for delivery and fixing those that broke down. His situation thus worked out quickly, since he not only found a skilled worker position, but moreover one that was a perfect fit for his previous training and experience. His situation further improved when he went to work for a major French automobile manufacturer that also made tractors:

> I just applied like that, then one day, um, a gentleman came to the apartment. Mireille's the one that saw him. He asked some questions, all that, and then he said: 'Say, well, your husband should come see us…' Ok, so

> I presented myself at the branch up there. [...] The director, he made me talk so he'd know what I'd done, all that. And whaddya know, he offered me a job! Plus housing!

This branch of the company was both a salesroom and a repair centre with a dedicated tractor repair garage where Roger was hired to work. They were given a small apartment in exchange for assorted services, mainly cleaning the offices and acting as superintendent on weekends.

If Roger was able to quickly find work that suited his desires, the same was not so for Mireille. First she found housekeeping work near their home. When they moved to the city they lived in a small, two-room apartment that Mireille's parents had bought for them, located between downtown and the train station. Mireille mainly worked as a housekeeper in hotels near the station, but she was not fond of the work: 'I wasn't in my element at all!' Then, she got a job at a grocer's, her time split between doing the owners' housework and working as a cashier in the shop: 'I didn't like that very much, either! [...] It wasn't that interesting, I didn't want to stay there'. She left the shop at the first opportunity, when she got a temporary sales job at a department store downtown. This was when she became pregnant, and about the time when Roger got his job at the tractor repair shop, housing included. This new apartment was welcome because their two-room apartment would have been too tight with the arrival of their first child. Mireille henceforth took care of the cleaning of the branch facilities in the evening and often helped by Roger after he had finished his own work. Mireille says that she worked 'like a maniac' during this period: she supplemented this work with other more or less lucrative activities, in private homes or in other companies, full- and part-time. This is how she came to keep accounts for the tax service and work as a 'paperer' (as she put it) for a printer, where she collated printed documents into signatures before folding and stapling them, among other tasks. As their daughter got older, Mireille gradually found more rewarding jobs, culminating in a job as a secretary in a marriage agency. As her activities became more regular and her pay more substantial, her income and Roger's together made it possible for them to consider buying their own house. Thus began a residential career that manifests Mireille's efforts to assert a social position closer to that of her family background.

Mireille and Roger's migration to the city did not unfold like a fairy tale... even if Mireille's parents provided housing for the couple at the beginning. Although Roger rather easily managed to reach a professional position meeting his expectations – a job as a skilled worker in a big company, meaning guaranteed job security – and to climb to a more comfortable position than that of his parents, this is far from the case for Mireille. She could rely on family resources – economic resources, for example, that made it possible for her parents to fund the purchase of their first apartment – but unlike Roger, she did not have the educational attainments that would have allowed her to find satisfying work quickly. She went from unrewarding jobs to positions that were hardly more satisfying and was obliged to accept work that did not really suit her. Likewise, she found herself relegated to a social position considerably less comfortable than that of her parents. The migration from the country, of which she had dreamed so much that she had made it a precondition for marriage, resulted in her social downclassing: her social position in the city was markedly lower than that of her parents in the country. Of course, her parents could help them in many ways, by giving them vegetables from the garden or taking care of their daughter Sonia during school holidays. And of course, no one states the difference in class position outright. This gap nonetheless did exist and would motivate Mireille to restore her social position to a level close to her origins through their residential trajectory.

A reclassing expressed mainly through the residential career

Ultimately the couple decided to have a house built. Mireille's professional situation improved: she had just been hired as secretary in a marriage agency on an open-ended employment contract. She was content with her professional situation, Roger's had been stable for a while, and they decided that the time had come for them to start the process of acquiring their own home. 'Well, may as well invest! Because we're not gonna spend our whole life there [in the apartment that came with his job]', Roger exclaimed in an interview, 'We were still earning money and then we said, after all, we've gotta...', he trailed off. A cousin already living in the neighbourhood where they would settle kept asking them, 'What are you waiting for to have a house built?' Especially, Roger added, since 'at the time [the late 1960s] it was affordable!' Moving to their own home would also help the family escape the restrictions of the workplace apartment, especially those imposed by the arrangement. Roger recalled,

> We were even sometimes required, except school holiday periods, to be present on Saturday – even if we weren't working! Yes, because every Saturday there was a representative, a used-car salesman, who was there to see customers, so I had to be there to close the doors and all that.

Their daughter Sonia, who was growing up, would also have a real room and would no longer have to make do with her cramped and hard to enter room under a Mansard roof. A real estate developer was offering row houses in a development that also included apartment buildings, not far from downtown. Roger went to study the situation on-site, in order to make a better choice.

> I'd spotted the plot. I thought, the land inclines toward the street, so we'll make the basement at ground level and then, since the land is higher behind, we'll be at ground level behind. The back of the house'll be at ground level. Because otherwise all the other houses, where it's so they don't have an incline, all that, well...

and Roger went on to describe the disadvantages of the other sites.

So although Mireille and Roger moved into their new house due to the practical considerations we have just seen, Roger says it was nonetheless Mireille who pressed them to committing to the venture. Roger was in no rush, especially since, as he put it, 'I was always good where I was, it didn't bother me, y'know. I was, well, happy th'way it was!' A few years later he would have little desire to leave this house for a more posh single-family home in a better-off residential area (more on this later). The neighbourhood where they bought their first house was a working-class neighbourhood, newly built on the outskirts of the downtown area but in continuity with an older neighbourhood. It mixed two types of housing: row houses with six to eight lodgings per row and apartment buildings. At first sight, the neighbourhood looks like a housing estate on the urban periphery because the four or five-story apartment buildings run along the main streets. Barely perceptible from the main streets, the row houses are lined up behind the residential blocks in a maze of narrow streets lending a residential air to the neighbourhood but not entirely managing to hide its modest character. The houses were all built from the same plan: they are narrow, with a basement and two upper stories, and one climbs stairs to reach the front door. A little yard separates the house from the street, interrupted by the driveway to the garage, which is in the basement. A few years later, this general layout would provide Mireille with a practical argument for leaving it for a nicer single-family home in a posher neighbourhood. When asked why she wanted to leave her first house for a single-family home, she replied: 'Well, because the house, it was a multi-story house, three stories. And we preferred a single-story house… firstly to have a nicer house, and then single-story'.

A nicer and single-story house, she said, carefully prioritising the two criteria: single-story, but above all a nicer house, with all the ambiguity that 'nicer' carries with it! And yet Mireille was comfortable in her neighbourhood, or at least had been able to build friendly relationships with some neighbours, such as the ones next door:

> Oh well yes, we'd help each other out! And the kids were always together. The boy next door, oh, he… when they came home from school he'd come to the house with Sonia – often! He was also all alone, that little boy, so he and Sonia were close.

Or the two women who lived in an older house with a yard neighbouring that of Mireille and Roger:

> They were our yard-neighbours, from the far end of the yard! Two women. […] We became great friends. So, they lived together, those two women, and they were physical and massage therapists. […] Whenever they had a little something they'd say, you've gotta come over, you've

> gotta come over! […] They'd give us massages. […] When we came home at night we'd see a little packet on the gate: there'd be a cake! It was great, they were exceptional people. And then we befriended each other!

And indeed, Mireille and Roger continued this friendship with their 'yard neighbours' up to their deaths and stayed in touch with their former next-door neighbours. Regardless, Mireille wanted to leave this first house for a real house in a nicer neighbourhood. Is that how we should understand it when she says 'a nicer house'? In all likelihood. The multi-story argument does not hold, since in fact the house they moved to also has three floors: a large basement, the main living space on the ground floor, and then, above it, a finished attic space that they almost only use as a guest room for family and friends. They got along well with their neighbours, so…? The house they moved into is indeed more imposing than their first house – and it is in an entirely different neighbourhood.

From a working-class neighbourhood to the well-off suburbs

Mireille does not prove to be very talkative, however, when it comes to her reasons for wanting to move to their current house, giving the answer quoted earlier and otherwise dodging the question. It is nonetheless clear that it was her decision. Roger did not want to leave his house or the neighbourhood and preferred to take the country air from time to time on a little farm he had restored near where he grew up. Mireille was the one who wanted the new home and chose its location. She who had established moving to the city as a prerequisite for marriage ultimately decided to leave a house located in a neighbourhood near the city centre to settle in a house in a suburb of the city:

MIREILLE: Yes, and I came back to the country… I wanted the city and I come back to the country…
HENRI: You leave the city…
MIREILLE: Yes, but while still staying in the city – it's the suburbs!

It is also true that Mireille henceforth had her own car, although the suburb she chose borders and increasingly melds into the city. What does Roger have to say about all this? 'Mireille thought, "Since we have the means… Well, then, let's do it!" Well yeah!', and then later:

> Let's just say that I was for everything that was economical, yeah. Yeah, yeah. Whereas Mireille is generous, all that… So she wants the best quality, the maximum, everything, basically! That's her choice. Yeah, yeah! We don't always agree about it. Well anyway. That's how it works, y'know.

When he uses the word 'generous' he most likely means something closer to 'extravagant'. But his explanation is anything but psychological; indeed, he went on to mention the gap between their social origins. 'She's the one that pushed me! I … I was happy with little, y'know. It's true, I got used to it in childhood. Because she lived at a higher level than me, over there with her parents, y'know'. Mireille is not only from a better-off farming family, in contrast to Roger, but she is an only child, and so she developed another relationship with consumption and spending than he did. While Roger sticks to a form of frugality typical of certain working-class milieu, Mireille does not hesitate to take on major expenses as soon as she has the resources allowing her to do so, although she does not explicitly proclaim hedonistic behaviour.[2]

Mireille does have financial resources that, when combined with the money from the sale of their first house, made it possible for them to plan on having a smarter home built in a more pleasant development not too far from downtown without worry. As Roger explained, trailing off: 'My mother-in-law was dying to get rid of the farm buildings. So we got some assets from that, which made it possible for us'. Mireille's mother still owned the farm, which she put up for rent; she only held on to the land ('You don't sell land!', she often said) but she gradually sold off the outbuildings. The revenue from these sales allowed her to facilitate her daughter's plans. Roger, once again: 'So Mireille demanded… she demanded flat roofing tiles! OK… oh right, that looks more posh'. Mireille wanted a bigger house, and even more so a house of a standing more in line with her taste: a more up-market house. The development they chose is in a village quite near the city that looks very different from their previous neighbourhood, devoid of residential blocks and with bigger houses, all single-family, built on more spacious lots. Mireille and Roger were moreover able to buy an even larger lot at the end of a dead-end street, which gives them even greater comfort and calm. Lastly, in addition to the financial resources Mireille's mother put at their disposal, Mireille herself was able to stabilise her professional situation. She had found a permanent job before they bought their first house, but the marriage agency where she worked closed and she found herself unemployed. She passed a hiring examination at the unemployment office that opened the way to getting a steady, albeit modest, job as a 'bookkeeper, administrative agent, if you like!' – an office job that she would hold until her retirement.[3]

Their professional and residential careers imply a degree of balance in the couple, all the more so as they shared chores in conformity with the traditional distribution of labour in working-class households: Mireille takes care of the inside and Roger the outside (or least until Roger got more involved in cooking since he retired). Their residential career nonetheless strongly attests to the inequality that remains between them and the advantages that Mireille's resources provided them. This inequality is what made it possible for her to impose a residential mobility that Roger did not want. This inequality is also what makes it possible for her to impose certain consumption choices – such as buying groceries at an organic grocer, choosing quality over price, redecorating the house often, frequently changing cars – that go against Roger's preferences.

ROGER: I like simple things, I do. And Mireille, she wants a lot of things...
HENRI: How is it that she always wins, then?
ROGER: Well, it was to have some peace that I gave in... because her, she never gave in. [But] she has a trump card.
HENRI: Oh, what?
ROGER: Oh, well, because, huh, she was the owner of the farm in Marson! So she says, it's my money! There you have it! She plays on that!
HENRI: The fact that she had more assets...
ROGER: That's it!

The difference in social background – being from two distant fractions of the farming work – mitigates the usual distribution of roles between spouses in working-class households. It is ultimately the lingering inequalities from their original social positions – the financial resources that Mireille can use at any time – that put her in a position to impose a visible return to her original social class that is predominantly manifested in the couple's residential career, through her relentless pursuit of reclassing.

Inheritance and reclassing

There are many strategies for returning to a social class after being downclassed, especially when it concerns intergenerational downclassing. Mireille and Roger's case is interesting because it demonstrates the specific role of inheritance, in the usual sense of economic goods transmitted from one generation to the next, can play in such reclassing strategies. Mireille did not benefit from any intermediaries (from social networks her parents might have had, for instance) who could facilitate her access to employment. Possessing neither adequate cultural capital (she has a minimal education and no formal professional qualifications) nor social capital she could use in the city, the only way she could re-establish her compromised social position was to rely on the economic resources that her parents could gradually pass along to her as the couple's situation developed. Firstly, Mireille's parents financed the small apartment in which they lived when they arrived in the city, then they helped them when they committed to buying their first house, and then, after her father's death, her mother helped Mireille (who had reached a professional situation she liked) to embody her on-going reclassing by facilitating the purchase of a more comfortable house, regardless of Roger's reservations. This house is the visible proof of the reinstatement of a social situation that migration to the city had compromised. Engagement in work – related to dispositions instilled by the farming world – surely played a role, but the economic resources provided by Mireille's inheritance were the decisive factor in the couple's social reclassing.

Notes

1 For an explanation of the French educational system, see the Appendix.
2 The word 'frugality' seems more apt for describing such economical behaviour than the word 'asceticism', used by Pierre Bourdieu (1978, 1984) to describe a particular kind of economising in the petite-bourgeoisie.
3 The ANPE (Agence Nationale pour l'Emploi; National Employment Agency) was the precursor to today's Pôle Emploi, the French unemployment office. It was still the ANPE when Mireille went in the 1970s and would become Pôle Emploi in 2008, after she had retired.

References

Bourdieu, Pierre. 1978. 'Classement, déclassement, reclassement.' *Actes de la recherche en sciences sociales* 24: 2–22.

Bourdieu, Pierre. (1984) 1985. 'The Social Space and Genesis of Groups. *Social Science Information* 24, no. 2: 195–220.

PART II

Gender relations and domestic space

12

INTRODUCTION TO PART 2

Gender relations and domestic space

Thomas Amossé, Marie Cartier, and Olivier Schwartz

This section of the book is devoted to how couples and families function, seen from the angle of gender relations. It concerns the gendered division of labour and household and parental tasks between domestic partners and is intended to contribute to the sociology of the working classes by exploring these couples' gender models, domains, and definitions of feminine and masculine.

Addressing these themes in the working classes amounts to looking at aspects of working-class lifestyles that often prompt incomprehension or scorn in higher classes. The working classes have strong and deeply rooted specificities in domestic gender roles. They became particularly prominent when new models began to spread in developed societies in the 1970s, typified by challenges to the gendered division of family roles and the idea of women's liberation. These models came from the most highly educated social categories, driven mainly by women among them[1]; at least initially, these models were much slower to seep into the working classes, which were typified by the resounding reproduction of their classic characteristics. This resulted in the image (widespread to this day) of these social classes as predominantly conservative on gender issues, an image that could only impede comprehension of how they function as families (Amossé and Cartier 2018).

This section of the book analyses these issues using the materials resulting from this study. The introduction begins with a brief reminder of a few earlier characteristics of the working classes where gender is concerned and then highlights what we found to be the most significant findings to emerge from the case studies. It is followed by six household portraits.

DOI: 10.4324/9781003330073-14

Review of a few characteristics of the working classes

Historical and sociological literature on labourers, and working-class people employed by industrial companies in general, describes two well-known characteristics in these groups.

First and foremost, a sharp division of labour between genders: men's function in the family is principally defined by earning an income and contributing qualities that were traditionally associated with the masculine: strength, courage, and endurance (especially where work was concerned), while women are left with domestic tasks (home upkeep, feeding, running daily lives of family members), parental duties (childcare and rearing), family financial management, and interactions with public institutions, which are all defined as feminine. Numerous authors emphasise how sharp this division is, and how much it has been maintained.[2]

From this first characteristic comes another concerning the place of women in the family, which is both central and ambivalent. It is central because of the degree to which their families rely on them (it is their work, energy, and skills that provide family members with a degree of security in their daily lives), their role in the family, and the power that they wield (as the one to govern the household, in a variety of ways). But it is also quite ambivalent. They bear heavy material and mental burdens that are weightier still when the conditions of the family's economic existence are insecure and they must face the resulting challenges alone. These domestic duties complicate their access to paid employment, subject them to heavy constraints when they do have a job, and contribute to impeding their chances of professional success. Although they give them power in the home, they also have the consequence of demanding that women put themselves in the service of their families in order to live up to expectations, with the potential risk of never being able to do something for themselves.[3]

Both of these characteristics regularly appear in the literature on labourers and working-class employees. They are 'traditional' characteristics, by which we mean historically recurrent in these groups. To them should be added a third point, important to what follows. As we mentioned earlier, the most highly educated women were the main force behind challenges to the gendered division of roles in the family that began in the 1970s. Studies conducted in the 1970s and 1980s demonstrate how socially situated this process was. Working-class women of the time were much less involved in this movement. When one study asked female labourers and basic employees what division of food preparation and childcare tasks they thought 'normal' between spouses, only a minority responded in favour of an equal distribution, even if they worked full-time, which contrasts with the responses of women with high educational attainments.[4] An interview-based study of female labourers and basic employees working in offices likewise stresses that it is 'exceptional for [interviewees] to manifest demand for greater sharing of tasks with the husband: in most cases, the interviewed women consider household tasks to be their province and accord great importance to their responsibility to maintain their homes' (Daune-Richard 1984, 49). Among employed working-class women in the 1970s and 1980s, the gendered division of tasks in the family was still largely accepted, including its major characteristic – the attribution of the bulk of daily household and parental labour to women. There are probably several explanations for these findings, and insight from our research allows us to highlight one of them. For members of the most modest social groups, the division of roles between men and women may provide access to one of the few rewarding identities available to women and men. Just as there may be a form of prestige in completing the checklist for virility, women in these social groups may find legitimacy in taking proper care of their families and homes.[5]

What the case studies contribute

The working classes of contemporary France are indeed the heirs of the working classes of earlier periods that presented these characteristics. Households consistently function according to a sharp division of labour between genders (a division that was still acceptable to women themselves in the 1980s) with resulting effects on the place of women in the family. This begs the question of whether these characteristics are still typical among the contemporary working classes, and what the case studies have to teach us about it.

We should emphasise from the outset that recent studies have demonstrated that a great many of the aforementioned characteristics still unquestionably apply to the working classes of today. INSEE's 'Emploi de temps' surveys show that the percentage of time that men devote to household tasks is the lowest among working-class men, a sign that the gendered division of tasks remains strong (Cartier, Letrait, and Sorin 2018, 70–72). A recent study on childrearing norms in the family shows that this division is still widely accepted by working-class women (Court et al. 2016).[6] Other research shows that, far from liberating women, new forms of working-class housing situations may prolong or increase the sharply gendered division of labour (Lambert 2015, Gilbert 2016). If we focus more closely on the most fragile fractions of the working classes, the Collectif Rosa Bonheur's work shows that women's place in domestic work, and anything to do with the household's survival more broadly, is central today and that they accept this centrality (Collectif Rosa Bonheur 2017). The contemporary working classes clearly preserve some of their older characteristics, and this is even truer in their most insecure fractions.

So what do our case studies have to tell us? We will see that they are no exception to what has just been said, but they reveal the greater complexity of today's working-class lifestyle landscape within the fractions targeted by the study – not the least secure fractions, but the less vulnerable fractions with a modicum of stability. These case studies provide several examples of the reproduction of traditional or older characteristics of the working classes in this fraction, in line with what has just been said, but several also manifest developments and change. They demonstrate the reproduction of working-class traits concerning responsibility for housework and gender models but also show recent challenges to these models and how they have been redefined. When it comes to gender relations in the domestic space, the working classes of today are not as immobile or as homogeneous as some might be tempted to claim. As we will see in the following case studies, they live in ways that reproduce, change, and reconfigure the previously documented characteristics.

Men who contribute to housework and child care

Starting with changes, the first is in how men behave towards housework and raising children. Several of our case studies contain men who contribute substantially and regularly to some of these tasks, confirmed by their wives or partners. In the home of Eric and Cécilia Dufar (library caretaker and supermarket cashier), for example, Eric (age 41) cooks and eats lunch with their daughter who comes home from school to eat, usually cooks dinner, does some (albeit limited) cleaning, and is usually the one to go to parent-teacher meetings.[7] In the home of Cécile and Jean-Marc Pilier (hairdresser and supervisor for a private security company, around 30 years old, with a toddler), Jean-Marc does the grocery shopping and cooking and minds their son when his work schedule allows it.[8] In the home of Nicolas and Stéphanie Fontaine (he is a public service maintenance technician, and she is currently on maternity leave; three children), Nicolas was the main minder of their first child and did a majority of the housework for several years, while Stéphanie came home late from her middle-management job at the unemployment office after an hour and a half commute.[9]

None of these situations has altered the centrality of the woman in running the family (not even the third example), a point that we will return to later. But the men in these households do make substantial contributions to running the home that are recognised as such by their partners. 'He's the cook!', Cécile says of Jean-Marc, and she stresses that he took care of their son as a baby. And although Cécilia openly reproached Eric of some failings in front of the interviewer, she gives full credit to his contributions, saying 'he does lots of things' and 'If you ask him to do something, he does it, he's present, you can't call him lazy'. We have focused on the six case studies in this section, but we could also cite other households in other parts of the book. For example, in the home of Myriam and Nicolino Sanatanazefi (a part-time cleaning woman and a lorry driver, two children), most of the housework falls to Myriam, but Nicolino often cooks dinner, sets the table, and does the dishes, and Myriam acknowledges his responsibility for these jobs. Although our handful of examples is obviously not enough to induce the scale of the phenomenon, they do demonstrate a challenge to the strict division of labour in the home that, as detailed earlier, is a classic characteristic of the working classes. This makes them an indication of changes occurring in conjugal arrangements and men's behaviours in at least some of this class group. These observations align with findings from our statistical analyses: comparing 1974 to 2010, male labourers and basic employees came to devote an average of 30 minutes more to household tasks per day, half to shopping, cooking, or cleaning and half to looking after the children.[10]

The case studies also help us to make out some elements that might explain these developments. For one thing, they (unsurprisingly) demonstrate the influence of wives and partners' wage-earning work on men's new attitudes. If Eric Dufar does not want his daughter to have lunch at the school cafeteria, he has to take responsibility for it himself, since Cécilia's work schedule means that she can't. Nicholas Fontaine has no choice but to do housework and mind his son, since Stéphanie returns so late from work. Since Jean-Marc Pilier often has the whole day off (because he frequently works nights and weekends) and Cécile works days, it's logical that he does the shopping. Given their working hours and those of their partners and the demands of family life, all three men had to contribute. The scale reached by women's employment in the past few decades has decisively influenced men to adopt more participative attitudes towards domestic and familial labour. This does not mean, however, that it has only arisen from constraint. For men like this, it could also be a way to reach their own goals: guaranteeing children the presence of a parent (Eric Dufar's case), making homeownership possible by sharing housework so both members of the couple can earn an income (Cécile and Jean-Marc Pilier's plan), or simply earning their partner's appreciation, as we saw in several instances.

The case studies highlight another determinant element in these developments: these men's partners clearly express a demand for men to participate, and they evidently have means for ensuring it is understood. Cécilia Dufar says it would be intolerable if Eric 'didn't help out with anything'; Cécile Pilier wants to avoid a return to the 'macho' model where 'women take care of the house'. And it is evident that both of them have resources for making themselves heard in case of major disagreements with their husbands over how things work in the couple. Cécile claims to be so determined that she is ready to fight about it ('if we have to fight, too bad, we'll fight') should Jean-Marc fall back on the classic paternal attitudes he grew up with as a child when dealing with their children, and especially their two daughters. It is even clearer in Cécilia's case. When she and Eric separated (on his initiative) a year after the birth of their daughter, Cécilia managed to take care of herself and her daughter on her own, refusing help from her parents. When they got back together, she says that their relationship was changed by the knowledge that she could materially and psychologically get by without him. They both know that she is capable of living without him, and now she has, in her words, 'power over him'. The case study shows that Eric makes an effort to contribute to housekeeping because of this situation, to reduce Cécilia's dissatisfaction. The participation of Cécile's and Cécilia's partners in housework and childcare cannot be understood independently of Cécile's determination and Cécilia's upper hand. And once again, the significance of their paid employment is evident. Cécilia was able to survive Eric's departure because she had a job (as a full-time supermarket cashier), and Cécile probably has the confidence to face down Jean-Marc at least partly because of her job (as a full-time hairdresser). The contributions of the men to domestic labour cannot be dissociated from these two traits in their partners: the women demand more participation of their partners, and their employment gives them resources that lend clout to their demands.

Women's refusal of the more negative forms of the division of household labour

As the previous section hinted, working-class women have also changed, and the qualitative research produced several findings on the subject.

One is demand from some women that their partners participate in housework and childcare. It appeared clearly in several case studies. It was mentioned earlier in relation to couples where the men do make meaningful contributions, but it was also expressed by women who have not been able to get their partners to do more. In either case, a number of interviewed women condemned, often quite explicitly, situations where all housework fell to them while their husbands or partners spared themselves most of the trouble. For example, when interviewed, Régine Leblanc (46 years old, childminder, husband a public transportation driver, two young-adult children) expressed clear discontent with her husband, who does nothing around the house, and referred to this domestic labour as 'my chores'.[11] When Laeticia Kergal (age 27, currently unemployed following several warehousing jobs, husband a delivery driver, one daughter) cannot get her husband to chip in as much as she would like, she tells him she's not his 'maid'.[12] All domestic labour falls on Nadège Lancel (currently a homemaker, husband heavy goods vehicle driver, two children), protests her partner's complete lack of involvement in managing household finances, which fall entirely on her although they are in a delicate financial situation: 'Patrick doesn't worry about anything! I'm the one who's worried all the time, stressed out'.[13] To state it plainly, though, neither these women nor the preceding group demands the equal distribution of housework that is so distinctively associated with women with high educations. Rather than speaking in these terms, they protest the significant imbalance in how this work is divided, to their detriment and exhaustion. They see it as proof that their partners are inattentive to them, but rather than asking for an equal division of this domestic labour, they only ask for a less unequal division (Cartier, Letrait, and Sorin 2018, 78).

While this reaction differs from that of women from the highest social categories, it also differs from the most common attitudes of working-class women in the 1980s. The women discussed here do not contest the principle of the division of domestic responsibilities according to gender, but instead reject a strict form that subjugates women. The literature on working-class women in the 1980s mentions no such protest; on the contrary, it highlighted how widely accepted this division was by women in this social milieu. It seems that sensibilities have changed over the past few decades, although our data is insufficient to gage the extent of this change. It may have been favoured by the massive entry of women into paid employment and by the spread of the idea of equality of the sexes throughout French society as a whole (Kaufmann 2003, ch. 5, Clair 2011).

These last three cases also reveal another manifestation of this change. In one way or another, Régine Leblanc, Laeticia Kergal, and Nadège Lancel are all women who do not have paid employment outside the home. At the time of research, Nadège was a homemaker, Laeticia was unemployed, and Régine was a childminder, working from her own home. If, as we have seen, the division of labour between the sexes is expressed in the working classes in a strong injunction to take charge of housework and childcare, this injunction is even stronger for women in such situations: since they are always at home, their families and friends see them as being in a position to fulfil this role. Their reactions to this injunction are significant. None of them challenges the central role they are assigned in the domestic space – they are actually deeply invested in it. But their way of talking about it reveals a distinct refusal to allow themselves to be put in the constant service of their family or let the family dispossess them of the possibility of also being able to devote some time to themselves, at least occasionally. This refusal is expressed in certain practices. Two of them have a regular activity outside the home that they would never give up: Régine regularly practices archery in a club, and Nadège goes to Zumba classes twice a week (other case studies provide other examples of the activities favoured by working-class women today). Their discourse on the subject is also important. When Régine talks about archery, she calls it 'my sport'; she insists to her family that she is more than a wife and mother, that she is also a paid worker. Laeticia explains that she is set on making her partner understand that she cannot always be at his disposal when he comes home and that he has to accept that there are certain times that 'are my time' (Masclet 2018). In word or deed, they demand the possibility of not always belonging to their families. The possibility for members of a couple to have domains of their own within that relationship, which the sociology of the family has shown to be characteristic of representations of middle- and upper-class couples in recent decades, seems to have been appropriated by some women in the working classes (Singly 1984, Kellerhals et al. 1982).

So once again, a particular form of the gendered division of labour is no longer the rule. As we stated earlier, the women in this study did not demand an equal division of housework, but they did object when the division of labour took the form of complete housework avoidance by men that put them in constant service to their families without the possibility of taking time for themselves. This repudiation was not evident in studies conducted in the 1980s.

One condition and a few traits that have lasted in the working classes

The case studies thus contain indications that there have been shifts in working-class lifestyles and sensibilities, including indications from several women in the study (presented below) who clearly stated that they did not want to reproduce their mothers' situations. This leads us to the following observation: if one considers these developments (more participation by men in housework and childrearing, women rejecting an excessively imbalanced division of household tasks, women's demands for some time for themselves), the lifestyles and sensibilities of a portion of the working classes have gotten more similar to those of the middle classes. Once again, we can see the complexity of cultural boundaries between social class groups.

That being said, it should be restated that the couples in this study also still have characteristic traits of the working classes insofar as the issues that interest us here are concerned. Remember that the situations in which they find themselves are sharply marked by the difficult living conditions characteristic of this class group, including unemployment, atypical working hours, and tight financial resources. For example, although she is very attached to her independence and had paid (but insecure) work for several years already, Laeticia Kergal is still struggling to put unemployment behind her, and this situation, compounded by the birth of her daughter, traps her in the unwelcome role of housewife. Nadège Lancel has been at home since the birth of her second daughter (who is now three) and would like to resume her previous work as a housekeeper, but her partner's irregular and unpredictable working hours as a lorry driver make it difficult so long as their daughter is not big enough for school; even if this is probably only part of the explanation (see below), she is nonetheless pulled into the position of housewife. Nicolas and Stéphanie Fontaine's situation (mentioned earlier) is also telling, despite an atypical aspect related to Stéphanie's career. Reading the portrait of this couple from modest backgrounds will show readers how their situation was initially characterised by a substantial engagement by Nicholas in daily household operations and Stéphanie's professional rise into management at the unemployment office, but their positions were reversed by constraints engendered by the purchase of a house that were especially burdensome for Stéphanie, since they could only afford to buy one an hour and a half from her job. With their second and then third child, Stéphanie grew intolerant of the long commute and how it ate into her time with her children and began a career change to become a childminder, thus shifting the couple back to a classic division of domestic labour. The burden of economic constraints turned the woman's career and the sharing of housework into a mere interlude.

In addition to the persistence of specific economic conditions, the case studies also demonstrate the persistence of some ways of functioning and being in the working classes. First of all, the sharply gendered division of domestic labour is manifestly still the model in several of the studied households, so women are responsible for most domestic labour, childcare and rearing, and management of household finances and interactions with public institutions for the couple. Régine Leblanc is not unique in our sample: six of the seventeen case studies with information on the subject have couples that function this way. In no way do the previously described changes to male behaviour eclipse this seemingly contrary observation that many contemporary working-class men are still very little involved in everyday parental and domestic tasks. The same finding emerges from statistical data from INSEE: in the categories of labourer and basic employee, women continue to devote nearly twice as much time to domestic tasks as men.[14] This low involvement does not necessarily bother their wives or partners. Although, as we saw above, it does raise protest from some (four of the six case studies in this section), others accept it: this is the situation in two of the portraits, in a logic where the women in question subscribe to the role of household manager and procure self-esteem from doing this work well. In any case, the sharply divided form of the gendered division of roles continues in part of the working classes.[15] And more generally, in nearly all the case studies – even in those of couples where men make a significant contribution – women hold a central position in the family that, as we saw earlier, is a classic characteristic of the working classes. Women are the ones who usually do most of the everyday housework and childrearing, and even when their partner shares this labour (as with the Dufars and the Piliers), they are the ones to bear the mental load of ensuring the household runs smoothly. One more point should be stressed: as mentioned above, women in the working classes may find rewards and satisfaction in assuming the role traditionally associated with their gender by doing necessary household and family tasks well. Many women in the study identify with this model, even if it is only one component of their social identity. It is found in the relationship many of them have to housework. Neither Cécilia nor Régine nor Laeticia nor Nadège put down housework – on the contrary, it is important to all of them, even declaring they enjoy it sometimes. Nadège says she 'adores' cleaning, Cécilia refers to her' cleaning and says she likes doing it, Laeticia spends considerable time on it and also refers to it in the possessive ('my cooking', 'my cleaning'), and Régine is clearly invested in it as well. Their complaints about their husbands' lack of involvement in domestic labour is not because they shun these tasks; Régine calls them her 'chores' to express frustration at her husband's indifference, not to devalue the work itself.

This identity model is also found in the extent to which Régine is invested in motherly duties for her daughters, whether it involves their education or nourishment (she was always insistent that they return home from school for lunch). In addition to allowing the family to adapt to her husband's difficult work schedule, Nadège finds being a housewife is also a way to devote herself to these tasks, which is why it was easy for her to pivot to this situation when her second child was born. The couples from working-class backgrounds that are at the heart of this study clearly reproduce certain ways of functioning and being that are fundamental characteristics of the working classes.

The diversification of definitions of feminine and masculine in the working classes

All this leads to three main points.

First of all, the case studies clearly invalidate the image of the working classes as conservative and implacably faithful to classic models of gender in the family, regardless of whether this image came from social prejudice or from sociologists of the working classes. This leads to the hypothesis that lifestyles and sensibilities relating to gender have changed in recent decades. In some cases, men's behaviour and the way domestic partnerships operate have moved away from the sharp division of gender roles, and women are protesting the most subjugating forms of this division and demanding more time for themselves. These changes seem to come from within these classes and are manifest in some women's defiance of earlier or traditional characteristics of the working classes, ultimately bringing some working-class women's reactions close to those of middle-class women.

At the same time, the case studies also show that the contemporary working classes do not simply follow a basic logic in gender roles. Although the previously stated changes are important, they do not put an end to working-class people reproducing the traditional characteristics of the class group. On the contrary, some of these characteristics are still quite discernible in their lifestyles and reactions: a sharp division of gender roles is still fundamental in many couples, women still commonly hold a central position in the family, and many women still embrace a feminine identity in which enduring domestic and familial roles bolster their self-worth. Where gender models are concerned, the contemporary working classes are manifestly sites of both transformation and reproduction.

As a consequence of this ambivalence, today some forms of working-class life present two characteristics on these matters. One is a great diversity of situations, ways in which couples operate, and lifestyles among working-class individuals and couples, depending on the extent to which they have been impacted by these transformations and reproductions. This is crystal clear in the following group of case studies. Concerning men who contribute to daily household tasks, for example, there are major differences between the Piliers, who share an ambition for social ascension that leads them to agree on shared responsibility, and the Leblancs, who have underlying tensions due to his reproduction of a classic masculine position and resultant unresponsiveness to her demands. Likewise, there are significant differences in the kind of feminine identity assumed by the various women in the study. Nadège Lancel identifies with the home. Cécile Pilier identifies with paid employment and the rejection of being shut up in the house, and in their own ways, so do Régine Leblanc (her paid work is important to her, even if she works from home) and Laeticia Kergal (who is stuck at home, unhappily unemployed). Insofar as gender models in the couple are concerned, the diversity of ways in which working-class people operate is clear. The second characteristic is the consequence of a working-class person shifting towards middle-class patterns while also reproducing some working-class traits, or of the reproduction of working-class traits by a person who also disputes at least some of those traits. It results in people with hybrid lifestyles that combine some typical working-class traits with traits more associated with other social groups. The case studies provide several examples of this. The femininity of Régine Leblanc is both typically working class, in the depth of her investment in maternal, domestic, and housekeeping tasks, and similar to that of the middle classes, in her insistent demand for autonomy within the family. Laeticia and Nadège also show signs of some form of hybridity. Likewise for the men: Eric Dufar has a combined masculinity, a man who regularly contributes to domestic tasks traditionally defined as feminine while also strongly asserting his virility in certain areas. Where gender models are concerned, the contemporary lifestyles of the working classes are also characterised by the existence of such socio-culturally in-between situations.

Reproduction, change, hybridisation, heterogeneity: working-class life, in its many forms, presents all of these characteristics today, meaning that it is rife with complex logics.

Comments on the presentation of the following household portraits

Contrary to the approach taken in the other two portrait groupings, the next six case studies are not presented in a thematic progression. We thought that if we were to try to present them according to the extent to which they manifest the processes explored in this introduction, we ran a chance of emphasising the differences between them – some incarnate change, others represent reproduction and classic characteristics – and thus fuel the class-centric value judgements to which the sociology of gender relations is only too susceptible where the working classes are concerned. Consequently, we opted to present the portraits in alphabetical order rather than organising them thematically.

Notes

1 On the role of women in higher social categories in this process, see Singly (1984).
2 In 1987, the authors of an analytical review of studies on labourers (Herpin et al. 1987) observed that the exclusive consignment of women to domestic tasks is considered a major characteristic of the labouring lifestyle in nearly all the works comprising their chosen 'literature of reference' on the topic (only one, Halbwachs 1933, did not raise the subject). These texts are Halbwachs (1913 and 1933), Lynd and Lynd (1929), Chombart de Lauwe (1956), Hoggart (1957), Young and Willmott ([1957] 2011 and 1973), Gans (1962), Bourdieu ([1979] 1984), and Caplow et al. (1982). The study's authors found that a majority of these works mentioned child-rearing falling to mothers as well. For an in-depth study emphasising these phenomena in nineteenth and twentieth century France and England, see Scott and Tilly (1978).
3 This ambivalence emerges sharply from the literature. The central position of the figure of the mother in labouring families is often emphasised: see especially Hoggart (1957, ch. 2), Young and Willmott ([1957] 2011), Elias and Scotson (1965, ch. 4), Scott and Tilly (1978), Verret ((1988) 1996, ch. 3), and Schwartz (1990, ch. 3 and 5). But the same texts, as well as others, also emphasise the weight of the constraints and forms of dispossession that this position entails for women: see Hoggart (1957), Chombart de Lauwe (1956, p. 55–60), Haicaut (1984), Verret (1988), and Schwartz (1990). For more on this position and its changes in the working classes, see Schwartz (2018).
4 We should add that it was a non-negligible minority, but it is considerably higher among more educated women (Kellerhals et al. 1982, 158–159).
5 Kellerhals et al. thus speak of the possible 'gratifications' of 'domestic life' for working-class women, which they also stress comes at a 'considerable cost' for them (1982, p. 142).
6 When the mothers of the studied families wanted help with their domestic work, they asked daughters rather than sons (Court et al. 2016).
7 See 'Keeping the conjugal peace: A compensatory domestic equality' by Olivier Masclet.
8 See 'A business that works: Breaking away from the family model, relying on family help' by Violaine Girard and Maulde Urbain-Mathis.
9 See 'An interlude of equality: "Stéphanie is there with the children, she can manage the homework"' by Muriel Letrait and Marjorie Tilleul.
10 Analysis of the *Emploi du temps* surveys from 1974 to 2010, by Amossé and Brousse.
11 See 'The power of two femininities' by Marie Cartier.
12 See 'Being a mother and unemployed: Resisting being stuck at home' by Angel Baraud.
13 See 'Being a housewife: Between permanence and evolution of a traditional role' by Maulde Urbain Mathis.
14 Average time spent is over 4 hours a day for women and under two and a half hours for men (analyses by Amossé and Brousse of the 2010 *Emploi du temps* survey).
15 The gap between gender roles can even run quite deep in some contexts, with a heavy component of masculine domination, as shown by Benoît Coquard's work (2019) on young rural working-class couples.

References

Amossé, Thomas, and Marie Cartier, eds. 2018. 'Ménages populaires.' Special issue, *Travail, genre et sociétés* 39.

Bourdieu, Pierre. (1979) 1984. *Distinction: A Social Critique of the Judgment of Taste.* Translated by Richard Nice. Cambridge MA: Harvard University Press.

Caplow, Theodore, Bruce Chadwick, Howard Bahr, and Reuben Hill. 1982. *Middletown Families: Fifty Years of Change and Continuity.* Minneapolis, MN: University of Minnesota Press.

Cartier, Marie, Muriel Letrait, and Matéo Sorin. 2018. 'Travail domestique : des classes populaires conservatrices?' *Travail, genre et sociétés* 39: 63–81.

Chombart de Lauwe, Paul-Henri. 1956. *La vie quotidienne des familles ouvrières.* Paris: CNRS.

Clair, Isabelle. 2011. 'La découverte de l'ennui conjugal. Les manifestations contrariées de l'idéal conjugal et de l'ethos égalitaire dans la vie quotidienne de jeunes de milieux populaires.' *Sociétés contemporaines* 83: 59–81.

Collectif Rosa Bonheur. 2017. 'Des "inactives' très productives". Le travail de subsistence des femmes de classes populaires.' *Tracès. Revue de sciences humaines* 32. DOI: https://doi.org/10.4000/traces.6862.

Coquard, Benoît. 2019. *Ceux qui restent. Faire sa vie dans les campagnes en déclin.* Paris: La Découverte.

Court Martine, Julien Bertrand, Géraldine Bois, Gaële Henri-Panabière, and Olivier Vanhée. 2016. 'Qui débarrasse la table? Enquête sur la socialisation domestique primaire.' *Actes de la recherche en sciences sociales* 215: 73–83.

Daune-Richard, Anne-Marie. 1984. 'Activité professionnelle, travail domestique et lignées féminines.' In *Le Sexe du travail,* Grenoble: Presses Universitaires de Grenoble.

Elias, Norbert, and John Scotson. (1965) 1994. *The Established and the Outsiders.* Thousand Oaks, CA: Sage Publications.

Gans, Herbert. 1962. *The Urban Villagers: Group and class in the life of Italian-Americans.* Glencoe: The Free Press.

Gilbert, Pierre. 2016. 'Classes, genre et styles de vie dans l'espace domestique.' *Actes de la recherche en sciences sociales* 215: 4–15.

Haicault, Monique. 1984. 'La gestion ordinaire de la vie en deux.' *Sociologie du travail* 26(3): 268–275.

Halbwachs, Maurice. 1913. *La classe ouvrière et les niveaux de vie.* Paris: Alcan.

Halbwachs, Maurice. 1933. *L'évolution des besoins dans les classes ouvrières*, Paris: Alcan.

Herpin, Nicolas, Olivier Choquer, Liliane Kasparian and Daniel Verger. 1987. 'Les conditions de vie des ouvriers.' *Les collections de l'Insee, Série M* 126.

Hoggart, Richard. 1957. *Aspects of Working Class Life.* London: Chatto and Windus.

Kaufmann, Jean-Claude. 2003. *Sociologie du couple.* Paris: Presses Universitaires de France.

Kellerhals, Jean, Jean-François Perrin, Geneviève Steinauer-Cresson, Laura Voneche, Geneviève Wirth. 1982. *Mariages au quotidien.* Lausanne: Editions Favre.

Lambert, Anne. 2015. *'Tous propriétaires!' L'envers du décor pavillonnaire.* Paris: Seuil/Liber.

Lynd, Robert, and Helen Merrell Lynd. 1929. *Middletown: A Study in Modern American Culture.* New York: Hartcourt, Brace, and Co.

Masclet, Olivier. 2018. ' "C'est mon moment". Le temps pour soi des ouvrières et des employées.' *Travail, genre et sociétés* 39: 101–119.

Schwartz, Olivier. 1990. *Le Monde privé des ouvriers. Hommes et femmes du Nord.* Paris: Presses Universitaires de France.

Schwartz, Olivier. 2018. 'Les femmes dans les classes populaires, entre permanence et rupture.' *Travail, genre et sociétés* 39: 121–138.

Scott, Joan, and Louise Tilly. 1978. *Women, Work, and Family.* New York: Methuen.

Singly, François de. 1984. 'Accumulation et partage des ressources conjugales.' *Sociologie du travail* 26, no. 3: 326–345.
Verret, Michel. (1988) 1996. *La Culture ouvrière*. Paris: L'Harmattan.
Young, Michael, and Peter Willmott. (1957) 2011. *Family and Kinship in East London*. Oxon: Routledge.
Young, Michael, and Peter Willmott. 1973. *The Symmetrical Family*. New York: Pantheon Books.

13

BEING A MOTHER AND UNEMPLOYED

Resisting being stuck at home – Laeticia Kergal and Valentin Dufour

Angel Baraud

Laeticia is 27 years old. She grew up in Brittany with her mother and her stepfather, who owns a small fishing business. After earning a vocational *baccalauréat*, Laeticia went through a string of insecure shipping and handling jobs. She met Valentin, a delivery driver, at a nightclub in 2012. He was living with his parents at the time, and after dating for several months, he moved in with Laeticia. The apartment was half way between their jobs, and they were both working full-time. They 'settled in' and went clubbing less often. In 2014, Laeticia learned that she was pregnant, so they moved into a single-family house in a suburban town closer to Valentin's job, and Laeticia found herself at home. At the time of the study, she had been unemployed for a year, alternating unemployment with maternity leave. The birth of their daughter Shayna accentuated the division of household work, thus pushing each a little closer to traditional gender roles.

How did Laeticia, who had thus far attached great importance to the independence granted by her work, adjust to this new situation, which she does not want to become permanent? How do they manage the consequences of this imbalance between their professional situations? While Laeticia has the experience of being stuck at home, finding herself in a professional situation marked by uncertainty and doubt while ensuring nearly all the housekeeping and parental work, Valentin continues his work as a delivery driver and maintains rooted and rewarding forms of external sociability, especially thanks to their move. This imbalance has suddenly raised several points of contention in the couple, which has become increasingly tenuous as a result.

DOI: 10.4324/9781003330073-15

Staying economically independent in difficult conditions

Being economically independent through employment is of capital importance to Laeticia. This principle is based on two things: she does not want to be reliant on anyone, neither her mother nor her partner, and she attaches particular importance to being able to spend her money as she wishes without having to justify it to anyone. This desire for independence is central to her relationship with work and is also the basis for her judgements of others. Her conflictual relationships with her sisters, particularly her explanations for their disagreements, illustrate the strength of her commitment to economic independence through employment. Laeticia criticises her older sister for judging how she spends her money and claims that she has 'never asked anything of anybody'. She also laments that her little sister is 'spoiled super-rotten' and that it is 'difficult to show her the value of money' as a result. She thinks that it is unfair that some people have money without really deserving it, meaning without working for it. This is the reproach she makes of 'people in council estates' and 'members of parliament' alike. Certain elements in her family and employment history explain why money earned though employment is so important to her and so central in her evaluation of herself and others.

Laeticia was young and still in school when she started her first job while. She spent her childhood in Brittany with her mother and stepfather. Her stepfather made it a point of honour that she and her older sister 'work so they can have what they want' and to this day Laeticia considers this a positive part of her upbringing. When she was 14 she started working in her stepfather's fishing business on weekends, making fishing nets on piecework. She said the job was 'hard but paid well'. Laeticia experienced economic independence very young: she could buy 'whatever [she] liked' thanks to the money earned this way, which meant clothes and make-up. It also made it possible to save money for larger expenses and thus experience other forms of independence, particularly being able to get around without having to rely on her parents or friends since her income let her buy herself a scooter. This purchase was especially helpful in obtaining freedom of movement because she lived in a rural area poorly serviced by public transportation.

This strong aspiration for economic independence is also part of her family history. Laeticia has a very close relationship with her mother that is based in part on similar experiences. Her mother's employment and residential histories were marked by relationships with men that were characterised by violence upon several occasions. When Laeticia was two years old, conjugal violence prompted her mother to leave her father (who had an electrical business in greater Paris) and move back to Brittany, close to her parents. Sometime later she remarried the man Laeticia now calls her stepfather. Her mother's employment situation is still insecure today, and Laeticia identifies with her trajectory:

ANGEL: What did she [your mother] do before?

LAETICIA: She was trained as a secretary but then my mother did a lot of odd jobs. She never actually had a set job. And then when you turn 50, well, you don't know anymore… To change careers at 50, it's even harder than at 28. So… it makes me sad because my mother moved for my stepfather and she doesn't have friends anymore, she doesn't go out, she's not enjoying life, and it bugs me. I'd really like for her to enjoy her life – she's 50 years old, like, shit! Enjoy it, shake it up, get out! But no. When she used to go out and all that fairly often before. That's why we were pretty independent. But… and it's the same for… I've shut myself in since we're here.

This desire to not be economically reliant on anyone nonetheless conflicts with her history of insecure employment. Laeticia has done paid work for 15 years but has never held a formal full-time job. After having gradually increased her hours in the fishing business, she worked there full-time earning a vocational *baccalauréat* in trade and logistics. At the same time, she was also working nights as a 'cleaning woman at the spa'. Altogether, she worked nearly ten years making fishing nets, but since this job was undeclared, keeping it depended on maintaining good relations with her family, especially since her stepfather was also her boss. When this relationship became strained, she decided to quit. Through the employment office (Pôle Emploi) she found a job packing orders in a candy company not far from home. She was promised an open-ended employment contract that never came, so she ended up working three back-to-back limited-term contracts, for a little less than a year each, from 2011 to 2013. And although she managed to hold on to her financial independence through work for several years, the employment market in which she found herself (low-skill jobs, a lot of temping and insecure jobs) prevented her from having a steady job, and the assurance of a long-term income that comes with it.

When Laeticia learned that she was pregnant, she was finishing her third limited-term contract at the candy company. She and Valentin decided to move to be closer to his workplace and rent a bigger house with room for their daughter. This decision meant that Laeticia would not request a new contract, and she found herself unemployed. This new situation, marked by uncertainty about the future, stirred up all the contradictions and hesitations typifying Laeticia's relationship to work and employment, which were already perceptible in her account of her teenage years, especially at the key moment of choosing her educational track at the end of *collège*.[1] Laeticia was interested in archaeology at the time and wanted to go to a generalist *lycée*, but her *collège*'s guidance counsellor declared that her marks were not high enough to succeed in an academically oriented *lycée*, and her friends and family could not understand why she would strike out on a path that did not lead to a paying job. She ultimately had no choice but to enrol for a BEP trade and logistics. Her thwarted aspirations to academic and professional qualifications were revived by her recent experience: the degree she earned only allows her to hold shipping and handling positions, and her recent attempts to go back to school have not worked out. Throughout the interview her discourse on employment fluctuated between resignation (characterised by an instrumental conception of paid work) and aspirations based on a conception of employment as a means to fulfilment, doing something she likes, and getting recognition (Nicole-Drancourt, Roulleau-Berger 2001).

> Yeah, it annoys me, actually, because I want to do something with my life and now I'm going to end up… I mean, I'm not saying that it's pejorative to work in a factory or anything, because so long as you've got a job, you've got money, you pay your bills. I tell myself, so long as there's money coming in, but… I don't want to end up like that. It's not what I want to do, I want to have… something I like. Not working to work. So that's what annoys me, actually.

Today, Laeticia plans on using this period of unemployment to change directions, acquire new qualifications, and renew with her desire to not 'stay at the bottom of the ladder'. However, the conditions for resuming her studies are not adapted to her family situation, and she is once again having difficulties with the school system. Her first aim was to set off on a path she 'really likes', but she could not enrol in a CAP-earning pastry programme because, being over 25, she was no longer eligible for financial assistance and could not afford to commit a long period without an income. So she turned to a BTS in administrative assistance, in a programme alternating classroom time with hands-on paid work experience that would allow her to pursue a degree while earning an income, but this project fell through because she could not find a business to host the internship component.

Thus, while Laeticia sees holding down a job as the best – and only – way to maintain her financial independence and get recognition (she only makes plans for employment), the possibilities opened by the democratisation of education have gradually shrunk, thus increasingly raising the spectre of two other perspectives she finds much less appealing: being a stay-at-home mother or having an unskilled, insecure job.

Finding oneself 'at home', a gendered consequence of the birth of a first child

While the concomitance of the birth and decision to move plunged Laeticia into psychological as well as material uncertainty about her professional future, the consequences of the birth of their first child on Valentin's professional situation were much less perceptible. After earning a BTS in negotiation and client relations in 2011, he set out to find a sales position. He was unemployed for a year, but failing to find sales work, he decided to 'return' to the company where he had done the on-the-job portion of his sales training, but this time as a delivery driver, because 'I knew they would take me'. At the time of the interview, he had worked for them for three years on an open-ended employment contract. He sees some advantages to the job, especially the working hours, but he mostly stresses the lack of recognition.

ANGEL: And you get bonuses if you cover a lot of customers?

VALENTIN: Nah, that's what's a shame. Because sometimes... That's the problem, actually, in this company, you work so hard, you end up at 65, 70 [packages delivered per day], something extraordinary where you worked hard nonstop, and they don't say anything, zip, whatever. But then the day when you end up with 65, the next day you've got 40, they'll hassle you, all that, tell you 'Nah, stick around to lend a hand, go do things here and there', all that. They'll get up your nose because you haven't done enough. [...] When ultimately, no one says anything to you because when you've done 65, they don't give a damn.

After their daughter was born, Valentin delayed his plans for professional development. It was important that he keep his income to be able to support Laeticia's hopes to go back to school in a work/training programme.

VALENTIN: Nah, I am staying a deliveryman for now. I've got an open-ended contract, anyway, so you see, I've got [job] security. [...]

ANGEL: Yeah, that's lasted... two years. Yeah, so for the time being, you're staying with that...

VALENTIN: Yeah, yeah, I'm staying with that and then we'll see later with Laeticia because with the baby we can't afford both of us doing something just now [Laeticia was enrolled in a BTS at the time]... because, well, where income is concerned, even if it's a work/training programme, you don't earn a bundle either, so...

At the same time, the fact that Laeticia is at home has also helped him to improve certain aspects of his job. He comes home for lunch every day, for example, and Laeticia prepares the meal and waits to eat with him at 2 in the afternoon. Eating at home allows Valentin to take a real break midday instead of eating hurriedly in his truck. He also believes that this arrangement (and Laeticia's work) helps him avoid 'giving' an hour a day to his boss.

The decision to move and not request a new limited-term employment contract radically transformed Laeticia's everyday life and the kind of work filling her days, and she experienced a new form of domestic enclosure in the months preceding our interview. First of all, her job at the candy factory had brought her a significant form of recognition, despite the insecurity of her contract. She felt a degree of pride in not 'making mistakes', unlike the 'other girls'. Because of this she was given 'responsibilities', put in charge of foreign shipments and orders from 'big companies like Lafayette [department stores]'. She was engaged in her work, establishing a 'system' for organising labels that allowed her and her co-workers 'to go faster', for instance. Laeticia prepared orders with five other 'girls'. There was some rivalry in the group due to productivity demands that put employees in competition with each other, and the gendered division of labour tallied with hierarchical relations, leading to jealousy. It was nonetheless also an important base of sociability: there was a 'good atmosphere' and they 'planned quite a few things among co-workers', like 'having some beers Thursday nights'.

The move that was seen as advantageous for Valentin nonetheless put Laeticia farther from her family and friends, further deepening her feeling of being cut off. Their house is just a few kilometres from Valentin's job, but also quite near his parents, brothers, and paternal grandparents. Laeticia's mother and friends, mostly former co-workers and friends from *lycée*, live about fifty kilometres away. With this move Laeticia was not only cut off from the working sphere but also her main spheres of sociability. On top of that, moving into a suburban housing development limits her options for going out and having friendly relations with the neighbours. Her account of her days is marked by boredom and a feeling of isolation:

> Oh, am I bored. [...] Val, when he gets home, he says 'Yeah, go out, enjoy yourself' – well fine, what am I supposed to enjoy? Lézac!?[2] So, anyway, my friends aren't near, I've got one friend who isn't far, Camille, but she's pregnant, she's due in a month.

When Laeticia does go out, it is mainly with her partner and often with his friends or family. Valentin has personal hobbies, mainly tennis, which is very important to him. It is the primary explanation he gives when his family declares he would be better off working for the national train company, the SNCF, like his father. Indeed, his current job has set daytime working hours, so he does not have to work nights or weekends. Playing tennis brings him a form of recognition in a socially diverse male social setting. He is proud to have risen quickly in the rankings when he returned to competition and that the Lézac club asked him to join. Sport also helps him to 'decompress after work' and release some of the stress from his job, which demands constant efficiency. Lastly, playing tennis, like his job, is a significant basis for male sociability. He goes out regularly with his tennis friends.

Lastly, the division of domestic work in the couple reasserts the characteristics usually attributed to men and women, particularly the interior/exterior distinction, which compounds Laeticia's feeling of being shut in after having been in the habit of going out with friends (Testenoire 2006). Laeticia orders their groceries online, for example. She is the one who knows the household's needs for the next two weeks because she is practically the only one to do the cooking; Valentin is charged with going to the store to pick up the order. He also has to do the dishes and take out the trash daily. Laeticia takes care of all the other domestic tasks every day (cleaning, laundry, etc.).

Laeticia now finds herself in an ambiguous position: what was supposed to be a time for her to change careers is becoming a period marked by uncertainty because of the difficulties she encountered in going back to school, and she is trapped between her desire to resume work and her investment in motherhood. This ambiguity can be found in the string of administrative statuses that have defined her situation since she stopped working. After two months of unemployment (during which she received return-to-work benefits [Allocation de retour à l'emploi]), she went on a four-month maternity leave with support from the child benefits office (Caisse d'allocations familiales). At the end of maternity leave, she went back to job-seeker status. Although her employment situation did not change that year – she had no job – the status under which she was remunerated fluctuated between active worker looking for a job and mother of an infant. Women with limited educations in the market for insecure jobs are particularly subject to this porosity between unemployment and inactivity (Maruani 2011) from which Laeticia is currently suffering.

Resisting being stuck at home

Laeticia is currently invested in raising her daughter and keeping house. She prepares all Shayna's meals herself, cooks for herself and Valentin, and vacuums and dusts daily. She enjoys some of these tasks and feels a certain pride in having a nicely arranged and well-kept home. Despite all that, the rhetoric of pleasure does not change her conception of the work that she does every day. Much of what she says and does signal resistance to the unequal division of domestic and parental work and most of all her hope that this situation be a temporary exception in her life course and her relationship.

Laeticia and Valentin have discussed and formalised the distribution of domestic and parental work, but it is still prone to conflict. Each of them presented their formal division of work caring for Shayna: Laeticia cares for her during the day, Valentin feeds her in the evening, they take turns giving her a bath (every other day), and on weekends they alternate getting up early. Valentin did not mention any problems with this organisation of parental work, but Laeticia did. She stressed the fact that far too often she has to tell, ask, or remind Valentin that he has to do something. She moreover regularly uses possessive pronouns to designate the tasks she does at home ('my housework', 'my cooking', etc.). In other words, she is the one carrying the mental load of the household's domestic and parental organisation.

ANGEL: Yeah, and so you've got the impression you fight a little?

LAETICIA: Yeah, that's it, what annoys me, actually, is repeating myself, and he says, 'Yeah, you're a pain, you're always repeating the same thing'; 'Well yeah, but if you did them I wouldn't have to repeat myself'.

By starting conversations and sometimes fights, Laeticia reminds Valentin of his obligations as father, because they 'both made Shayna', and fights against the routinisation of this domestic arrangement that she wants to be temporary.

Laeticia does not think of her domestic and parental work as something she unconditionally owes to Valentin; she does not want to be 'his maid'. One of her main strategies to maintain this conception concerns how household expenses are shared. Indeed, although her income is currently lower than Valentin's, she makes it a point of pride to pay exactly half of their common expenses. She thus leaves no opening for economic dependence to take root, which could follow the rather classic form holding that she owes it to Valentin to do all the domestic and parental work because he ensures the household's financial well-being. By paying for half the expenses, she also maintains her self-image as an active woman able to provide for her family's needs. She moreover regularly reminds Valentin that this situation (her unemployed, him working outside the home) is temporary. She experienced this double burden while she was working and compares her past situation to that of Valentin today, an indication that she does not consider masculine and feminine roles to be strictly different and complementary.

> I say to him, 'What are you going to do when I go to work?' Honestly, when I was working I'd come home, I'd do the housework, I'd make my dinner, all that. [...] I really don't think he has anything to complain about – the house is kept up, I take care of the baby, his laundry is clean, I mean, you see? [...] OK, I don't work, but I put in a day's work at home, I think it's well kept...

Laeticia mainly sees the work that she does around the house as a responsibility to her family. She has taken on many time-consuming activities to provide Shayna and the household a certain quality of life, especially where food and decoration are concerned, and this despite their limited economic resources (Valentin earns about 1,500 euros a month). For instance, she makes homemade baby food for Shayna's health and to accustom her 'to the taste of vegetables' so she will like to eat them later, but it also saves a considerable amount of money, about 120 euros a month according to her calculations. Her scrupulous accounting and anticipation of household expenses are also part of this dynamic. Lastly, Laeticia also spends a notable amount of time online comparing prices and thus saving them more money.

Just as Laeticia does not see her domestic work as something she owes Valentin, nor does she see it as time for herself (Masclet 2018). She thus tries to arrange for time to do things she likes, such as time for personal hobbies. However, the fact that she takes on nearly all of the mental charge of domestic organisation makes it very difficult, even impossible, to arrange for this time 'for herself' in the home. This is how she described the challenge:

> I really like… yeah, like I told him, 'When you get home, if I go upstairs, leave me an hour or two alone in the bedroom'. I do my nails or I read – I love to read. Leave me alone in peace just an hour or two. But you know, when he says 'Yeah, take an hour or two for yourself', when I'm here, he calls up to ask me things every five minutes. He says 'Nah, but you should take some time for yourself', but when I take time for myself he calls me every five minutes.

Laeticia goes out periodically, but her outings are not part of the household routine the way that Valentin's tennis is. It seems as if they are often subject to negotiation, and Valentin tends to panic when she goes out. This gives Laeticia the impression that she cannot 'have any time to herself'.

> I once had a hairdresser's appointment on a Saturday morning, so he was watching the baby, and for an hour he harassed me on the phone, he was calling and I didn't answer. And then when I got home he says, 'Well why didn't you answer?' I tell him, 'Ah, that was my time for me, I told you'. 'Well yeah, but after two hours I was starting to worry, I couldn't see you coming'. I tell him, 'What, do you think it takes half an hour at the hairdressers?' Pffff… see, every time I take some time for myself, he's still got to… even when I'm going shopping and all, 'Where are you? Whatcha doin'?'

These various forms of resistance, which are more or less effective, are ways in which Laeticia distances herself from the model of the housewife as one who lives only through and for her husband and children and thus maintains her self-image as an economically active and independent woman, despite her material circumstances.

The egalitarian model is very present in Valentin and Laeticia's relationship. They make most household decisions together, and both emphasise the importance of both parents contributing to raising their daughter. This model is moreover fuelled by Laeticia's desire for independence and rejection of conjugal dependence. Despite all that, there are many obstacles to putting this model into practice. And even if Valentin makes an effort (he delayed his plans for professional development, no longer goes out to clubs, and participates in some activities and decisions concerning Shayna), their unequal engagement in the employment market, especially the obstacles Laeticia runs up against in her desire for 'professional success' in the world of insecure jobs, contribute to accentuating gendered behaviours shaped by their previous experiences. Ultimately Laeticia finds herself in charge of the vast majority of domestic and parental work. She tries to balance this situation by trying to fix Valentin in the home (especially through raising their daughter), securing his engagement (Schwartz 1990), and trying to arrange for some time for herself. All of Laeticia's efforts to block the normalisation and routinisation of inegalitarian domestic arrangements engender frequent arguments in this couple that is struggling to stay together.

Notes

1 For an explanation of the French educational system, see the Appendix.
2 The town name has been changed to help preserve anonymity.

References

Maruani, Margaret. 2011. *Travail et emploi des femmes*. Paris: La Découverte.

Masclet, Olivier. 2018. '"C'est mon moment". Le temps pour soi des ouvrières et des employées.' *Travail, genre et sociétés* 39: 101–119.

Nicole-Drancourt, Chantal, and Laurence Roulleau-Berger. 2001. *Les Jeunes et le travail 1950–2000*. Paris: Presses Universitaires de France.

Schwartz, Olivier. 1990. *Le Monde privé des ouvriers. Hommes et femmes du Nord*. Paris: Presses Universitaires de France.

Testenoire, Armelle. 2006. 'Éloignés au quotidien et ensemble. Arrangements conjugaux en milieu populaire.' *Cahiers du genre* 41: 117–138.

14

THE POWER OF TWO FEMININITIES – RÉGINE AND HERVÉ LEBLANC

Marie Cartier

Régine Leblanc, a 46-year-old childminder, takes care of her household's errands, meal preparation, laundry, budget, and dealings with governmental administrations. She also has a vegetable garden, takes the cars to be inspected, and attends homeowners' association meetings. Régine often uses the word 'chore' when speaking of these tasks. As a childminder, she cares for several children aged three months to three years in her house and loves to take them out 'to clear my mind of housework' and not be 'shut in' at home. Proud of her income, she thinks of herself as actively employed, even if it is at home. On the weekends when she does not have an archery competition, she likes to go out and see people. She recently let it be known to her husband, a public transportation driver for a city in western France, that she was 'fed up' with being 'left with the chores'. But at the same time, though their eldest daughter had just moved out of the family home, Régine endlessly asserts her 'role as mother', her homemaking, cooking, and budgeting skills, and how much she enjoys 'playing waitress' at her husband's *pétanque* club. How to characterise this style of femininity? Since Régine defines herself as a woman mainly through her maternal and domestic activities, in line with a style of maternal femininity regularly observed in the working classes, how to account for her great attachment to her income, her distanciation from domestic 'chores', and her investment in a sport for middle-class men?

Régine and Hervé are both originally from the Côtes d'Armor, a department of Brittany. She has a BEP degree in the garment industry, and he has a CAP in butchering.[1] They met while both working temporary jobs in a food plant in the 1980s, following a period of unemployment. A move to the greater Parisian area and the occupational engagement of Régine meant that they were ultimately able to attain relative economic and social stability thanks to their combined incomes. After living ten years in a social housing estate in

DOI: 10.4324/9781003330073-16

Seine-Saint-Denis, they were able to buy an apartment in Nantes when they were about 35, which they then sold in 2008 to buy a 90-m^2 single-family home in a development in the suburbs of Nantes. Régine Leblanc's domestic and parental activities, her perceptions of them, and the relationships she has with her husband and daughters are characterised by the reproduction of a working-class style of femininity marked by a strictly gendered division of roles. At the same time, Régine is also characterised by practices and dispositions that are out of step with this working-class style of femininity.

Mother ...

Régine and Hervé Leblanc moved to Seine-Saint-Denis in 1989, after Hervé got a bus-driving job for a sub-contractor serving the Paris airports. Régine waitressed for two and a half years for a restaurant at Charles de Gaulle Airport, a job she liked for the contact with a largely foreign clientele. When she was 24, she gave birth to their first daughter. Far from her family in Brittany and unable to find childcare for her irregular hours, she had to give up working outside the home. She got a home-based childcare licence but could not set up a stable business in the public housing neighbourhood where she lived. Their second daughter was born three years later, in 1994. Régine thus spent several years at home and did not resume paid employment until the younger daughter began school in the late 1990s (as a part-time ironer at dry cleaners). When she speaks of it in retrospect, she emphasises the negative consequences of this period without active employment, which forced her to enrol in social security through her husband and deprived her of her own income, condemning her to 'a stingy life' and making her 'lose out for retirement'. Her priority investment at the time was in her 'role as mother', which she asserts as a central aspect of her identity. The idea of 'depending on cafeteria personnel' was alien to her, and she preferred to provide nutritionally balanced and sufficiently copious meals for her daughters herself ('That's my role as a mother! It's... it's part of who I am!'). To this nourishing dimension of 'the role of mother' was added an attention to childrearing and education that Régine also highlights when speaking of her years without outside employment or working only part-time.

> And after, they had their own school hours and I had to be available, and to chaperone them on school trips, because I sometimes didn't have a job... and so I was practically at the disposal of the husband and kids but, uh, I still favoured the role of mum above all, y'know! I wasn't just good for cooking and doing the laundry, either. So I took care of their upbringing, the school part, parent-teacher meetings, doctors' appointments.

Régine carefully kept up with her daughters' homework, making them recite poetry they had to learn by heart, for instance. Fearing that their younger daughter might be dyslexic (when she was three she mispronounced certain words), Régine consulted a paediatrician who recommended that Estelle see a speech therapist; she would do seventy sessions from the age of four. Régine was determined that her sessions be on Saturday mornings, not during the school day, because she remembered three of her elder daughter's classmates in year 2 of school who missed class for speech therapy and had to repeat the year.

The centrality of the familial and maternal role can also be read in her motivations to return to paid employment. Concerned by her financial independence as a woman ('not relying on spousal benefits'), Régine also tried to improve the family's living conditions and meet their daughters' consumption needs: her relationship to paid employment is thus shaped by the demands of her role in the family, according to a model observed among working-class women throughout the twentieth century (Scott and Tilly 1978, Daune-Richard 1983).

> I had to find a job, I had to have an income, I had to pay into retirement, and for my daughters, I had to work it so I wasn't always saying "no", because after a certain age – birthday parties, gifts for friends, all that – if you don't have the budget for it you say no, and you prevent them from accepting the invitation and all that, and that, I couldn't.

When Hervé got a job as a bus driver in Nantes and they moved there in 1999, Régine passed up a minimum-wage job selling fabric until eight at night and became a licenced childminder instead. This job let her earn an income while continuing to provide lunch for her early-teenage daughters at home. They would only start eating at a cafeteria in *lycée*. Certain that they did not appreciate the experience, Régine concluded: 'That confirmed my quote-unquote "belief" that it was better to eat at home!'

Domestic tasks are distributed quite unequally between her and Hervé. 'For him, he married a woman, she takes care of everything, y'know! Like his mother did. *I* take care of *everything*, right? I raised our daughters'. She sometimes complains about it (we'll come back to this), but at the same time she gives herself over to these domestic and parental tasks with verve and skill, as can be seen in the following quote, wherein she mentions her husband's tastes and a dish she had just cooked for him for his return home from work.

MARIE: And your husband doesn't like vegetables that much either, right?

RÉGINE: [Hesitates] Oh, he's no fan, y'know! And then, he really prefers a big dish of pasta or... well, rice is good, he loves it, so I favour, now that there's often only two of us at the table, I favour lunches with rice more than pasta! We do have pasta, y'know, I've got some, like when our daughter comes to eat here sometimes, well, we can eat pasta because she prefers it because of her allergies, but otherwise... I prefer to make us rice when I have the chance. Over there are stuffed zucchini from granny's garden. I took the

> filling from two herbed sausages that I bought, I blended that with the core of the zucchinis in a thing for babies, over there, voom voom.

Since their eldest daughter left home, Régine does the supermarket shopping every two weeks. She appreciates not having to go weekly. Hervé's contribution is limited to buying the bread every day. Régine relates with satisfaction that she was able to lighten her domestic work thanks to the acquisition of a freezer when they moved into a single-family house.

> Well, as soon as we knew we'd be moving there, I wanted a big one, I wanted to be able to buy a months' worth of meat in there, I wanted to be able to... grow things and freeze them.

Régine is also proud of her role as manager of family financial resources. She 'carefully' manages family income and expenses. She organises, plans, arbitrates, and economises. She makes consumption choices based on balancing quality and price and avoiding 'useless' purchases and 'waste'. Having noticed that the low-consumption light bulbs from IKEA that are supposed to last eight years actually burned out after three months, she regularly returns them for new ones ('I use after-sales service', she says). For the past 15 years, she systematically saves the refund coupons from the supermarket checkout and sends them to the companies for reimbursement, received months later. This money goes into an account reserved for special expenses. She regularly participates in the online consumer forum *C'vous*, run by a major national grocery chain, where she gives housekeeping, cooking, and shopping 'advice' and 'tips' to other users in hopes of drawing praise from other 'consumers', to the point that some have become 'friends'. Her participation in this forum confirms her positive investment in such domestic tasks. She does not denigrate cleaning activities, which she performs meticulously while doing her utmost to make them easier.

> One night to descale your toilets: Using a little mister bottle of vinegar lets you get under the rim, and pouring a bowl of vinegar into the bowl all night, bingo! Good-bye to bad odours and hard water deposits. In the morning, a good scrub with the toilet brush and a little flush and that's all the work, toilets like new! Happy 'less tiring chores', girls!
>
> *Posted on the C'Vous forum by Régine on 4/11/2014*

Another message attests to this same concern with lightening housework as well as her high cleanliness standards. It also illustrates the importance she attributes to the quality and durability of household appliances:

> Comforter in the washing machine with 5 tennis balls, which drives the drum, slowed by the weight of the wet comforter: it comes out

> well-drained and doesn't take too long to dry afterwards. It's more practical for saving time than taking the car to a dry-cleaners (and this twice) and ends up being much more economical, too. Think about it!

When another user of the forum indicated that she had damaged her washing machine doing this, Régine replied:

> That's awful! What brand is this washing machine that's so fragile? I want to avoid that brand if I need to replace mine, which is aging well after ten years of use already, and the comforters every three months... There's no way I'd buy a washing machine that's not sturdy! I already have the problem with a bad sewing machine from Darty [*an appliance chain*]... and I'm having a tough time of it! Buy well.

Discussion on the C'Vous *forum, 3/11/2014*

Régine invests her domestic skills in the school parents' association and her husband's *pétanque* club and repeatedly stresses her 'pleasure' in doing so:

> I was somewhat part of the parents' scene, helping without being a member. I'd sew for hours, without regard for the time, little trinkets for the Christmas fairs... I'd do it for fun! I was a mother and I embraced my role of mother! So I'd do all kinds of tinkering, lots of sewing, everything I knew how to do, tons of *crêpes* like that to sell at the Christmas fair and all... So I gave, y'know, time, time, time! But I had fun.

This taste for domestic and maternal activities recalls the working-class style of femininity identified in many studies (such as Schwartz 1990; Le Pape 2006).

... and competitive archer

One of Régine's activities nonetheless seems out of step with this maternal and homemaking-based style of femininity: she has been in an archery club for 18 years. In 2012, she went twice a week (Tuesday from 8 to 9 pm and Thursday from 7 to 9 pm). To every parent who wants to hire her as a childminder she explains that they must pick up their child by 6:15 on Thursday nights. On weekends, she regularly participates in competitions. She discovered the sport when she was living in greater Paris. While going about her everyday business she used to pass an archery centre where 'people seemed to be having a good time'. As soon as she got her job at the dry cleaners, after several years off the job market, she had the income to 'give herself' a membership in the archery club, which agreed to let her bring her children. She likes the mental and physical effort that archery demands, but also the competitiveness ('winning') and the walk from target to target outdoors in the right seasons. When I asked Régine what her husband thought about her engagement in this activity, she unhesitatingly replied, 'He didn't see why I shouldn't do it, given that he had *pétanque*. I never had any problem on that point'. She calls it 'my passion' and 'my sport' and the topic came up very quickly in our earliest exchanges for the study. She also mentions it on the *C'Vous* forum. It is an aspect of her identity that is very important to her. Through archery, this activity 'for oneself' (Masclet 2018) that takes her out of the home several times a week, Régine has attained physical autonomy from the home and domestic work. Finding such time for herself must be related to the fact that Régine only has two children, which is few and represents a considerably lighter domestic workload in comparison to that of working-class mothers of earlier generations. Several times Régine mentioned her mother, overwhelmed by the work of raising seven children, as a counter-example. She laments the fact that her father forbade her mother to work as a farm worker outside the home, thus condemning the whole family to a life of poverty. Her disposition to use a sport to get some space from her domestic role also comes with an assertion of independence in the couple, a freedom of choice and movement relative to her spouse. When their desires for vacations diverge (whether to travel abroad or not, go with the *pétanque* club or not), she has no compunctions about going off on her own or letting him go alone. In our first interview, Régine admits that she had let Hervé know that she was 'fed up' with the fact that he does not do any more housework today than in the past.

> Twenty-five years of living together, he plays *pétanque*, he plays poker, he plays Ping-Pong, some works council meetings at work once or twice a month, and other than that [*sarcastically*] Daddy's in his place in the couch, ever since the girls were little. A spectator of things. Player, spectator, not at all in the 'being responsible for' mind-set. When it comes to running the household, stuff like that, well, he counts on me! Now sometimes I try to pass him the ball a little – sometimes I don't make him dinner [*with satisfaction*]. He ends up doing it because he'd really like to eat! [*laughing*].

Now that their daughters are young adults ('we finished childrearing'), Régine thinks that she has 'matured', and she would like her husband to contribute more to tasks around the house. If we connect this complaint to her investment in an activity 'for herself' (archery), it is conceivable that they refer not only to a passing phase of being 'fed up' with imbalanced domestic task distribution but also a disposition to independence that is as typical of her style of femininity as maternal devotion and domestic skill. Her style of femininity seems to be a real hybrid: the central position accorded to the nourishing and material dimensions of her maternal and familial role is accompanied by a vigorous assertion of independence.

Childminder: an occupation with ambiguous effects on gender relations at home

Régine's practice of the occupation of licenced childminder, for a year in greater Paris and ever since her move to Nantes in 1999, favoured the hybridity of her style of femininity. The job entails caring for several pre-school-aged children in her own home for what can be long hours every week. By definition, it leads women to perform tasks resembling those that they (have) practice(d) as mothers, but professionally. Although regulations now forbid minders from 'doing housework' during working hours and stipulate a focus on care for the small children themselves, minding children still requires the performance of material and relational domestic tasks that increase as the number of children in care rises. In comparison with a mother working outside the home, Régine's maternal and domestic tasks lasted longer and proliferated when she became a childminder. By its very nature, this occupation actually strengthens the gendered division of roles and tasks in the family. Speaking of the case of a two-year-old girl that only arrived at 10 in the morning and was consequently off schedule when it came to lunchtime, Régine emphasises the difficulty she has in coordinating the schedules of everyone she has to feed.

> She'd eat a little bit later than us sometimes, but since I had babies that were slow to … feed – it's slow for babies, with a spoon… And we eat too: there were also my girls, who came home from school, who came home to eat. It was also economical for us to be… home, to serve everyone, the husband, both girls, the babies, and the little one who'd arrive at the end of the meal – she'd eat the end of her meal with us, anyway. But still, it was tricky, that little girl. We had trouble… Our day was… disrupted relative to the non-respect of her life, I mean, of her schedule.

Other than the nature of the tasks, the work setting (the home) can also contribute to re-enforcing the imbalance of task distribution in the family. Indeed, it tends to blur the boundaries between tasks related to the job of childminding and those relevant to domestic work for family members. Husbands and children might provide less help in such a situation than they might for women who work 'away from home', either because the mother's presence in the home increases the chances of forgetting her occupation (since she is 'at home'), or because all domestic tasks are henceforth considered to be related to her job as childminder. We can see this phenomenon of blurred boundaries and resultant misunderstandings that ultimately increases the domestic load on mothers in the following account, in which Régine describes a tense moment with her husband and daughters that ended in explanations.

> Because a daughter complains, the other daughter complains, the husband complains… 'Well, what about me in all that?! Can't you see I'm trying to

> earn our living here?!' The time comes when you have to confront them! 'I've got this, this, and that to do! That there is my job, this is not my job, this is my job, that's not my job! You can help me with this and this, y'know! That's family, it's not mine!' And so we managed … […]. Hervé can help me by buying the bread when he comes home from work, that saves me from going out just for that, when it takes me 20 minutes to get myself and all the kids dressed [*to go out*]… It's ridiculous, just to go buy bread… every day.

So while the occupation of childminder tends to strengthen Régine's disposition to prioritise her maternal and familial role in practice, it also fuels the blurring of boundaries and family tension. This situation leads to thought and discussion on the respective roles of childminder and housewife. Distancing herself from the nourishing role of mother, although it is dear to her, Régine indicates that although she prefers home cooking, she also regularly buys frozen pizzas.

> You just can't! You only live once, y'know! There's only 24 hours in a day, you've gotta sleep, y'know! It's not possible to cook 24 hours a day, only homemade, only fresh, only things not bought at the store, blah blah… That time is over and done with. We work! We don't have time, so we also buy frozen food sometimes – for the family! Not for the little ones I watch, but for the family.

Throughout the interviews, it seemed that doing archery helps Régine to dodge the obligation to prepare family meals every weekday and even openly assert the limits of maternal devotion:

> On nights when I do sports, or I go shopping, and/or I haven't got time to cook… Because we're expected to work 15 hours a day, we wives, y'know! Bring the groceries into the house… so already, you've got to waste your time in the aisles, to buy them; after you've got to… wash them, prepare them, chop them, cook them, and after… Well, we go to bed, it's 11 at night, we haven't even rested! Didn't stop to breathe, catch your breath. I said 'Enough of all that – the freezer will help me out!'

Despite the fact that her work takes place in her place of residence, being a childminder leads Régine to see herself as a woman who is active outside the home and to assert it to friends and family. Her income's significant contribution to the family budget also favours such a self-identification. Régine is thus unlike some childminders she knows, who see this income as supplementary ('pocket money'): it is central to the couple's lifestyle, not only allowing them to consume certain goods and services 'as a treat' but also giving them access to credit and property ownership.

> These days I get 1200–1300 euros a month, that my sisters – cashier/shelver in a store, or another one who works in a factory, or another who's at a retirement home – they make between 900 and 1400 euros. I said, 'Well, I'm in the average'. And like for retirement, I know that I earn and contribute as much, too. I'm in the norm, I've got an income. It's my occupation, my income, I assert it! And then, without that, we wouldn't make it [...]. I'm attached to my income. I don't call it a bonus or a supplement – no, we need it for the homeowner's loan, to buy... We had to justify that I had 3–4 contracts [*with parents, to mind their children*], pay stubs. We had to make 12 pay stubs, multiplied by three families – 36 pay stubs to the bank, to say I was solvent. It's important! If we don't have a decent income, how can we plan purchases, loans, car/real estate, all that? How can you live normally without an income? I know it's impossible, I experienced it, so I'm attached to my income.

Régine's protest of the burden of domestic tasks she has to ensure often takes a generalising turn. She often says 'we' or 'one' rather than 'I', as if she were speaking in the name of a group of women who have both domestic and paid work, which today is most women (Maruani 2011). More concretely, this 'we' also refers to her fellow childminders, who she meets when taking the children for a walk and fresh air, or at events for minders held by the municipal government. Régine complains about the imbalanced distribution of housework at home with her peers. After letting her husband know she was 'fed up', she explained that she had spoken about it with other minders, who 'backed' her protest and quest for recognition. The social backgrounds of childminders have become more diverse in recent decades, as a rising proportion possesses educational attainments and some are in a domestic relationship with mid-level workers and managers (Devetter 2012). The occupation is now a social space that is shared with middle-class women, either colleagues or employers, that may pass the norm of gender equality along to other women with more limited formal educations. It is also important to stress the 'professionalisation' process (Aballéa 2005) that home-based childcare work has undergone since 1977, when the number of mandatory training hours to earn the licence increased, and again in the 2000s, after the signing of a labour agreement and a new requirement of written employment contracts, as childminders went through the process of appropriating salary rights (Cartier 2015). In the 2000s, Régine Leblanc learned how to negotiate contracts with parent-employers.

When questioned about the training she received, she first cited the legal training in glowing terms:

> It was comforting, the fact to be able to… not choose or impose, but to be able to tell parents, 'Well no, I can't accept that', or 'Yes, I'd really like that!', or 'I can also offer you this version…' Anyway, negotiating things with families is easier since the training, and that's thanks to the session with the lawyer […] She made me comfortable with the problems I'd had. It's easier to set limits with the families, too… On running over-time, non-respect of this or that… It's easier to get respect when you know what you've got rights to, what you don't have rights to.

The rhetoric of 'rights' and 'limits' ('to set limits') used here to speak of the working relationship with parent-employers is reminiscent of Régine's previously cited discourse on conjugal and familial relations and domestic work. Ultimately, Régine's search for independence has gone from one social scene to the next since the late 1990s, from leisure to domestic to professional. Régine does not mention the training sessions on various aspects of the work itself (how to communicate with babies, but also how to balance family and work) that non-profit organisations and Mother and Child Protection Services (Protection Maternelle et Infantile) offer childminders, taught by experts from the social sciences (psychology, sociology, education) that come from the educated middle classes. These training sessions also contribute to spreading various and sundry gender norms among childminders, from exultation of women's natural maternal devotion to feminist calls to 'think of oneself'. Both the disposition honouring the maternal and familial role above all and the disposition to assert independence and the limits of devotion were strengthened and legitimised in this training.

Régine Leblanc presents a hybrid style of femininity developed in the 1980s–2000s, in a relationship where neither partner had significant educational attainments. From the stable working classes, their trajectories are marked by the development of subaltern jobs in the service sector and migration to cities far from the rural areas from which they came. On the one hand, Régine asserts in word and deed a style of femininity revolving around motherly devotion and acceptance of her spouse's complete disinvestment in housework. In light of the available research on the gendered social relations in the households of various social classes, we can speak of a working-class style of femininity for which the desire to have her children eat at home rather than the cafeteria could serve as a symbol. On the other hand, Régine also manifests in word and deed, and just as vigorously, a quest for feminine independence that is simultaneously corporeal, financial, and symbolic. It consists of setting limits on maternal and familial devotion, first of all by practising a sport but also by using her professional activity and the resources it provides to maintain the limits of her devotion on the scene of daily domestic life. In this second facet, Régine's femininity resembles that of active and well-educated women of the middle classes. This hybrid femininity and the contemporary restructuring of gender in the French working classes more generally are not exclusively the outcome of longer educations. Still other processes may be at their root. This was what I wanted to suggest when I emphasised the ambivalent effects of working as a childminder on gendered social relations at home; far from merely consigning women with little formal education to the home, domestic tasks, and motherly devotion, this occupation may have unexpected liberating effects, despite the low opinion educated middle- and upper-class men and women (including some feminists) often have of it.

Note

1 For an explanation of the French educational system, see the Appendix.

References

Aballéa, François. 2005. 'La professionnalisation inachevée des assistantes maternelles.' *Recherches et Prévisions* 80: 55–65.

Cartier, Marie. 2015. 'Les assistantes maternelles ou la subordination chez soi? Socio-histoire d'une relation d'emploi depuis 1977 en Loire-Atlantique, Volume 2.' Habilitation à Diriger des Recherches in sociology, Université de Nantes.

Daune-Richard, Anne-Marie. 1984. 'Activité professionnelle, travail domestique et lignées féminines.' In *Le Sexe du travail*, Grenoble: Presses Universitaires de Grenoble.

Devetter, François-Xavier. 2012. 'Qualité de l'emploi et des conditions de travail des professionnel-le-s de la petite enfance.' *Politiques sociales et familiales* 109: 9–22.

Le Pape, Marie-Clémence. 2006. 'Les ambivalences d'une double appartenance : hommes et femmes en milieux populaires.' *Sociétés contemporaines* 62: 5–26.

Maruani, Margaret. 2011. *Travail et emploi des femmes*. Paris: La Découverte.

Masclet, Olivier. 2018b. '"C'est mon moment". Le temps pour soi des ouvrières et des employées.' *Travail, genre et sociétés* 39: 101–119.

Schwartz, Olivier. 1990. *Le Monde privé des ouvriers. Hommes et femmes du Nord*. Paris: Presses Universitaires de France.

Scott, Joan, and Louise Tilly. 1978. *Women, Work, and Family*. New York: Methuen.

15

A BUSINESS THAT WORKS

Breaking away from the family model, relying on family help – Cécile and Jean-Marc Pilier

Violaine Girard and Maulde Urbain-Mathis

Cécile and Jean-Marc Pilier, both about 30, live with their three-year-old son Luc in a suburban town in western France. They own a three-room house that they are gradually renovating, and their financial situation is stable. They both have open-ended employment contracts, so their incomes allowed them to obtain a loan with no difficulty. But if their income is regular, it is nonetheless low: Cécile earns 1,200 euros a month and Jean-Marc earns 1,400, which was low enough to make them eligible for an interest-free loan when they bought their house. The family experiences economic limitations; Cécile speaks of privation (especially for want of being able to go out to eat) and indicates that they try their best to not be 'spendthrifts': 'We pay attention, we pay what has to be paid first'.

Cécile is a hairdresser and says she loves her job. She likes the contact with her clients and appreciates the creative side of her job. Working outside the home seems to be a foregone conclusion. As for Jean-Marc, he is chief of security for a subcontractor hired to work inside a pharmaceutical facility. They both speak of their jobs in the register of vocation, and both plan to advance in their careers. Jean-Marc was recently promoted to team leader, and Cécile says she would like to open her own hair salon one day. As a couple, they are pursuing plans for family success. With this comes a desire, especially strong in Cécile, to not copy their parents' conjugal model, especially in the distribution of household and childrearing tasks. This is partially explained by the considerable tension between Cécile and her parents when she was a young adult and rejected her father's control over her comings and goings and the company she kept, especially after she had met Jean-Marc. How does this refusal (or at least partial refusal) to reproduce the working-class family legacy play out, and how is it experienced? The trajectories of Jean-Marc and Cécile Pilier provide an

DOI: 10.4324/9781003330073-17

opportunity to explore an apparent paradox. Although they clearly took their distance from the lifestyle of the previous generation, they ultimately settled near Cécile's parents and rely heavily on them for help. This refusal to reproduce their parents' model is thus not experienced as a conflict or a break; on the contrary, immediate family is a determinant form of support for the couple that allows them to project themselves on a path to social ascension.

Refusal to reproduce traditional parental roles

Cécile and Jean-Marc Pilier met when they were about 20 and were part of the same gang of friends. They lived with their respective parents at the time, Cécile in a working-class town in the rural periphery of a city in western France, and Jean-Marc in the centre of a rural town forty-some kilometres to the south. Both are from families of the stable working classes, although their parents did have to deal with health and employment issues. Cécile grew up in a family working in labour and small-business ownership. Her father was a worker in a major local paper company and was laid off when it closed in 2013, just three years before he was planning to retire. Her mother was from a family of small independent business owners. She started working as shop assistant in her parents' bakery and then drove the mobile shop truck on its rounds until health problems reduced her mobility and obliged her to stop. Jean-Marc's father was not home very often when he was growing up, because, as a framer working in construction, he was often away on a job, and he died at retirement age. Jean-Marc's mother was a cleaning worker, and his sisters are a warehouse handler and an auxiliary nurse who had a shoulder injury and was reclassified in hospital administration; they all live near each other in the town where he grew up. While neither Cécile nor Jean-Marc was exposed to family problems as children, Cécile still harbours a deep sense of injustice concerning how her father blocked her access to independence as a young adult. She ran up against her father's authoritarianism after she met Jean-Marc, when he refused to grant her freedom so long as she lived under this roof. 'I was a girl, I was his responsibility', she said, stressing that things were different for her younger brother, who still lives with their parents. Her father was opposed to her 'sleeping over at Jean-Marc's', thus giving the impression that he rejected her boyfriend. Cécile's mother agreed to let Jean-Marc visit when her husband was not home, but the bond of understanding with her daughter did not go so far as defending her in front of her husband. This situation quickly led Cécile to look for a place where she and Jean-Marc could move in together. They did so after barely a year together, in 2005, which in retrospect she says was rather 'hasty'.

From this period, Cécile retained the desire to not reproduce such parental roles in her relationship with her partner or as a mother. She claims that she is prepared to argue with Jean-Marc over how to raise their children, counter to the submissive attitude she says her mother had, and all the more so if they have a daughter:

> If we have a daughter one day, well, we'll argue with each other, but I won't put her through what I went through! [...] My mother never stood up for me by telling [my father], "Listen, leave her alone". I've always said [to Jean-Marc], I'll never be like my mother, if we have to fight, too bad, we'll fight, but it's out of the question...

Cécile loudly and clearly declares her attachment to a norm of equality in how girls and boys are treated: 'A boy can do as many stupid things as a girl, I don't see what the difference is. And so I won't do the same thing as my parents, that's for sure!' By the same token, she also rejects a number of established conjugal roles characteristic of working-class households of her parents' generation. She especially dreads seeing Jean-Marc repeat a version of the childrearing model he grew up with, consisting mainly of intimidation. Jean-Marc is fully aware of this and mentions Cécile's fear of seeing him 'take the same turn' as his own father when he was a child, in whose presence, he explained, 'you mustn't move, you knew [it] at a glance'. Cécile requires that she be able to make her disagreement known in the home and intervene to change her spouse's attitude. Although she has noticed that he has many personality traits in common with his father, she intends to prevent him from being 'very authoritarian' with their son. This is a major issue in the household, to the point that Cécile exclaimed once in an interview, 'It's almost couples therapy, what we're doing!'

Other than this tension over how to raise children, Cécile would also like to tear herself away from certain social factors that could be passed along. She is particularly concerned that their son not have the same difficulties in school that her husband had when he was young. Jean-Marc left school at 16 and managed to earn a CAP in automotive bodywork after two years of training, but he had been oriented to this field by default and did not enjoy working in the sector.[1] As he put it himself, 'I hope [my son] won't have a school career like mine'. Since Luc was starting nursery school the year after our interviews took place, they were both a little apprehensive, dreading being 'summoned' by the teacher if their child does not 'keep his nose clean'. Cécile mainly expects her son to put a good effort into his education and school – 'he can do what he wants but he's got to work hard'. She says she is proud of having pursued her education through a vocational *lycée* rather than through apprenticeship – 'I was really in school for three years', and she went on to mention that she had maintained good relations with her old teachers, who invite her to sit on the entrance board for the vocational *baccalauréat* in hairdressing every year. This pride, combined with educational attainments higher than those of her husband, explains why she can't see herself as a stay-at-home mother. On the contrary, time seemed to drag on while she was on maternity leave and she cites an 'essential' need to work outside the home, 'to see people', by which she means contact with the clientele of the salon where she works. She describes her occupation as a calling – 'I was a pain for my parents since I was six, saying "I want to be a hairdresser"' – and says she also likes its 'artistic side'. Moreover, her full-time employment is determinant in their ability to achieve the status of homeowner. In describing household expenses, she explained that 'Everything is calculated with both of our incomes', thus confirming the importance of women's incomes in property acquisition in the stable working classes (Lambert 2015).

Cécile has distanced herself from some norms that are more traditional in working-class households of the previous generation. But rather than manifesting itself in tension, this distance re-enforces the Piliers' shared plan for a respectable life. Cécile intends to make their couple the site of a significant change in the division of domestic tasks. For although female employment is in continuity with their family legacies, since both of their mothers worked outside the home, Cécile's way of identifying herself through her job leads her to break with their parents' model, which exonerates men of the vast majority of domestic tasks. She sums up this division of roles with the following formulation: for the 'machos' (men of her father's generation), 'women take care of the house'. Jean-Marc's unusual working hours give him more time to do the shopping in the daytime, so she grants him the lead role in provisioning and meal preparation –'he's the cook!' She also insisted that he take care of their son when he was an infant after coming home from work. Jean-Marc himself emphasises that he 'contributes more' than his father, meaning that in addition to taking charge of certain tasks, his investment in the home is very different than his father's, since he devotes time to his son, especially by regularly taking him to the park to play.

Lastly, Cécile means to give an egalitarian image of their couple by insisting on their shared engagement in conserving household resources. She enjoys speaking of how their accounts are organised, because 'we share everything'. They each have their own savings account, plus a joint account. When she mentions transfers between accounts, she speaks in the first-person singular and does not consult her husband for his advice on account management. Although she is the one to manage the household accounts, in accordance with a 'traditional' role for women in the working classes, she systematically tries to manage transfers so that both savings accounts will have the same balance (Schwartz 2018). This way of pooling incomes, divvying up expenses and keeping savings equal, is very close to the domestic budget management norms taught by institutions counselling the working classes. Ana Perrin-Heredia (2011) describes these norms as following 'a principle of resource mutualisation' wherein household expenses are undifferentiated regardless of the gender of the earner or spender, which presupposes that household members do not see money as being gendered.

Advantages from help from the family

Although the couple claims with a certain measure of pride that they have grown away from their parents' conjugal practices insofar as the gendered division of roles is concerned, Cécile and Jean-Marc still maintain strong ties with their immediate families.

Their attachment to staying geographically close to their parents' homes attests to this fact. For example, Jean-Marc considers himself 'an expat' despite the fact that he lives less than an hour from his mother and sisters. The couple settled about 7 km from the town where Cécile grew up and works and where her parents still live. They are very present in the young family's everyday life.

The help of Cécile's father, now retired after a period of unemployment, seems determinant in the couple's successful residential path. In 2012, Cécile and Jean-Marc became owners of a small, old, three-room house of 80 m^2 requiring significant renovation (electricity, insulation, new finishing of walls, floors, and ceilings) with a 600-m^2 yard. The work was still underway three years after they moved in because they decided to do the work themselves in their free time to stay within the 120,000 euro budget advised by their real estate credit officer. One year, for example, Jean-Marc deprived himself of his usual two weeks of summer vacation. The effort required for all this work would not have been sustainable without the help of Cécile's father, however. She explained that they learned a lot of essential things 'with my dad, and the internet – we watch quite a few videos'. In addition to his advice, her father lends a hand for the big jobs, to the point that at the time of interviews, the couple had delayed their plans to lay a new wooden floor because Cécile's father had hurt himself slightly and could not help them for a little while. Cécile salvaged and repainted her maternal grandparents' kitchen cabinets while waiting to be able to buy 'a real coordinated kitchen'. They also turned to Cécile's parents when they needed to change both of their cars, because they had 'money set aside' and could help by allowing them to avoid taking out a bank loan and having to pay interest. Cécile does not see this arrangement as a form of direct financial assistance on the part of her parents, however. She is very clear that it is a loan, not a gift, since they pay down this debt to her parents every month. Lastly, Cécile's parents frequently look after Luc, a great help in balancing domestic and work constraints, especially given Jean-Marc's irregular and unusual working hours. A childminder cares for Luc during the week, but they call on Cécile's parents every Saturday, when she always works at the salon.

This multi-faceted help from the family allows Cécile and Jean-Marc to avoid turning to commercial services (such as child care on Saturdays and tradesmen to work on the house), but it is not seen as undermining the couple's virtue in the pursuit of their path of social ascension: 'We are proud to say that we did it ourselves', Cécile declares of the renovation, 'at least we didn't hire anyone, it's easy. [...] We've had so much dust!' There is also an ascetic morality of expense management alongside this family help that allows them to save money. Counter to a hedonistic vision of money, Cécile claims to be particularly attached to savings so they would be able to handle the unexpected and explains that they do not live beyond their means: 'When we can, we can; when we can't, we can't'. Cécile presents the far-sighted attitude she espouses as being related to the fact that they 'get by on their own', by which she means that they alone are responsible for their situation. Since both of them work, she says they 'don't have a right to anything' in terms of public assistance despite not having 'huge incomes'. Ultimately, not relying on outside help is a key component in their social position: they emphasise succeeding on their own as a source of social value.

Maintaining gender roles in the domestic space

This desire to rise socially co-exists with the partial continuity of a gendered distribution of roles in the couple's family. They are both in heavily gendered occupations – hairdressing and security – and each experiences different work-related constraints that have to be managed within the domestic sphere. Cécile works on Saturdays, when she entrusts Luc to her parents. Jean-Marc is in a different situation, because he often works nights and weekends in an irregular schedule that changes every month. Even if he proves to be available for ensuring certain tasks during his time off, particularly the shopping, cooking, and picking Luc up from the childminder on his days off, Cécile is the one in charge of many aspects of domestic management, mainly but not limited to budgeting and bank accounts. She also says that because she works near home, she uses her lunch break to go home and tidy up or do chores so she will not have to do them at night. The interview with both members of the couple made it clear that Cécile is the one who takes care of their son: she gets him up from his nap and is in charge of snack time, choosing the time and snack and feeding it to him. Their description of the time devoted to raising Luc also reveals that Cécile takes care of him most often inside the house, while Jean-Marc favours trips to the park. Ultimately Cécile does not challenge these differences in domestic roles, since what seems to matter the most to her is that Jean-Marc do more than their respective fathers did.

Another bond in their relationship seems to lie in Jean-Marc's engagement in advancing professionally, which re-enforces their efforts to pursue a path of social ascension. Although school was difficult for Jean-Marc, he proved to be motivated to obtain his first formal educational attainment attesting to his skill in the security sector. He took a six-week course for professional qualification as a security officer funded by the national employment office (Agence Nationale pour l'Emploi), which made it possible for him to set himself apart from his former co-workers without qualifications and be promoted to better positions. A few months before the interview, he 'went up a grade' and became leader of a team of 25. Although he has ambivalent feelings about this promotion – he would like 'to stay in contact with the team' and not 'change status' in the eyes of his co-workers even though he 'became the boss' – this change in jobs demonstrates his implication in an occupation that requires considerable availability given the variability of the working hours. In contrast, Cécile, who has worked in the same salon for 12 years, chose to favour her 'family life' when she had an opportunity to advance professionally a few years earlier. Her mother's parents were small-business owners who ran a bakery, and her grandfather had bequeathed a business space to her when she turned 24 so she could open her own salon as owner. Her parents supported her plans to set up her own business, and she went so far as to file a financial plan with the bank before she abandoned the project. She said she made this choice because 'I mostly wanted to have a baby, and that was my priority'. The importance of having a steady income was another barrier influencing her choice to give up on the project, as she mentioned how important the financial stability of being an employee was to their path to homeownership. The fact remains that the contrast is great with her husband, who manages to reconcile the role of father with investment in a career that comes with heavy constraints on his time.

Having to compromise between keeping a gendered distribution of tasks and the practical demands of managing help from the extended family (dropping Luc off at her parents' every Saturday, for example), Cécile finds herself in the midst of a family organisational system wherein the major demands mostly fall to her. 'My parents are a little intrusive', she conceded, explaining that they have gone on vacation all together but she does not want to do it again, to avoid having to keep certain hours or justify meal times. 'Sunday's the only day we are all together as a family', by which she means her, her husband, and their child, and she admits that they try to protect this day from her parents. Jean-Marc is the only one with a leisure activity outside the home, playing badminton once a week in a sport club. Cécile sometimes finds respite from her family obligations by setting aside time exclusively for her and Jean-Marc. She allows herself to ask her parents for more help, or hire a babysitter, so they can go to a restaurant together, because, as she says, 'it's important to be able to go out, just us two'. Cécile especially appreciates these evenings and cites 'the pleasure of being served, of not having to cook'.

Cécile tries to keep a distance from her parents, and she determinedly refuses to allow the male authoritarianism she attributes to the past to be reproduced in her household. Aspirations to social ascension are combined with refusal to continue operating in the same way as the previous generation, but without breaking family ties. On the contrary, the household's domestic arrangements rely on help from the family, and such help, both financial and organisational, is an essential resource in the working classes. The couple wants to maintain its independence, however, and confirms its engagement on the path to social respectability. 'It's a matter of pride to say we are getting by on our own', Cécile declared, making the observation that they do not rely on social assistance or direct financial assistance from their families. Additionally, the couple takes care to arrange for time together, without their extended family, to go out to eat. This management of leisure activities attests to how engaged they are in freeing themselves from the 'traditional' conjugal model: if their working-class backgrounds explain their rather sharp division of domestic roles, the desire to preserve a space for themselves as a couple is a telling reflection of the aspiration (particularly strong in Cécile) of having some time free of domestic constraints.

Cécile thus seems to be at the head of a successful enterprise: happy with the domestic organisation that she put in place since the birth of their son, she pursues their shared engagement in home renovation and mentions her desire for a second child. To do all that, however, she had to put her plans to open her own salon on hold, the only project that was hers alone. Indeed, since she is already shouldering the major share of the family's plans for social advancement, she doesn't think starting her own business is possible.

Note

1 For an explanation of the French educational system, see the Appendix.

References

Lambert, Anne. 2015. *'Tous propriétaires!' L'envers du décor pavillonnaire*. Paris: Seuil/Liber.

Perrin-Heredia, Ana. 2011. 'Faire les comptes: normes comptables, normes sociales.' *Genèses* 84: 69–92.

Schwartz, Olivier. 2018. 'Les femmes dans les classes populaires, entre permanence et rupture.' *Travail, genre et sociétés* 39: 121–138.

16

AN INTERLUDE OF EQUALITY

'Stéphanie is there with the children, she can manage the homework' – Nicolas and Stéphanie Fontaine

Muriel Letrait and Marjorie Tilleul

Nicolas and Stéphanie Fontaine have been together for 20 years. They have three sons, aged 10, 3, and 18 months. Stéphanie is currently on parental leave, which Nicolas really appreciates: 'Everyone's comfortable. It's so... well here, you see, I get home, and it's really nice'. They live in a small town of 3,500 inhabitants where they had a house built while Stéphanie was pregnant with their first child. Since she has a post-secondary degree, she was able to get a middle-management position at Pôle Emploi, the national unemployment office, while Nicolas, who left school early with no formal qualifications, is a public-sector maintenance worker who left a career as a dance instructor after an injury. Since Stéphanie's job was far from home, he got there well before her in the evening, and for three years he took care of many domestic tasks and their first child until she got home. The situation changed when their second child was born, and now she is more present at home and performs the majority of domestic and parental tasks. This inversion of situations may well become permanent because after the birth of their third child, Stéphanie decided to extend her parental leave and took a course to become a childminder, with the idea that she could change careers to devote herself to her children and their education, much to Nicolas' relief.

A meeting thanks to a shared passion

Stéphanie has a much higher education and reached a much better professional position than Nicolas, but their social backgrounds are quite similar: both come from the stable fractions of the working classes strongly rooted in the civil service. Nicolas' father worked in a variety of low-skill jobs before ending up as a municipal dump truck driver, and his mother was a secretary in the public

DOI: 10.4324/9781003330073-18

school system. Both of Stéphanie's parents ended up as local-level civil servants. Her father was a tradesman for several years before becoming head of municipal technical services, and her mother, who was a housewife when Stéphanie was a child, was hired as a cleaning woman in a town hall and later moved into an administrative job. Nicolas had a sister, now deceased, who was a schoolteacher, and Stéphanie has a brother who is a bus driver.

They met through a common passion for acrobatic swing dance. They were both living in the outskirts of Paris, where they grew up. Nicolas was 21 and Stéphanie was 18. They both practiced acrobatic swing intensively and gave classes every night and weekend. Nicolas was invested in the activity professionally, while Stéphanie only did it for fun.

Nicolas threw himself into dance when he was in *sixième* (just starting secondary school), practicing six hours a day because he loved it and was hoping to make a career out of it since he had difficulty at school.[1] This choice led him to quit school at 16, since the long hours spent practicing every week had put him even further behind. When they first started seeing each other, Stéphanie was still in *lycée* and Nicolas was supplementing his work as a dance instructor with subsistence jobs: 'I could just as well work as a trash collector as a waiter, as anything'. Thanks to his athletic performances and the comfortable income they earned him, his situation was somewhat better than Stéphanie's at the time. Comparing him to other teachers, she vaunted his skill: 'Practically the only one who could show us how to do the moves was Nicolas'. However, having failed the examination that would have allowed him to become a state-accredited instructor, Nicolas could not find a way to enjoy institutional recognition for his work. Six years after they met, his situation stabilised when he was hired by the Ile de France region as a contractual maintenance technician, with working hours allowing him to continuing giving classes in the evening and during vacations.

Stéphanie began dancing later, when she was 15. She made rapid progress and at 18 was confided with introductory classes, which were unpaid but let her take other classes for free. Unlike Nicolas, she did well in school and said she 'loved school, so it went really well'. She stated that she would have liked to become a *lycée* teacher or university professor, but was dissuaded from engaging in lengthy studies for financial reasons. After earning a *baccalauréat* in Economic and Social Sciences, she enrolled in university and earned a DEUG in Economics and Business Management while also working as a salesperson in a clothing store and giving dance classes nights and weekends. After getting her DEUG she found a subsidised job at Pôle Emploi and then, after being hired in a management position on an open-ended employment contract, she took a correspondence course to obtain a *licence* in Economics and Management.

For a few years, the couple enjoyed a combined income that placed them closer to the stable middle classes than the working classes, and they experienced upward social mobility thanks to Nicolas's two incomes and Stéphanie's job.

Fleeing the 'rotten banlieue' but moving farther from work

They moved in together when Stéphanie started working at Pôle Emploi and lived in the public housing apartment of her grandfather, who had recently died. They had to move out two years later, around the time of their marriage, because the lease in his name expired, so they rented a privately owned apartment where they stayed for three years. Stéphanie has bad memories of this apartment, which she described as 'almost insalubrious' because it was damp and hard to heat. At the time their lives revolved entirely around their shared passion, dancing, to which they devoted all their evenings and weekends. When they learned they were expecting their first child, they decided to buy their own home and move. Stéphanie stopped teaching dancing at this time. After a long search for housing and constrained by their limited financial resources, they ultimately decided have a house built in a small town 80 km from Paris: 'In budgetary terms, we couldn't stay close to Paris while being in a nice neighbourhood', Stéphanie explained, adding that she did not want their child to grow up as she did, in what she called 'the rotten *banlieue*'.[2] Given their respective workplaces, they determined they would not go farther than that.

Their desire for a large family manifested itself upon acquisition of this custom-built house: they had the possibility of having large rooms, but they preferred several small rooms to be able to house several children. They chose the town so that their children could have happy childhoods there and not be bored as teenagers. Remembering her boredom as a teenager in her parents' house in a rural village in 'the middle of nowhere', Stéphanie told her husband: 'I'd really like to build in the country because I think it's better for kids, but in a setting where you can still find everything for children later. Not little like so, but teens'. They have a very pleasant home, but it has the drawback of being an hour and a half from Stéphanie's job, and so she suffered from not being present enough for their first son as a baby:

> Actually, I came home… The morning I'd get him up, I'd drop him off at day care, I'd come home at night to give him his bottle and put him to bed. So you see, it's true that it was really, it was… I really missed not being able to do more than that.

When their child started school, their work constraints – due to Stéphanie's long commute and Nicolas' long work days, starting one job early in the morning and giving dance classes every night – prompted them to opt for a private school because it was 'the only one to offer child care before and after school'. Although this decision consequentially meant additional expenses, they had few regrets because of the rumours circulating about the public school in town: 'Let's just say that it wasn't run well'. In order to be able to spend one day a week with her son, Stéphanie decided to put all her working hours into four days a week to have Wednesday off. This choice resulted in her working very long days, since she had to leave home at six in the morning and returned at eight at night, and she increased her investment in family and home on Wednesdays.

Toward greater equality?

When their son was four, Nicolas broke a heel and had to stop teaching for several months. When he had recovered his employer announced that he did not want to rehire him and was keeping his replacement, who was cheaper. Like other dancers from working-class backgrounds who were able to move socially upward through dancing while being aware of the precarity of their new position because they are at the mercy of physical injury (Sorignet 2016), Nicolas had to abandon his career and found himself with only his job as a maintenance worker for the region. He was able to get a position closer to home and obtained permanent status after passing a public service examination. Despite the stability offered by the protective status of his new job, the loss of his job as dance instructor made their monthly income drop by about 1,000 euros a month. During this period, he refocused on his family and spent more time caring for their son, becoming much more present than Stéphanie at home.

While Stéphanie was never home before eight, Nicolas started work very early in the morning and came home around four in the afternoon, which favoured his investment in family and domestic life and the abandonment of a 'traditional' model of household task distribution in the couple during this period. He took responsibility for a large share of the housekeeping and shopping and looked after their son until his wife came home from work. Stéphanie nonetheless continued to manage administrative business and doctors' appointments for their son. She seems to have suffered from being less close to their son than Nicolas at the time: 'I mean, he really had a special relationship with Nicolas, who was with him much more often, I admit'.

The couple's return to a more traditional arrangement

This period of Nicolas making the most significant contribution to domestic tasks lasted three years, because when their eldest was seven they had a second child, after trying for some time. Even before Stéphanie became pregnant they had decided that she would stop working for a few years if they were to have another, so she could make the most of his or her childhood: 'I said no, I don't want that, I did everything to not go through that again, because I wanted to be able to enjoy my children'.

It might seem surprising that Stéphanie was the one to interrupt employment when she was the one with a management job and was much better paid than her husband. This situation is far from unusual, however, since it is quite rare for men to take parental leave. Only one in 100 fathers with a child of three or younger does so, as compared to one woman in four (Boyer, Nicolas, and Robert 2013), despite the fact that since the early 2000s there are more couples in which the woman has a higher education than her male partner than the reverse (Bouchet-Valat 2014). Women whose employment situations are better than their partners' are less likely to alter their career paths after the birth of a second child: while one in four women in this situation change careers after a second baby, only one in two women with qualifications equivalent to or lower than her husband's does so. But even in this scenario, 'the birth of children often leads to an adjustment in women's engagements and plans, in favour of the family and to the detriment of the professional sphere' (Guichard-Claudic, Testenoire, and Trancart, 2009). One other thing might have encouraged Stéphanie to take this parental leave: she does not like her working conditions or the atmosphere in her department at work. As a supervisor at Pôle Emploi, she disagrees with upper management's way of doing things: 'as soon as something goes wrong, they want to blame someone, and that's not at all my style'.

Since she suffered and felt guilty because she did not see enough of her older son when he was a little, Stéphanie enjoyed being able to make the most of the second and having more time for him. She has the feeling that she is making up for lost time:

> It's going to be four years now that I can be here for him. May seem like nothing, I missed his early childhood but not the rest. So I got him back in CE1 [*age 7–8*], you see, which still let me make up what I might have missed and what he might have missed, I think.

She also mentioned financial reasons as a justification for this parental leave, since their respective working hours would have obliged them to spend 8–900 euros on childcare if they had hired a childminder.

After having contributed significantly to housework and care for their older son, Nicolas cut back his participation because Stéphanie is at home more than he is, thanks to her parental leave. She said that in their couple, 'tasks are shared but without knowing that you're the one that'll do this, you're the one that'll do that, basically. It's whoever's there that does it, and does it when it needs to be done'. Nicolas' employer also contributed to this return to more traditional gender roles by changing his working hours. Nicolas was used to starting early in the morning and having his afternoons free, but other hours were imposed on him with the excuse that his wife was at home. He put it this way:

> And then the other twit shows up: "oh, well, presto, you're wife's there, come on, blah blah blah… We're gonna put you in the afternoon". But that doesn't work for me because for me, finishing at six, seven at night, that… I basically can't do anything at home anymore.

Nicolas currently works Monday and Tuesday 9:30–6:00, Wednesday 6:30–5:00, and Thursday and Friday 6:30–2:00.

Stéphanie had planned to resume work at the Pôle Emploi at the end of her parental leave, but she found herself pregnant again. Although it was unplanned, the couple greeted this third child joyfully – Nicolas calls it 'the miracle baby' and Stéphanie declares that they are 'overjoyed' to have their three children. Stéphanie's gynaecologist was adamant that she not take any chances with her third pregnancy, so she prescribed sick leave to start just when she was to resume work. At the end of this pregnancy, Stéphanie did not intend to return to the pace she had when her eldest son was a baby, and childcare for two pre-schoolers is even more complicated and costly, so she decided to take another parental leave. During the leave she earned a CAP in Early Childhood Development and passed the examination to be a nursery school classroom assistant (ATSEM). Stéphanie was not afraid to go back to school while caring for two pre-school-aged children. She is full of energy and has always mixed employment and studies. Having worked while in school and often studied while she was working, she accumulated qualifications and working experience. Stéphanie decided to change careers and start training to become a child-minder, favouring her family life over her career. This desire to shift her focus to her children and family is also explained by a sad situation in the family, since Nicolas had lost his mother, sister, and father over the previous ten years. After all this mourning, the couple's priorities have shifted to enjoying the present and the family. All of their decisions seem to be guided by a concern with making their children happy and celebrating family life, even though they still have financial limitations because of the drop in income since Nicolas' accident and Stéphanie's parental leaves.

Meals are planned 'according to what the children like' – especially the picky eldest – although Stéphanie acknowledges that sometimes 'it depresses me to not be able to eat other things'. Unlike the working-class women that take their nourishing role very seriously and prefer that their children eat at home to be sure that they are eating balanced meals (Stettinger 2018), Stéphanie explains that her school-age children come home for lunch because she thinks that it is 'nicer' for them. But like these other mothers, she is attached to respecting her children's tastes. During her pre-school assistant training she did an internship in a school where she was able to see that mealtimes were more rigorous than at her house:

> I worked there so I know, it's relatively good anyway, it's balanced. But still, they watch over them a fair bit – no, I think that they might sometimes even eat better at the cafeteria. Because they'd make less of a fuss [there], I think. At home they know we'll cave in, that we're more mellow.

Television programmes are also chosen according to the eldest son's tastes. Nights that are not school nights they watch all-ages shows that he likes, such as *Koh Lanta* (a reality show based in Fiji) and *The Voice*: 'he likes it a lot, so fine, let's just say that we half watch it, it just happens. We're with them, we're all together'. Their outings (walks in the country, bike rides, ice skating, swimming) are opportunities to 'get together with the children around something they really like'. The children also weigh on the choice of vacation destinations: despite their young age, the older two give their opinions and, according to Stéphanie, the family makes the decision 'collegially'.

Stéphanie's schedule revolves around the school schedule so she can devote herself to the children, housework, and household administrative obligations. She nonetheless insists that Nicolas not shirk at helping her when he can. In the morning, she tidies and cleans the house after bringing the older boys to school, takes care of the 18-month old, and then picks up the older two for lunch. After eating, she takes the ten-year old to the neighbour, who brings him back to school. While the younger two are napping in the afternoon, she does the laundry, ironing, and administrative tasks and sometimes orders groceries online from a supermarket on Nicolas' route, so he can pick them up in the evening on his way home.

An unequal investment in the children's educations

At 4:30 in the afternoon she brings the younger children along when she picks up the eldest from school, except on the two days a week that Nicolas leaves work earlier and can help her out and take care of them after their snack. The other days Stéphanie tries to arrange it so they play together so that she can devote herself to supervising the homework of their ten-year-old, who does not care much for school and is not very independent. Before she went on parental leave, the homework help came from Nicolas, who has very unpleasant memories of this time, perhaps because it brought up bad childhood memories. The fact that Stéphanie can ensure this task moreover seems to be the main reason he appreciates her parental leave. Watching over his son while he did his homework was a burden; he thinks that he is less patient than she is, and since he cut his education so short he probably also feels less able:

> No question I wouldn't have the same patience. When I was doing his homework with him at the beginning, well, the kid blubbered all the time… I can't afford to spend two hours doing homework, he's not independent enough to do that, you see? Because phew, gotta stay calm. Stéphanie's got patience, even if sometimes she snaps, but I swear, if you saw… No, no, if I could, yeah, Stéphanie, I'd really have liked her to not work.

Nicolas puts his teenage years in good light by claiming that he enjoyed youth more than Stéphanie and the interviewer, who pursued post-secondary studies and are closer to the middle and upper classes than he is. He somewhat condescendingly compares their respective youths to his own, as attests his use of the word 'robotic' to speak of students that conform to the scholastic norm:

> You, you were a little… well, a normal person is rather robotic, I mean, you get up in the morning, bam, school; bam, homework, check! You see, it's really… It's really squared away, what you've got. But from another perspective, did you really make the most of it? Maybe in what follows that'll help you out, that's… that's for sure, but I think that as for me, what I had in terms of experience, I'd say I experienced other things.

Nicolas presents a rather positive version of his path; he 'really made the most of it' and found work afterward.

> It's what I did, y'know, but there it is, I don't pay much attention to what I do, but anyway, today, I've got a job, I had a different experience than normal people, you see what I mean? That's it.

The idea of enjoying one's youth before giving oneself over to heavy work evokes the observations of Richard Hoggart (1957), with the difference that Nicolas realises the importance of succeeding in school.

Stéphanie may be patient and perseverant, but homework time is an ordeal for her as well:

> For four years I fight with him every day, every day, every day to do his homework, to push him, so he won't be held back, to not… to bring him to the speech therapist, to bring him to the shrink, to… anyway, here and there, it never stops.

She even sometimes asks Nicolas to take a turn so she can 'breathe' a little.

Since she started caring for the children full-time, Stéphanie has few personal pastimes. She loves mysteries and says she manages to find only a few minutes to read in the evening, while showering (by wedging her book in the medicine cabinet), while getting dressed, and over breakfast twice a week. This is possible because Nicolas takes care of the children before work on the days that he starts at 9:30 and brings her breakfast in the bedroom so she can read while she eats. Stéphanie also sometimes goes for coffee at a neighbour's house after taking the children to school in the morning, but she also presents this as a favour to her youngest child, so that he can have contact with children other than his brothers, since the neighbour is a childminder. Stéphanie feels close to this neighbour, who also has a post-secondary education. Far from being outliers, both of these women are part of a generation where half of all child-minders possess a *baccalauréat* (Devetter 2012). Ultimately Stéphanie has more affinity with her than with the other mothers at the school, who did not pursue educations, and says she finds it pleasant 'to have conversations where the level is a little higher'.

Stéphanie's parental leave brought them back to a system similar to that of their first years living together, with a traditional gendered arrangement of domestic roles. Stéphanie takes care of the house and children, and Nicolas presents himself as being the sole provider of income for the household, saying he currently earns 1,600 euros a month while Stéphanie 'earns nothing'. Stéphanie describes things differently: 'So, since I'm here at home, [...] I don't have full pay', but she adds up the various benefits she receives for parental leave and family benefits and concludes that 'for me, the fact of being at home with the children, I have roughly 800 euros coming in'. Household revenue has dropped considerably without Stéphanie's income, a drop in financial resources that was temporarily balanced by the inheritance Nicolas received following the deaths of his parents and sister. They are now digging into their savings and have to pay attention to all their expenditures, from grocery shopping, vacations, outings, and leisure activities to the children's extracurricular activities.

Nicolas's holidays do not always fall at the same time as school holidays, so he takes advantage of them to increase household income by doing renovation work while Stéphanie looks after the house and children alone. 'Whenever I'm on holiday, well, I work at someone's place or... I don't do anything at home, Stéphanie does everything inside and me, I work outside'. The extra income from this work thus allows them to go on holiday with the children.

The excessive cost of a professional career

The fact that Stéphanie's mother was at home when she was a child may also be a factor, as Stéphanie could have been influenced by this model of the family. As we saw, although Nicolas accepted responsibility for most of the housework and does not resist helping her out when he is home, Nicolas seems to prefer that she stay home. Research has already highlighted the fact that some working-class men are open to doing domestic tasks, at least from time to time and in their partner's absence (Cartier, Letrait, and Sorin 2018). Nicolas supervised their son's homework during the few years of their 'equality interlude' when Stéphanie's schedule was heavier than Nicolas', but was very relieved when Stéphanie took over, finding her more skilled for the role than he. Stéphanie's greater success in school allowed her to obtain a better job than Nicolas, but it is also why he values her return to the home. The main reason that Nicolas cites for this does not correspond to a traditional working-class perception of gender roles – it is because of her scholastic skills, not because she is a woman, that she should be more present at home. For all that, Stéphanie does not experience her new situation as downclassing. To the contrary, owning their own house lets her think of them as upwardly mobile: 'So in a way we're still relatively proud of what we've been able to create, if only to have a house for the children, you see? I mean, we started with nothing. We were both in council estates'. Nicolas and Stéphanie's story thus resonates with a finding of Claudine Attias-Donfut and François Charles Wolff (2001): 'Being a homeowner is an important element in subjective mobility, just like the success of family life'.

Owning a house and raising children in a pleasant environment, quite different from the council estates of their own childhoods, was indeed a priority. But their financial means obliged them to live in a small town far from their jobs, especially Stéphanie's. Since the town is small, it is unlikely that Stéphanie could find a job appropriate for her qualifications. The cost of a professional career has proven too high for her. The distance between home and work makes it especially difficult to reconcile her professional life with her family life.

In this sense, even if it should not be read solely in terms of renunciation and a return to traditional sex roles, this case illustrates how difficult it is for working-class women to have a career. Doing well in school and obtaining a good professional position may not be enough. Despite her degrees, Stéphanie has not managed to have a career. She pays dearly for the couple's obligation to buy a house so far away from their respective workplaces.

Notes

1 For an explanation of the French educational system, see the Appendix.
2 The *banlieue* is the word given to areas on the outskirts of cities dominated by council estates, often associated with poverty and hooliganism. We chose to leave it in French rather than translate it as 'suburb', which has a very different socio-economic connotation.

References

Attias-Donfut, Claudine, and François-Charles Wolff. 2001. 'La dimension subjective de la mobilité sociale.' *Population* 56-6: 919–958.

Bouchet-Valat, Milan. 2014. 'Les évolutions de l'homogamie de diplôme, de classe et d'origine sociales en France (1969–2011) : ouverture d'ensemble, repli des élites.' *Revue française de sociologie* 55: 459–505.

Boyer, Danielle, Muriel Nicolas, and Marie-Josée Robert. 2013. 'Les pères bénéficiaires du complément de libre choix d'activité.' *l'e-ssentiel* (CNAF):131.

Cartier, Marie, Muriel Letrait, and Matéo Sorin. 2018. 'Travail domestique: des classes populaires conservatrices?' *Travail, genre et sociétés* 39: 63–81.

Devetter, François-Xavier. 2012. 'Qualité de l'emploi et des conditions de travail des professionnel-le-s de la petite enfance.' *Politiques sociales et familiales* 109: 9–22.

Guichard-Claudic, Armelle Testenoire, and Danièle Trancart. 2009. 'Distances et proximités conjugales en situation d'homogamie et d'hétérogamie.' In *Entre famille et travail*, edited by Ariane Pailhé and Anne Solaz, 187–207. Paris: La Découverte.

Hoggart, Richard. 1957. *Aspects of Working Class Life*. London: Chatto and Windus.

Sorignet, Pierre-Emmanuel. 2016. '"Si j'arrête de danser, je perds tout". Penser les mobilités sociales au regard de la vocation d'artiste chorégraphique.' *Politix* 114: 121–148.

Stettinger, Vanessa. 2018. 'Mère "je fais tout". Des pratiques éducatives populaires en tension.' *Travail, genre et sociétés* 39: 83–99.

17

KEEPING THE CONJUGAL PEACE

A compensatory domestic equality – Cécilia and Éric Dufar

Olivier Masclet

When asked about sharing housework with her husband, Cécilia Dufar, a 40-year-old supermarket cashier, replied, 'I can't complain'. She presents her husband Éric, age 41 and caretaker of the town library, as a 'man who's active around the house'. 'He does lots of things', she said, citing cooking, cleaning, and home improvement. 'If you ask him for something, he does it, he's present, no-one can say he's lazy', she added. Éric's everyday involvement emerges strongly in interviews with the couple. Since their daughter Louise, age 10, stopped eating lunch at the school cafeteria, he took charge of preparing her lunch and eating with her at home daily. Every day he also cooks dinner and tidies the kitchen. He regularly mops, cleans the toilets, and hangs the laundry when Cécilia cannot take care of it herself. Every week he does the shopping at the Leclerc shopping centre. He is also the one who takes care of maintenance and repairs for their two cars. Not only does he do his share of household tasks, but many are traditionally feminine chores that are rarely interchangeable between men and women (Zarca 1990, Brousse 2015), like mopping and handling relations with the school, a responsibility he ensures by attending parent–teacher meetings, usually alone and sometimes with his wife.

Although the equality between them is far from perfect – Cécilia does more chores than Éric and she carries a heavier mental load – it is palpable enough to singularise them as an exception to the traditional masculine and feminine models fating men and women to opposing and non-interchangeable gender roles. Interestingly, Éric and Cécilia's educations and jobs are not ones that bring them into contact with the middle classes, which would increase the likelihood of their encountering other, less divided gender models (although such models hardly guarantee of equality in housekeeping: Singly 2007). Both possess low-level educational attainments, and although they hold steady jobs,

DOI: 10.4324/9781003330073-19

both work as unskilled or low-skilled executant employees, a category that statistical studies always show to have more prominent domestic inequalities relative to higher-skilled social spheres (Cartier, Letrait, and Sorin 2018). How, then, to explain this greater equality in the Dufars?

Several elements seem to help answer this question. The first is rooted in Cécilia's personal history and the history of their relationship. Her socialisation led her to reproduce the model of the housewife, while certain challenges in their conjugal relationship made her want to emancipate herself from it. This ambivalence explains the importance she accords to daily household tasks as much as her refusal to be 'the maid'. The second element concerns their occupational situations. Although they both hold unskilled service jobs, their conditions have increasingly diverged. While Éric manages to find certain gratifications in his work, the same cannot be said for Cécilia, who feels belittled by her condition as subaltern worker. She expresses on the domestic scene complaints originating in the working scene and comes up with ways to put it symbolically right by buying a lot of clothing and feeding her taste for fashion and celebrities with magazines and television. Éric's heightened contribution thus appears to be a compensatory effort, since he is happy with the balance he has found at work, while she expresses growing personal dissatisfaction as well as a desire for a change of scene.

A stable working-class household

Éric has a BEP in plumbing and heating. He described how his schooling was disrupted by the death of his father, an ailing alcoholic, when he was 12. He repeated the school year and chose to orient his studies towards plumbing, like one of his friends. His father had worked at the counter of the PTT (Postes, Télégraphes et Téléphones; the public postal, telegraph, and telephone service), and Éric does not know how far his education had gone. His mother, who is now retired, started working in a garment factory at age 14 and stopped to be a housewife when she got married. Éric grew up in the house his parents bought in a suburb of the regional capital where he lives today. His father's death upset the family balance. His mother supplemented his pension by minding children in her home then found a job as cafeteria worker for the city.

Just like his elder brother, a roofer by training who became a motorcycle salesman, he began his working life in construction, although he would have preferred to join an élite police unit like the BRI (Brigade de Recherche et d'Intervention, Research and Intervention Brigade) or GIGN (Groupe d'Intervention de la Gendarmerie Nationale; National Gendarmerie Intervention Group). The first time he 'went up to Paris' was to do his mandatory military service 'with the CRS' (Compagnie Républicaine de Sécurité, Security Company of the Republic). Assigned to the highway brigade, he felt like he was in his element: 'the top speed, the sport...' He decided, however, to return to his hometown in west-central France rather than try for a military career in greater Paris, where he did not know anyone. For over five years he held a variety of construction jobs, always as a temporary worker. He sums up his life at the time in three words: 'work, sport, party'. He played basketball three times a week and ran daily to train for marathons. He went to nightclubs every Saturday night, and that is how he met Cécilia, through a basketball team-mate ('"You know this girl? She's my sister" – She's cute – that's it'). Aged 26 at the time, he applied for a job posted by the city, in hopes of landing a steady and 'more mellow' job. He wanted to escape the temp jobs that he describes as physically wearing ('the jackhammer all day, at the end your whole body is shaking'), demanding very long hours ('we might begin at seven, end at eight at night, sometimes Saturday, too… that's temping, you're tied up'), and of poor quality ('we did shitty work'). He also had hopes of 'developing' his employment conditions. Hired as a municipal agent, he was first assigned to the technical service as a cleaning and maintenance worker and then passed an internal competitive examination to climb the ranks (technical deputy, then skilled technical deputy). He spent nearly nine years in the technical service, bad years that Éric described as troubled by tense relations with older workers. As an athletic young man refusing to define himself through the traditional practices of his peers (hunting, drinking, an established lifestyle), the tensions made it difficult for him to fit into the shop ('it was fine with me, they made me do things that you had to go out for'). One co-worker with whom he got along fairly well (he was also athletic) encouraged him to apply for a new position as caretaker of the library, and he got the job in 2008. It was attractive for its many benefits: it came with housing, irregular hours allowing him to free up personal time, a locally prestigious cultural facility as workplace, no boss on his back.

Cécilia is year younger than Éric. Her parents were immigrants from Portugal, her father a skilled worker and her mother an unskilled worker in the same small factory. In an interview, Cécilia describes herself as a borderline student who 'barely barely' passed. Today, she says that she would have been better off going to a vocational high school like her friends, rather than going to the university-track generalist *lycée*.[1] For her parents, however, there was no question that she would go as far as the *baccalauréat* and follow in the footsteps of their oldest son. He passed the *baccalauréat* on the second try and then passed the competitive examinations to become an auxiliary and then full nurse. Cécilia says that he earns a good living today as an independent nurse. 'He succeeded', she said, while she describes herself as 'the black sheep'. Conflict with her parents began to fester in her adolescence, and Cécilia quit school in her first year of *lycée*, around the age of 16.

For ten years she went through a string of unskilled short-term jobs that included cashier, housekeeper, receptionist, and waitress. She tried to escape this insecurity by going for a BEP in secretarial work. She got it when she was 25, but her letters applying for secretarial jobs went unanswered. She started temping at an Intermarché, a grocery chain, and after a year, they offered her a permanent position: 'I got my first open-ended employment contract when I was thirty years old', she said, her voice revealing her distress that it took so long. It was a part-time contract for thirty hours a week. After another year she got a full-time contract that let her coordinate her hours with Éric's. She does not work on Wednesdays and begins and ends her workdays at set times, either on the morning shift (9:15–3:15) or the afternoon shift (2–8). In exchange for this regularity, she agrees to work every Saturday afternoon (from 2 to 8).

So, nearly ten years after they got together, this is how Éric and Cécilia finally managed to acquire stable employment situations. As caretaker Éric earns 1,470 euros a month plus an annual bonus of 1,200 euros. Cécilia's income is close to 900 euros a month, and she gets a 13th-month bonus. They nonetheless feel that they 'live well' and get by without too much difficulty, largely thanks to the fringe benefits of having employer-provided housing: they pay neither rent nor utilities (water, gas, electricity) and can thus devote a larger share of their income to consumption and leisure than many other workers and employees like them, with few or no formal qualifications.

To stop being an 'obsessively tidy' woman

It is out of the question that they call upon the domestic services of someone else. Cécilia explained that housework does not bother her. She thus devotes a good part of her Wednesdays, when she does not work, as well as Sundays and vacations, to indoor chores. 'I like to do it', she declared, 'I like to empty the cupboards, sort, organise'. She does it at her pace, often while listening to music channels on the television. She does 'her' housecleaning more extensively on Sundays than other days, vacuuming, cleaning the windows, scrubbing the bathroom, ironing and changing the sheets,

> because on other days, I work, I don't want to… If it's really dirty I'll give it a spray of [*cleaning product*], sure, but… I don't want to do it every day. I don't want to, I'm tired, I wouldn't have the patience to do it every day, quote-unquote "like my mother". But on Sundays it doesn't bother me, no, I like it when everything's all clean.

This housekeeping activity is just one aspect of Cécilia's domestic work, since the everyday management of people and things also falls to her. She manages household finances, keeps an eye on Louise's school affairs, takes care of paperwork, and writes important letters. For example, when Éric learned that a caretaker job had become available, he immediately asked for Cécilia's help: 'Holy shit! I go home, I say, "Cécilia" – because Cécilia knows how to write really well, she has pretty writing and all, I said "Grab a piece of paper right now, write my letter here and now!"' She is also the one to prepare the weekly shopping list and make appointments with doctors or teachers, even though Éric usually accompanies their daughter alone. When all is said and done Cécilia performs more tasks than Éric and emerges as 'the family secretary' (Siblot 2006), with all that presupposes in terms of nearly constant attention to household needs.

Cécilia makes the best of her larger share of domestic work, heavier in quantity as well as responsibility, and does not demand that Éric do as much as she does, partly because she thinks that she is in many ways more meticulous than he ('He does the laundry when I ask him to, but it's not really his thing'). Her 'taste for doing', inherited through the gestural socialisation provided by her mother, moreover explains why she does not see the imbalanced distribution of household and parental tasks as a problem. She does not demand behaviour traditionally expected of women from her husband, but she could not abide it if he 'didn't help out with anything' or boxed her into the dominated identity of wife at the service of the household by adopting a passive everyday behaviour.

Cécilia has the kind of ambivalence that many daughters manifest towards their mothers where housework is concerned. They may reproduce some of their mother's behaviours while at the same time deeming them negative. Almost despite themselves, and despite their desire to free themselves from the maternal model, they repeat the habits they saw at home as children (Kaufmann 1997). Cécilia describes her own mother as an 'obsessively tidy' woman who spent long hours cleaning and re-cleaning the house, thus paradoxically reigning over 'her' home as both 'maid' and 'boss' of the place and its occupants. She explained that she suffered from her mother's authoritarian behaviour, which she blames for her failure at school and somewhat hasty departure from the family home: aged 25 and unemployed for two years, she pressured Éric to get an apartment with her so she could escape her mother.

She found herself trapped in the house in turn, however. When she speaks of herself in the first years as a couple, she uses the same words she used to describe her mother: 'cleaning, cleaning, cleaning'. Without a job, she spent her time doing housework, hiding in it to compensate for her isolation and difficulties in making an independent life, or at least one less tied to her partner:

> I was unemployed, and yeah, I'd wait for him. He'd go to work, I'd wait for him; he'd go work out, I'd wait for him; we only went out with his friends, you see... It's really destructive, that kind of thing. I became obsessive, but that came from my mother because she, she'd sweep, she'd vacuum, and she'd mop every day, and I became that way, y'know, which is, well, kind of stupid.

Her return to work was the achievement of her aspiration to not end up a housewife. Her mother had stopped working at the birth of her first child, devoting herself to ten years of life in the home that she endured with difficulty.

Cécilia described her mother as depressed and mean, pitting father and children all against each other. Cécilia was hired as a cashier shortly after the birth of Louise, and she refused to be tied to motherhood, despite her mother's pressure to take care of her child full time. When six-month-old Louise was hospitalised for two days, Cécilia said her mother told her, '"Your daughter could have died but you preferred going to work!" The guilt she dumped on me… it was horrible, horrible!' She arranged things with Éric so she could keep the job and managed to obtain an open-ended contract.

A year after Louise was born, they separated. This challenge forged new dispositions in Cécilia: she refused help from her parents, found the strength to get an apartment in her own name, and discovered that she knew how to get by with a child on her own. The break-up helped her to gain independence. When Éric came to her a few months later wanting to give their relationship another try, she accepted, but the relationship would not be the same. Once she had been forced to assert herself, she says she 'got power over him':

CÉCILIA: Bit by bit we rebuilt our life. I was doing fine at my place and then, he came back… Fine, we still loved each other. I told him, 'I would really like to try again, but it's my place, you come to my place, it's not your place, it's mine' […].

OLIVIER: But what did you want him to understand when you told him that, 'OK, you come back, but it's "my place"'?

CÉCILIA: I wanted him to understand that I'm the one taking the upper hand. He'd screwed me over, completely. At first I thought I couldn't live alone, without him, with a baby in my arms. He really screwed me over and I wanted him to understand that I'd taken the upper hand, that I was able to get by without him and that now I was the one who'd decide and that it was my place and that, y'know, I'd get power over him. Because, you see, I'd always been in his shadow. When we were together I relied a lot on him, and I was the maid, the obsessively tidy one. And so when you get dumped like that, overnight, with a baby, you don't know where you are anymore… There were some really hard times, seriously hard.

Cécilia still has high standards for the upkeep of 'her' interior today. She cannot stand clothes lying around, dusting that needs to be done, disorder and uncleanliness that interfere in the home. The difference is that she now 'runs' the housework by taking advantage of her partner's participation. Even if they now live in an apartment that comes with Eric's job and no longer at Cécilia's place, she more or less explicitly assigns him chores that he performs without balking. On Fridays, he does the shopping, scrupulously respecting the list. He takes pictures of Cécilia's toiletries to avoid making mistakes, and when he cannot find them, he shows the picture to a supermarket employee rather than asking for women's products by name. On Saturdays, while Cécilia works, he vacuums, gives a quick mop, and cooks dinner, so when she comes home from the supermarket after 8 in the evening, the house is orderly. When it is not tidy, she chastises him. On Sundays, he takes part in the big cleaning when he comes back from his run. Although he very actively contributes every day and thinks that this is 'normal', he still sees housework as a feminine thing, to the point of still considering it as 'Cécilia's housework'.

Éric seems to appropriate this work by masculinising it. When he talks about it, it is always in a virile mode: he goes the shopping 'at full charge', shakes out the comforters and mattresses that are 'too heavy for Cécilia', scrubs the floors 'like a lunatic', and so on. In many ways, he manifests the 'moral for activity' described among industrial-era workers (Weber 1989, Schwartz 1990): he occasionally does 'side jobs' (he does plumbing 'under the table'), thinks little of passive activities like watching movies, using a computer, or reading a book ('I can't! I've gotta move!'), and does leisure activities outside of the home (weight training, basketball, and running twice a week). Their relationship history makes sense of his making the home into a new field for exercise: his return to Cécilia and the power she gained over him are both elements explaining his housekeeping good will. This history is also a factor in his efforts to compensate for the widening differences in their working conditions, as he says that he wants to 'relieve' her.

Jobs offering unequal potential for self-worth

Éric works full time while Cécilia's contract is for 30 hours a week, but the way they see it, the employment constraints are not the same: they are worse for Cécilia. She works six hours straight with only short breaks and comes home from work exhausted and demoralised. She works the multimedia department register and takes care of printing digital photographs. She does not complain about this position, which shelters her from the much greater noise and bustle of the grocery department on the ground floor. But despite the fact that she describes her position as a niche inside the store, she says she can no longer tolerate being cashier. Several times in our interviews she repeated that she 'really likes the contact with customers', but also that she 'hates them' and 'can't stand with their faces anymore'. Her occupational wear and tear come as much from her working conditions as the unrewarding aspect of the job itself: the bonuses do not go far enough to make up for the minimum wage she is paid every month, and Cécilia says that 'you can't stay a cashier your whole life'. She says that a lot of cashiers today are students, because 'that costs less'. Those unable to leave their cashiering jobs are 'jaded'. She dreads becoming an 'old-timer', an attribute stripped of any positive connotation when she says it.

The year before, she had replied to an advertisement from a company hiring a commercial secretary. She explained that she took all the tests and 'everything was OK'. She cast the job in very positive light: 'I had an office to myself,

1,800 euros net, 35 hours, plus a bonus for every five appointments made'. She backed down when faced with what seemed like mission impossible to her: she had to land dozens of interviews every week… Cécilia did not want to give up her open-ended contract at Intermarché for, as she said, 'a job where I knew I wouldn't make it. Maybe I underestimate myself…' Éric encouraged her to look for other leads, but Cécilia justifies her choice saying that Intermarché is 'a little cocoon', and she has 'her little routine'. 'To drop everything, completely transform my life, I dunno…' She resigns herself to her cashiering job even though she can no longer stand working in a supermarket where, like other women in similar jobs (Benquet 2009), she says she endures a low salary, the remarks of supervisors, and no freedom, trapped at her register (she cannot take a smoke or bathroom break when she wants).

Éric's work comes with more advantageous conditions: His job includes an apartment, his income is higher, and he is a civil servant, with all that entails. But it also has its share of constraints, related to his choppy working hours, the fact he lives at his workplace, and his subaltern position in the job hierarchy. Depending on the week, he is on the job from 7:30 am to 4:30 pm with a break from 12:30–1:30, or 8:30–12:30 and 4:00–7:00 pm, and all working days he must do a final round at 9:00–10:00 pm. Unlike his previous job with the city technical services, he no longer has a precise job to perform, but rather a variety of little jobs that are not very physically demanding and do not require much technical knowledge (he delivers the mail, changes light bulbs, does basic maintenance and repairs like re-gluing carpet, removes bulky objects, delivers orders, oversees security, and opens and closes the library). In a work environment divided into several sections ('Youth', 'Literature', 'Audio', and so on), his job not only seems secondary, but also rather lonely; he said that, 'Other than the other caretaker, I don't have any co-workers', although he works in a library with 82 employees. In his first six years as caretaker, Éric explained that he 'threw himself into the job', running from office to office to make himself 'useful'. He stopped when he learned that people made fun of him, calling him the 'building roundsman'.

But unlike Cécilia, he manages to keep the limitations of his job in check. For one thing, the athletic habit he developed in childhood is today an essential outlet for fleeing his tether to the workplace and symbolically bolstering himself. Sport provides him with another social scene, escape, and many gratifying resources. He constantly opposes his taste for physical effort to the supposed 'softness' of certain other employees that spend all their time 'in books'.

For another thing, he tries to enrich his work by offering a range of services that go beyond his job description, including carpentry (he builds displays and shelving for books), painting (he did some painting in one of the library sections), and electrical work (he installed additional lighting for an exhibit). In a given week he estimates that he spends 'almost 50%' of his time on such activities not in his job description, which he says are a way to make his job 'more interesting'. They are more technical than the tasks he is formally assigned, and they give him a chance to build another kind of relationship with library employees, who see him less as 'the handyman' and a little more as a 'co-worker'. In a working environment that is hierarchical and heavily feminised (around 90% of the library employees are women), he is trying to shift the balance in co-worker relations so that their differences in status, gender, educational level, and how they relate to written culture do not stand between them as much. He also gets involved in organising regular exhibits in the library lobby, an investment that earns him a degree of recognition. Éric is always invited to the VIP dinner at a restaurant on exhibit opening days. He was officially named 'exhibit preparator', and his boss is pressing their higher-ups to move him up the pay scale. She also includes him in the monthly 'news meetings' for municipal elected officials and office staff.

Yearning for elsewhere to make up for a subaltern status

The divide between working conditions has deepened in the couple: while Cécilia suffers from holding a wearing job marking her abandoned aspirations to occupational qualifications, Éric has acquired rewarding resources in and outside of work. This divide regularly prompts Cécilia to engage in a 'polemical practice of speech' (Schwartz 1990, 329). For example, she reproaches her husband for 'taking it easy at work' (he has access to a space that he converted into a little shop for himself) or being 'too nice for his own good' with his boss, and she comments sarcastically on all his efforts 'without earning a penny more'. She also criticises him for doing 'too much sport' and giving her too much laundry to wash ('filthy athlete stuff') or not looking after Louise enough, even though she keeps her daughter close to her in a thousand little ways.

Suffering from her cashiering position, Cécilia withdraws into her activities in the home: housework and watching television occupy most of her time. She built an imaginary world as if to compensate for her occupational dissatisfaction. She watches *Reines du Shopping* (Queens of Shopping) on the channel M6 when she gets home from work, and every week she buys the fashion and 'people' magazines *Closer*, *Public*, *Oops*, *Voici*, *Glamour*, *Be*, *Cosmopolitan*, and *Gala*. These magazines give her more than the illusion of being close to celebrities; they give her access to certain models of elegance and beauty to which she tries to conform. She has several celebrity-focused websites in her 'Favourites' folder that offer multiple models for readers to identify with, and she uses them to build her own 'look'. Making a didactic use of these websites, she explains that she really likes 'to look at celebrities' faces, actually, their dresses, how they're made up, how their hair is done [...] It's just to look at fashion, like, girl-stuff [...] It gives me ideas, to change hair colour. [...] When I see Nabila [*a pop starlet*], that was my inspiration [...] She's pretty, she's only 21 [...], she creates buzz – she's right, I'd have done the same thing'.

She goes to the salon once a month and devotes part of her budget to working on her elegance: 'I buy a lot of clothes. I admit it, I admit it, I admit it. I have a closet full of coats, I could dress all of France, but... I love coats, I love bags, I love shoes'. She says she is not one of those women who neglects her appearances for lack of taste. Her physical appearance and the way she dresses are a way to avoid being associated with subaltern workers, who garner little respect and low pay, and to 'disidentify' herself from the stigma of economic and aesthetic poverty associated with the 'working class' (Skeggs 2015). She finds an escape in the models for dress and personal care provided by the media, models that incarnate her desire for another life.

At the same time, she has not entirely come to terms with her aesthetic pretentions. She fears gossip and the idea that someone might think that she immorally tricks people by mudding the waters of social judgement with her appearances. At the time of research, she was in conflict with Éric's brother (the motorcycle salesman) and sister-in-law (a nursery school assistant, ATSEM), who she said despised her and Éric.

> She's a sphere who does nothing to lose weight and who eats enough for four and who judges everyone and who takes herself for a high-society lady and who's only an ATSEM and who really loves to judge others, who thinks that nothing bad could ever happen in her life, that she'll stay married her whole life to Laurent, that she'll spend her whole life in a bubble... Well yeah, yeah, they show off. They treat us like shit. Because we have nothing in our lives, we dress well, we treat ourselves, but alongside that we don't have anything, we're nothing. It's all appearances but after that, there's nothing. That's what they think.

Cécilia, who has internalised her detractors' point of view, is afraid of accusations of pride: she herself says that they are 'only' a cashier and a caretaker and are thus scarcely allowed to look any more fashionable.

Led to live beyond her means by her need to escape her position as a lowly executant employee, the image she wants to create for herself and her husband (who she often criticises for his poor taste and '*beauf*' appearances[2]) endlessly exposes her to fear of being called out, mocked, or the object of sarcastic silence. These negative feelings poison her life and trap her in a distant, even hostile, relationship to the real world outside.

By putting himself under the command of his wife who assigns him domestic chores, Éric tries to restore balance with Cécilia. He has to take account of the unrealised social and professional aspirations she bears, all the more so as Cécilia openly expresses her dissatisfaction by demanding that he not put her down through selfish or negligent behaviour. Cécilia 'controls' the household and finds a point of pride – inadequate but nonetheless real – in the flawless execution of everyday chores. If Éric values his relationship, he has to demonstrate his good will. This man, with so many traits reproducing the classic virile working-class male model, is led to genuinely participate in everyday domestic chores out of a realistic principle that does not necessarily have much to do with the 'middle-class' ideal of shared domestic labour. This realistic principle – the quest for domestic peace – explains his active yet docile contribution to domestic work. He more or less consciously tries to sooth Cécilia's unhappiness and prevent her from turning into an 'obsessively tidy' woman – or from being overcome by the desire to really act on her dream of change, for that matter.

Notes

1 For an explanation of the French educational system, see the Appendix.
2 '*Beauf*' took its current meaning from Cabu, a cartoonist, who used the common contraction for 'brother-in-law' (*beau-frère*) to refer to a racist bigmouth character, and the term has since come to mean a boorish working-class lout.

References

Benquet, Marlène. 2009. 'Nathalie M. Le refus d'encaisser. Propos recueillis par Marlène Benquet.' *Travail, genre et sociétés* no. 211: 9–24.
Brousse, Cécile. 2015. 'Travail professionnel, tâches domestiques, temps "libre": quelques déterminants sociaux de la vie quotidienne.' *Économie et Statistique* 478–480: 119–154.
Cartier, Marie, Muriel Letrait, and Matéo Sorin. 2018. 'Travail domestique: des classes populaires conservatrices?' *Travail, genre et sociétés* 39: 63–81.
Kaufmann, Jean-Claude. 1997. *Le Cœur à l'ouvrage*. Paris: Nathan.
Schwartz, Olivier. 1990. *Le Monde privé des ouvriers. Hommes et femmes du Nord*. Paris: Presses Universitaires de France.
Siblot, Yasmine. 2006. '"Je suis la secrétaire de la famille!" La prise en charge féminine des tâches administratives entre subordination et ressource.' *Genèses* 64: 46–66.
Singly, François de. 2007. *L'Injustice ménagère*. Paris: Armand Colin.
Skeggs, Beverley. 1997. *Formations of Class & Gender: Becoming Respectable*. Thousand Oaks, CA: Sage.
Weber, Florence. 1989. *Le Travail à-côté, Étude d'ethnographie ouvrière*. Paris: INRA.
Zarca, Bernard. 1990. 'La division du travail domestique: poids du passé et tensions au sein du couple.' *Économie et Statistique* 228: 29–40.

18

BEING A HOUSEWIFE

Between permanence and evolution of a traditional role – Nadège and Patrick Lancel

Maulde Urbain-Mathis

Nadège and Patrick Lancel and their two daughters live in a suburb of a city in western France. Their eldest, Noémie, is 14 and is Nadège's daughter from a previous marriage. The second, Louise, is three. Patrick is a lorry driver, and Nadège was a salesperson and housecleaner before becoming a housewife upon the birth of Louise.

The family lives in a recently built public-housing single-family home with adjoining garage, surrounded by a yard. It is a five-room house (three bedrooms, a dining room, and a living room) that includes two bathrooms, two water closets, and a kitchen. Nadège and Patrick had moved there a year and a half before the study was conducted, fleeing what had become an uncomfortable situation: problems with neighbours that 'made [Nadège's] life miserable' and a failed attempt at homeownership. And so the family moved a few kilometres away, across the river separating their old and new towns. The move left Nadège feeling torn in two. By crossing the bridge she feels like she has changed geographical areas and abandoned her mother, who stayed behind. Nadège tries hard to keep several everyday activities in the town where she used to live: her grocery store, her doctor, her hairdresser, and Noémie's *collège* and gymnastics class. Leaving was painful, but they find their current housing development respectable. They were able to move there thanks to a couple of friends who backed their social housing application to municipal authorities, thus avoiding the distress that would have been caused by moving to the stigmatised social housing neighbourhood closest to their previous residence.

Domestic work in Nadège and Patrick's home reveals some changes in the roles traditionally observed in the working classes. Nadège is quite invested in her role as housewife and devotes most of her day to her roles as mother, wife,

DOI: 10.4324/9781003330073-20

and daughter, roles giving her some status, but her well-being is not entirely melded with that of the family. Her interest in personal fulfilment is most strongly expressed in a search for conjugal happiness and time for herself. How can a conception of domestic organisation based on a sharply gendered division of roles coexist in the same marriage with an attitude including more contemporary norms of self-care?

A family in difficulty

Although moving to a house in what Nadège calls a 'quiet' neighbourhood permitted them to avoid socio-spatial relegation, their life course remains fragile at best. Indeed, they have very limited financial resources: Patrick earns 1,500–2,200 euros a month depending on the trips he makes, to which are added 129 euros a month in child benefits from the Caisse d'allocations familiales (CAF; Family Allocations Fund) and 100 euros in child support from Noémie's father. They have trouble making ends meet: their low income combined with the year that Patrick was unemployed after being laid off drove them to use the food bank at the social assistance centre (Centre communal d'action sociale; CCAS) in their former town.

Concerning education, Patrick has a CAP in mechanics and Nadège a BEP in sales. She cut her studies short, while studying for a vocational *baccalauréat* in the service sector (the *bac* STT).[1] She now regrets this choice that she cannot really explain, and although she understands that earning the *baccalauréat* would have allowed her to earn a better living, she does not really see herself going back to school. Nadège sees her professional future as working as a cleaning woman in a school, like her mother. As to Patrick, despite what he terms a 'difficult' educational career, he expresses no regrets and no ambitions for professional development: 'I stopped in *cinquième* [age 12–13] [...], I was manual'. Patrick mentioned that his parents sent his 'delinquent' brother to a private school to 'straighten him out', which suggests that the family might have had some resources, but solid data is lacking on Patrick's social background. Nadège came from the upper working classes: her father, who is now deceased, was foreman in a local factory and her parents were able to buy a house, where her mother still lives. It has been another story for Patrick and Nadège, who seem to have more difficulty achieving stability than their parents, since their respective separations and their relatively late start on a relationship have prevented them from being able to follow through on their home-buying plans, denied a bank loan because of their ages (Nadège is 39 and Patrick 46). This failure attests to how costly a divorce can be for social classification in the working classes. Nadège quickly relativised the failure, however: 'it's nice to have a house, your own home, but it's a lot of nuisance'. Nothing in their attitude suggests a search for social ascension, for themselves or their children.

Being a housewife: from giving to others…

Conforming to a classic conception of running a household, Nadège is deeply invested in her role of housewife while Patrick assures the role of breadwinner by ensuring the means to feed his family (Blic and Lazarus 2007, 82). Nadège's attitude reflects several ways in which she gives herself over to the service of the members of her family.

She is the one 'who does everything' in the home, as she likes to point out. She does the cleaning, washing, shopping, and cooking and declares she 'love[s] to clean'. Patrick is in charge of tasks outside the house and those Nadège thinks are dangerous: home improvement, fixing the car, mowing the lawn, tidying the garage. The couple thus has a traditional conception of the distribution of household tasks that opposes women's work (inside the home) to men's work (mostly done outside). But because Patrick often works irregular and variable hours, he is away a lot, and when he is there, he is often too tired to do the jobs that fall to him. Nadège is thus forced to 'muddle through' and perform some tasks she considers outside her 'domain', like doing small repairs in the house or mowing the grass. Ultimately, only repair of the couple's three cars remains exclusively Patrick's area, because of the practical knowledge from his CAP, but here, too, he lacks time and struggles to get it done, to Nadège's great regret. Despite the significant load that housework represents – she refers to it as 'a chore' – Nadège does derive satisfaction from it. By doing everything every day, she has an overview of everything that happens inside her house and manages to obtain some authority there: thanks to her devotion, she feels that she is the one 'who wears the trousers'.

Although Nadège had to become a housewife when Louise was born because of Patrick's irregular working hours, she does not present it as a choice made unwillingly. When she was younger, however, Nadège imagined herself in an occupation that is difficult to reconcile with her current-day dedication to the home: firefighter. Her hopes of practicing this occupation were probably not very realistic given her social environment. Indeed, her ex-husband as already a firefighter and adamant that they not have the same occupation and forced her to give up on this plan, threatening to quit if she passed the qualifying exam. Thoughts of becoming a firefighter would thus remain a 'dream', but Nadège does not express great regret about it either and today seems to have found her work as a housewife to be the basis for social respectability. She willingly vaunts this role and rejects other figures of women's work, incarnated by Patrick's ex-partner, herself a firefighter in the same station as Nadège's ex-husband. Nadège condemns her lack of investment in her home, where 'she didn't do anything!', and jokingly contrasts it to her own dedication: 'when we were first together, when I'd cook for him, he couldn't believe it! Hey, maybe that's why he gained weight… it's kind of my fault!' The ultimate proof of her housewifely respectability can be read on her husband's belly, and Nadège is proud of it: her husband is well fed and her house well maintained.

The burdens she bears are heavy, however. Nadège sees the family as a space for solidarity and protection where she plays a determinant role. She is responsible for household balance and she values this role, although it is challenging to keep the family on track given its social and economic fragility. It is an arduous task and Nadège lives under pressure from which Patrick is sheltered. Keeping the budget falls to the mother, according to traditional working-class family practices, and it is a heavy responsibility for Nadège to bear, as in so many low-income households (Blic and Lazarus 2007). Far from enjoying the situation, Nadège describes her stress from managing the household budget:

> Patrick doesn't worry about anything! He doesn't give a damn, as they say. He's got an income, he's not sick, he's got a job. Everything's fine! He's never worried! I'm the one who's worried all the time, stressed out, and him, 'It's nothing, no big deal!' [...] I worry about the fact that I don't work, so it's always 'Are we gonna make it through this month?', 'Might another setback come crashing down on us?'

Nadège is worried about their future because the household income is low without a second wage-earner, while Patrick 'doesn't worry about anything' because responsibility for keeping their budget in the black does not fall to him.

Nadège's care for her mother since the death of her father is another source of anxiety. Their relationship used to be difficult, and tensions were at their worst when Nadège was a teenager. Her mother was very restrictive about her going out but lax with her brother: 'I didn't have the right to do anything! [...] It's maybe because he's a boy, but he was allowed to go out. When he wanted to come home, he'd come home at... later than me, he was allowed. It was more mellow. Then it was... our parents told us, "listen" – well, especially my mother – "He's a boy, y'know, you're a girl"'. Their relationship has evolved for the better today, but Nadège would have liked a little more acknowledgement of what happened in the past: 'I have the impression that she forgot how she used to be with me'. Despite that, Nadège puts time and energy into protecting and helping her mother through everyday ups and downs. Her mother does not have a driving licence, so Nadège takes her to the store and doctor. She also goes with her when she has administrative procedures to deal with. 'Looking after my mother isn't easy', she stresses, and is a daily burden. It is even more difficult because she is the only child that still lives near their mother, since her younger brother and sister moved several hundred kilometres away, and sibling relations have degraded. Among other things, she reproaches them for asking their mother for money and putting her in a difficult financial situation that

Nadège then has to settle, such as the time she had to help pay off a loan that her mother took out for her brother.

Nadège thus gives a lot to the family as a group, because 'when the fact of paying is a chore instead of a power [...], the wife is the one that tends to do it' (Trépos et al. 2009). Despite the load she carries, she is proud of her implication in the domestic sphere and rejects other models of women's work. The only professional future she imagines concerns domestic-like work in her daughter's school by becoming a cleaning woman, which shows just how highly she regards the housewife model. Despite her significant domestic constraints, she manages to find satisfaction and prove her respectability.

...to looking after oneself

This form of self-sacrifice conforms to a traditional working-class conception of the role of the woman in the home, but she combines it with clear concern for herself. Indeed, despite all the devotion that Nadège demonstrates to her family, she still pursues personal well-being. Nadège first actively expressed her individuality in the realm of marital happiness, when she left her first husband to get out of an unhappy marriage. She felt as if her mother pushed her into it too young, encouraging her to commit rapidly to married life out of what was likely hopes that she formalise the relationship, so that Nadège would be sleeping with her husband rather than a mere boyfriend. So Nadège got married 'to make [her] mother happy' and probably also to escape her control. She got bored in the relationship and ended up getting close to Patrick, a friend of the couple (and husband of one of her ex-husband's co-workers), and she ended up moving in with him and putting an end to her first marriage.

Nadège is bitter about her upbringing, and her divorce from her first husband could be seen as revenge for the traditional model for raising girls, which she blames for her unhappy marriage. Without fully realising it, however, she tends to reproduce the same model with her own daughters by allowing them little freedom. She sees the outside world as a threat, a perception that justifies her very close control over their activities and undermines potential for upward social mobility. For instance, she delayed Louise's entry into pre-school for a year out of fear of confiding her to strangers. It is at an entirely different level with Noémie, who is 14. Like her mother before her, Nadège is raising her just like the miners' daughters Olivier Schwartz met in northern France in the 1980s, limiting her time out and forbidding access to a sexual life (Schwartz 1990). Noémie is only allowed to go out on the street in front of the house, and sometimes Nadège jokes that Noémie will be sent 'to a convent'. Nadège regularly spies on Noémie's diary and telephone to make sure is respecting the limits she has imposed. This is how she recently discovered a text message sexually propositioning Noémie, sent by a friend Noémie's age who Nadège knows well. Nadège was very angry and demanded an explanation from her daughter, who refused to talk about it and went to live with her father for a few days. He is more tolerant where his daughter's sexuality is concerned; a few months earlier he had even suggested that she get a prescription for the pill, which Nadège had categorically refused on the grounds that their daughter was too young – unconsciously reproducing the child-rearing model that she condemns, despite herself. There are several things that could be preventing her from realising it. First of all, not having a son means that she is not confronted with the fact that the restrictions she imposes on Noémie are related to her gender. Secondly, by refusing to raise her hand against Noémie, she has the impression that she is 'cooler' than her own mother, who 'hit' her; this effort to break with a harshly criticised traditional child-rearing method allows her to think that she has succeeded in setting herself apart from her parents. Lastly, there is Nadège's social ageing: she thinks that the outside world is much more dangerous now than it was when she was young, which justifies her restrictions. Despite the conflict that it has already created between her and Noémie, Nadège is attentive to keeping her daughters close to her and within what she sees as the protective domestic space of the family.

Her divorce was thus an infringement of her familialist values. Daring to challenge her marriage destabilised the entire protective space in which she held a rewarding role. When she started seeing Patrick the risk became even greater:

> It wasn't easy! I'd just gotten married in 2000, I had a two-year-old, and well, we got together in 2004. I told him, "I've got a family, it's not for a one-night stand". And then, well, it's been eleven years now.

Her respectability as wife and mother was undermined as a result. Her divorce was most costly because it hurt her reputation as a woman in her home village. Nadège went against a social prohibition in her immediate environment: '[My ex-husband] insulted me, he called me a slut – even in front of my father'. There were rumours about her relationship choices that would reach the ears of the CCAS administrator with whom Nadège had already worked. She internalised this prohibition, and her decision to openly pursue her relationship with Patrick gives her the feeling she 'sinned'. She defends her decision to favour her own conjugal happiness, but refuses to accept that it might make her less respectable as wife and mother. This position is expressed most vividly when Nadège speaks of her very tense relationships with Patrick's mother and sister, who have trouble accepting the blended family. While preparing for their wedding, Patrick's mother wanted Nadège to wear a suit rather than a dress, since it was a second marriage. Nadège refused to cave in to her mother-in-law's demands and chose to wear a traditional white dress instead. More generally, Nadège feels as if she and Noémie are excluded from his family. For instance, Patrick's mother did not give Noémie a birthday present the year of the study, and Nadège said she was ready to decline any gifts for Louise: 'You don't do "we'll do one, but not the other"'. Nadège was also very hurt that Patrick's sister once called her a 'hanger on'. She is very upset that the sister did not stand up for her and is determined to defend her choice to build a new family.

Nadège devotes considerable time to her role of mother, daughter, and wife, but is nonetheless driven by a quest for time for herself. This is the second element revealing the importance she accords to her personal fulfilment. Twice a week she does Zumba, a combination of dance and aerobics where class participants go through several routines to a soundtrack of Latino, African, Middle Eastern, and hip-hop music for strength and cardiac training. Unlike more classic dance forms, the goal is not to perfect your moves, but to let go and burn off energy, which makes it possible to say that it corresponds to certain traits of working-class taste. Nadège signed up for Zumba in her new town in a class where the researcher was also enrolled, which is how the research relationship developed. Twenty to thirty women attended each session, with a core group of fifteen regulars that faithfully attended every class as well as weekend events like the local Zumba party held by Daphnée, the instructor. Some of these women have been friends and neighbours for years, and others (like Nadège) did not know anyone before they began. A friendly atmosphere developed quickly and participants soon became closer, leading them to stay in touch on social networks outside of class time. Their average age is about 40 and they are all mothers, but their social backgrounds vary widely: the instructor Daphnée is a chemist for a local company; Brigitte, a social worker; Angela, a foster carer, and Clara, who works in a bank. It is a chance for Nadège 'to see people', as she puts it, and arrange for a social space of her very own. It is also an opportunity to allow her to treat herself by buying Zumba-brand active wear, which she buys on sale through the company website or used from other women (of higher social position) in the class, and she hides the expense from her husband as best she can.

For Nadège and the others, Zumba is an opportunity to set aside time just for oneself, away from domestic constraints; as an official Zumba post that Daphnée shared on the group's Facebook page in 2015 put it, 'You dominate the world 23 hours a day, but for one hour you are free'. Nadège sometimes has to skip it on nights when Patrick comes home late, which she hates to do. In order to get away more easily, she eagerly bought a Cookéo do-it-all kitchen appliance that chops, blends, stirs, and cooks with the push of a button. Classes are at 7 in the evening, so she sets it before leaving home and the meal is ready when she returns. Nadège prefers eating unprocessed foods and not having to watch food as it cooks. In addition to freeing up time, she says the appliance also makes it possible for her to eat more 'healthy' in order to lose weight. Although she is proud of having a well-fed husband who 'gained weight' since they got together, she tries to keep a diet that will lose her a few pounds. To reduce their caloric content she updates dishes with rich sauces, which the working classes have traditionally appreciated out of a preference for nourishing and inexpensive food (Bourdieu 1984). She gets her recipes from a Facebook group for sharing Weight Watcher's recipes converted for Cookéo machines. According to Nadège, who seems to have some rudimentary knowledge of nutrition, adapting recipes is rather simple: 'You don't use any oil and you put in more vegetables than starch'. Facebook group members support each other's efforts to lose weight: 'And you see that there's some that lose hope because they aren't losing weight, you give them a little boost'. Zumba participants also commonly have this kind of exchange. Conversations about food are frequent and often pick up the discourse forbidding junk food, although many of them like it, condemning it even if they 'can't resist' sweet treats. One of the goals of doing Zumba is losing weight and sculpting the figure, and indeed, three participants are obese and have even had stomach reduction surgery to help them lose weight. This attitude aligning the body to an aesthetic norm is connected to the transformation of certain domestic norms. Taking the time to sculpt and care for one's body is itself a form of emancipation from domestic injunctions. Nadège is particularly attentive to her appearance, wearing makeup and regularly changing her hairstyle. Losing weight is probably also a way to make the time she takes for herself visible.

Nadège and Patrick's lifestyle reveals fresh perspectives on traditional domestic operational model, not breaking with it but integrating new norms. Nadège is the one behind this development, in the same way that she is behind her recipe for boeuf bourguignon, a traditional beef stew that she converted to a lower-fat version using her Cookéo. 'I made a boeuf bourguignon for my mother last time, and she knew that it was something like that'. Nadège adapts her recipe to new values and injunctions: freeing up time to take care of herself and her appearances. The recipe is a success, if even her mother, a key figure in her apprenticeship in domestic norms, could not guess at the changes she had made! Likewise, Nadège does not try to profoundly alter the traditional model, a rewarding source of respectability for her, but she does change it by including new norms of self-care. Her quest for personal fulfilment may run counter to traditional values, but she does not reject them. She usually finds a compromise between giving of herself and caring for herself, more often than she puts them in opposition. Nadège has made the family the ultimate protective space and a site of solidarity, but is not prepared to sacrifice her individuality to it. She sets aside time for herself, by allowing herself the pleasure of practicing Zumba.

Note

1 For an explanation of the French educational system, see the Appendix.

References

Blic, Damien de, and Jeanne Lazarus. 2007. *Sociologie de l'argent*. Paris: La Découverte.

Bourdieu, Pierre. (1979) 1984. *Distinction: A Social Critique of the Judgment of Taste*. Translated by Richard Nice. Cambridge, MA: Harvard University Press.

Schwartz, Olivier. 1990. *Le Monde privé des ouvriers. Hommes et femmes du Nord*. Paris: Presses Universitaires de France.

Trépos, Jean-Yves, Isa Haddad, Aurélien Lambert, Fanny Liebelt, Soumia Nifri, Serena Roumens, and Maria Scheerer-Molnar. 2007. 'Les marquages conjugaux de l'argent en milieu populaire.' *Le Portique* 19. https://journals.openedition.org/leportique/1191.

PART III

Triangular social consciousness and institutional 'goodwill' – the reconfiguration of relations with other social groups

19

INTRODUCTION TO PART 3

Triangular social consciousness and institutional 'goodwill': the reconfiguration of relations with other social groups

Marie-Hélène Lechien and Yasmine Siblot

This third and final section explores households in our study in terms of their sociability practices, how they relate to institutions, and how they position themselves in the social space. In the 1950s through the 1970s, French and British sociology described this positioning as being structured by the opposition between 'Us' and 'Them'. Richard Hoggart postulated that 'most groups gain some of their strength from their exclusiveness, from a sense of people outside who are not "Us"'. He argued that the 'Us' of the working classes is rooted in 'the strength of the home and neighbourhood' that 'arises partly from a feeling that the world outside is strange and often unhelpful, that it has most of the counters stacked on its side, that to meet it on its own terms is difficult'. This world of 'Them' consists of bosses and public officials such as policemen, teachers, social workers, and magistrates (Hoggart 1957, 62).

Although Hoggart's analysis is historically and nationally situated – especially in its references to the English labour movement and its repression, which are important for understanding the strong mistrust of the ruling classes – it was widely adopted in France, and the work of Pierre Bourdieu (1984) and Michel Verret (1979, 1996, 1999) also emphasised the practical and symbolic distancing of the dominant. The living conditions and lifestyles of French labourers from after the war through the 1970s were thus seen in terms of the Us/Them opposition. It was (and still is, to a degree) used as a template for reading the social world, taken as a view that persistently characterises the working classes' relationship to other social groups. Paul Pasquali and Olivier Schwartz have demonstrated that this is probably because *The Uses of Literacy* managed to describe 'what it is to experience the world as a labourer' to the satisfaction of sociologists close to Pierre Bourdieu, including Jean-Claude Passeron, who worked on its translation and publication by Éditions de Minuit.

DOI: 10.4324/9781003330073-22

'Miraculously', according to Pierre Bourdieu, Richard Hoggart 'recovered a cultural experience' from people close to him and avoided traps like class prejudice and populism encountered by sociologists and intellectuals in general when they study 'the people' (Pasquali and Schwartz 2016, 28–29).

What comes under this Us/Them opposition? To what extent is it still operational today? Does it always play out through 'familialism' and 'localism', or, in other words, does it still privilege a dense sociability within the extended family, workplace, and place of residence as forms of protection within the in-group that developed to counter domination, but also as autonomous cultural traits? In *The Uses of Literacy*, first published in 1957, people live in relatively homogeneous neighbourhoods, the men all working in the same factories and the women working on building and maintaining family respectability, the main 'biographical programme' in which they could invest.

And yet, as the introduction of this volume pointed out, a number of social, economic, and cultural transformations have altered the logics internally structuring the working classes and their relationship to other social groups in France, both before and after the 1960s. They seem first of all to attest to a gradual upheaval of lifestyles within every class and class fraction and their proximity to each other: the improvement of material living conditions and access to consumer goods and services, the dissociation of place of residence and place of work with the construction of major council estates, the 'medicalisation' of life with the establishment of a universal public healthcare system and greater attention to health, the generalisation of access to secondary education and the gradual opening of post-secondary education, the development and diversification of sport and leisure activities, and the spread of a 'mass psychological culture' (Castel and Le Cerf 1980). In the mid-1970s other, much more ambivalent processes began to transform working-class living conditions: public policy and private sector initiatives to make modest renters into homeowners, the impoverishment of public housing neighbourhoods, the decline of subaltern jobs in industry and their rise in the tertiary sector, unemployment and the precarisation of employment, destabilisation of 'the wage-earning society', and restrictive migration policy. And then, in the late 1980s, began the withdrawal of public services from rural areas and urban peripheries, areas where the working classes are over-represented; the weakening of unions and political parties claiming to represent 'labourers' and 'the working-classes'; and the reconstruction of a political far right and the rise of political options blaming 'immigrants', 'benefits scroungers', and 'council estate youths' for the problems of French citizens. These transformations take many forms, renewing economic domination while strengthening cultural 'porosity' between social groups (Schwartz 1998), which calls for study of contemporary forms of the division between Us and Them.

Furthermore, in France as in Britain, the sociology of the working classes developed at a particular moment, during the historical interlude of housewives

(Maruani and Meron 2012). Women's resumption of paid work outside the home in the 1960s also redefined the Us/Them divide and how working-class people experience interactions with 'the world outside'. In the stable fractions of the working classes studied here, where both partners are usually employed, we wondered what consequences come of more frequent interaction with the middle and upper classes, particularly for the women in basic employee jobs who encounter them most often. These relations may be based in face-to-face interactions or in greater exposure to dominant norms resulting from the tertiarisation of jobs held by members of the working classes who adapt to socially diverse clienteles, but may also develop through rising working-class recourse to services ensured by people from the middle and upper classes (in education, health care, banking, etc.). This leads one to wonder how familialism and localism have been reconfigured, given this expansion of lived social space and women's new relationship to the home now that they attend school longer and keep their careers (albeit rocky ones) even after becoming mothers.

The seven portraits following this introduction begin to answer these questions about relations between the working classes and other social groups. The ethnographic case studies reveal four processes: the erosion of 'Us' and the 'triangular social consciousness' becoming commonplace (Collovald and Schwartz 2006); transformations in local sociabilities and community engagements; the reconfiguration of familialism and the affirmation of a variety of forms of educational goodwill; and, more generally, exposure to institutional norms (in health and hygiene, child-rearing, psychology, greater professional and geographical mobility, and so on) that may become common aspirations. While some of these processes have already been identified, we propose what may be a new articulation distinctive to these stable fractions of the working classes.

The process that runs through the largest number of portraits (and not just those in this section) is the spread of a tripartite view of the social world in the stabilised fractions of the working classes. This split into 'Them/Us/They' is probably not new to the working classes, which have been affected by divisions separating the French from immigrants, the respectable from the unrespectable, the established from the marginal, and the like, but it has grown since the 1980s.[1] 'Them' no longer means members of the middle and upper classes, but rather groups and individuals incarnating 'the pressure from below' (Schwartz 2009) – unemployed people or 'non-workers' who don't pay taxes, people who don't own their homes, teenagers and 'council estate youths' presumed to be violent (in elementary and secondary school, recreation centres) and to drag educational quality down. 'Them' designates dominated groups that have become more visible because of their stigmatised over-exposure in the political field and new social integration policies, with the spread since the 1980s of an injunction to autonomy and expanding control measures to catch 'frauders' (Duvoux 2009). In contrast, 'They' refers to groups and individuals holding dominant positions in a social order that the studied households feel is unfair but against which they feel powerless. While they are sometimes close and incarnate, especially at work or in the local social space, the dominant are generally vaguely identified and seen as distant, such as 'bosses', 'stockholders', and 'politicians'.

Some of the processes might seem contradictory, especially those leading to investment in private happiness at the level of the family, couple, or individual (home ownership, tightening sociability in around school and children's activities, 'time for myself' practices for men and women alike[2]) and those attesting to involvement in a network of acquaintanceship or even collective activities in the public space (in the neighbourhood, at work, in community groups). Another contradiction exists between sociability practices demonstrating the relative continuity of a working-class in-group and others suggesting that barriers between social groups are falling. Such paradoxes came to light partly due to our decision to conduct the study through household studies. They explore all the representations and practices defining a social condition, in its private and public, individual and collective dimensions, through conjugal relations and the stakes of inter-generational transmission. The research design thus allowed us to circulate between the perspectives of each member of the household and between social scenes that are more diverse than those seen in sociology of the 1950s–1970s, which favoured the work and sociability of male labourers. Due to their role as mother and/or the nature of their work, women are more exposed than men to the institutional norms that determine the common framework of existence of all families (school, medical institutions, governmental institutions and public services, banks) and, ultimately, other groups' norms. It is possible that their greatest and oldest familiarity with legitimate norms is manifest in 'filtering work' and the selective appropriation of such norms that the case-study approach brings to light. In other words, the feeling of being on the wrong side of power relations and an outsider relative to another insider group is not incompatible with women in these families being exposed to institutions over the long term and adopting their norms. Men in these stable fractions of the working classes are also exposed to such norms, notably in the professional sphere where management and work organisation promote norms of 'self-mobilisation' (Villette 1988) that are prominent in the mechanisms for internal promotion encountered by several men in our study who are working as skilled labourers for mid-sized to large companies.

The seven portraits in this section could be ordered in several ways. We chose a progression starting with the strongest 'Us' to the most flagrant 'I', from the individuals most integrated into occupational and activist groups to those the most invested in psychological therapies whose conception of the self was adopted from the register of the individual 'biographical turn' and self-transformation, quite present in the middle classes. Nonetheless, these portraits suggest a less linear and unequivocal reformulation of the sociability practices and relationship to other social groups than this progression would lead to believe:

although there is an observable decline in localism, a perception of dominants little coloured by antagonism, and notable institutional goodwill, the people we interviewed do not necessarily try to escape their class or turn their backs on any collective. The ways they use psychological tools indicate tensions and frailties specific to the working classes, even the stable fractions, including degrading working conditions and professional conflicts, children more likely to be in difficulty at school, and a greater risk of social fall in case of a negative life event such as divorce or unemployment.[3]

Declining localism, triangular social consciousness, and ordinary altruism

The first two portraits stand out for their strong sense of 'Us' combined with union and professional collectives. Chantal Monlouis, a hospital laundry worker and labour union activist with the CGT, and Alain Rigaux, a tourist coach driver also member of the CGT, both work for large organisations where union engagement remains high and works councils ensure workers advantages, occasions to socialise, and a sense of security.[4] Although the top management in both organisations seems out of reach and Alain thinks the 'stockholders' of his transportation company decide its future on their own and in a rather opaque way, both Chantal and Alain manifest the feeling of a collective and personal capacity for protest, a 'mobilised relationship to their condition' (Siblot 2018). They live in dissimilar geographical configurations. Chantal lives in a housing estate in greater Paris. She came to mainland France from Guadeloupe, and her family socialisation gave her a particular relationship to public institutions: she 'gets her rights recognised' and actively calls upon municipal resources for assistance with schoolwork and leisure activities for her children. Alain and Nathalie Rigaux live in a post-industrial town in a rural part of the Nord region of France, where they were born. Although Nathalie also uses town resources (she goes to the library regularly), local institutions offer much less in terms of redistribution and protection. Despite these differences in usage of institutions, both households relate to their immediate neighbourhoods in the same way, exhibiting little or only the most selective localism, since they keep the people with whom they share residential space at a distance. Chantal describes her neighbourhood's 'little Africans' as being left to their own devices, and Alain calls his neighbours 'non-workers', hostile spectators to his own respectability as a 'worker' ('They watch us leave for work, [...] I've got the impression that I'm disturbing them because I leave early in the morning, I see them, the ones that are there without doing anything'). Alain has several friends in town (they go fishing together, mostly), but most are also co-workers and fellow union members.

The affirmation of an 'Us' at work through activism, rather rare among the case studies overall, does not exclude the possibility of a triangular social consciousness, which is present in nearly all the households we met. Rejection of 'benefits scroungers' comes along with rejection of 'politicians', typically perceived as 'in their own world' and not recognising the value of 'workers'. Despite this defiance, all households in the study vote regularly and are involved in 'unexpected associative engagements' (Misset and Siblot 2019): many volunteer to coach or take care of paperwork in sport clubs, others are active in village fête committees or patient associations, and a majority of women are active in school parents' associations. Such engagements could be referred to in terms of ordinary altruism or civic sense, in that the interviewees in this kind of engagement do not usually hold high positions in these organisations; they are less likely than the middle and upper classes to accumulate positions in multiple community groups, making their contributions harder to see. This form of altruism often presupposes resources of autochthony (that one member of the couple is from the town where these engagements take place) and so a certain kind of localism, but in form different than that presented in *The Uses of Literacy.*

Indeed, the third portrait, of Samuel Bidaud (skilled labourer) and Vanessa Le Coz (skilled basic employee), shows that localism can come with residential mobility. A couple in their thirties who grew up in the 'village', they have also lived in big cities and abroad before returning to their hometown and becoming members of the community bar, run as an association by a couple of pensioners working to maintain social ties among residents.[5] This household also highlights the challenges in renewing the electorate for the left, since Vanessa and Samuel disagree over the far-right political party Front National and some local friendships going back to childhood. They are both moving away from the partying 'working-class bohemian' lifestyle (Mauger 2006), and Vanessa devotes an increasing effort to their daughters and the schooling of the eldest.

Broadening sociability and institutional goodwill

The next two portraits depict the same redefined localism. Jean and Manou Audouin now live in Jean's home region, but Manou made a significant move (from Martinique to the mainland) and as a couple, they followed the demands of Jean's career as a lorry driver to other parts of the country.[6] Myriam and Nicolino Sanatanazefi live in the town where Myriam was born; Nicolino is from the overseas department of La Réunion and drives a lorry.[7] Both of these couples have developed deeply split sociabilities that are maintained by the women, who were able to avoid a certain 'domestic enclosure' (Lambert 2016) through community engagement. They became housewives when they moved in with their partners and had children, but both became active in town educational associations and institutions and draw 'resources of mobility' from them (Retière 1994): at the school for one and sociocultural centre for the other, they forge relations with middle-class parents, teachers, teaching assistants, and social workers. Having acquired a small capital in social relations and having been encouraged to go back to school (Myriam earned a modest vocational degree in early childhood development) or professionalise (Manou became a foster carer), they assumed administrative responsibilities in their respective organisations, where the upper- and middle-class parents seem to see them as 'democratic and anti-racist totems', since Manou is black and Myriam's father is Algerian. Their social networks are thus no longer exclusively defined by the social in-group: while one has an in-group of childhood friends (who helped Myriam earn her driving licence, get a job in a cleaning company, do Zumba – in other words, get out of the house) and the other an in-group of neighbours in insecure situations (women from the French Antilles and sub-Saharan Africa who help Manou to 'not get too white'; they swap favours and discuss personal things), they both also socialise with school parents from the upper and middle classes through their associative involvements.

Although both of these women manifest limited, modest forms of educational goodwill, their experiences nonetheless help us to see how hard the families we met try to play by the rules for schooling and support their children's academic success. All of the portraits in this section confirm the scale of labour families' educational goodwill, which has already been identified by several earlier studies (notably Terrail 1984, Lahire 1995, Millet and Thin, 2005, Poullaouec 2010), and demonstrate that it is equally true for parents who are basic employees (in these examples, working in a cleaning company and personal services). This internalisation of the longer educational norm plays out in a variety of ways, and its social effectiveness presumably varies considerably depending on the family configuration: oversight of homework can sometimes be distant, or only in subjects the adults think they understand well, and can quickly become an ordeal or a chore when parents yell and children cry, and oversight of friendships, bedtime, and screen time can in some cases be quite lax. But other interviewees (Chantal Monlouis, Vanessa Le Coz, Sylvie Barderon) gave detailed accounts of their children's schedules and notes, all the calls and meetings they had with teachers to negotiate their being put in the 'right' classes, and repeated family discussions over the importance of school and having diplomas; it bears emphasis that they were all women, and that the fathers we interviewed, although they consider school important, generally spend little practical or mental time on their children's educational success. The mothers rarely miss parent-teacher conferences, and nearly all are involved in the school parents' association, which has a lower barrier to entry than many other community groups.

A new definition of familialism can be inferred from these engagements in or close to school. The importance given to family relationships, especially with the elders, has not flagged, and many of the couples we studied live near their aged parents. They helped watch the children when they were little, and are then helped in turn, although family unity can sometimes feel like a burden, like when young couples' parents/in-laws go on vacation with them. Here again, the interviewed women regularly spent more time caring for elders, but men also 'lend a hand': Alain Rigaux looks after his parents and helps look after his mother-in-law. Material tasks in the homes of elderly parents are delegated less in the working classes than in the upper and middle classes, where they are usually ensured by domestic workers and home care service providers. Siblings are less included in these exchanges, since they are often fewer and more scattered, both geographically and socially. Relations can be tense when siblings judge one another by their social positions (as is the case for Myriam Sanatanazefi and Jean Audouin) and according to how much help they agree to give their aged parents. Sibling relations can also be intense but selective, as shown in the example of Manou Audoin, who is only close to some of her sisters, with whom she meets up regularly in and around Paris ('we talk, we squeeze together'). Their familialism consequently tends to shift the focus to children and their activities in and out of school, and reach into the 'restorative' dimension of the household for employed women, as described in the second section of this volume.

The 'psychologisation of experience' in the working classes

Finally, in the last two portraits, Sylvie Barderon, a cleaning woman raising her son alone, and Philippe Chapalain, a skilled labourer married to Marianne Chapalain, auxiliary nurse, describe their experiences of psychotherapy in similar ways: it helped them to get back on track, and marks a change in their lives, a before and after.[8] Their stories allow us to see two ways in which 'mass psychological culture' has reached working-class milieus (Schwartz 2011). The first is through support for people in insecure situations by social workers, doctors, and psychologists. Sylvie Barderon, a former hairdresser who got into a destructive relationship after her divorce, gradually got out of unemployment, depression, and alcoholism by reaching out to social and medical institutions for help. The second is via the 'industrial psychology' (Boltanski 1987) propagated in the workplace, in this case as part of mechanisms for internal promotion in an automotive factory. Philippe Chapalain was a rank-and-file labourer who was singled out by management and groomed to supervise other labourers. He was subsequently treated for obsessive-compulsive disorder, and now speaks of his perception of psychology (of which he used to be wary) in terms of a genuine conversion in how he sees himself and others. He tries to bring the perceived benefits of his therapy, which are mostly relational in nature, to his factory supervisory work. Does it help him to listen to labourers better, and make him refuse to pressure them for greater productivity, as he claims? Or does it favour acceptance of management policy by strengthening his moral and individualising worldview? Although we cannot speak to the effects of the psychologisation of his experience, we can observe that Marianne Chapalain, who also received psychological care after a suicide attempt she attributes to the deterioration of her working conditions, has turned to a form of collective wellbeing by joining the union. Other factors relating to the penetration of mass psychological culture into the working classes should also be highlighted: all occupations dealing with early childhood, even subaltern ones, implement psychological knowledge transmitted in training and through the institutional supervision of childminders and foster care providers, occupations held by Manou Ardouin and other women in our study. Another factor is that some parents have encountered the psychologisation of their children's difficulties at school (Darmon 2001, Morel 2014) – notably Alain and Nathalie Rigaux, Sylvie Barderon, and Philippe and Marianne Chapalain – when teachers and counsellors advised them to seek psychological counselling for their children. Likewise, psychological norms in child-rearing have been widely disseminated by the media, through radio programmes in the 1960s–1980s (Cardon and Laacher 1995) and, more recently, television. Myriam Sanatanazefi provides an example of this, as she draws heavily from the programme *Super Nanny* to train herself in the norm of 'governance by speech' in her relations with her children (Serre 2009, Garcia 2011). The last factor in this psychologisation of experience is undergoing psychological therapy, as several men and women interviewed for our study had, which leads them to psychologise their life experiences and ways of understanding the world in varying ways, depending on their own life courses and therapeutic situations (Arborio and Lechien 2019).

Notes

1 For more on this, see Lechien and Siblot (2019).
2 Among interviewees, these practices are developing and are no longer such 'guilty pleasures'. Whether they occur at home (playing games on the telephone or tablet, scanning interior decoration websites, participating in online consumer forums) or outside (Zumba class, choir), they could be interpreted as the assertion of a right to be unavailable to their spouses and children. They are also part of a rationale of breaking with their subaltern wage-earning condition (Masclet 2018).
3 See the first section of this volume.
4 See 'Being a respectable woman: Between stigma of housing estates and the union in-group', by Yasmine Siblot, and '"Simple people"? A local labour family, between social reproduction and openness, by Antoine Younsi and Anya Bouamama.
5 See '"It's really important to be able to grow": Social ambitions and political disappointments in a working-class household' by Tristan Poullaouec.
6 See 'Always between two worlds: The split local social life of a couple', by Clément Degout.
7 See 'The cleaning woman and the school parents' association: Multipositionality in the working classes', by Olivier Masclet and Gérard Mauger.
8 See 'Getting back to a "normal life": Biographical disruptions and "institutional goodwill"' by Vanessa Stettinger, and '"I've had two lives": Self-improvement work and the infiltration of psychological culture into working-class worlds' by Séverine Misset.

References

Arborio, Anne-Marie, and Marie-Hélène Lechien. 2019. 'Que font les usages "psy" aux classes populaires?' Paper presented at the seminar 'Une société d'individus, c'est-à-dire?,' CERLIS, 16–18 January.

Boltanski, Luc. (1982) 1987. *The Making of a Class: Cadres in French Society*. Translated by Arthur Goldhammer. Cambridge, UK: Cambridge University Press.

Bourdieu, Pierre. (1979) 1984. *Distinction: A Social Critique of the Judgment of Taste*. Translated by Richard Nice. Cambridge, MA: Harvard University Press.

Cardon, Dominique, and Smaïn Laacher. 1995. 'Les confidences des Françaises à Menie Grégoire.' *Sciences humaines* 53: 10–15.

Castel, Robert, and Jean-François Le Cerf. 1980. 'Le phénomène "psy" et la société française. Vers une nouvelle culture psychologique.' *Le Débat* 1: 32–45.

Collovald, Annie and Olivier Schwartz. 2006. 'Haut, bas, fragile: sociologies du populaire.' *Vacarme* 37: 50–55.

Darmon, Muriel. 2001. 'La socialisation, entre famille et école. Observation d'une classe de première année de maternelle.' *Sociétés et représentations* 11: 517–538.

Duvoux, Nicolas. 2009. *L'Autonomie des assistés. Sociologie des politiques d'insertion*. Paris: Presses Universitaires de France.

Garcia, Sandrine. 2011. *Mères sous influence. De la cause des femmes à la cause des enfants*. Paris: La Découverte.

Hoggart, Richard. 1957. *Aspects of Working Class Life*. London: Chatto and Windus.

Lahire, Bernard. 1995. *Tableaux de familles. Heurs et malheurs scolaires en milieux populaires*, Paris: Seuil/Gallimard.

Lambert, Anne. 2016. 'Échapper à l'enfermement domestique. Travail des femmes et luttes de classement en lotissement pavillonnaire.' *Actes de la recherche en sciences sociales* 215: 56–71.

Lechien, Marie-Hélène, and Yasmine Siblot, eds. 2019. '"Eux/nous/ils"? Sociabilités et contacts sociaux en milieu populaire.' Special issue, *Sociologie* 10, no. 1.

Maruani, Margaret, and Monique Méron. 2012. *Un Siècle de travail des femmes en France, 1901–2011*. Paris, La Découverte.

Masclet, Olivier. 2018. '"C'est mon moment." Le temps pour soi des ouvrières et des employées.' *Travail, genre et sociétés* 39: 101–119.

Mauger, Gérard. 2006. *Les Bandes, le milieu et la bohème populaire. Étude de sociologie de la déviance des jeunes des classes populaires (1975–2005)*. Paris: Belin.

Millet, Mathias, and Daniel Thin. 2005. *Ruptures scolaires. L'école à l'épreuve de la question sociale*. Paris: Presses Universitaires de France.

Misset, Séverine, and Yasmine Siblot. 2019. '"Donner de son temps" pour ne pas être des "assistés". Bénévolat associatif et rapports à la politique au sein de ménages stables des classes populaires.' *Sociologie* 10, no. 1: 73–89.

Morel, Stanislas. 2014. *La Médicalisation de l'échec scolaire*. Paris: La Dispute.

Pasquali, Paul, and Olivier Schwartz. 2016. '*La Culture du pauvre*: un classique revisité. Hoggart, les classes populaires et la mobilité sociale.' *Politix* 114: 21–45.

Poullaouec, Tristan. 2010. *Le Diplôme, arme des faibles. Les familles ouvrières et l'école*. Paris: La Dispute.

Retière, Jean-Noël. 1994. *Identités ouvrières. Histoire sociale d'un fief ouvrier de Bretagne 1909–1990*. Paris: L'Harmattan.

Schwartz, Olivier. 1998. 'La Notion de classes populaires.' HDR thesis, Université de Saint-Quentin en Yvelines.

Schwartz, Olivier. 2009. 'Vivons-nous encore dans une société de classes? Trois remarques sur la société française contemporaine.' *La vie des idées* 22 September 2009. https://laviedesidees.fr/Vivons-nous-encore-dans-une.html.

Schwartz, Olivier. 2011. 'La pénétration de la 'culture psychologique de masse' dans un groupe populaire: paroles de conducteurs de bus.' *Sociologie* 2, no. 4: 345–361.

Serre, Delphine. 2009. *Les Coulisses de l'Etat social. Enquête sur les signalements d'enfant en danger.* Paris: Raisons d'agir.

Siblot, Yasmine. 2018. 'Entretenir un rapport mobilisé à sa condition sociale en milieu populaire. Engagement syndical et sociabilité parmi des ouvrières de blanchisserie.' *Sociétés contemporaines* 109: 65–92.

Terrail, Jean-Pierre. 1984. 'Familles ouvrières, école, destin social (1880–1980).' *Revue française de sociologie* 25, no. 3: 421–436.

Verret, Michel. (1982) 1999. *Travail ouvrier.* Paris: L'Harmattan,

Verret, Michel. (1988) 1996. *La Culture ouvrière.* Paris: L'Harmattan.

Verret, Michel. 1979. *L'Espace ouvrier.* Paris: Armand Colin.

Villette, Michel. 1988. *L'Homme qui croyait au management.* Paris: Seuil.

20

BEING A RESPECTABLE WOMAN

Between stigma of housing estates and the union in-group – Chantal Monlouis

Yasmine Siblot

'Hello, love [...] I'll get back to you, my pet!' This affectionate exchange over the telephone took place between Chantal Monlouis, a worker and secretary of the CGT (Confédération Générale du Travail; General Confederation of Labour) union branch of a hospital laundry, and an experienced union employee who called to remind her of a meeting. This style of interaction dominates in this little union branch and reveals how important sociability is to its members, women with low occupational skills who in many cases are immigrants or children of immigrants residing in massive housing estates in the outskirts of Paris. The in-group atmosphere of activism provides them with a socially reassuring setting. This portrait of Chantal reveals a real contrast between this intense workplace sociability and her withdrawal on the residential and family scenes. It also reveals the importance of union engagement for some fractions of the working classes, low-skilled public-sector workers in this instance (Pignoni 2016), and its contemporary forms. Although Chantal has appropriated a discourse critical of the socially dominant 'Them' in and outside of work, to the point of vaunting the 'Us' of workers with her colleagues in the comfort of an in-group of 'respectable women' (Skeggs 1997), she also has a 'triangular social consciousness' (Collovald and Schwartz 2006) in common with other union members and keeps the less secure fractions of 'the estates' at bay. While asserting the ability to 'get rights recognised' (Siblot 2006), she moreover manifests institutional, and especially educational, goodwill.

Workplace-based research

Since this portrait is based on a study conducted in a workplace, not in the domestic space of a household like others in this volume, further details on

DOI: 10.4324/9781003330073-23

the research relationship are called for. I first met Chantal Monlouis in 2005, while conducting a study on the CGT union. She was one of a group of female laundry workers in a training programme held at a local union office near their workplace, and they encouraged me to look into their branch and visit their 'factory'. The laundry where they work is a public industrial establishment with 120 employees, nearly all of whom are labourers (and female labourers at that[1]), who wash the sheets and work clothes of a number of Parisian hospitals. Divided into three services (sorting, washing, and 'finishing' – drying and folding), work is mainly done on an assembly line at a set pace, and it is hard in many respects (difficult positions, repetitive movements, heavy loads to carry, hot and loud). Most employees enjoy the status of civil servant, although 15%–20% of them work on limited-term contracts or as temporary workers, and union membership is high (around 40%). In 2013, I renewed contact with the people I had met in 2005–2007, in order to deepen the analysis of their trajectories, and Chantal Monlouis – union secretary since 2007 – facilitated this return to the field.

Chantal has daily office hours, and I spent a half day per month with her for a little over a year. I interviewed her twice, but most material comes from informal conversations and repeated observations of practices and relations in the small group of activists that spent time in the office during their breaks and for meetings. Although I was warmly welcomed, I was no longer seen as a young person of no particular social position, as I had been in the first phase of research: I was questioned about my professional status, family situation, and place of residency, and I was kindly but explicitly kept at a social distance. Traits that might have brought us closer (being close in age, women with children) led to conversations in which the disparities of our situations were endlessly emphasised. Family life, school, housing, and leisure-time pursuits were discussed in detail, but the initially planned visits to their homes were always put off for later. The way they delineated the boundary of the study and kept it contained to the workplace seemed to reveal their desire to protect themselves from my potentially disparaging social judgement. The experience of being put at a social distance when I returned to the field moreover helped me to understand that my previous assessment situating them in the higher fractions of the working classes had been inaccurate and that their position was actually distinctly lower, Chantal's included.

A stable position at the bottom of the ladder

Chantal was born in 1963 and was 52 when we last met. She is from Guadeloupe, where she grew up in a small rural village. Her father had been a farm worker on a banana plantation until he moved to the mainland in 1974, as part of a wave of emigration from the French Antilles (Condon 2008). Thanks to the support of a sister-in-law, he was able to get a job as a service worker in a hospital on the edge of Paris, where he was then given a permanent job and worked until retirement. Her mother joined him a year later with their children and also tried without success to find work with the AP-HP (Assistance Publique-Hôpitaux de Paris; Public Assistance-Paris Hospitals); she finally found work with a hospital cleaning subcontractor. When Chantal arrived in the Paris area at age 12 (in 1975), she was quickly guided towards the typist/steno track in school, but she failed the CAP. She then went through a string of insecure jobs, some in secretarial work: a subsidised limited-term contract in a *collège*, a replacement worker at an alarm manufacturer, and various low-skilled manual and service jobs (mail sorter, housekeeper). She was living with her parents in a housing estate on the edges of Seine-Saint-Denis (north of Paris) when she met her future partner in 1986. Robert was one of her brothers' friends, born in Martinique in 1956, who moved to the mainland in 1974 with no formal educational qualifications. Shortly after arrival, he was hired by a hospital, and he has worked as a transporter at the same hospital in the inner suburbs of Paris ever since. They moved in together (without marrying) and, in 1989, obtained a two-room apartment in a housing estate in the inner ring of the Parisian suburbs. They lived there for more than ten years while waiting for new housing, a wait that dragged on despite the birth of their daughter Cynthia in 1998 and their son Brandon in 2000. They finally got a four-room apartment in a dilapidated housing estate where they still live; although the estate has since undergone major renovations, it still has a reputation for drug trafficking and violence.

After several spells of unemployment, Chantal applied to work at the laundry in 1989, on the advice of an aunt who worked there already. Her first attempt failed, but she was hired as a limited-term contractual hospital worker in 1990 and then became permanent in 1991, a civil servant with the category-C job of 'professional laundry worker'. After several seniority-based promotions, she reached the level of 'master worker' and an income of 1,400 euros a month (near the maximum allowed salary), like her partner. She has limited perspectives for promotion: she made an unsuccessful bid in the competitive examination to become an auxiliary nurse, does not feel up to civil service examinations for administrative work, and does not want to take the technician's exam, which would put her in the position of shop supervisor, a job that she thinks would be untenable. The status of laundry worker theoretically offers the possibility of retiring at 55 (due to the acknowledged demandingness of the job), but Chantal's broken employment history prevents her from being able to enjoy a full pension at that age like her co-workers, so she will keep working as long as she can.

Chantal and Robert have an assured but limited income: about 2,800 euros a month plus child benefits (for two children), but no housing assistance. They have no capital, have no plans to become property owners, and their consumption practices are economical without being marked by privation: they buy groceries from the estate's supermarket, wear inexpensive clothes, go out infrequently, and only take vacations every two years – a trip to the French Antilles made possible by the support provided by 'subsidised leave', which is granted to certain civil servants originally from overseas territories who work on the French mainland. These trips are still costly regardless of the financial aid, and most of the couple's savings get spent that way.[2]

Although these elements undisputedly keep the household out of the upper fractions of the working classes, Chantal and her family are nonetheless far from the insecure and impoverished fractions and are situated truly in the middle of the contemporary working classes. Their case is a gage of how decisive job stability is for couples with few qualifications and no other economic or cultural resources: more generally, their overall relationship to public institutions (and Chantal's in particular) is a key resource in their current situation and how they relate to the future, even more so than their civil servant status.

An engaged relationship with institutions

Chantal's father was a member of the CGT union, but she says he was never really an activist. She describes him in the same terms she uses for her partner, 'a simple union member', and remembers no conversations about unionism with him or union-related events or practices. It does seem, however, that her family (which includes many hospital workers, including her father and some aunts) passed on a disposition to call upon public institutions, more out of a legacy of civil service than from unionism. In addition to familiarising her with governmental administrations, this family socialisation led her to consider the resources of public and social services as 'rights' rather than 'hand-outs' (Siblot 2006, Cartier, Retière, and Siblot 2010).

So it is that one of her aunts, a laundry worker, encouraged her to apply for a replacement position at the AP-HP, with a future permanent position in mind. When she and Robert got together, she was still living with her parents and siblings in a housing estate, but they soon applied for public housing through the AP-HP, the municipal government, and a variety of low-income housing authorities. Although their application to the hospital's human resources office would never bear fruit, they finally obtained a two-room apartment in a municipally operated housing estate, and then, after repeatedly renewed demands at city hall, a new assignment to a larger apartment after their children were born, a four-room apartment on the fifth floor that Chantal describes as pleasant despite the lack of elevator and its location in a 'difficult' neighbourhood.

This engaged relationship with institutions is clearly expressed in how their children are raised, especially where school is concerned. Chantal and Robert have no formal educational attainments, and although Chantal attended school longer than her partner (until she was 18), she did not have a good relationship with the scholastic institution: she went directly to *collège* when she arrived in mainland France at age 12 and immediately had difficulties.[3] In *quatrième* (when she was 13–14), she was put on the vocational track and studied for the CAP examination in typing and stenography at a vocational high school. She claims she was really interested in 'the occupation of secretary' and thought she would succeed given her high marks in French (she makes few errors), but she narrowly failed the examination two years in a row because of her mathematics score, which she thinks is deeply unfair. She still has a lack of confidence where scholastic evaluations are concerned, as attest her remarks about an internal competitive examination at the AP-HP for which she sat but without much faith she would pass: 'It was really easy, but I flunked'.

Both children attended their neighbourhood public schools, and Chantal follows their education as best she can, lamenting the fact that Robert fobbed this responsibility off on her. Trying the limits of her academic baggage (in subjects other than French, that is, with which she feels much more confident), she at least ensures that they do all their homework and seriously restricts the time they spend away from home, in the neighbourhood. She has also long been invested in school parents' associations and was (re)elected every year to the boards of the primary school and, later, the *collège*. This provided her with a better understanding of the school system and, more importantly, privileged relationships with the schools' teachers and administrators, a sort of school 'colonisation strategy' (Zanten 2012). Although she is still very concerned about her children's education and often feels helpless, her assiduous presence made it possible for her to handle several sensitive situations by appealing to school employees for their help. For instance, in 2013–2014, Cynthia was in her first year of *lycée* and her marks began to drop; she and Chantal wondered if they should request that she repeat the year. A French teacher encouraged them to take this step and assured them that teachers would support her. The same year Brandon, who was part way through *collège* (*quatrième*, 13–14 years old), was punished several times for 'doing stupid things', stopped studying, and announced he wanted to take a vocational path the following year, split between *collège* and a vocational high school. Distraught, Chantal was ready to agree when the head teacher of the *collège* called to convince her otherwise, wanting to give Brandon 'a last chance', and she is very grateful for it. A year later she seemed happy with those decisions, although both children have marks that she finds a bit 'close'. This relationship of yielding to actors in the scholastic institution comes with her relative internalisation of legitimate child-rearing norms, like speaking with children and giving them 'choices'. As a result, she finds herself out of step, sometimes even in conflict, with her partner, who espouses a more traditional child-rearing style. Chantal criticises him for only intervening to punish Brandon by yelling and sometimes insulting him. She tries to convince him to attend certain appointments at the *collège* and to spend more time with their son.

This relationship to school comes paired with intensive use of local institutional options. Chantal enrols her children in a variety of free public organisations based in the *collège* and the neighbourhood's community centre for help with homework and their many leisure-time activities. Cynthia dances and sings and Brandon plays basketball and handball all thanks to programmes offered by the municipal youth services, and they regularly go off to camp or travel thanks to youth programmes offered by the municipality at very attractive rates. This is how Cynthia was able to go to the United States for 116 euros, the rest paid for by the city and the Conseil Général of their administrative department.

While she vaunts the city's initiatives for young people, Chantal is evasive when it comes to political news and her own opinions, sharing her union colleagues' marked scepticism of the political world. She says she votes regularly – and 'for the left'. She knows that the mayor of her city is in the Parti Socialiste (Socialist Party), but she has never been close to a particular party and keeps up with political news only sporadically, through 'news alerts' from her telephone service provider or by watching television while doing something else. The only newspapers to be seen in the union office are the free ones distributed in public transportation. But her positive relationship with public institutions and her use of local services led her to get involved in the neighbourhood events committee and attend a variety of municipal ceremonies, such as one held for the families of *collège* graduates. Chantal's account nonetheless reveals a strong contrast between this presence in the neighbourhood's spaces of institutionalised sociability and her limited interactions with other residents outside these scenes.

The stigma of housing estates and limited sociability

Although Chantal has lived in the neighbourhood for more than 15 years, her relations with the neighbours seem to be rather limited and marked by a concern with distinguishing her family from the most insecure families in the estates. This is especially so for those to whom she referred twice as 'the Africans', before moderating her statement by stressing that there were also 'good people' amongst them. This term targets big families whose children she thinks are poorly raised: for example, Chantal is exasperated by parents that let their children cut the line to serve and re-serve themselves huge portions from the buffet at the neighbourhood party. She mostly refers to the boys and teenagers outside the estate late at night as 'little Africans', seeing them as potential delinquents and fearing their bad influence on her son.

Her concern with distinguishing her family from the 'Africans' is ambivalent, however, because it touches on her experiences with racism, since she and her whole family are seen and identify as black. Along these lines, she mentioned the difficulties they encountered while looking for their first apartment, when some landlords turned away 'people with origins' (her expression), among which she counts herself, and she spoke explicitly of 'discrimination'.

This experience is one she partly shares with some insecure families in her neighbourhood, leading her to express solidarity with them, but she also harbours a feeling of racial and residential stigmatisation that spurs her to hold them at a distance.

So although she speaks highly of getting along with neighbours and helping each other out, and she encourages her colleagues with young children to ask help from their neighbours when they have childcare problems (implying she did so herself in the past), she nonetheless communicates a sense of relative isolation in her neighbourhood. She only mentions one old, close friend ('my friend') with whom she spends a little time every day after work: they meet up on an underground platform and commute home to the estate together, chatting a bit more there before going home to perform their domestic chores.

Chantal mainly spends her social time with her mother, her sister who is a single mother with a son Brandon's age, and her younger brother, who all live together in a housing estate apartment in a bordering city. Their close relationship is mainly kept up through daily telephone calls, periodic outings to things like the cinema, and regularly helping each other out (Chantal's mother took care of the children when they were little, and Chantal gives her money when she needs it, because her pension is small). This family sociability is selective, though, and Chantal has little contact with her other siblings. Likewise for her partner, who is closest to one of his brothers and an aunt (Brandon's godmother), who both live in Martinique. They see each other once a year, either in Martinique or in Paris, and communicate through the application WhatsApp.

Chantal's social relations outside of work thus seem to be limited, all the more so since she takes care of nearly all the domestic work and thus has very little time for herself: 'I handle everything', she said, listing the shopping, meal preparation, and housework, not to mention the paperwork for governmental administrations. She also feels that she has little help from Robert with raising the children, be it material assistance, school, or their leisure activities: 'It's like I was alone with my kids', she says. At the time of research, she was actively encouraging him to reinvest himself in his relationship with his children, especially their son, and contribute to helping them with their homework and keeping an eye on their friendships. More generally she laments the fact that their relationship has withered, and she criticises him for turning into a 'homebody'. Robert works early in the morning and comes home early in the afternoon; Chantal calls him a little later to wake him up from his nap. She says that when she comes home at night, he has not done a stitch of housework, and her efforts to start a conversation remain fruitless. She said that she asks him, 'So, did you have a nice day?', and starts talking about what she did, but he only responds in monosyllables. They do not go out often, except to play trifecta with a neighbourhood friend, and he rarely accompanies her and the children when they go to see family, a film, or a show. Chantal says she is 'resigned' to this situation, but she bemoans it. She emphasises that 'he wasn't always like that': she wanted to 'enjoy him' and her 'youth', and it was only after 10 years together that she decided to have children (she stresses the fact that it was a choice), when he would have liked to have had them earlier.

Rethinking union engagement in light of all these elements – social and professional position, relations with institutions, neighbourly and family sociability – lead to an illustration of how this engagement acts to uplift social standing and confidence, not only for the status of worker, but also for the status of 'respectable woman' (Skeggs 1997).

Union practice and sociability: respectability of class and gender

Chantal became a member of the CGT as soon as she began as a replacement at the laundry, in 1990. There was a major strike at the time, during which personnel blocked the site for several weeks, demanding the creation of a new status specifically for laundry workers in public hospitals. 'Status of what? What's a status?' Chantal laughingly pantomimed her reaction at the time, as a young insecure employee coming out of a long period of unemployment beginning to learn about the demands of employees and unionists. Chantal described how it had been impossible to not join the strike and very tricky to not join the union and explained that she quickly became a full-fledged civil servant the following year (with most of the other contractual workers), a change they won thanks to their mobilisation. She became shop steward in the early 2000s and was elected union secretary in 2007.[4] The CGT was the majority union (followed by two other unions, Sud Santé and FO), with about 25 members in 2005 as well as 2015 (newcomers replacing the departures), and is led by a committee of representatives. Every afternoon Chantal has office hours to receive workers and prepare meetings. She never mentioned any health problems, so I was slow to catch on to the fact that she has a partial disability that limits her ability to work in the same laundering post all day, due to 'musculoskeletal problems' and vascular issues.[5] Other members of the shop committee also periodically take 'representative' hours to attend meetings or meet with management or workers.

Observing office hours and meetings facilitates identification of the union practices of these public-sector workers. For one thing, it is a shop-based unionism, focussed on working conditions and defending the worth of workers (Beaud and Pialoux 2012). If stewards have to attend some meetings outside of the laundry (with the larger union organisation or joint advisory bodies with hospital management), most of their union work takes place in-shop. Protests against declining numbers of workers, complaints when machines malfunction, and objections to the practices of shop supervisors are as many motivations to act and make demands by bursting into the management office, directly confronting people in positions of responsibility, or scheduling more formal meetings. At the hospital scale, and in alliance with workers from other laundry facilities, it is also a matter of getting recognition of the value of the labours of workers charged with washing the laundry, a devalued 'dirty job' (Hughes 1996). Chantal regularly invites unionists from other sectors to visit their shops so they will be aware not only of how hard their work is, but also how technical it is and the volumes they handle.

In addition to defending workers as a group, unions provide more individualised support to employees with problems at work, and sometimes beyond work. Workers threatened with sanctions, in conflict with their superior, or having trouble finding housing or escaping debt call upon Chantal (and the other representatives that help her with the job) during office hours. If she thinks that the case is morally defensible and relevant to the union, she does her utmost to help that person 'get their rights recognised', whether it be in their relations with hierarchical superiors or social services. Chantal thus not only distributes information on the rights that come with their 'status', but she also tries to convey an active relationship to these rights.

Despite their work promoting workers as a group and providing more individualised support for recognition of their rights, representatives (and especially Chantal, because she ensures the daily office hours) run up against repeated accusations from rank-and-file members and other workers that their union position allows them to avoid the constraints of working on the shop floor and even obtain privileges (Mischi 2011). In February 2014, for example, a conflict erupted between Chantal and a young union member, Fabien, who thought that she 'wanders around' too much. It lasted several weeks, with Chantal refusing to 'let it drop' until Fabien apologised publicly. This is an example of how union members emphasise their technical skills and endurance at work: mastery of machine operation, not 'shirking' by drawing out breaks, and not complaining when in pain are among the norms that the activist core tries to embody and maintain, and these values likewise have deep roots in the working classes.

Indeed, stewards differ from other workers in their familiarity with issues beyond those concerning the laundry and in their relationship to speech and the written word – Chantal in particular is proud of her writing prowess and ability to adopt a rather formal linguistic register when interacting with management. But, like other shop committee members, she stays away from legitimate culture: she reads little, mostly union documents and virtually nothing with no bearing on work; she likes R&B and variety music (in one of her infrequent outings, she and her daughter attended the live musical tour of *Violetta*, a successful television series for young adults); she relaxes by playing on her phone or computer; and she and her co-workers often discuss their opinions of various television series (mainly game and reality shows).

Union sociability is driven by Chantal and other shop representatives (all women, save for one man who stays in the background) and can generally be understood as an assortment of tastes and norms that add up to a 'style of working-class femininity' (Avril 2014), a form of respectability with many constituent parts. Conversation and relations are first of all structured by esteem for their role of mother responsible for household management: workers have the right to wash and dry their personal laundry on-site twice a week, so the table in the union office is regularly covered by laundry to be folded, an activity that is often accompanied by discussion of family and swapping tips on running a home. Chantal also frequently calls her children from the office (to verify they are home from *collège*, have found something to eat, are doing their homework, etc.). The office is well organised, clean, and aired out, the dishes are clean, and Chantal has brought in a variety of decorations (plants, madras placemats). Regardless, this in-group atmosphere is not only focussed on reminding its participants of domestic and maternal norms, since it also promotes corporeal norms in terms of work on appearances: although they wear a uniform or coverall over their clothing and clogs or sneakers, all of these women carefully style their hair and wear jewellery, and some even wear makeup, despite the heat. They compliment each other on their clothes and accessories, which are attentively selected and updated. Chantal, who is a bit heavy, wears colourful roomy shirts, leggings, and earrings that are all clearly inexpensive but quite varied. Her very long hair is meticulously dyed and straightened (unlike her sisters, her hair is relatively straight thanks, she says, to her grandmother of Indian descent). These women also hold conviviality in high esteem, so their conversations are dotted with friendly digs at one another and the CGT regularly holds parties for union members and the personnel. Lastly, a central element in the ties uniting these workers is their great attachment to having a job and being independent. Half joking, one union member, a mother of young children who went back to live with her parents, once said she regretted not having a 'love guy' who took her away for weekends and gave her gifts, to which Chantal and other representatives shot back in the same tone 'You mustn't be a kept woman', and insisted she should always hang on to her job, and the rights and 'debit card' that go with it.

Although the union functions in some ways as a place for reminding members of the class and gender norms of a dominated position, it is thus also a space for affirming a hybrid respectability that values intra-feminine groups and material independence, at a considerable distance from family and residential settings.

Notes

1 Seventy per cent of 'production' employees are women. Male workers primarily hold specific positions at the beginning and at the end of the laundry chain.
2 The employer pays for the airfare and gives employees a trip allowance.
3 For an explanation of the French educational system, see the Appendix.
4 Stewards are designated by the union. They can intervene in a range of problems that might occur in shops, and attend informational meetings held by management.

5 This is a category of occupational disability resulting from repetitive movements, which are extremely common in the laundry sector (Garoche 2016).

References

Avril, Christelle. 2014. *Les Aides à domicile: un autre monde populaire.* Paris: La Dispute.

Beaud, Stéphane, and Michel Pialoux. (1999) 2012. *Retour sur la condition ouvrière. Enquête aux usines Peugeot de Sochaux-Montbéliard.* Paris: La Découverte.

Cartier, Marie, Jean-Noël Retière, and Yasmine Siblot, eds. 2010. *Le salariat à statut. Genèses et cultures*, Rennes: Presses Universitaires de Rennes.

Collovald, Annie, and Olivier Schwartz. 2006. 'Haut, bas, fragile: sociologies du populaire.' *Vacarme* 37: 50–55.

Condon, Stéphanie. 2008. 'Travail et genre dans l'histoire des migrations antillaises.' *Travail, genre et sociétés* 20: 67–86.

Garoche, Bruno. 2016. 'L'exposition aux maladies professionnelles. L'importance toujours prépondérante des troubles musculo-squelettiques.' *Dares Analyses* 081.

Hughes, Everett C. 1984. *The Sociological Eye: Selected Papers.* New Brunswick, NJ: Transaction.

Mischi, Julian. 2011. 'Gérer la distance à la base. Les permanents CGT d'un atelier SNCF.' *Sociétés contemporaines* 84: 53–77.

Pignoni, Marie-Teresa. 2016. 'La syndicalisation en France. Des salariés deux fois plus syndiqués dans la fonction publique.' *Dares Analyses* 25.

Siblot, Yasmine. 2006. '"Je suis la secrétaire de la famille!" La prise en charge féminine des tâches administratives entre subordination et ressource.' *Genèses* 64: 46–66.

Skeggs, Beverley. 1997. *Formations of Class & Gender: Becoming Respectable.* Thousand Oaks, CA: Sage.

Zanten, Agnès van. (2001) 2012. *L'école de la périphérie. Scolarité et ségrégation en banlieue.* Paris: Presses Universitaires de France.

21

'SIMPLE PEOPLE'? A LOCAL LABOUR FAMILY, BETWEEN SOCIAL REPRODUCTION AND OPENNESS – NATHALIE AND ALAIN RIGAUX

Antoine Younsi and Anya Bouamama

Born, respectively, in 1964 and 1966, Nathalie and Alain Rigaux are both from the Cambrésis, an industrial region in the north of France. As children they took the same school bus. Twenty years later they met again, at the home of the bus driver that had taken them to *collège*, who was a friend of Nathalie's family and co-worker of Alain. They were married two years later and had three sons between 1994 and 2002: at the time of research, Thomas was 21, François 18, and Julien 13. About a year after meeting, they decided to move in together to be closer, since she was a domestic worker in Paris and he was a lorry driver. Alain's parents and aunt helped them to find their first apartment in a small town in the Cambrésis. This town was centrally located between each of their families, which factored into their choice. It seems that proximity to services (schools, doctors, shops) were also decisive factors, since Nathalie did not have a driving licence and would have to raise the children mostly alone while her husband was on the road. While Nathalie was pregnant with their third child, the family moved to a bigger house nearby that belonged to one of Alain's cousins, and they still live there today.

At first glance, the Rigaux family is a 'simple', 'traditional', and 'normal' working-class family, at least according to their oldest son, a university student who was the main informant for this portrait. The family incarnates the familialism and localism supposedly characterising the working-class lifestyle, since the spouses have the same social and geographical background and share the same local network of relations and acquaintanceships. In addition to this local rootedness and attachment, the family lives according to traditional gender and inter-generational relations. In the background, Nathalie Rigaux is a housewife who works to maintain the family 'Us' through her devotion to her children and husband as well as to her mother and in-laws. But the 'traditional'

DOI: 10.4324/9781003330073-24

traits characterising this family's practices and worldview are reshaped by social change and opening: these 'normal people' are not so 'simple' after all. For one thing, the 'capital of autochthony' (Retière 1994, Renahy 2010) does not preclude residential mobility insofar as Nathalie is concerned. Secondly, in parallel with the strongly gendered division of roles and the family 'Us', Nathalie and Alain are both culturally open minded. Lastly, although the family 'Us' extends into Alain's significant professional and union sociability (which contributes to the denunciation of a 'Them' consisting of bosses and stockholders), residential localism has disappeared, fallen victim to industrial relocation. If the Rigauxs do not closely follow traditional working-class practices, it is because the economic context changed, as the industrial decline of the town has transformed the condition of the local working classes and their neighbourly relations.

Local roots and mobility

From local labouring families (Retière 1994, Renahy 2005), Alain and Nathalie's local social roots go deep. Nonetheless, they both went farther afield before becoming a couple. Alain has a CAP and BEP in electrical mechanics.[1] After finishing school, he left for his mandatory military service, which he then voluntarily prolonged another two years. During this period he earned the full range of driving licences. Confronted with the limited number of jobs in electrical mechanics, he decided to go into heavy goods transportation. In 1988, when he was 21, he got a job with the transportation company for whom he works to this day. After a long spell as a bus driver for a line operated for the SNCF (the national train company), for the past 15 years he has been a tourist coach driver.

Nathalie has a *cértificat d'études* (a primary-school diploma) and started a vocational *lycée*, but left her studies in cooking and early childhood education after six months to try her luck on the job market. From 18 onward she went through a string of jobs: nursery school assistant, babysitting, cleaning at the school or town hall. She spent summer vacations with her mother, who was a building superintendent in Paris, and ended up finding work in Paris herself by word of mouth. She is the one who went the farthest from the Cambrésis, since she was a domestic worker for a family in Paris for eight years before going back north, looking after the children and housework (cleaning, ironing, cooking). Ever since, she has been a housewife, which she considers to be a 'real job'. She also does three hours of house work for an elderly person, under the table. Nathalie would have liked to become a childminder but did not complete the process, which she though too complicated: obtaining a licence from the Council of the administrative department depends on repeated interactions with the early childhood specialists of Mother and Child Protection Services, who assess the safety and cleanliness of applicant's homes, along with their 'educational capacities'.

All three sons were educated at the same private Catholic school and the nearby public *collège*, but on different paths. Thomas was the most academically successful: he went on to the public *lycée* in town and then enrolled in the Université de Lille, where he earned a *licence* degree in History and Geography. Describing himself as fascinated by history, he says he has wanted to teach it since childhood. At the time of research he was preparing to sit for the CAPES exam (prerequisite for teaching at the secondary level) in History and Geography, seeing himself as a teacher like so many good students from working-class backgrounds (Hugrée 2010). As for François, after *collège* (where Nathalie says he got 'good guidance') he went into the Compagnons du Devoir to earn a BEP, in line with the family's labouring history.[2] For three years he alternated between periods getting on-the-job experience as a solderer and periods of classroom learning with the Compagnons, across the department and elsewhere in France. Julien was midway through *collège* (*quatrième*) at the time of research and was struggling, so his scholastic future was uncertain. Upon the encouragement of his teachers and the family doctor, he had just started seeing a psychiatrist.

A traditional family 'Us'?

Their eldest son, Thomas, put us in contact with his parents, who he presented in these terms: 'You'll see, they're simple people'. To his thinking, simplicity resides in the 'classic' character of his family, sheltered from any 'major shake-ups' of biography, temporally and materially 'settled', with a 'traditional', 'basic', 'normal' lifestyle. 'It's always worked out well, even very well, it's simple that way. [...] There's no complications, weird questions or other things to wonder about. There's dad, mum, the brothers, the grand-parents, and it goes on from there', he added, with a slightly far-off but affectionate expression on his face, as if he was both honouring and regretting his family's stability and social modesty.

It is true that this family's stability, the distribution of household tasks, and the somewhat quaint charm of the house (plus Nathalie's involvement in the parish) all correspond to the common image of the 'traditional' French family, rooted in a rural town that is losing its industry. The Rigauxs seem to have put the founding and perpetuation of the family at the centre of their lives. As we saw earlier, their place of residence was chosen mainly according to their desire to stay close to their respective families, whose help with the children was invaluable to Nathalie (babysitting, transportation for outings and seeing friends).

This 'traditional' character is also found in the gendered division of labour: wage-earning for him, domestic for her. Alain had a steady job when they became parents, while Nathalie (who had previously been a basic employee) seemed to resign herself to being a homemaker. This resignation also results from Alain's decision to go from driving a local bus route to driving tourist coaches, meaning that he would be away from home frequently, sometimes for long periods, although it also gives Nathalie a degree of everyday autonomy (Testenoire 2006). According to Alain, 'someone who lives with a coach driver is subject to the system. Either she gets used to it or, among us, those who don't get used to it get divorced'. So Nathalie does the real domestic 'job' (as she puts it) almost entirely herself. Unlike her husband, she says, she never has a day off. Thomas says that she devotes herself to 'running the house' the whole week long, with 'heart' and 'self-sacrifice'. She gets up at 5:45 to make her sons' breakfast before waking them. Once they have left the house, she does the dishes, cleaning, ironing, and laundry. Even if the housework is often quite unequally shared between them, Alain claims that he does his share 'equitably' when he is there. Regardless, the division of household tasks is still markedly gendered. Even if Alain does cook or start a wash from time to time, some tasks are only done by Nathalie, such as mopping or ironing. Other activities, typically seen as masculine, fall to Alain: yard work, home and automotive maintenance, and the main grocery shopping that requires a car. The lack of a driving licence, the gendered division of labour, and Alain's working hours limit Nathalie to activities in the private sphere.

Nathalie clearly also shoulders most of the care and childrearing work for the household and the extended family. Alain freely admits that the gendered division of roles extends to parenting:

> Raising the kids, I didn't contribute that much, I was absent a lot for that, [...] I can almost never manage to get to school meetings, the school, all that... I'm not... I can't manage to participate in all that, it's Nathalie...

Nathalie has demonstrated educational goodwill throughout their schooling, both materially (giving her time and energy to school outings and activities) and in more legitimate ways (helping children with homework, keeping up with their notes, and reading stories to pre-schoolers). Both of these dimensions of her investment in school led to more contact with educators:

> They need mums to go to sports, they needed mums to go to the museum, for example, to the library, so it's the same, it's always the same mums [...]. Plus the end-of-year field trips [...]. After that, well, Mother's Day it's the same, there's roses, so you gotta wrap up the roses, for Father's Day it was boxes of chocolates, so you gotta wrap the boxes of chocolates.

Nathalie is just as devoted to her children and husband in her own household as she is to her mother, an 80-year-old widow who lives a five-minute walk from the Rigaux house but is having increasing difficulty getting around on her own. Nathalie helps her out several times a week, going out for a walk or to the library together, and doing her dishes every two days and her cleaning once a week. Alain takes care of 'provisioning' 'granny' by doing her shopping as soon as he is able. They have agreed that they will visit her regularly to avoid the retirement home. Alain also helps maintain family ties by frequently helping his sister and parents. The Rigauxs are close to Alain's parents, who are 70. They are still independent, but Alain regularly helps them with yard work and home maintenance. They see Alain's parents twice a week plus occasional dinners (as a family or even with Alain's co-workers), holidays, birthdays, some outings, and their annual holiday in the Dordogne.

The Rigaux family only goes on holiday once a year. For the last ten years, they have rented an apartment in the Dordogne with Alain's parents. This new family tradition is an opportunity to get together while sharing the costs (the grand-parents pay for the rental) but is even more important for the time spent socialising together over meals, visiting to charming villages, castles, and markets, and enjoying group activities like fishing and cookouts. Nonetheless, Nathalie has mentioned wanting to change destinations. She'd like to go to the Vendée, where she and Alain have already been, but their holidays depend on his parents so they do not really have any say. Even Alain seems to find these holidays a little burdensome, although he does not dare say so outright: they participate in the intense familialism, composed of exchanged affections and favours, partly out of routine or even out of obligation and indebtedness that they are hard pressed to escape.

Finally, the sphere of the Rigauxs' family 'Us' is enlarged by Alain's professional sociability. The couple is old friends with Henri – the bus driver responsible for their meeting – and his family. Nathalie has also known them for a long time, since she used to mind their children. The two families maintain very close ties; even today, the children call Nathalie's mother 'gran'. Henri and his wife are each godparent to one of the Rigaux boys, François and Julien. When their parental constraints began to lighten, the two couples went on holiday together for five consecutive years, in the Vendée. They still see each other quite often, to share a meal or lend a hand (work on the house in exchange for vegetables from the garden). The strength and longevity of their bond lead the Rigauxs to say they are practically family: 'Well, we say friends, but...because you can't say they are family... but we are more part of the family than friends'. Furthermore, Alain's company's works committee plans dinners and trips for current and retired members, often held at a park (such as a zoo or amusement park). Alain invites Nathalie and his parents to the dinners. The trips are an opportunity to see each other and spend a day with the kids.

The Rigaux family is thus primarily characterised by a strong family 'Us' and the constraints imposed by Alain's job (trips and absences of irregular frequency and length), which have contributed to structuring the family – especially the division of roles and chores in the couple and their social relations.

Several elements in how this family functions reveal its typical aspects: Alain and Nathalie's desire to maintain strong family ties (sometimes at the cost of their own aspirations), the absence of social mobility, the gendered division of roles and labour. However, Nathalie and Alain's reflexivity concerning how their family functions illustrates one of the ways in which they are more distant from the classic family 'Us'. Nathalie, who worked for ten years before moving in with Alain, has no intention of being restricted to the role of housewife and wants symbolic recognition of her domestic work as a 'real job'. Alain is aware of how unfair this gendered division of labour is, and, in an effort to lighten or perhaps deny it, speaks in terms of 'equitable sharing' of housework when he is home.

The second way in which they diverge from this traditional model can be seen in how each of them implements autonomous activities alongside their domestic and professional obligations. Despite her short education, Nathalie likes to read and distinguishes herself from the figure of the woman trapped in the home by getting involved in cultural activities (being active in the church, investing in the school by reading stories to pre-schoolers, going regularly to the library). In this she is closer to another traditional female figure – the woman engaged in altruistic activities and upkeep of family cultural and social capital – more often found in middle and upper-classes than the working classes, although she is entirely responsible for domestic work rather than delegating it. The trips Alain takes as driver are an opportunity to get away and demonstrate curiosity in culture (visiting museums, cultural outings, cycling, and the like during his time off). The internet also facilitates his work, since he is on a social network for drivers, works out his itineraries, plans his activities, and discusses with drivers across Europe. He is moreover moved by a practical working-class relationship to knowledge that favours a form of autodidacticism (cooking classes during his time off, a working-class technical culture updated through use of the internet on top of mechanics and tinkering, occasionally reading books on gastronomy and medicine at the library).

This individual openness to culture by both members of the couple leads us to emphasise their relative distance from the 'traditional' family model. Thomas's success in school thus seems to be a consequence and a source of development in the family's practices and relationships: he is close to his mother, who he supports affectively by frequent visits home, and he confides in her; he tries to avoid discussions with his father, especially over politics, and failing that, tries to moderate what he calls his father's sometimes 'borderline' views on immigration. The family 'Us', understood as turning in on (or even isolation within) the private sphere and support of loved ones, thus also comes with individual social openness. But it also goes hand in hand with Alain's feeling of belonging to a strong professional 'Us'.

A strong professional 'Us' and opposition to 'the stockholders': a traditional worldview

As we have seen, the Rigaux family 'Us' is shaped by Alain's job and suffused with his professional sociabilities. Shifting focus, it quickly becomes evident that Alain's occupational identity is governed by the logic of familialism, this time applied to the working sphere. Alain opposes two antagonistic families, of a sort. The first is that of drivers, the 'closed circle of coach drivers', a 'group', a 'big family', that can be studied at many scales. The second is composed of company stockholders who to Alain's thinking form a 'family' in that they are few, united, and granted a nearly mystical power; they impose their interests on employees and profit from their labour. This compounds two classic dimensions of working-class worldviews: the importance of work in the definition of masculine legitimacy and the activation of an 'Us/Them' opposition in perceptions of the social space.

Alain says he spends seven months of the year with his coach-driving peers. Over the course of the year, he claims he spends more time with them than his wife: 'We are [together] constantly, it's as if, [laughing] it's not like we're married, but still [...] Over a year, if I really think about it, I'm more often with my colleagues than with Nathalie'. When he leaves on a 'trip', he is often accompanied by a co-worker, which creates close ties: 'a crew, that's a week, a week together. [...] In the same hotels, we've got the same coach, we're side by side'. Additionally, the crew (whose size and composition varies according to the trip) is part of a larger group, the 'family' of tourist coach drivers in the company. There are about ten of them in this 'voyage section', where Alain frequents fellow drivers with whom he's worked for thirty years and a few young drivers that the old-timers have to train. Being in this section favours the inclusion of young newcomers into Alain's work-family 'Us': 'Even with the young ones who come in, we never push them aside, never'.

The strength of the ties and integration of a family 'Us' in the working sphere is more than the closeness fostered by such work and the longevity of the relations; it also includes the nature of the ties developed with co-workers. Firstly, there is an erasure of the boundary between family and professional life: 'We all have each other's phone numbers, we know what the others are doing, we know the kids, [...] we talk about everything, family, kids, the problems we might have, sickness, death'. Secondly, the bonded group of drivers helps each other out considerably. Whether is be technical advice, swapping clients for practical reasons, or arrangements to free up schedules for leave time, it seems as though they all give themselves to satisfying the desires of the others: 'We work things out between drivers, too. If you wanna do this, want me to do that, a given client, we work it out between us. That's, that's kind of a family'. The last factor favouring the strength of their ties is going out together when off the clock. Several times Alain told us that he does things alone with his co-workers outside of work: 'We go out to dinner, ok we don't do it often, only 2–3 times a year, but when we aren't working at night we go out, my co-workers and I go out and about'.

Alain defines one last 'Us' that surpasses competition between companies and even borders: the 'big family' of drivers across Europe. It, too, is rooted in forms of sociability and mutual help that he has experienced with drivers from other countries, met on the road and online. Alain is on an online social network of European drivers where they share 'everything: tips [where to find good parking lots, bars, and restaurants], problems, breakdowns, hotels, what we think about hotels, we make notes, "don't go here anymore"'. On top of their practical use, such networks act as places of discussion, exchange, and sociability. They thus help to unify their various users and let them arrange to meet online or in parking lots or restaurants while on the road. On those occasions, the language barrier and competition between their companies are superseded by membership in the 'big family' of drivers, united by the same love for their occupation (both driving and life on the road), the lack of immediate hierarchical oversight, their interest in mechanics, masculine sociability, and the relational aspect of tourism transportation:

> We talk about vehicles, we look at the coaches, we talk about what's new, there's always something to see, always something to learn [...]. We always come across people we know, we're always in the coach parking lots, anyway there's no place in Europe where we don't talk to each other, even when we don't understand each other. [...] You come and have a drink, a coffee, a beer [...], we always manage to understand each other, to eat... [...] It's kind of a closed circle, coach drivers. It's a group [..]. It's a big family, even if we're competitors'.

The second 'family' in Alain's working world appears when he speaks of various union actions in which he participated against the major groups that have run the company he works for. In reference to family and professional 'tradition', Alain quickly joined the CGT – the only labour union active in the company, of which Alain says 99% of the employees are members, which attests to the persistence of unionism among skilled labourers in certain sectors (Pignoni 2016). A rank-and-file member, Alain presents his union as a 'very united, very hard-line' political force that knows how to make itself heard. Alain's company had a different name from the mid-1960s until 1993 and was apparently rather prosperous. In 1993 it was purchased by another company, which ran it for about ten years. A few years in, the union discovered 'a dirty secret' when it found out that a company affiliated with the parent company was renting them equipment at prices 25% higher than the going rate: 'They were the ones running things and the ones who took the money, and us, we were the ones that straightened it all out'. Thus began a struggle between the union and the parent company that ended with the purchase of his company in 2003 by someone who already owned another transportation company. Despite a few glitches – the buyer was slow to introduce himself to the drivers, having started with 'the office' and management – Alain was happy with the new owner. The new boss was a former driver himself, closer to the employees: 'The current boss [...] was a coach driver. His father, who built the [other] company, was someone who knew how to work, basically'.

Lastly, during our research in 2015, the RATP (the train network for metropolitan Paris and its further-flung suburbs) became the majority shareholder, at 54%. A period of wavering ensued, during which Alain and his co-workers wondered what would go wrong ('what sauce they would eat us in'). He thinks that 'it's always the same system': behind the string of acronyms the company has had through the years, with each successive owner, there is always a hidden 'family of stockholders', 'millionaires' who 'run the world'. This frequently mentioned 'family of stockholders' is a metaphor; it is nameless and seems to Alain to be moved by the perpetual lure of profit and managerial logics that has consequences on his work: 'They're people who want to make money money money, the stockholders, on the back of the worker'. Beyond this activist and moral denunciation of stockholder domination, the opposition between the word groupings 'people' and 'the worker' demonstrates Alain's perception of the antagonism between these two 'families'. For him, stockholders do not work, and this opposition between workers and non-workers is the foundation and fault line of his perception of the categories 'Us' and 'Them' in the working sphere. We should also point out that the same interpretation is applied to categorising bosses: the previous boss was accepted because he was 'a former driver', the son of someone 'who knew how to work':

> That was a boss we'd see very day; this will be a boss, but one directed by stockholders, there'll be a financial lobby behind it. If, by the end of the year, the accounts aren't good, they throw the director out and replace him with another, who tightens the screw.

So, after the family 'Us', Alain's second 'Us' is based on his organised professional group. This group of belonging and sociability is also 'like a family' for him – they are close to each other, do things outside of work, share objective working conditions, belong to the same union, and are friends who are familiar with each others' lives and help one other. This family-like aspect fades as the scale widens: the crew, tourist coach drivers in France, all bus drivers in France, European bus drivers. The meaning and structure of this 'Us' comes from its opposition to the 'family of stockholders' and bosses who 'get rich without working'.

'Non-workers', uncomfortable neighbourhood relations

The 'Us'/'Them' opposition structures Alain's view of his working world, but also how he relates to his neighbours and the town where they live. In opposition to 'those who work', in which he counts himself, he places two diametrically opposed figures: the 'big bosses' and the 'unemployed', who 'are there without doing anything' and 'never work'.

The biggest bosses locally are those of the old factories of the Cambrésis, chief among them Chappée stoves, Seydoux cotton goods, and Simons tile. Their factories long drew people to town, but their closure dragged it into decline. While their activities were being moved offshore, 'all these big bosses sold everything [...]. They went outside [of France] because French workers were too expensive [...], that's what made the town decline'. This plunged the town into 'not having anything to do': 'Once the factories had left it was over, we didn't have any more jobs, people found themselves without anything to do'. Alain includes himself in this 'we' ('we didn't have any more jobs'), thus marking the local impact of this industrial policy and his sense of local belonging. On the other hand, when he speaks of 'people' facing unemployment, he excludes himself because he thinks that not having anything to do is synonymous with incivility.

If the unemployed are presented as victims of structural change ('we have huge drug, alcoholism problems, all that, people who unfortunately are out of work have nothing to do'), they are also stigmatised as troublemakers: 'if people are working, they don't think about committing incivilities, doing damage, they have other things to do than loiter in the streets'. Alain sometimes discredits the unemployed in general, but his representations of his neighbours and their interactions most clearly conveys how he distances himself from the 'Them' of 'non-workers':

> It's like we should do like the neighbours, like, stay home [...]. In how people see us, yes, we bother them. We bother them, I have the impression that we bother the people who are around me, [...] I've got the impression that I'm disturbing them because I leave early in the morning, I see them, the ones that are there not doing anything [...]. We don't see people. And then, they avoid us [...]. They never talk to us, they never work, they're not people who work, they don't work and then, I dunno, they run away...

Alain implicitly decries an inversion of the norm of activity since, to his thinking, he is the one who is watched, observed, avoided, 'bothers' his neighbours, almost at fault for working. He takes his distance from a neighbourhood transformed by the industrial decline of the town, now a 'dole town' populated by 'non-workers'. He describes it as a 'dead town' that is emptying, noting all the houses on the market and shop closures.

In this rural region undergoing deindustrialisation, the Rigaux family seems to demonstrate the persistence of a 'traditional' working-class lifestyle: high esteem for male labour, feminine and maternal devotion in the background, identification with labour, sociability among labourers and the union, and local roots serving as a social system of resources and constraints. But this family is more complex: each spouse has developed practices that open them to culture in addition to their embraced roles within the family 'Us' and that move them away from relations with neighbours. The neighbourhood no longer functions as a relatively homogeneous social space where they can confide in each other, help one another out, socialise, and gossip: localism no longer exists in this form, and the division between 'Us' and 'Them' now plays out in an opposition between 'workers' and 'non-workers', also reflecting divisions within the working classes. This opposition appears in the values that the Rigauxs try to pass along to their children: they insist on hard work and school, the only things they think are likely to provide them with an occupation and keep them away from the 'Them' of the unemployed. Thomas, a university student in Lille at the time of research, seems to be the only one to be on an ascending trajectory accompanied by a degree of social and geographical uprooting. François's technical studies and Julien's trouble in school seem to put them both on trajectories of social reproduction. Here again, however, we have to ask if this social reproduction is as simple as all that. The experience of the youngest son in school illustrates the psychologisation of academic failure, the negative face of scholastic democratisation. As to the middle son, his training prepares him to be a skilled labourer in an ascension within the labouring world, carrying on his father's aspirations and taste for the technical, but within a 'society of degree-holders' (Millet and Moreau 2011).

Notes

1 For an explanation of the French educational system, see the Appendix.
2 The Compagnons du Devoir is a non-profit journeyman training association for the manual trades, offering a particularly traditional training through a series of apprenticeships all around the country.

References

Hugrée, Cédric. 2010. '"Le CAPES ou rien?": parcours scolaires, aspirations sociales et insertions professionnelles du "haut" des enfants de la démocratisation scolaire.' *Actes de la recherche en sciences sociales* 183: 72–85.

Millet, Mathias, and Gilles Moreau, eds. 2011. *La Société des diplômes*. Paris: La Dispute.

Pignoni, Marie-Thérèse. 2016. 'La syndicalisation en France. Des salariés deux fois plus syndiqués dans la fonction publique.' *Dares Analyses* 25.

Renahy, Nicolas. 2005. *Les Gars du coin. Enquête sur une jeunesse rurale.* Paris: La Découverte.

Renahy, Nicolas. 2010. "Classes populaires et capital d'autochtonie. Genèse et usages d'une notion." *Regards sociologiques* 40: 9–26.

Retière, Jean-Noël. 1994. *Identités ouvrières. Histoire sociale d'un fief ouvrier de Bretagne 1909–1990.* Paris: L'Harmattan.

Testenoire, Armelle. 2006. "Éloignés au quotidien et ensemble. Arrangements conjugaux en milieu populaire." *Cahiers du genre* 41: 117–138.

22

'IT'S REALLY IMPORTANT TO BE ABLE TO GROW'

Social ambitions and political disappointments in a working-class household – Vanessa Le Coz and Samuel Bidaud

Tristan Poullaouec[1]

Both born in 1980, Vanessa Le Coz and Samuel Bidaud live with their two little girls in a small, recently built house in the administrative department of Deux-Sèvres, in western France. The area's employment rate went from 5% in 2008 to 8% in 2016, but it still offers more employment options than the rest of the 'Vendée choletaise' (Chauvet 1987). A major centre of the footwear and clothing industries until the 1990s, the area still benefits from labour-dependent industry in other sectors (food, tyre, leisure watercraft, and motor coach manufacturing). Samuel's parents lived in this town when he was born, and Vanessa's (who were originally from the department of Finistère) moved there when she was three years old. Vanessa and Samuel met at the town youth centre in 1995, when they were 15. Their weekly 'dinners with [their] mates' assemble their childhood friends, all born in the 'village', which is how they refer to their part of town. Their siblings all live within 3 km.

This local rootedness is precious to both of them, even if they have travelled extensively. Their accounts of their lives stress the geographical and professional instability that delayed their moving in together and having children. How to understand the apparent paradox between their desire to move around and their return home? It is as if their love for travel, begun by Samuel, was overcome by plans for small upward social mobility, mainly at Vanessa's initiative. Their family histories shed some light on their need to get away. Aware of the duality of his family's legacy, Samuel's reflexivity illustrates a form of psychologisation of experience that is found in some fractions of the working classes today (Schwartz 2011). As for Vanessa, she is deeply invested in 'growing' professionally and ensuring their daughters' success in school, transferring her disappointed hopes in higher education to them. Lastly, this aspiration is challenged by their repetition of a binary representation of society split between 'Them' ('white collars',

DOI: 10.4324/9781003330073-25

'bosses', 'politicians') and 'Us' ('co-workers', 'mates', 'local families'), further complicated by the temptation to vote for the far right, which also puts them in opposition to foreigners, 'Roma', 'gypsies', and 'Muslims'.

Delayed cohabitation

Both left home to live elsewhere for quite some time, and they only 'got together' in 2005, ten years after they met. They lived and travelled in Australia for nearly a year before moving back to Deux-Sèvres together. They speak of their time in Australia as marking the end of youth and the beginning of their conjugal, residential, and professional stability. Samuel described his earlier lifestyle this way:

> It's that a moment comes when, dying of boredom in this Podunk town, you think, "well, alright then, I'm going to see what it's like elsewhere, but I'm going to go looking far, far away". […] Yeah, I'd come back to my mum's. I'd set aside every other pay check, I'd take off with my benefits, and then I'd take off to enjoy my youth.

Vanessa was the one to describe their return: 'And after, when we were back, we said "Well hey, it's time, we've travelled together, we did what we wanted to do, why not have a baby?"'

Prior to that, Vanessa's life had been turbulent, although many details are missing in the interviews. At age 19, Vanessa left her *lycée* in Maine-et-Loire for another in a large town in Brittany (probably as a boarding student), where she got a General *Baccalauréat* two years late.[2] She started a *licence* in sociology in Rennes but soon quit; she had been working at McDonalds to pay for school and found it more interesting. A year later, she went to England to be an au pair and met a Peruvian man to whom she was married for a short time. She spent nearly two years there before moving to Paris, where she enrolled in a hospitality school on a one-year qualification contract.[3] She had 'really struggled to find an apartment' and happily left Paris to live in her hometown, where she found a receptionist job in a budget hotel. When she returned from Australia, her good relationship with her new boss helped her rapidly become head receptionist for two hotels, and she worked up to 45 hours a week in 2007–2008.

In 2009, when their eldest, Manon, was born, Vanessa decided that 'it's just not possible to work weekends, holidays', and so she turned to office work, taking a continuing education course for accounting assistants at a national agency for adult education (AFPA) near Nantes. Shortly after, she was happy to land an open-ended employment contract in the purchasing department of a commercial furnishings manufacturer very close to home, although it was not in accounting. Although she clearly expresses her regret at not having persisted in sociology at university, she is proud to explain how she became a supply technician:

> Still, I really grew, really grew internally, actually. Because going from data entry to thinking a little more, having responsibilities, in five years, it's really not bad. Plus... Well, I don't know, it's also because I wanted it, because it's something I wanted, too. And I still want it, to progress a little in work. Even with the girls [her children]. For me, it's, like, really important to be able to grow. Even if, you know, I didn't have a lot of school, I mean, I didn't go far in school. But if there is a way to grow with a company, you can do it, I think. Well, I mean I think it's doable. Well, I succeeded, at least. Samuel will tell you about it, too, it's the same for him – he succeeded in doing that quite a bit himself. Even if we are still low-level employees, labourers.

This small promotion should be contextualised in the restructuring of her company. In debt and trying to expand in Asia, the industrial group was pinched by the economic crisis and saw its revenues cut in half. Executives closed two of four factories in France, putting 200 employees out of work. Many left her factory around the time she arrived:

> the old-timers couldn't stand it – it didn't work at all like it used to, it was no good. They were unhappy, basically. That wasn't the case for me, so that's also why I was able to grow, because if everyone were there in place, I wouldn't have grown that way. So I got there at the right time.

Samuel has a vocational *Baccalauréat professionel* in Mechanical Production and speaks of his educational path realistically and without regrets: 'I did a BEP, and then a *bac pro*. After that I had the possibility of going back to the general track, but since I liked it a lot, I left to put it into practice'. In his 20s, Samuel alternated between long trips (travelling for several months at a time in French Guyana, South America, continental Africa, Madagascar, Cambodia, and Laos) and limited-term employment contracts for 6 months as a turner and milling machine operator while living with his mother. He was proud to be working for his 'fourteenth company', which designs and manufactures precision cutting tools for the automotive and aeronautic industries; he had been there a year and a half at the time of interview.

In 2010, the company was bought by a major Swedish group, which was in turn bought two years later by the dominant multinational company in the sector. The new owners cut 1,000 jobs worldwide in 2015, 45 of which in France, so Samuel was also hired in a context of restructuration. Having already worked in this domain, he was rapidly promoted to production team supervisor, like so many workers with vocational *baccaluaréat* degrees (Misset

2009): 'I don't "do management" with my guys - I bring them their work, I explain what to do'.

He highlights the importance of the technical knowledge, research and development, and closeness between higher-ranking technicians and engineers that is involved in his work: 'We aren't at the base of a machine working the line. Gotta use yer hands and brain'.[4] Nonetheless, he thinks that his status, alongside his professional sociability, places him clearly on the 'blue-collar' side rather than with the 'technical managers that've never made anything':

> I manage to take in theory and convert it into practice. But yeah, above all without doing any management. [...] I certainly don't go near that. Or clients, either, [...] I'll never have a client on the line, and so much the better!

Deep down, his greatest source of professional satisfaction is undoubtedly the feeling of having a sought-after qualification that protects him from boredom and unemployment.

> Oh, well, for me it's a party because I have knowledge that's worth its weight in gold today, on the market. And for a dead end, I think I'm pretty lucky! [laughing] Because they stuck me in a dead end, [but] I liked my line of work, and so it makes me happy. So yeah, it's the tops. As far as I'm concerned, it's the tops, it's really tops. And then, we're also in a region, the West, that's hugely industrial so it's really easy to find [work].

Tensions from their family histories

Between the two of them they earn a little over three thousand euros a month. Vanessa took part-time maternity leave since the birth of Jade, their second daughter, in 2014, so she does not have to work on Wednesdays; her drop in income is compensated by the Child Benefit Office (CAF, Caisse d'Allocations Familiales). Their trajectories of small upward social mobility probably explain why Vanessa and Samuel do not regret returning to the hamlet where they grew up: they say they are very attached to it because of family and friends.

Life has been no picnic for them, however. Samuel's mother died in 2012, at age 72. She was widowed when Samuel's father, a farmer, died when was 4. Three years later she remarried a man 15 years her senior who kept the local bar. Her death plunged Samuel into a depression that was 'healed' through psychiatric treatment and medications (antidepressants, anxiolytics, sleep medications). 'I was unemployed at the time, and so my psychiatrist goes, "I think you'll stop treatment the day you find a job you like"'. However, his troubles clearly go deeper than that.

The same year Samuel and Vanessa were separated for about a year, most likely after the death of his mother. Among the causes for the separation cited in the interview are Samuel's depressive and moody inclinations, along with arguments about household finances related to their not having a joint bank account (Vanessa blamed him of not wanting to share household expenses equally). Samuel took off to Madagascar for a while.

> I realised that I was depressive ever since I was a kid, due to the death of my father when I was four and loved ones who wanted to protect me but ultimately imposed taboos around my father's death, taboos around the family.

Today, Samuel is rather talkative about his family history and social position. One of his brothers took over the family livestock farm, another manages a small farm and garden equipment shop, and the third works as a glazier, 'so, pretty manual jobs, basically'. The man he calls his 'adoptive father' had children of his own who have become 'teachers, upper management'.

> So there was also, at a time, at the time, you see, when the family blended, I was young and so I benefitted from both, I'd say. But there was a degree of shock [laughing]. Wow! [...] Yes, a culture clash. And then, on my adoptive father's side of things, the marriage wasn't necessarily taken well either, since he remarried a farmwoman, a widow, who had a farm on her hands and kids, too. So not necessarily taken well on his side, either.

Since his mother's death, Christmas dinner no longer brings all the siblings together: 'When I still had my mother, we did that as a family, with them. But, y'know, it was kinda... It was kinda... dismal [laughs]'. Samuel thinks that the age difference and being the youngest explain why he is not very close to his brothers, other than the one 'that's just above me'. He was never close to his stepfather's children, either, where social distance is added to the mix. Samuel's inheritance made it possible to lighten the bank loans to buy and expand the house where they now live. They bought it below market price because it had belonged to his mother, who had purchased three houses in the hamlet to let as a supplement her retirement. This inheritance objectively improved Samuel and Vanessa's situation. Since their household income level makes them non-taxable, they can afford to set aside 200 euros a month with an eye to another purchase: Samuel wants a larger house in the hamlet, while Vanessa dreams of a studio in Nantes, a major nearby city, as a source of additional income.

The death and dealing with the estate were trying for Samuel. Neither he nor his mother had fully grieved his father's death, which he described as 'a burden that dragged us both down'. Settling the estate raised tensions between the two older brothers, but Samuel watched without getting involved and stayed on good terms with both. He was mostly worried about not being able to overcome his illness, because several members of the family had already suffered from depression. Although they were separated at the time, Vanessa was very supportive in his fight against depression, making the first appointments with the family doctor and then helping him regain self-confidence. Following a family conflict between her sister and their parents, she herself was considering counselling from a mental health service centre, because 'I've got too much of a knot in my gut ever since. It's starting to bug me, I've gotta do something'.

Vanessa's parents got married, found steady jobs, and had children in rapid succession in the early 1980s, when they were in their 20s, and arrived in the region shortly before the recession impacted local industry. Settling into Vanessa's hometown, her father became a maintenance worker for Michelin and her mother an office worker in the procurement division of a supermarket. When the interviewer remarked upon the similarities in their jobs, Vanessa concurred but sought to distinguish her path: 'Well, it's not the same because she's in a supermarket, but it's the same sort of work. Except she's been doing it as long as I have, you see'. Vanessa's father encouraged her to pursue her studies. Although she thinks it is important to follow Manon's schoolwork and has gotten involved with the school parents' association, she sometimes distances herself from her father's childrearing style, marked by an engagement in education but including practices that were 'dissonant' with new pedagogical methods (Kapko 2012):

> I had to know my history lessons down to the last detail. It didn't make any sense because I didn't understand anything about what I was learning, it was memorisation. And so I didn't want to do it, either... So [with Manon], I just want to try to make her understand how you have to learn, basically.

It is likely that Vanessa and Samuel are not on the same wavelength when it comes to the orientations their children should take in school. Vanessa has already noticed a difference between their approaches:

> I'd do anything for her to make it, I think [...] Anyway I'll try to be more on top of her. I think it's more important for me than for Samuel - 'Yeah, you can be a hair stylist, we don't care, y'know'. Oh no! Pain in the ass! But still, I didn't do it myself. I mean, I didn't do it? I only got my *bac* and I think that I might have been able to do something else'.

This regret that she cut her studies short drives her plans to have her prior experience validated so she can change employers someday without taking a drop in income: 'I'm lacking my *bac* plus two [years of post-*bac* study], basically', she explained.[5]

Avoiding conflict at work

Vanessa is rather satisfied with her professional situation, however: 'I can't complain', she said several times. She uses the same expression to relativise the unequal sharing of domestic chores between her and Samuel and the ends of the month 'in the red', and when assessing her income and working conditions. Nonetheless, at work, 'people complain, but they don't say anything': 'I've been there five years now and there hasn't been a single raise'. At another site, the restructuring led to stoppages due to the presence of a local union section, 'But that's them – us, no', Vanessa explained, adding, 'Samuel'd tell you, "That's the Vendée for you"'.[6] There are no union members where she works, and she does not want to get involved 'for the collective':

> Even me, I know… I would really have liked to be on the works council […]. And then I thought, that's enough, if I do the works council plus my 28 hours of parental leave, well, my job… for one thing, I wouldn't be doing it any more, and then, after that, well my professional goals will take a heavy blow, basically. […] I think that someone that doesn't have that ambition - to grow professionally - or who says 'It's a lost cause in this company anyway' [could get involved in the union]. Anyway, for me, I know that I'd be like that, if I didn't have any professional ambition.

Samuel has experienced several social conflicts in his company, but he speaks of interpersonal conflicts, which he puts at the same level, in greater detail. For example, his manager had a 'tiff' with one of his co-workers: 'And so afterward, it's funny, they each came to see me to tell me what happened. I'm still the go-between in situations like that'. He also mentioned a former employer that made the unequal salaries of employees in equivalent positions public information: 'It was clever. The bosses' goal, it's to divide so as to better conquer'. On their side of things, some employees had managed to get their hands on the income tax declarations of the company's top three executives. Arguing that he tries to avoid 'jealousy', 'resentment', and 'a mess among employees', Samuel has resolved to no longer get caught up in this kind of confrontation: 'Now, [whistles] - if there's a conflict, I just back away [laughs]'.

The weakness and limitations of unions also figured into his resolution: 'They're unions that lined up on the bosses' side', he said.

> When they're the ones that ask us to work 42 hours a week, they made it really clear that if we didn't do it we were putting the company in danger, or things like that. So you see, it was… we had the boss's line coming from the union.[7]

'A vote to provoke'

The voting record of the canton where Samuel and Vanessa live has never escaped the right, which in that region means primarily a Christian democratic inclination. As in several other departments in western France, however, the far right made a breakthrough in 2015, with a backdrop of high abstention: in their town the Front National's (FN) list for the regional election received 25% of the vote, as compared to 7% five years earlier. The issue came up rather early in the first interview with Vanessa, who was 'super-astonished' by the FN's results in her town: 'But we haven't got any… I mean, there aren't a lot of foreigners here. We haven't got troubles like they might have in big cities with the Roma or foreigners'.

Vanessa is not particularly interested in politics. Or rather, she prefers to pay attention 'to what's going on around me and how it happens': 'After, what's going on in the world, I mean, in the world or in France, politically, it's such a disaster right now…' She voted for the first time in 2012. On previous occasions, she had been abroad or too far from her polling place and had never thought to authorise someone to vote in her place. She has voted for the left and far left:

> But you see, in the presidential elections, the last ones there, oh, well, I was sure of it! I was all, "Oh, well anyway, the far left can't lose, it's got to [win], it's not possible [for it to lose]. People are too bad off, something has to happen".

She and her father shared disappointment and a temptation to abstain in the general election:

> God knows he said a thousand times 'No, it's super-important to vote, blah blah blah', and there he goes and starts not wanting to do it anymore, or almost, to say, 'No, this is unbelievable!' Almost saying that he'll go vote FN, basically. The other day he said, 'But no, but actually, I could never, like, I'll never go vote for the FN, I'd rather not vote at all'.

She says she's 'disgusted' and seems to be at a loss: 'I don't get it, I don't understand anything anymore', 'I have the impression that we have no power'. In the future she is thinking of leaving her ballot blank, but Samuel (who long voted a blank ballot before starting to vote for the left) 'lectures her', explaining that it serves no purpose. In the departmental-level elections, he voted for the far right – although, according to Vanessa, 'it's just to shake things up'. She does not approve of his vote, but she tries to protect Samuel's image by stressing that the FN's strength is the simplicity of its message, an argument that has emerged other studies as well (Braconnier and Mayer 2015):

VANESSA: I think there are things, he agrees with them on certain points, basically. But… but not on everything, of course, on anything racist, fascist and racist, he doesn't, but there are things he believes in, basically. But they know how to sell themselves very well, y'know. After, I think that, you see, it's stupid, but they are maybe the only ones, when you look at what's happening, I mean, when you look at what they can do, they're the only ones that are… that are real, not real, but understandable. Actually, they are the ones you can manage to understand the best, basically.

INTERVIEWER: Yeah? When they speak?

VANESSA: When they speak, yeah. And it's stupid, y'know, but there's plenty of people that think, 'Well yeah, hey, there's like some things where they're not wrong [in a disgusted tone]. Ultimately they want to do something, basically, to try to do something new'. But no! There's more to it than that, behind it all. I mean, I'll never get to that point.

Samuel was not that embarrassed to explain his vote to the interviewer the first time they met. It was an act of 'anger' that he described in a humorous tone: 'I wanted to see what it'd be like: "Oh shit, I did it!" [laughing]'. He was doubtlessly trying to be reassuring when he added that he would go and 'vote for the left in the general election if there's a real problem'; 'I was also raised that way, to think to the left, so…' The arguments he gave went through three phases over the course of the interview. After positioning his vote as a strictly tactical move to make his disappointment with the left heard, he tried to position himself relative to the ideas backed by the FN but ended by discussing a very specific local and familial example at length. This explanation mainly illustrates the current-day difficulty in maintaining votes for the left, regardless of the political legacy of parents.

SAMUEL: Yeah, to be provocative, yeah, that's it. A vote to provoke.

INTERVIEWER: Out of disappointment?

SAMUEL: Yeah, that's it. Maybe also to show the socialists in power that, well, that's it, we're… that the voters they aren't getting on the left anymore, well, they didn't go to the far left or [centre] right […]. Yeah, I voted for the [Socialist Party], for Hollande. I was happy, but then I saw that they cut [welfare] benefits, I saw they cut lots of things. Like apprenticeships for young people, things that make me sick at heart, basically. Because, see, I've got a BEP with a *bac pro*, and today […] employers don't take apprentices anymore because they're too expensive'.

Beyond disappointed ideological inclinations, this case shows that the FN vote may also express resentment related to the rift between the working classes' stable and vulnerable fractions, which does not necessarily come with racist justifications:

> It's the same, I'm not against immigration but I think that it was done badly, basically. After, I think it's done badly when you see in Calais what can happen. […] So my brother, he had things stolen twice in a

> row - he has a sheep farm, he had sheep stolen. [...] So the cops came and gave us the whole, 'Oh well, when all's said and done, now that [...] there are strict laws for slaughterhouses, Muslims can't come buy their sheep directly anymore because the sheep's tails have to be long [can't have been docked], there has to be a prayer toward Mecca, all that has to be done. So since they don't have the right anymore where veterinary things are concerned, now gypsies steal sheep to sell them to Muslims'. So somehow, if his things are being stolen, it's because the laws are poorly made.

The intention is not to present Samuel's vote as an expression of complete agreement with the ideas of the far right supposedly typical of the contemporary working classes, but rather to show how such a vote can be made at a given moment in political history by someone possessing a set of social attributes that are currently commonplace in some working-class fractions: both members of the couple are employed, with modest educational capital, stable professional positions, aspirations to upward social mobility, recent access to homeownership, and disappointment in unions and left-leaning political parties.

Notes

1 The interviews and their initial analysis were conducted by Sarah Delcroix in May 2015.
2 For an explanation of the French educational system, see the Appendix.
3 Qualification contracts are fixed-term employment contracts for people up to age 26, based on alternating between training courses and a job and culminating in recognised qualifications.
4 This is a common posture among young qualified workers with vocational *baccalauréat professionnel* degrees (Eckert 2006).
5 Young labourers with higher educations are more likely to pursue continuing education (Poullaouec 2004).
6 The Vendée is a neighbouring department, just to the south, where Stéphanie's employer is located. It is known for its conservatism.
7 In contrast to the legally mandated workweek of 35 hours for non-management job categories.

References

Braconnier, Céline, and Nonna Mayer. 2015. *Les Inaudibles.* Paris: Presses de Science Po.

Chauvet, Alain. 1987. *Porte nantaise et isolat choletais. Essai de géographie régionale.* Maulévrier: Hérault-Editions.

Eckert, Henri. 2006. *Avoir 20 ans à l'usine.* Paris: La Dispute.

Kapko, Séverine. 2012. *Les Devoirs à la maison. Mobilisation et désorientation des familles populaires*, Paris: Presses Universitaires de France.

Misset, Séverine. 2009. 'Proximité professionnelle et distance scolaire: les jeunes ouvriers qualifiés et leurs trajectoires.' *Revue française de pédagogie* 167: 59–71.
Poullaouec, Tristan. 2004. 'Les jeunes ouvriers et la "formation tout au long de la vie": promotion ou insertion?' *Formation Emploi* 86: 53–68.
Schwartz, Olivier. 2011. 'La pénétration de la "culture psychologique de masse" dans un groupe populaire : paroles de conducteurs de bus.' *Sociologie* 2, no. 4: 345–361.

23

ALWAYS BETWEEN TWO WORLDS

One couple's split local social life – Manou and Jean Audouin

Clément Degout

'We freaked out. Jean thought "No, I can't imagine myself with a black woman," and I thought, "oh my God, no way, I could never live with a white guy!"' Manou and Jean Audouin met in a city in central France in 1998, a year after Manou had migrated to the mainland from Martinique. She was 24, he 38. As Manou's description indicates, their relationship was anything but a foregone conclusion; given the great differences between their backgrounds, such a relationship seemed inherently delicate to each of them and their families. Nonetheless, it all went quite quickly according to Manou: in the year that followed, they moved in together and got married 'like a formality, like in Las Vegas'. They had their only child, a daughter, the year after that. In addition to the significant differences between their backgrounds (Antillean working-class and rural white working class), their age difference, and the fact that they were older when they moved in together set them apart from their siblings.

After several moves to different towns due to Jean's lorry-driving jobs, they settled in his home region. They live in a town of barely 5,000 inhabitants in a rural department in western France. Manou had a *baccalauréat* in business but stayed at home after they met, until she got a foster-care licence in 2010.[1] She now cares for minor children in placement by the departmental child protection services (Aide sociale à l'enfance: ASE), who she takes into their home for an income below minimum wage. After a string of lorry-driving jobs, Jean is now employed as a full-time conveyor of new buses with a side activity as self-employed lorry-driving instructor, which is barely profitable. He is often on the road to other parts of France, while Manou's work makes her place of work and residence one and the same.

The quest for independence at or through work is a very present theme in interviews with the Audouins that makes particular sense in the context

DOI: 10.4324/9781003330073-26

of their respective occupations, which are situated according to gendered and racialised divisions of the job market. Their differing ways of relating to wage work and the domestic space are also seen in their local civic engagements and more broadly in their split sociability with local friends. They have different ways of seeing and speaking of how they relate to other social groups, especially where the insecure fractions of the working classes are concerned.

Getting out of the house

Manou's narrative of her occupational trajectory places it in the logical continuity of her volunteering activities and past jobs, up through her acquisition of a foster-care licence and her investment in an undervalued occupation for which she has found meaning – helping young people in delicate social and affective situations, 'working for the government', and reporting to the state.

Their 2005 move to Jean's home region coincided with their daughter starting school, and after having spent several years at home Manou said she felt useless and frustrated. She also described her isolation broken only by Jean's parents, who live on the same street and who she helps often. In order to escape a life limited to the home, and based on her skills and naturalised taste for childcare, she became intensely involved in early childhood organisations in the region, initially without pay. As a volunteer in the sociocultural centres of a neighbouring town and then their own, she was an active member of the school parents' association while participating in a variety of local programmes for childrearing such as the 'parents' café'.

These activities allowed her to build what would become the couple's main network of friends. She mainly met other married women through these engagements and furthermore discovered that they have 'real jobs', paid employment (Lambert 2016). She decided to go on the job market herself. She earned a BAFA (brevet d'aptitude aux fonctions d'animateur, a certificate qualifying her to work in a supervisory capacity with juvenile publics) and returned to her town's sociocultural centre, this time as a paid youth counsellor. She even joined the centre's board as treasurer. After meeting other couples in which both work outside the home, she came to see the material and symbolic importance of her paid activities as recognition for her work as well as a reduction of her financial dependence on Jean.

Her contribution to household income allowed her to break with the classic heterosexual marital model wherein *he* brings in money and *she* manages domestic affairs – a model she considers 'old-fashioned French' and tries to avoid. Although the job of youth counsellor was insecure, it was, as she put it, a way 'to associate the useful with the pleasant'.

While Manou's local engagements were a gateway to employment, they also contributed to her inclusion and position in the local social world, leading her gradually towards social work. At the town sociocultural centre, she was thought to be the one with the best relationship to 'kids from the zone', 'problem kids'. She put the good relations with those she calls 'social minima' to advantage, explaining this proximity by pointing out that she was the only black person in the office. This observation and suggestions from her co-workers got her thinking about social work and getting licenced for foster care.

Through these activities, Manou thus arranged spaces of sociability for herself outside the home, while seeking recognition of her care work through public employment. Being hired as a foster carer by child protection services gave her a professional view of the families whose children are in placement and confided to her today – she generally speaks of them in psychological terms and regularly refers to individuals' family histories. Working for state social services gave her skills and experience, and indeed she speaks of the minors in placement in a register of expertise: one child had 'self-destructive behaviour', and a pregnant girl she supported through the birth of the child had 'adolescent behaviour' rather than 'maternal behaviour' and exposed her child to 'situations of risk', and it was impossible for such a helpless mother to build a 'soothing environment' for her child.

The professional legitimacy of this view is nonetheless undermined by the subaltern position of foster-care providers in the field of social work.[2] Manou's search for independence at work is manifest in her accounts of conflict with her hierarchical superiors. She describes herself as a 'loudmouth' who complains to her superiors by registered mail or requesting a meeting. She described the screening process as an invasive procedure that she resisted somewhat by denying social work inspectors access to her and Jean's bedroom. She also tries to formalise her professional relationships to get a grasp of what is expected of her work (especially informal expectations), by requesting access to behavioural counsellors' and psychologists' job descriptions, for example. On her own initiative she writes up weekly menus, activity schedules, and detailed accounts of daily expenses, which she posts on the refrigerator and files away, and she slips analogies between running a household and a business into her speech. This all means that she is ready to 'provide her accounting', a sign that she feels invested with a responsibility through her relationship with the state. For example, she insists on full traceability of how she spends the monthly fostering allowance issued to cover the costs of children taken into the home (in addition to her salary). This assiduous management of financial resources is an indication of this responsibility. Speaking of the children confided to her by child protection services, she asserts that this way, she does 'not teach children to be future dole dossers'.

Furthermore, Manou's professional relations with her peers are also conflictual. She claims her co-workers boycotted her because they had different conceptions of working as a group. She refers to an institutional definition of child protection service teams, which group her with skilled workers (behavioural counsellors and psychologists), which she opposes to the informal foster carer help and information network, whose invitations she has always declined.

She stopped attending practical analysis workshops, where violent arguments frequently erupted, which she suspects may not respect confidentiality. By emphasising her involvement in the institutional organisation and her concern to 'advance the occupation' at the cost of relative isolation, she thus stresses that she does not feel that she belongs to foster carers as a professional group.

This conflictual situation arises from two ways in which she tries to set herself apart, rooted in the position of foster carers. Her professional position places her at a *de facto* distance from parents whose children were taken into state care, while she is trying to free herself from a morally discrediting image of foster carers as the mercenaries of social work, unskilled workers doing it 'for the money'. She sets herself apart from her peers by highlighting her vocational rather than instrumental relationship with the job and getting the similarities between her life history and those of children in placement acknowledged. Over the course of her stories, she mentioned the violence one child was subjected to, the self-harming of another, and one adolescent's experience of migration and foreignness, all situations that activate memories of her own childhood. This proximity sometimes upsets her to the point of having to stop caring for certain children, but it is also the basis of her legitimacy through experience-based knowledge. Manou thus sees herself in an intermediary position, between the groups that encounter each other in social work.

Neither a civil servant nor on the dole

He alone in a lorry, she without anyone telling her what to do in her house, Jean and Manou both value their independence at work much more than any form of professional sociability, marking a common aspiration to escape certain forms of subordination, which in Jean's case ties back to his farming background (Gollac and Laulhé 1987). Jean's taste for solitude and travelling also reflects the freedom of movement and use of time allowed to men by women's presence in domestic spaces; the imaginary of the road and the possibility of the unexpected contribute to the construction of certain forms of masculinity (Testenoire 2006). Jean describes his 'family responsibilities' as rootedness by obligation but hopes he will someday be able to renew his experience as a lorry driver in England, taking off alone with his pack for several months, muddling through and learning some English, to 'feel free'. His worldview and life course are configured around respect for work and freedom, refusal of state services in the form of welfare benefits or the sheltered status of civil servant, and rejection of the traps of consumption. He cited the example of 'ladies' at the supermarket checkout: 'They open their wallets, they've got 30 loyalty cards, "Now where is it...? Ah, Super U, there it is!" Oh, they've got no problem, the shops, they've got no problem finding them, those people, because they're enrolled everywhere'. This form of social virility (the principle behind his social and moral positions) is manifest in his praise of risk-taking and, combined with his capital of autochthony, probably contributed to his becoming sought after for associative and political responsibilities.

Jean contrasts the freedom and adventure of the road to the figure of the civil servant at his desk, the archetype of a monotonous risk-free life. His creation of an independent and audacious self-image involves his working conditions as well as his employment status and relationship to being an active worker, which is accompanied by discursive condemnation of welfare assistance, state protection, and labour law. To Jean's thinking, getting by through work means taking initiative and risks to create your place in the job market, in accordance with the idealised narrative of the entrepreneur. He moreover knows the story of the town's great industrial family quite well and lists off the locations of statues of the automotive company's founder, his wife, and his heir in their town and the neighbouring one, where he was born. He vaunts his self-employed teaching activities rather than his wage-earning job as conveyor, although the latter represents the vast majority of his income and the former barely turns a profit. He presents himself as lucid, albeit economically wronged, about transformations in employment. Locally, he expresses solidarity with business owners and executives in industry for their 'flexibility' in face of social security 'taxes' and 'bureaucracy', rather than with the demands of workers, who were 'paid, don't give a damn' until they were laid off when the factory closed.

In this way he paints an image of himself that is far indeed from the figures of the civil servant and welfare recipient. His representation of the civil servant is mainly based on the lives of his siblings, who are municipal technicians, a nurse, and a social worker. His summation of their occupational situations boils down to employment security that he considers out-dated, a guaranteed comfortable lifestyle and retirement, linear careers, and boring day-to-day jobs. In the town's stricken industrial area, Jean identifies the figure of the 'benefits scrounger', even among his neighbours. He thinks he can legitimately set himself apart from them because he went through several periods of unemployment himself and noted how easy it would have been to 'let [himself] go' without sacrificing comfort thanks to state assistance.

These representations of work and this relationship to the state have a strong impact on how he conceives of their 14-year-old daughter's education. Jean was frustrated and scarred by his own painful experience of school, which still leads to humiliating situations when, for instance, he has to prepare official documents required by his clients or Manou corrects mistakes in his text messages. He is not invested in following his daughter's education, unlike Manou, who ensures the supervision of schoolwork despite her own disinterest in school. Manou also supports a greater range of options for their daughter's studies in the future than Jean, who expresses reticence to the idea that their daughter adds on to a (hypothetical at this stage) general *baccalauréat* by pursuing post-secondary studies like most of her older cousins. Instead, he urges her towards vocational training and rapid entry into the employment market. He wants her to work summers, and since she is too young to have a paying job, he assigns her jobs around the house so he will not see her 'pissing around'.

While Manou's investment in local early childhood organisations, which she described in a vocational register, was a path to employment and a resource for developing friendships for the couple, Jean's local engagements manifest his curiosity about experiencing responsibilities in associative organisations and municipal government, an excursion to the land of local dominants. Although he never expands on these subjects, he widely uses the lexical field of curiosity and discovery and situates himself as an outside observer for whom these are relatively alien spaces.

His first engagement came out of a desire to not let himself go during a stretch of unemployment, by looking after his body. He enrolled in the municipal swimming club, whose board was empty and on the verge of dissolving, so he became vice-president. From this position, he was offered a place on the list of the sitting mayor, 'rather to the left', in the last municipal election. He was elected but devotes little time to the position because he is often travelling for work and is mainly 'sent' to commemorative and festive events, thus ensuring a representative role. He also minimises this engagement, which he never brings up spontaneously, and stresses that he will not run in the next election.

Above all, Jean tries to depoliticise his municipal mandate by classifying actions and elected officials according to their technical skills and praising the 'stars' in each domain:

> So on the [municipal] council, there, we've got the mayor, who's… who's competent, basically, maybe he could be more laid back. You can sense that he's always a little stressed out all the time – he's not relaxed enough for me. But mostly, everyone around him, his council members… his deputies, y'know. There's one, chief deputy, he's, like, a star. He's a star. Then there's another who looks after green spaces, he's a former agronomic engineer. [Jean describes an 'ultramodern', 'environmental, functional, and economic' invention of this man] You realise that around you, you really need to have a bloody competent team, y'know. […] That's when you realise that it's not left/right, y'know, don't give a damn about all that.

Disputing the validity of the left/right split in the municipal as well as the national political space, he developed an analogy between managing a town and a company. Despite his restraint speaking on the subject, Jean's office does confer him with additional and potentially prestigious status. He nonetheless has an outsider's experience of local spaces of power through his municipal functions, such as serving as an *ex officio* member of the local *collège* board as representative of the municipal counsel: 'You don't understand a thing, you have a drink, and you go'. Manou expresses a frank disinterest in politics and they do not discuss Jean's office between them; for that matter, they both only vote in 'important' elections. This political ambivalence is symbolised by the campaign poster for the mayor and his list (including Jean), which is tacked to the inside of the living-room cabinet door.

Classifying oneself and others in a housing development

Manou and Jean's distinct relationships to domestic spaces, revealed by the issues of wage labour and local engagements, reflect how they relate to sociability in the local area and with friends, which is likewise inflected by gender and race. Rather than a narrative of solitude and (entrepreneurial) adventure, Manou describes her social position as distinctive, a bridge between different social worlds. Just as she sets herself apart from the families involved with child protection services without fully identifying with her foster-carer peers at work, her management of the couple's local sociability highlights her social ease and her ability to move among several worlds without ever identifying herself with any of them.

Although they have a shared and asserted taste for spending time with friends, Manou and Jean do not feel like they fully belong to any of the local groups with whom they socialise – a social landscape that they laid out quite clearly. They are always in an in-between position, between distinct worlds with social and racial boundaries, from a culturalist perspective. They are neither the 'benefits scroungers' nor the 'environmentalist bourgeois' that they frequent in turn. They have one foot in the mutual support networks of working-class neighbourhood women from the Antilles and sub-Saharan Africa, the other in town organisations where they see members of the white middle classes.

Some of their social interactions and the figures fuelling their perceptions of their social position relative to other groups are rooted in the very local space of their housing development. Manou and Jean own their house, one of the biggest on the street. In addition to this notable property is Jean's status as elected municipal official, which means that neighbours sometimes seek him out with roads problems or questions about the fate of town-owned land. Their street is lined with single-family homes occupied by owners and renters, including some for low-income social housing, and runs along the sprawling site of a major automobile factory that has been abandoned for several years. Until it starting running into difficulty, the automotive industry employed a significant percentage of the town's working population and was largely responsible for the town's by attracting working-class families from elsewhere in Europe and the world. When it closed it left high unemployment in its wake.

In the social and ethno-racial typology that emerges from the discourse of Jean and especially Manou, the street brings together the white middle classes, often retired, and white and non-white working-class households, a significant proportion of which on unemployment or working multiple insecure jobs. Manou and Jean's perceived (or created) social distance is not set in stone and is not always obvious. For instance, a 'white neighbour woman' initially intimidated Manou, who described her elegant clothing, confident gait, and cool expression to me; she made Manou wary of potential racist remarks or behaviour. Developing a friendship with this woman ultimately took time and the mediation of other white friends met at the school parents' association. The part-time occupant of the low-income housing property across the street from them is the couple's standard figure of the foreigner who 'takes advantage of the system'. They relay each other in describing his 'strategies' for making the house appear to be occupied full-time: they have noticed lights and the furnace on when the house is empty, in order to have believable electric bills.

Although he is an elected official, Jean does not try to socialise with neighbours, who he prefers to keep at the 'right distance' through cordiality and discretion. Manou has become part of the network of neighbourhood women from the Antilles and sub-Saharan Africa. These relationships are quite active in the daytime when Jean is not home and consist of helping each other out: picking up a package or mailing a letter on the road into town, picking up the children after school, dropping off spare vegetables. They provide Manou with an opportunity to speak in Creole, and the everyday character of these interactions and the free time shared by children in the little-travelled street has made them close through sharing their life stories, celebrating each others' birthdays, and visiting each others' homes.

This is the space of everyday sociability that Manou expanded when she took on local engagements. If her daytime activities and this network of mutual assistance make her presence and (paid and unpaid) work in the home tenable, she nonetheless refers to other forms of sociability in contact with the local white upper-middle classes to create the image of a 'bohemian' 'communal' life to which she says she aspires. These sociabilities are shared by the couple and play a central role in how Manou shapes herself and presents a pleasant, even festive life and a desire to 'not get all worked up', an aim shared by Jean.

Compartmentalising and moderating friendly relations: management of local sociability

Jean maintained ties with childhood friends in his home region, and he sees them from time to time but not frequently. Since they moved to the town ten years earlier, Manou is the one who has developed and maintained their friendships. She experiences and portrays their friendships in terms of two complementary approaches: valuing the diversity of the people they meet and keeping the times and spaces spent with each group sharply separated according to social criteria.

'It's *boat people* [in English] at our place'. As proof of how diverse their friends are, Manou lists willy-nilly their 'Russian, Angolan, Antillean, bourgeois, homosexual friends' that have recently come to the house. Among those with whom they spend the most time – who Manou refers to as 'friends' with no further qualifiers – are four heterosexual couples, the wives of which Manou met through the school parents' association. All white, they are teachers, architects, accountants, and private-sector managers, and Manou and Jean characterise them by their financial ease and familiarity with legitimate culture. They regularly get together for dinners and theme parties ('Ugly night', '1970s night') at each other's homes. Parties, laughter, games, and skits are the basis of these friendly relationships and why they are important for Manou. This involves avoiding serious conversations, especially about politics, which could make the ambiance tense. These times are deliberately distinct from relations with the Antillean and sub-Saharan women in the neighbourhood, who are mostly unemployed or work insecure jobs.

Manou explains this division of local sociability in two ways. In a culturalist rationale, she thinks that these two groups have different ways of being friends and having fun and that they would tire of each other. Both of them outline these cultural differences, which involve class and race relations and concern dietary practices, the acceptable degree of spontaneity or planning in inviting or visiting others, what can be laughed about, and marital and family relations. The tight control that 'bobos' have over their food contrasts with Manou's practices as the self-declared 'queen of canned goods' and promoter of hedonism. She describes them with a sense of humour suggesting an indulgent but distinct distance:

MANOU: I've met some women from the Antilles, because I thought, 'At the very least I've got to find people from my culture'. I never found anyone from Martinique, but I found [people from] Guadeloupe and Guyana, Gabon, and Togo. Because, well, I had to frequent blacks, too, so I wouldn't get too white. So, we're still friends. We're still friends, y'know, no matter what. It's complicated sometimes because they can be really invasive, like in the Antilles. The French are more likely to call before coming, the Antilleans and Africans just show up at any time – which I wanted to avoid in the Antilles. Which I'm putting back into place in France, despite myself. [...] [One friend from the Antilles] came to the school parents' association but she didn't like it. [Another] came, too, and she didn't like it. I think that it's a question of affinities, and then... They don't fit in there, they say it's not for them. Do you understand, or not?

CLÉMENT: So, these women are on unemployment?

MANOU: Women from the Antilles, Africa. But it's true, it's really another world. The girls at the parents' association, they're activists, and often environmentalists, you see. You know, the type to... well, bourgeois hippies, like, bobos. You know the sort… They try to be bourgeois but environmentally conscious at the same time, some kind of huge mix that you don't know what it is, exactly [laughing]. But I like it. I like that world. Our friend didn't like it, he took off because of that, he didn't like that population one bit.

CLÉMENT: Which friend?

MANOU: The one that took off. He said he was fed up with them. He can't stand this population. He wants a lighter population. It's true that it's sometimes heavy, but oh well… Gotta constantly think green, organic… He gets sick of it. […] He wants to be left in peace if he wants to eat a pizza covered in streaky bacon and cheese, with crème fraîche. To not be hassled with all this organic stuff. If he wants a Coca-Cola, he drinks his Coca-Cola. No one asks him if organic Coca-Cola is made with caramel…[…] I frequent those people, but I don't do that, y'know. I don't get worked up about it. If you gotta eat hotdogs, I'll eat hotdogs, y'know. But when we go to our friends' everything is… gotta eat sesame seeds, gotta eat organic vegetables, gotta belong to the CSA. Because there's the CSA and all that. And is… is there any spontaneity in all that?

So while she defines two groups of friends in relation to each other, she places herself in an intermediary position and does not fully find her place with either. Her discourse is structured by the idea that she is caught between Antillean working-class culture and white middle-class French culture, and looking for an autonomous zone between them. This desire to escape classification and attribution plays out in her relationship with her husband and with her extended family, which demand that she do constant adaptation and concession work. Sometimes her investment in this work is positive, as is especially clear when she describes her special relationship she had with the children and families served by child protection services early in her career.

By presenting such a detailed account of the couple's quest for independence, be it at work or in their social interactions, Manou thus shows that her migration and the intersecting relationships of gender, race, and class lead her to develop a relationship to other social groups that differs from Jean's. While some categories make sense to both of them – civil servants, the unemployed, 'benefits scroungers', Antilleans, Whites – there are stark differences in what is at stake behind these designations. In this sense, Manou's desire to control her story is expressed in the density of her speech filled with anecdotes and word play, in her refusal to let Jean – who is much less talkative about himself – talk about her, and in her rejection of his definition of 'Antillean culture'. Using friendship to redefine her social position and exhibiting her ease in mutually exclusive social worlds whose codes she has mastered had led to a strongly compartmentalised sociability that is tempered by the need to keep some time and a space for oneself.

Notes

1 For an explanation of the French educational system, see the Appendix.
2 On the competition and struggle for legitimacy between various social-work occupations – especially among newer, unskilled occupations (see Ion and Ravon 2012).

References

Gollac, Michel, and Pierre Laulhé. 1987. 'Les composantes de l'hérédité sociale: un capital économique et culturel à transmettre.' *Économie et statistique* 199–200: 95–105.

Ion, Jacques, and Bertrand Ravon. 2012. *Les Travailleurs sociaux*. Paris: La Découverte.

Lambert, Anne. 2016. 'Échapper à l'enfermement domestique. Travail des femmes et luttes de classement en lotissement pavillonnaire.' *Actes de la recherche en sciences sociales* 215: 56–71.

Testenoire, Armelle. 2006. 'Éloignés au quotidien et ensemble. Arrangements conjugaux en milieu populaire.' *Cahiers du genre* 41: 117–138.

24

THE CLEANING WOMAN AND THE SCHOOL PARENTS' ASSOCIATION

Multipositionality in the working classes – Myriam and Nicolino Sanatanazefi

Olivier Masclet and Gérard Mauger

Born in 1979, Myriam works for a cleaning company. Nicolino, born in 1976, is one of 100 lorry drivers in a transportation company. They met in June 2000. They first moved in together in Myriam's mother's home and then, when Nicolino got an open-ended employment contract, moved into subsidised public housing not far from the centre of a major city in west-central France.

Because motherhood then seemed to be in order, Myriam immediately stopped the pill: 'I didn't see myself without children. As soon as he got a permanent job, I stopped the pill right away'. Morgane was born in 2004 and their son Nicolas in 2007. They married ten years after they met: 'Marriage costs money', they explained, so they 'put children first'. They got married after saving enough to pay for it, even if it was after the children had been baptised. A display cabinet in the dining room has three shelves overflowing with souvenirs and the top shelf is devoted to their wedding, exhibiting material traces of their investment in family including photographs of the newlyweds and wedding party, the bride's hairpiece, and the wedding dinner menu.

Once she had gotten her driving licence, Myriam got a part-time open-ended employment contract in a cleaning company: She works there 38 hours a month, plus an additional four hours a day handling the trash in an apartment building and two hours a week (under the table) in a hair salon. She would like to work 'more hours', but 'not in cleaning': other than offering working hours allowing her to look after the children, the appeal is purely economic ('Let's just say I'm not on the lookout for more cleaning hours'). Lacking any possibility for subjective investment in work, Myriam's daily life is guided by a quest for private happiness.

Her social life is not limited to family circles, however. She assiduously frequents a social universe that is culturally and economically far from her own,

DOI: 10.4324/9781003330073-27

that of the school parents' association, which expands and diversifies the social surface area that she occupies. There she finds recognition denied by her cleaning job. In what follows, we will explore the effects of this 'multipositionality' (Boltanski 1973), a property typical of the dominant classes but seen here in a working-class version.

A cleaning woman's expanding 'social surface area'

Since direct perceptions assume particular importance, the visible and tangible environments of the people individuals meet can shape their vision of the social world. Over the course of the interactions that develop in this environment (a space that may be small or large, diverse or not), individuals have real experiences, if not of the social world, at least with the fraction of it to which they are exposed (not to mention the imaginary experience of the social world represented in film, television, and books). Over the course of experience with the people they encounter and the classifications they make of them, individuals internalise schemes of perception (worldviews), evaluation (ethos), and action (way of being) – a cluster of dispositions that are both generic and specific. In Myriam's case, this worldview is more implicit than explicit: indeed, for her, the contrast between 'Us' and 'Them' is both manifest and seen as such, although she can hardly be said to have an explicit class consciousness and/or worldview of antagonistic social classes in opposition to each other.[1] This working-class 'Us' – socially homogeneous, composed of their respective families, a family of sisters that are close friends, and, tangentially, members of the football club of which Myriam is vice-president – is in opposition to a 'Them' that is socially quite different and approached only by Myriam in the school setting.

The couple is homogamous, and their respective familial universes (socially quite similar in terms of jobs held, income, and educational attainments) place them within the working classes. Nicolino (age 38) was born on the island of Réunion, a French overseas department in the Indian Ocean, where his parents still live. His father (age 60) is a lorry driver for a public works company. His mother has no formal educational attainments and 'works in cafeterias'. Nicolino is the second of six children; his brothers are labourers and low-level employees and his sisters are housewives. The youngest sister has the *baccalauréat*, but Nicolino barely knows her.[2] The couple has regular news of the family in Réunion via Facebook.

Myriam knows little about her father, an unskilled labourer who migrated from Algeria, now a pensioner. He abandoned her and her mother for a younger woman from Algeria with whom he had four children, and Myriam sometimes 'bumps into them by chance'. Her mother (age 67, of French descent) is also a pensioner, a former unskilled assembly-line worker in a factory that ran two eight-hour shifts a day, meaning workers like her mother alternated weeks working mornings and weeks working evenings. Myriam has three half-brothers from her mother's previous marriage to an unskilled labourer, but she has little contact with them. She is out of touch with Patrice (45), who left school and is a lorry driver. Didier (44) is a labourer in woodworking and has a son and two daughters. Michel (43) is an unskilled labourer in the agro-food industry, where he works the night shift 'cleaning tanks'.

Myriam's friends, who she met when she was about ten and who the couple sees regularly, are from the same social world. They are five sisters who grew up in the difficult neighbourhood where Myriam's mother settled after her separation. Four of them are older than Myriam, work as cleaning women, and are married to labourers or lorry drivers. The youngest, Aurélie (28) earned a *baccalauréat* and had recently gone back to school. They introduced Myriam to the football club and a dance class, where she frequents others from her working-class universe.

The couple's council-estate flat is near the part of town where the middle and upper classes are concentrated, so Myriam's participation in a school parents' association, which is characterised by a mix of social positions, exposes her to economic and cultural domination. How to account for her determination to seize the opportunity to frequent middle- and upper-class parents and occasions for social decompartmentalisation that present themselves to her? It can be seen as an opportunity to 'do something other than housework' (as a housewife or as a cleaning woman), an expression of educational goodwill, or perhaps a consequence of belief in the declared principle of equality among schoolchildren's parents (or, more specifically, their mothers).

Myriam possesses the attribute of being the mother of a student, which comes with the right to join the association. The openness that seems to be indicated by this unifying label and the image it fosters of the parents' association as a socially neutral place seems to allow and even justify her presence. This is why Myriam, who started 'lending a hand' whenever needed (school trips, baking cakes, putting makeup on the children for events) as soon as Morgane started nursery school, accepted the head teacher's suggestion that she be a candidate to the school board. Once her son began school, she connected with a classroom assistant and the head teacher of the nursery school. She is currently an elected member of the school board of the primary school attended by both of her children. In September 2013, she became president of an association that she and a few other parents founded to counter the new head teacher's refusal to hold the school festival in June. The same parents are also elected members of the school board, 'people who', Myriam says, 'all have good jobs'.

OLIVIER: It's men and women?
MYRIAM: Well actually, there's 16 of us and only one man!
OLIVIER: Do you know what they do for a living?
MYRIAM: Well, most of them are schoolteachers. Of the 16 there's eight, no, more than that, even, from eight to ten schoolteachers.

OLIVIER: And their children are in the school?
MYRIAM: Yeah, yeah, but they're more *collège* teachers.
OLIVIER: So they are actually *collège* instructors…
MYRIAM: Instructors, yeah… Last time I was adding it up and I think, there's half of 'em that're schoolteachers. I'm surrounded by schoolteachers. We've got a lawyer. I keep good company, huh? I've only got professionals around me. We've got a nurse, so, schoolteachers, a lawyer, a nurse, umm… something like a banking job… No, no, I've got people who all have good jobs all around me. And from Nicolas' class, since nursery school, there's people… surgeons, teachers, nurses, lawyers, only pretty highly placed people.

And yet Myriam was the one elected president of the parents' association. To understand this seemingly improbable situation, research would have to be done with other association members, but it is possible that Myriam serves as a democratic totem. By electing a cleaning woman as president, the association displays the democratic image it wants for itself while delegating some of the drudgework to her (such as doing the rounds of shops to find raffle prizes and free ingredients for making crepes). In this position, she asserts that being the parent of a student is the sole criteria for legitimating membership, while by the same token she evades the implicit criteria of class position, or more specifically the cultural capital possessed (which is important to ensuring its transmission to children and its conversion into educational capital). Meetings are held at the school – 'I've got the right to go there, I've got keys'. Meetings to prepare for school board meetings are held in a bar, and the meeting is usually followed by 'a little dinner with each other, in a restaurant. We elected parents get along really well with each other, yeah, yeah, it's brilliant'. Association parents do not see each other outside of these meetings, however.

Their considerable contact with the virtual social worlds seen on television – a permanent guest in the home (Masclet 2018) – makes one wonder what place they occupy in Myriam's worldview. Television's imposing presence (the three sets in Myriam and Nicolino's home are on 12–14 hours a day) leads one to consider it tantamount to a member of the family, or rather several members of the family, since everyone has their own set and programmes. One wonders what the consequences of this near-constant presence of familiar actors, singers, and hosts might be. While it is true that 'oblique attention' (Passeron 1970) is possible – 'we're after background noise', says Myriam, 'it's a presence' – there is nothing to prove that this is always the case. Myriam and Nicolino's uses of television are not all that casual. Women's series open a wide range of possibilities for identification along with escapism and entertainment (Mauger and Poliak 1998). Myriam prefers the soap opera *Les Mystères de l'Amour* to *Desperate Housewives*. It is set in a posh neighbourhood, and her favourite character is Olga, who is unabashedly uncouth (she 'pulls no punches', according to Myriam) and jumps at every opportunity for a drink and to sexually exhaust her partners, but she also likes Hélène, who she describes as 'a saint'. In addition to entertainment, Myriam can also be credited with ethical uses of television. The French version of the programme *Super Nanny*, for example, is an opportunity to learn about psychological interpretation and behaviour:

> I learned things watching that. It's not just to watch, it's that you learn things – how to talk to your child, how you should do things, to punish or not, to force or not, stuff like that. She taught us a lot of things.

Far from being seen as consistently part of the world of others ('Them'), the realm of television offers opportunities to use corporeal resources: this is notably the case in programmes featuring song, dance, or beauty competitions, which rely on natural and thus randomly distributed attributes such as a good singing voice. Generally speaking, mass culture absorbed via television seems to be a resource that can be opposed to school culture, simultaneously allowing someone to be like everyone else and distracting them from failure in school.

Social and moral classifications

Myriam applies economic and cultural criteria to her classifications: they are intrinsic to the objectification of disparities between living conditions. Although she never mentions her North African roots, which are perceptible in her given name, one might nonetheless think that, in conjunction with her unfailing educational goodwill, they might also help to make her an anti-racist totem to other school parents.

Overlying the usual criteria for social classification, Myriam's moral classification is less related to disparities between conditions and based more on modes of self-presentation in everyday interactions ('down-to-earth'/'stuck-up'). She uses it to classify school parents as well as the 'Us' group. Myriam sorts the parents' association into two groups: those who reduce or deny the gap between living conditions and the social distance resulting from it (who she thinks they are 'nice' and 'open') and those who highlight them by disrespecting her or being inconsiderate. She was elected to the nursery school board for the three years Morgane was in pre-school but did not want to run for the primary school board when Morgane went there: she 'didn't feel like it', the parent representatives seemed 'really hoity-toity' and she did not know any of them. But when her son started nursery school in 2010, she once again ran for school board, upon the invitation of the head teacher: parents there 'aren't toffee-nosed', are 'open', 'warm', 'down-to-earth', 'really laid back', she explained. Myriam's presence in this social world is thus subject to suspension of the relationship of domination. Belief in the declared principle of shared humanity supposes that the dominated have a certain interactional style. The objective domination has to be reduced or denied, or as Myriam described it, that 'they talk to me normally, basically'. 'We use [the informal] *tu* with each other, kiss each other in greeting'; 'they could look down on you - but don't at all'; 'yes, they've got money, but they're, like, really down-to-earth'. But by the same token, domination led her to choose exit over voice or loyalty (Hirschmann 1970) when she was put down by 'stuck-up' parents who 'look down on you' and 'think they're really somebody because they earn more money'.

Although Myriam's moral classification is discriminatory when it concerns the local bourgeoisie and petite bourgeoisie ('Them', 'people with good jobs' or that 'have means', including nurses and teachers), she applies the same classificatory order within the working-class 'Us' group – but in this case, the operative criteria is 'respectable', not 'down-to-earth'. The moral case Myriam mounts against the most impoverished fractions of the working classes picks up the theme of welfare dependency: 'they are over-protected, they get too much help, they have the right to God knows how many things [...] They get so much a day to do nothing while we slave away a work to earn pennies'. The daughter of an Algerian immigrant married to a man from Réunion, Myriam nonetheless continues along the same lines to condemn an 'excessive' immigrant sub-proletariat: 'we've got to do cleaning', she said, 'if we sent foreigners back home there'd be more work for us'. This moral condemnation of some people's laziness and cheating and the injustice done to those like Nicolino and herself who 'work, don't cheat, and don't get assistance' allows her to assert her position among the 'respectable' fractions of the working classes. This same honourability is nonetheless contested in the very family into which she was born: her youngest half-brother's partner, who is a lower-level employee with a *bac technologique*, is condescending towards Myriam and thinks she lives off the dole. Inversely, Myriam expresses admiration for the family of her friend Sandrine, the fourth sister in the family of friends. She is also a cleaning woman, and she is married to Richard, who is originally from Martinique, a lorry driver like Nicolino, and black skin like him, too. Myriam speaks of them as 'good parents': 'they are really into school', she explained, contrasting them to the other sisters who are 'more ready make concessions to their children'. They managed to raise their children 'the way you should'; 'they are all doing well', although 'the girls are really into school and the boys a lot less'.

Working-class multipositionality: economic ethos, scholastic strategies, and the rewards and preservation of the in-group

The dichotomous and compartmentalised social universe where Myriam and her classifications develop permit us to identify her various registers of practice, on the school scene (where she is faced with 'Them') as well as the professional and family scenes (the world of 'Us'). Although Myriam's alternation between the two obliges her to 'produce the personality that suits each place and occasion' (Boltanski 1973, 16), it does not seem to produce a split in the habitus or role distance. Indeed, Myriam generally stays in what she understands as her place while adapting to the scholastic scene and the people she sees there. Her quest for scholastic wellbeing for herself and her children is probably consolidated by her assiduous presence on the scholastic scene and the encouragement she finds there.

Within the family, the adjustments Myriam has made to deal with economic constraints define an economic ethos characterised by the tension between necessary asceticism and intentional hedonism. She maintains a tight budget for 'ordinary' family expenses while arranging for the extraordinary (setting aside money for ten days at a holiday village in the summer and 'romantic dinners at a restaurant'). The collectivisation of resources (which add up to less than 2,000 euros a month) is the rule for this couple: 'it's not my money or his money, it belongs to both of us'. Perpetuating men's delegation of (economic) power to women, Nicolino lets Myriam 'keep the accounts' and 'plan' the family budget. Once the automatic payments have been made, the remainder is used 'to do whatever we want' (leisure and set aside as savings): 'everything is calculated', 'we don't spend money for nothing' she explained. As far as the children are concerned, Myriam tries to strike a delicate balance between her desire that 'they not want for anything' and her determination to 'not give in entirely to the children'. Asceticism is imposed by economic necessity: 'we don't have enough money' (for the cafeteria, summer camp), 'we do everything we can, but then, we're limited, too'.[3] While endeavouring to satisfy their material needs as best as possible, they also try to avoid negative economic classifications and resulting shame in the scholastic space by allowing them to 'be like everyone'. For birthdays, for example, 'the problem is that we are surrounded by people with good jobs and us, we can't… well anyway, we're obliged to follow', Myriam explained. These tensions between aspirations and necessity are at the principle of the inculcation of an economic morality adapted to constraints: according to Myriam, one must not 'give in entirely to the children' but instead 'teach them what things cost and that there are limits'. Accordingly, she criticises Catherine, the second of the family of sisters, whose son 'does nothing':

> He could have gone really far because he's very intelligent and all, except he didn't want to do anything. And so he hangs around… well that's it, they didn't have enough character to set him straight. And since he was really little… they went along with everything he wanted. Now he's 19, and they still always go along with him.

Myriam works hard to reduce cultural gaps as much as possible, if not to close them, through her efforts to educate herself, supervise her children's schoolwork, and participate assiduously in the parents' association. Myriam's attempts to escape the condition of housewife and/or cleaning woman suppose overcoming the handicaps of her lack of educational attainments, her aversion to school (she explained that she 'couldn't manage' to do well and 'didn't understand', 'it didn't interest' her, 'nothing registered', and she 'hated school'), and ultimately her lack of confidence. With the help of Aurélie (the youngest and most highly educated of the sister-friends), who 'wanted to get motivated together', she obtained her driving licence. With the backing of Mireil (another of the sisters, a cleaning woman who advanced to 'boss' in a cleaning company), she got hired on a part-time open-ended employment contract. With Nicolino's help and with the practical and above all symbolic support of a classroom assistant, a teacher, and the head teacher of her children's school, who strove to 'motivate' her by validating her vocation to 'take care of children' and crediting her with the ability to succeed, she studied on her own to take the examination for a CAP in early childhood development, without taking a preparatory course. She succeeded in 2014 ('They cried about it when I told them I passed').

The tension between her aversion for school ('For me who hates school, it was weird to dive back in') and her educational goodwill appear in her efforts to help her children with their schoolwork ('Every night, I tell 'em, "Homework!"'). Typically, the general tendency to longer educations and concern with avoiding unemployment for their children means at the very least consenting to children's pursuit of longer educations, if not implementing genuine family educational strategies. However, the difficulties encountered on this path soon remind parents of reality and bring them back to social reproduction strategies that tend to prioritise shielding their children from the ever-present threat of downclassing pulling towards the sub-proletariat ('dole dossers', or '*cas soc*' (social cases) in the indigenous lexicon).

Indeed, whatever educational goodwill parents might have, the chances of success in school depend on the family's cultural legacy. This legacy primarily concerns language: the spoken language of the working classes (including Myriam and Nicolino's) is not that of the school, which defines legitimate language and what it is to speak it well. This cultural legacy also includes experiences with school: Myriam's boils down to the painful ordeal of school rankings and the internalisation of unworthiness, resulting in a more or less explicit anti-school culture.

This unpleasant experience with rank in school is accompanied by indigenous theories. One such theory opposes recalcitrant and docile natures, incarnated here by their children: 'Nothing gets through' to their daughter, 'It just doesn't get through to her brain', 'she's not that into school', 'I think school will never be her thing', but 'it's easier [for their son] than for Morgane'. Beyond its performative character, this working-class version of the ideology of giftedness comes with consequences for learning: 'there's no point in persisting', that's how it is', 'Morgane's like me', said Myriam. Since Myriam's scholastic powerlessness is expressed in shouting ('If I speak nicely they don't listen'), the family's experience of schoolwork is also one of conflict, thus confirming the representation of learning for school as a chore. Having an 'allergy to school' is a variant of the ideology of giftedness: 'she's sad as a student', 'it won't do', 'she's not doing well', 'as soon as she enters the classroom she freezes' – despite the fact, Myriam explained, that 'as a child, she's joyful', 'she sings all the time', and incarnates 'a love for life'. The other indigenous theory of failure in school is a working-class variation of meritocratic ideology. Shifting the reason for this failure from a natural failing to a moral flaw, Myriam said that her son 'works better', but 'he is lazy'. While the working-class theory of cultural heredity (in its biological sense) has dire consequences (Myriam does not envisage lengthy studies for Morgane), it also authorises more favourable judgements of her daughter, such as the transmission of a taste for singing: 'We do karaoke together [...] On top of that, she sings well... better than me, at least'.

In addition to these uncontrolled effects of transmitted cultural legacy, moral education strategies intended to transmit a way of being can, to a greater or lesser extent, foster the docility the school expects in terms of politeness or work requirements (school is not for having fun). These dispositions are supposed to at least partly depend on rather strict rules for living, such as the hours imposed on children during the week because of school, but Myriam fears that being too strict might lead to rebellion. In general, the scholastic expectations of parents are not without anxiety or clumsy expression, and they seem to be aware of this: 'We pressure her, for sure, yes [...] I hollered twice really loudly, I was mad at myself for that...'. This can probably be attributed to their awareness of the high stakes of education and their powerlessness.

Ultimately, one might wonder about Myriam's practices as they are confronted with the cultural distance separating her from the world of the school's parents. She gets some symbolic and practical rewards from it: this extension of her social capital earned her the moral support of the teaching staff while she was studying on her own for her CAP in early childhood development. Myriam also derives symbolic gratifications that reassure her: she is vice-president of the neighbourhood football club ('They all wanted me to be president', she explained). However, the awareness of the cultural distance separating her from this world puts her in a position of give and take by trying to make herself useful while being prudently reserved, guided by concern with staying in her place. Myriam, who constantly excuses herself for 'being at a low level', avoids situations where she thinks she would be out of place: 'if sometimes they get together amongst themselves, like, they talk about teaching, because I can't understand a thing, well, like, I talk to someone else'. Likewise, she got along well with Morgane's teacher in CM2, who suggested they address each other in the familiar *tu* (rather than the formal *vous*), possible for her: 'but come on, it's Morgane's teacher, we can't act like we're friends'. Yet another example, for fear of making a mistake in taste, she passed along the responsibility for choosing a gift for a family that volunteered its yard for a parents-children event: the father is surgeon ('he could look down on you, but, like, not at all'), and she explained that

> I haven't got the same taste as them. Gotta say, they've got money so they've, like, got a taste for luxury, gotta say. I dunno the department stores, where he bought the vase. I don't buy vases at God knows how many euros.

All her efforts to educate herself, help her children with their schoolwork, and diligently engage in the school parents' association require that she also arrange spaces providing refuge from economic and cultural domination, with an in-group permitting the free expression of a working-class habitus, where she can have fun, clear her head with her girlfriends, and enjoy the everyday pleasures of being a mother. Generally speaking, the nuclear family seems to provide the ultimate shelter from limitations, norms, taboos, and institutional control (from work, school, and beyond): the in-group setting of the family serves to protect from the outside. Worker familialism is more a form of protection than a result of conservative principles, and it is maintained to this day (Schwartz 1990), the family being both a place of one's own and a place among one's own, protected from the outside world.[4] The weekend, family time, is characterised by a relaxing of schedules and dietary rules, and a freer use of televisual entertainment helping them to escape the stresses of everyday life; in Myriam's words, 'we relax, it's the weekend'. This is when she works with the football club, of which she is vice-president. She 'makes [herself] useful', running the snack bar and making crepes: 'It keeps us busy instead of sitting around on Sunday when you don't know what to do'. Like the football club, the Zumba class she attends is a working-class space (Myriam described it as 'evenings among girlfriends') mobilising (presumably natural) corporeal resources rather than economic or cultural ones. Dance allows her to escape the family in-group and free herself from the limitations of socialising with other social groups, making it possible for her to 'clear [her] mind' and 'have fun'.

Several consequences, some of them contradictory, of Myriam's multipositionality as cleaning woman and parents' association president can thus be highlighted. Although it involves an effort to acculturate, as seen in her educational goodwill – efforts to educate herself and her children – it also leads to *ad hoc* moral classifications of the people she frequents (down-to-earth/stuck-up) and interactional styles adapted to these classifications. The social decompartmentalisation implied by this multipositionality involves an improvised *modus vivendi* more than a split habitus – between goodwill and exit – adjusted to styles of interaction with people in high positions and the moral classifications she makes of them. Paradoxically, although this multipositionality prompts her to preserve in-groups among family and friends, in her case it attests less to a closure to the world of others than it does to an accommodation that allows her to manage the tension arising from worry over conforming to other people's norms. Lastly, the heterogeneity of the social space she frequents contributes to the renewal, if not re-enforcement, of a dichotomous vision of the social world, split into 'Us' and 'Them'. But insofar as the moral register of her classifications also extends to the working classes (where it opposes respectability and degeneration), Myriam's vision of the social world applies at least as much to those at the bottom as it does to those at the top.

Notes

1 Their expressed indifference and disinterest regarding institutional politics, by both Myriam ('we aren't very political') and Nicolino ('I'm neither right nor left, I don't really care'), probably stems from a feeling of incompetence. They have nonetheless voted regularly since 2007 and think that it is important to do so. By voting for the candidate predicted to win in the polls, they are most likely signifying that they are part of the majority and thus asserting their collective belonging.
2 For an explanation of the French educational system, see the Appendix.
3 The fluctuations in Myriam's income have dissuaded the couple from taking steps to become homeowners.
4 Transformations in this are rooted in a more egalitarian redefinition of the gendered distribution of domestic labour and the extension of the restorative function of the home to wage-earning women.

References

Boltanski, Luc. 1973. 'L'espace positionnel : multiplicité des positions institutionnelles et habitus de classe.' *Revue française de sociologie* 14, no. 1: 3–26.
Hirschmann, Albert O. 1970. *Exit, Voice, and Loyalty: Responses to Decline in Firms, Organizations, and States.* Cambridge, MA: Harvard University Press.
Masclet, Olivier. 2018. *L'Invité permanent. La réception de la télévision dans les familles populaires.* Paris: Armand Colin.
Mauger, Gérard, and Claude Poliak. 1998. 'Les usages sociaux de la lecture.' *Actes de la recherche en sciences sociales* 128: 3–24.
Passeron, Jean-Claude. 1970. Introduction to *La Culture du pauvre. Étude sur le style de vie des classes populaires en Angleterre,* by Richard Hoggart. Paris: Les Éditions de Minuit.
Schwartz, Olivier. 1990. *Le Monde privé des ouvriers. Hommes et femmes du Nord.* Paris: Presses Universitaires de France.

25

GETTING BACK TO A 'NORMAL LIFE'

Biographical disruptions and 'institutional goodwill' – Sylvie Barderon and Enzo

Vanessa Stettinger

Sylvie Barderon, a 48-year-old woman working as a house cleaner, used to imagine another life for herself and her children, but 'some are born into families that are predisposed to this kind of story'. She thinks she comes from a 'good' family of strong, hardworking people who 'don't have the habit of complaining'. She thought her life was off to a good start when she was 30, but it took an unexpected turn. 'I've had two lives, even three lives, actually!' she said. 'I had one "before", when I had a normal life with a normal job. I was a hairdresser'.

Sylvie Barderon's story is particularly interesting for what it shows of the social vulnerability of some of the people encountered over the course of this research. Although we place them in the stable fractions of the working classes, the vagaries of life (divorce, health problems, layoffs, debt) may destabilise them and drag them into insecurity. In early adulthood, Sylvie was positioned in a stable working-class household, given her and her husband's family situation, professional situations, residential setting, and strategies for raising their first child. But her life changed after their divorce. Its financial, geographical, and employment consequences led her to lose the social position that she had achieved in a stable and 'promising' relationship, as she described it. She went into depression and became an alcoholic. Social and legal services intervened, and with their help, she struggled to re-establish what she often refers to as a 'normal' family and professional life. She thus converts their supervision into support and demonstrates 'institutional goodwill' by conforming to the legitimate norms to which she has been exposed in her long-term repeated interactions with a wide range of social workers, teachers, and health professionals. While her account highlights how she gradually regained control over her life, it also reveals the challenges and her efforts to escape both the insecurity and

DOI: 10.4324/9781003330073-28

the institutional control that supported her for a time. Sylvie struggles to return to a 'normal life' and the social position she once had.

A promising beginning shattered by divorce

Sylvie Barderon grew up in northern France. She comes from one of those families that successfully, but not without difficulty, ascended socially by getting out of mining work (Leconte 2002). Her maternal grandparents both worked in mining as did her paternal grandfather, who had a well-placed job making it possible for his wife to not work. He was someone who thought ahead and had ambitions for his son: Sylvie's father avoided mining because he was sent to work for a printer when he was 14 and would make a career of it. Sylvie's mother also escaped mining and was a seamstress until her marriage. Sylvie's parents first moved into the house of her maternal grandmother in a mining town in northern France and then bought a new house in a neighbouring town. Becoming homeowners was expensive, however, and the arrival of children brought financial difficulties, so Sylvie's mother had to resume work. After the birth of their fifth (and last) child, she became a house cleaner.

Sylvie has happy childhood memories of sliding on slag heaps and vacations in Belgium. School went well; she liked it and was in the top ten of her class. Things changed in *collège*, and she had to repeat *sixième*.[1] Her *cinquième* was 'so-so, oof, really not great', and she reluctantly left to study for a CAP in sales. Sylvie loves hairdressing and began working in a salon when she was 14. She did a two-year apprenticeship in hairdressing there, where she says she flourished, and earned a CAP, but she did not manage to get a *brevet professionnel*. She worked all the while in the same salon, where she was never declared. She spent her income on outings, clothes, and getting her driving licence and bought her first car when she turned 18.

When Sylvie was 18, she met Pascal, who was working on a BTS in mechanical engineering. She was working a lot at the salon at the time and thought she was earning a good living. After a year, the young couple rented an apartment together. Their son Romain was born three years later, and his arrival was not particularly disruptive to Sylvie's working life. Romain went to day care while she was working and his grandmothers helped. They lived in a neighbourhood that Sylvie considered disreputable, 'where you mustn't raise children if you want them to be "normal", as they say'. So when it came time for Romain to start school, and after their request that he be allowed to attend a school outside their district was refused, they decide to move. Pascal was a breakdown mechanic in a big garage at the time but shortly thereafter got a job with the SNCF, the national train network.

Sylvie looks back on it as a good period. Both were working and earning a good living, Romain was growing up well and attending a school they liked, and their respective families helped them out. At 30, her life changed when she learned that Pascal was having an affair with the neighbour across the street, whose last child was Sylvie's godson. 'I was hurt, very hurt, deeply hurt. I didn't expect it at all, because she was 100 kg (220 pounds), she was a brunette, short, she had an ass like this!' Sylvie was very attentive to her appearances, both because of her job as hairdresser and because of remarks from Pascal encouraging her to watch her weight, not get fat, and stay 'feminine'. They divorced.

Sylvie says that her second life, quite unlike the first, began after the divorce. Although she was able to find housing through family resources (she went to live in her grandmother's old house), she suffered from the loss of the stability that came with her life in a relationship. Moving and changing schools disrupted her and Romain's lives. As time went by she lost interest in hairdressing: 'I let myself sink, sink, sink. [...] The divorce is a hole, it's rock bottom...' Very close to her son, she had good times with him but was lonely, having lost her network of friends associated with her married life (Martin 1993). 'I spent five years alone', she reported, 'I slept with Romain, so there were no men in my bed'.

Five years after the divorce, Sylvie met Artur, a beggar originally from Poland who panhandled in front of her grocery store. Even though she saw the social distance between them, she did not see it as a boundary: 'Now, I've changed. But then, I thought that anyone could fall on hard times, and it was brave to beg'. She attributes this relationship to her fragile psychological state at the time. Sylvie was soon pregnant with her second son, Enzo. For five years Sylvie lived under the grip of alcohol and blows from Artur, first in France and then in Poland. She gradually grew estranged from her family and her son Romain. She had doubts about her ability to perform her role of mother well: 'I thought that I was a bad mother and that I'd abandoned my son. [...] I was in my own world. I wasn't a normal mother, either'.

Called by the neighbours, the police intervened frequently over the years that Sylvie was dominated by Artur, and she also saw a few social workers at the hospital and at home, but this is not when she made her connection with social workers. After one of Artur's attacks, Sylvie and Enzo moved into a shelter for women with children, but she felt alone and unwelcome there and returned to Artur a week later. The three of them went to live in Poland shortly thereafter. After 'two hellish years' in Poland, Sylvie and Enzo were repatriated by the French Embassy and went to live with her parents. Relieved to be back home, she nonetheless suffered the backlash of the previous two years and fell into depression and alcoholism: 'I lost a year of my life, a year without memories, practically. Well, alright, I have memories, but I mean... yeah, they're patchy'.

Although Sylvie does not necessarily make a connection between her life course and that of her family, it should be pointed out that her family history is also marked by disruptive incidents. Her paternal grandfather lost his mining job due to silicosis and alcohol dependency and became a road maintenance worker. Health problems forcing Sylvie's father to stop all sport also made him depressed and alcoholic. Lastly, her brother Pierre was a drug addict who took his own life at age 35. Biographical disruptions are part of her family history. But the way in which Sylvie initially allowed herself to be taken into charge by an array of professionals and institutions and then took charge of herself distanced her from her family's fate. Sylvie developed a particular relationship to institutions that made it possible for her to gradually rebuild her life and once again do 'normal stuff, like normal parents should do'. Several years of regular meetings with social workers and exposure to the norms they advocate were a lifesaver for Sylvie.

Relying on social workers to rebuilt her life

Sylvie's third life began thanks to a social worker, 'someone incredibly great': 'So Mrs M. said, "Regardless, I'm going to give you a kick in the ass from time to time, it's worthwhile"'. This time Sylvie jumped at the opportunity. The social workers' 'it's worthwhile' had hit home. The guidance she received led her to an alcoholism recovery programme ('the best holiday of my life!'), a regularised situation with the unemployment office (Pôle Emploi) and the family allocations office (CAF), and back to work. She rediscovered the self-esteem that she had partly lost, along with certain resources allowing her to rebuild her life, which took the form of a house, a job, and psychological care. Three years after her return to France, Sylvie no longer drinks, has a home, and works as a house cleaner. She cannot resume work as a hairdresser.

> I lost a lot because of new techniques, styles – it changes, it evolves. When you're active you keep up bit by bit, you take classes, there's free classes, so you're always in continuing education when you're in it. It's like someone who goes to the factory and shouldn't tighten the bolts like that, he's got to tighten them the other way, it's the same thing. But when you've stopped for several years, you don't know what to do anymore.

Her cleaning job allows her a relatively stable income and lets her look after Enzo, who 'has behavioural problems' in daily life and especially at school, 'due to all the abuse he was subjected to'.

In addition to her social worker, Sylvie has an alcohologist, a psychiatrist, and a psychologist. She got assistance raising Enzo, who started seeing a behavioural counsellor, a psychologist, and a speech therapist. Sylvie developed a privileged relationship with the behavioural counsellor, Mr. Bernard, who is a constant pillar of support:

> I need something, I call. There's a problem, I call. Even if he's not there, there's the secretary. Even if the secretary isn't very comforting, she can't help me because she has no power, but just having her on the phone does me good. It's dumb, isn't it?

When I asked her, 'Do you feel like you're being watched?' Sylvie unhesitatingly replied, 'No, not by him. Oh, he lets me decide for myself. He gives advice, he helps me to make decisions. When I don't know what to do, I call him'. This counsellor incarnates help, protection – a reassuring masculine presence, for once. She even wishes that he were more present in Enzo's life, 'to do guy stuff' with him, 'talk football, talk basketball, talk wrestling, talk about men things'. Mr. Bernard ended up taking her to task so she would respect the boundaries of his professional intervention: 'I used to always buy him cakes or chocolates or… We even shared a king cake with him, stuff like that. And then one day he said, "You know, I break the rules with you". Normally he's not allowed'. Despite the fact that Mr. Bernard coordinated a closer relationship between Enzo and Romain, a move with which Sylvie disagrees, she still wants his counselling to continue: 'I'm always the one to ask for a renewal. Always'.

Sylvie's attitude towards social service workers allows her to confront the difficulties she faces and more generally shows the strength of her institutional goodwill to make it through hard times: she cooperates with them and aspires to normalisation or normality – at least as they are vaunted by state services today.[2] Sylvie is usually one step ahead of social service workers: she contacted municipal housing services to find a place to live, found psychological care for Enzo at a Medico-Psychological Centre (CMP) in a town closer to her job, requested a classroom assistant (AVS) to help Enzo overcome his difficulties in school and interceded with the school system hierarchy to accelerate the process, and fought for recognition of Enzo's disability and an overall care plan to address it.

Finding the right support

While rebuilding a 'normal life', Sylvie knows that she does not have all the resources she would need to do it alone. Her challenges and failures led her to understand that she would have to broaden her support network beyond social workers. In relating her request for psychological care for Enzo at the CMP, Sylvie revealed all the effort she had to go to and the alliances she had to forge so that it would be granted:

> When I went to see the CMP to have a psychologist, I was on the waiting list, no way, no way, no way. Mr. Bernard, he did what was necessary, too bad, still no way. I went to see the school doctor and I said "here's the story, blah blah". She [the school doctor] picked up the phone, called the CMP in front of me, and she said, "You've got to take Enzo now". Two weeks later I had a letter with an appointment.

Sylvie also knows how to ask people around her in other occupations for everyday help with her son. A woman who works at Enzo's school cafeteria is his babysitter after school, which is reassuring for Sylvie because she already knows Enzo and his problems. Enzo was also well supported one day when had to go visit his father, always a difficult time for him:

> I brought him to the outdoor centre, his counsellor was Lucie, his favourite, so much the better that day. Lucie took him under her wing and she knew very well that it was the fateful day, and that's that, basically. So it went fine. And the night before, the centre nurse took him aside to talk to him a bit. Everyone really chipped in.

The same is true for her legal issues. Her lawyer through the child protection programme for children living at home (Action éducative en milieu ouvert; AEMO) is also one of her employers, since Sylvie cleans her house. Her lawyer's partner defended her when she took Artur to court for violence. This proximity to her lawyers comes with some advantages:

> Theoretically I should pay part of the legal fees, but since I work for Madam and I've already filled in sometimes to do the ironing for her, they know me. So, they worked it out so I'd have full legal assistance. They worked it out so all my income wouldn't be spent that way.

Their relationship plays out in a private setting, which suits her. She also takes advantage of her relationships with 'the rich' to pick up 'nice clothes'.

The scale of the institutional and professional network that Sylvie has activated for her and Enzo's benefit can be seen as revealing her desire to rebuild a 'normal life', but also her fear of finding herself having to deal with her problems alone. She has the same approach to her financial situation. She manages her accounts somewhat offhandedly, calling on institutions to help her as need be, such as when her water or electric bills are in arrears. However, while Sylvie does build partnerships with a variety of professionals, she is more wary concerning her duties to 'the French state' and the school.

Strained collaborations

In her search for financial balance, a major criterion for her return to normalcy, Sylvie is careful to continue receiving certain benefits that allow her some flexibility. Although she now works, her modest income forces her to juggle several programmes so she will not end up in an imbalanced financial situation once again. While she is aware that some of these arrangements do not always meet the stipulated behaviour associated with the image of a good citizen, she blames her transgressions on the French state. She would like to keep her income low enough to benefit from the programme ensuring health coverage for the most disadvantaged (Couverture Maladie Universelle, CMU), for example, or pay the minimum for services offered through the school and recreation centre, 'Because actually, the money I earn on one side, I spend on private health insurance. See, it's ridiculous, it's stupid, it's French laws that are complete rubbish'. On the one hand, Sylvie is in debt, but on the other hand, she saves money so she can buy new furniture for her home, which is part of her quest for normalcy: 'Enzo and I managed to put aside 1300 euros. And with 1300 euros, I've got to buy two bedroom sets'. She knows that she cheats by not declaring all her income, but to her thinking, the French state makes her act this way: 'It's poorly designed, because I work, actually. So in France, you should not work at all or work a lot to really earn a good living. You can't be in the middle. Incredible!' Although Sylvie allows herself a few arrangements, she has a very moralist conception of money where her son is concerned:

> I owe nothing for Enzo, I pay cash on the nail. It's true, the kids, the cafeteria is paid, everything is paid on time – y'know, normal people, I think. You don't wait until they start looking at your kid funny at the cafeteria.

Sylvie walks a tightrope working with institutions to keep a balance that she knows is delicate: 'When you don't earn much you've got to be consistent. And once you've got a little problem, you plummet right away'. These difficulties in getting by raised a dilemma that remained unresolved throughout the study: work more to balance her finances, or keep taking care of her son? The two seemed incompatible.

> I wonder if I made a good or bad choice in my life. For now I'm happy with my job but wouldn't it be better to put Enzo aside and go off to work, taking up my old occupation again, for example?

Collaborating with the school system is also a source of tension for Sylvie. Despite the difficulties in getting recognition for all her efforts in getting educational support for Enzo and the progress she says Enzo has made, she nonetheless manifests the same institutional goodwill in her interactions with the school that she has established in her relations with social workers, although it's more of a burden where school is concerned. Indeed, Enzo has some disciplinary and scholastic problems, but Sylvie transformed interactions stemming from Enzo's problems into resources by reversing the initially negative personalisation of relations with the institution. Any conversation or meeting is an opportunity for Sylvie to use her relational skills to demonstrate her ability to listen and understand and how much effort she expends on her traumatised child. She thus ended up making close and long-lasting connections with teachers and other school staff so that Enzo is known school-wide, which provides some insurance, and then he breaks the rules because 'they know Enzo' and 'they know how he is'.

However, the world of school and cooperating with teachers worry and stress Sylvie, as highlighted by the following exchange with Enzo's teacher in the school planner, a notebook used for parent-teacher communication in French schools. When the teacher sent home a message saying, 'he interrupts, insults adults, including Mrs. X. This is completely inacceptable' and proceeding to detail how Enzo was punished for his acts, Sylvie replied, 'I am sorry and I hasten to punish him in turn'. She also expressed her availability to meet with the teacher 'to check in' and promised to speak with the psychologist about it.

When dealing with her son's teacher, Sylvie adopts a posture combining apology and acceptance of sanctions at home and at school. Such exchanges also reflect the tension she feels from maintaining a dual loyalty, towards the teacher whose judgements she says she respects and towards her son, who she is prepared to back when she and his teacher disagree. Sylvie admits that Enzo is not an easy child, but she thinks that his teacher does not recognise her efforts to help him:

> Even for homework sometimes, he's got it 'til 9 at night and Madam tells me he doesn't work enough at home. I say, be that as it may, I yell. I go home, I'm afraid to go home because I know I'm exhausted, tired, and I still have to yell to get things moving at home.

Sylvie is running out of patience and strength dealing with this chasm between Enzo's behaviour and the demands of school.[3]

When 'institutional goodwill' collides with excessively 'burdensome' oversight

Eight years after she was first taken into charge by social services, Sylvie thinks she is able to manage her and Enzo's lives on her own and no longer feels the need for their oversight. She thinks that the presence of social workers has become invasive and inappropriate in her life, practically negating the independence she regained thanks to them. If at one time Sylvie needed social workers to get back to a 'normal life', she now thinks that this can only truly happen if she takes her distance from them.[4]

Sylvie's collaboration with other kinds of institutional actors (especially social workers and psychologists) took a new turn when Enzo was taken into another programme, seeing a psychologist, a psycho-motricity specialist, a specialised teacher, and a (female) behavioural counsellor. This organisation's services were added to those of the AEMO, where Enzo was already working with a (male) behavioural counsellor and a psychologist, putting him in the care of a total of six different professionals. Sylvie did not manage to build a complicit relationship with the (female) behavioural counsellor the way she could at the AEMO, and dealing with all these professionals proved to be too burdensome. The annoyance began when the (female) behavioural counsellor labelled Enzo as a troublemaker at the cafeteria and after-school care centre, 'because whenever something happened, she'd always say it was Enzo's fault'. Sylvie will not put up with Enzo being given labelled as a bad kid and disagrees with the child-rearing norms that the counsellor tried to instil in her son:

> Giving presents, it's like his father! How many bottles of perfume did I get that ended up smashed against the bathroom wall! And flowers – every time I was beaten I'd get a gift, so it's pointless! I think it's not a good way to raise a child. It's true, y'know?! At after-school care, same thing, so he couldn't go anymore, so I found babysitters, I found nannies, I found…

Sylvie thus demonstrates that she is capable of passing judgement on the child-rearing methods that the professional wanted to instil in her and her son. Although she does not succeed in imposing her point of view – her ultimate move being to withdraw Enzo from the cafeteria and after-school care – she has managed to prevent this behavioural counsellor from coming to her home alone.

Enzo has two psychologists in the newer programme: one, affiliated with the CMP, who 'doesn't see what happens at home and who listens to Enzo', and the other, who 'comes to the house [and is] in a position to say, "You see, you should do it this way, and why did you do it like that, why didn't you do it like this instead?"' Sylvie soon became aware of how burdensome the situation was and how it did not, in fact, free her from supervising her son, which was her primary objective: 'it's true that they put everything in place, but despite that you've got to be home at least once a week because they come to your home. It's really a burden'.

Sylvie worked with these professionals to build a system to help her through daily life with her son. She thought of it as a way to free herself from the constraints of looking after Enzo without neglecting him so she could take on more cleaning work, but the help came too late. When she sees how surrounded she is by these professionals, she realises that they are more disruption than help and that she can never be a mother like the rest as long as they are around. Now she even feels judged by Mr. Bernard, who had been so important to her: 'He thinks I'm a bad mother'. Too inseparable, a mother who does not allow her child to grow, so 'He wants to send Enzo to boarding school to get him away from me'. She is upset by this state of affairs and does not know what to say to convince him otherwise. The latest word was that she and her lawyer were thinking about appealing the judge's decision to continue AEMO supervision. But while social workers are so concerned about her relationship with Enzo, it is remarkable that they are uninterested in her relationship with Romain. Her elder son was already of age when she came back from Poland. Although it took

Romain a few years to forgive his mother for 'having abandoned him', as Sylvie put it, she has a peaceable relationship with him today.

Sylvie's life course shows that although living with a partner provides certain women in the stable fractions of the working classes with 'shelter from the storm' (Fontaine and Stehlé 2014, Bonnet, Solaz and Algava 2009), it can also drag them into a process of insecurity, depending on the partner's situation. Eighteen years after her divorce, Sylvie Berderon has indeed re-established financial stability, but she has not returned to her previous standing as hairdresser and 'good mother'. The break with her former husband destabilised her for a long time, and it would be too simplistic to explain the resultant downclassing that Sylvie experienced with solely psychological factors (depression, alcoholism). Her low level of educational attainment and the insecurity of the job she held prior to her divorce also enter into the equation. To that are added the challenges of reconciling the needs of her son Enzo with the demands of her work, and the time elapsed since she was a hairdresser. The divorce put her up against her weak social resources. Today, despite the institutional goodwill that allowed her to partially rebuilt her life, Sylvie Barderon is still subjected to the goodwill *of* institutions, waiting for an entirely 'normal life' or at least a certified 'normality' declared as such by social services and the court.

Notes

1 For an explanation of the French educational system, see the Appendix.
2 Dalila Cabantous and Pierrine Robin stress that following a 2017 law (loi du 5 mars 2017), 'the submission of a case before the court is no longer conditioned by the gravity of the danger but by the parents accepting to collaborate with the Aide Sociale à l'Enfance [Children's Social Welfare] service to put an end to the danger' (Cabantous and Robin 2016, 72). The authors note the same change in the written documents of relevant professionals.
3 The research of Daniel Thin, among others, attests to the persistent gap between the child-rearing practices of the working classes and the expectations of the school system (Thin 2009).
4 Séverine Gojard speaks of the 'autonomisation of mothers', when they distance themselves from the models they used to form themselves: 'They tend to consider that their own skills dispense them from yielding advice they consider inappropriate' (Gojard 2010, 153).

References

Bonnet, Carole, Anne Solaz, and Élisabeth Algava. 2009. 'La séparation conjugale affecte-t-elle l'activité professionnelle?' *Document de travail (INED)* 164.
Cabantous, Dalila, and Pierrine Robin. 2016. 'Les ressources parentales au prisme des écrits professionnels : comment lire entre les lignes?' *La revue internationale de l'éducation familiale* 1, no. 39: 59–79.
Fontaine, Maëlle, and Juliette Stehlé. 2014. 'Les parents séparés d'enfants mineurs : quel niveau de vie après une rupture conjugale?' *Politiques sociales et familiales* 117: 80–86.

Gojard, Séverine. 2010. *Le Métier de mère*. Paris: La Dispute.
Leconte, Gilbert. 2002. 'De la mine au chantier : conversion et socialisation professionnelle d'anciens mineurs/futurs maçons.' *Formation Emploi* 78: 69–77.
Martin, Claude. 1993. 'Le "risque solitude": divorces et vulnérabilité relationnelle.' *International Review of Community Development* 29: 69–83.
Thin, Daniel. 2009. 'Un travail parental sous tension: les pratiques des familles populaires à l'épreuve des logiques scolaires.' *Informations sociales* 154: 70–76.

26

'I'VE HAD TWO LIVES'

Self-improvement work and the infiltration of psychological culture into working-class worlds – Philippe and Marianne Chapalain

Séverine Misset

Both originally from western France, Marianne and Philippe Chapalain met while Philippe was doing his mandatory military service. Before and after serving, he worked on an assembly line in a factory on the outskirts of the regional capital, and she did temporary jobs as a hospital service worker, a fresh BEP degree in hand.[1] Their respective employment histories are marked by promotion, since Philippe became a skilled worker in the same factory and Marianne is now an auxiliary nurse in a major geriatric centre. This ascension occurred alongside the birth of two daughters and new homeownership, which presupposed a considerable professional and domestic investment on their part.

What makes their trajectories singular, however, is that each has seen a psychotherapist, and they extensively psychologised how they relate to the world in our interviews. They provide an opportunity to study the concrete ways in which 'mass psychological culture' (Schwartz 2011) penetrates working-class milieus and explore its ever-ambivalent effects on professional, personal, and family spheres. Their accounts allow us to identify what their trajectories might owe to their educational and professional goodwill and regular interaction with people from the middle and upper classes, not to mention how their application of psychology to their experiences has softened their formerly ascetic dispositions.

An unexpected disposition to talk about themselves

Philippe was enthusiastic and talkative from our very first meeting and remained so throughout our encounters. Although I also spoke with Marianne, he was the main informant because of his disposition to talk about himself (which is useful when conducting research) and precisely because this openness was so unexpected. For all that, the similarities in their personal and professional

DOI: 10.4324/9781003330073-29

experiences and their great familiarity with each other's circumstances make it possible to analyse them as a couple rather than two individuals.

Philippe entered employment in November 1982, as an unskilled worker in an automobile factory, on the advice of an uncle who already worked there. Since he had not passed the examination for a CAP in automotive mechanics, he had no professional qualifications, and so this job was an opportunity not to be wasted, even if it was initially only temporary and at the bottom of the hierarchy. He had to leave his hometown, with which he has strong ties to this day. For four years (with the exception of his period of military service, 1984–1985) he lived in a single room and went home every weekend.

Philippe met Marianne during this period, which he described as pivotal, prompting him to 're-evaluate his life' professionally and personally. Although he was going through a rough patch due to the untimely death of his father in 1980, military service made something 'click', leading him to a healthy breakthrough in self-awareness. 'I must have thought, "shit, I screwed up everything before, I don't have a degree. What am I going to do for so many years... 20 or 30 years doing that..."'. So when he returned from the Army, Philippe worked hard to invest himself in his work so as to avoid 'spending my whole life on the assembly line'. His superiors considered him a valuable employee and he rose rapidly to a position with multiple duties, first as an Operator capable of working several stations of the line where he was assigned and then as a Monitor late in the 1980s. This put him in a position of responsibility over other operators, supervising their work, replacing them from time to time, adjusting the system when necessary, and training new arrivals.

Philippe was aware that his lack of a degree was a real impediment to his hopes for a rising professional career. Indeed, although he was not the only rank-and-file worker whose career advanced through Operator and then Monitor positions, he was not a 'skilled worker' yet, so he could not aspire to more enviable jobs (Misset 2009). So when he was offered a chance to go back to school for a BEP degree in 1994, he knew it was an undreamt-of opportunity for him to leave the line for good. With some trepidation he decided to accept his managers' offer, as he had always done, and went to *lycée* for a year to work towards the degree. The personnel manager, apparently desirous of this professional development, then suggested he pursue a vocational *baccalauréat* degree. Once again he was hesitant but ended up accepting the offer.

> I said, 'OK, I'll try, I'll give it a go'. I'm not the sort to say no. I'm more the sort to say, 'OK, I'll try!' Afterward, y'know, I won't have any regrets. [...] I was working on a *bac pro* MSMA, Maintenance of Automated Mechanical Systems. And since you have to have a BEP, that's why they directed me to a BEP first, to be able to pass... [The personnel manager] didn't tell me all that, but he knew very well where he wanted to lead me. But I didn't know that, and that's just as well.

Philippe is particularly grateful for the opportunity he was given to 'catch up' on his 'failure' in school. When he passed the *bac pro*, he passed three of its coefficients in one go. Although industry-wide agreements did not oblige his employer to grant him an equivalency, his accomplishment allowed him to reach the same grade as employees hired with a vocational *baccalauréat* in metallurgy, which meant a raise of 500 francs (about 75 euros) a month. More than that, he was promoted to the position of Electrician, classed as 'professional worker', which he would hold for four years until he became a System Operator, meaning that he was in charge of the operation and oversight of automated production systems.

In addition to the many forms of support he got from the company (bonuses, continuing education classes with engineers, internships in the maintenance service) without which this career would have been unthinkable, the Chapalains had to expend considerable effort themselves. He had been able to prepare for the BEP full-time thanks to funding from Fongecif (Fonds de Gestion des Congés Individuels de Formation, which pays an employee's salary so he or she can devote him/herself to training), but he took a two-year correspondence course through a national long-distance learning centre (CNED) to study for the *bac*, so he had to study after a full day at work, making it especially tricky to reconcile work and personal life.

Marianne also had an upward trajectory and went back to school. She aimed for an auxiliary nurse position from the outset. She traces this desire back to childhood, when she spent her vacations taking care of 'two old members of the family' in exchange for 'some change', which she said convinced her to turn to 'a human occupation'. After working a while as a temporary replacement worker, Marianne got a permanent job as hospital service worker in a retirement home near the major regional city. This was when the couple married and moved into a rental apartment, and then their house. Their eldest daughter was born a few years later, in 1989.

At the same time that Philippe was preparing his *baccalauréat* (1995–1997), Marianne studied for and obtained a state-sanctioned Auxiliary Nursing degree. Their first child was still a pre-schooler and they had just bought a 'rather dilapidated' house that they would renovate themselves. This intense and simultaneous investment aiming for an upward professional trajectory required several years of rigorous domestic organisation allowing each to study as necessary. As Marianne explained it, 'We coordinated between us at the time. My parents lived in the neighbouring [administrative] department, and every other weekend one of us took the little one to their place while the other stayed here to work'. It also presupposed waiting to grow the family, as the Chapalains' waited this period out before thinking about a new baby. The younger daughter was finally born ten years after the elder.

The Chapalain's personal and professional trajectories brought them in contact with psychologists several times. As is the case for hiring and professional development in many companies (Illouz 2007), Philippe had to take personality and psychometric tests over the course of his career. Moreover, his current job consists of ensuring the operations and oversight of automated machines in a production system that should safely manufacture a large volume of quality goods and supervising a handful of operators doing the manual tasks necessary to the system's smooth operation – which puts him in the category of professional supervisory workers that look after human matters at least as much as material matters (Wolff 2005). He says 'Ambiance is 80 per cent of the job'. As Monitor and then System Operator, Philippe developed relational as well as technical skills. So in 2010, when he was thinking about leaving the company, he looked into the possibility of becoming a special needs teacher. Philippe had learned in a skills assessment that this job was in line with the relational skills he accumulated throughout his career, but given his age (he was pushing 50) and the difficulty of giving up a relatively comfortable income while having to pay for his younger daughter's education, he finally gave up on the idea.

During the same period, Philippe experienced another major personal disruption, a particularly violent 'shock'. When he came home after a week in the hospital for a physical health problem, he did not recognise his living environment ('nothing was where I thought it belonged', 'it wasn't my house'). Marianne insisted that he contact a 'professor' to discuss the vaguely defined problems that consumed him and weighed on their family life. Philippe was quickly diagnosed with obsessive–compulsive disorder (OCD) and he joined a study testing a treatment combining anxiolytics and cognitive behavioural therapy. OCD has gradually taken over from the Freudian notion of obsessional neurosis and is used in the neurosciences and psychiatry to designate problems characterised by the unwanted and incessant occurrence of anxious thoughts (obsessions) that the sufferer tries to soothe with irrepressible rituals (compulsions) (Castel 2012). It could be described as an illness of hyper-control (Morgiève and Pelissolo 2016). The obsessions can concern a wide range of themes, often relating to filth, order, security, or responsibility, and awareness of the exaggerated or irrational character of the compulsive rituals is not enough to make them go away. In this paradigm, cognitive behavioural therapy is the treatment of choice (Morgiève and Briffault 2014).[2] Even if the discourse of a biographical turn is common among people with a chronic illness (Bury 1982), Philippe depicts starting therapy as a major change, making him say that he has had 'two lives':

> I did behavioural therapy, I learned to know myself, understand things, see things, and then… I've actually had two lives. I had one life before, one life now. And at the same time, there was the [economic] crisis that happened at the same time and… this therapy opened my eyes, made me understand things and everything that I… Everything I understand now, I didn't understand before.

Psychotherapy allowed him to learn about neurological and psychological mechanisms like privation, addiction, and how neurotransmitters work, and it reversed his opinion of 'shrinks', whose work he used to think was 'rubbish'. It also prompted him to revisit his past in light of this diagnosis. He attributes his failings in school and his OCD to childhood trauma from his alcoholic father, who seems to have been violent towards his mother and died early. Cognitive behavioural therapy gradually helped him to learn to manage his emotions, especially the negative ones and the 'fears' that drove him to develop 'control' mechanisms. A major part of therapy was thus learning to 'think positive' as much as possible, because, as Philippe often says, 'positive thinking is a resource for beating this illness'.

The contact with doctors, 'extraordinary people' who he seems to have deeply appreciated, motivated him to continue the experience by participating in clinical trials and getting involved in a group for people with OCD, giving him the opportunity to speak of his 'ordeal' ten or so times to help friends and families of people with the illness to understand it.

As for Marianne, she speaks of her job as a calling since early childhood and says that she likes it, even its more difficult aspects (patients that are burdensome or challenging to care for, such as those with Alzheimer's disease). She says that she is 'worn down' by the pressure on staff that has intensified in recent years, taking the form of insistent and repeated demands for unexpected replacements, absences that administrators think have become intolerable, and new inter-service mobility requirements that no longer take account of auxiliary nurses' desire to gradually progress towards less physically exhausting positions, to name a few. In this context, Marianne's supervisor has rebuked her for obtaining a certificate from the occupational doctor declaring her apt for work provided that she remains in the same service, which her superiors find constraining given the new flexibility requirements. She says her supervisor told her, 'You're a burden, a handicap, even, for the team, because you can no longer change services'. The situation worsened to the point that it drove her to attempt suicide in December 2015. After that, it was Marianne's turn to undergo psychotherapy for several months, although through her job she was already no stranger to the world of mental health and had been the one to encourage her husband to seek psychological care.

As their stories show, the specificities of the Chapalain's professional and personal trajectories (upward ascension, kinds of jobs held, following psychotherapy) accustomed them to introspection, and spending time with members of the cultural branch of privileged social milieus (education and health care) undeniably contributed to developing a disposition to talk about themselves that also explains why they agreed to participate in lengthy and recurring interviews with a sociologist. Philippe was particularly comfortable and willing to talk about himself and his mental state at length, which is rather rare among working-class men.

'Learning to indulge ourselves': a paradoxical conversion to hedonism

Philippe relates how his therapy engendered a radical shift in his worldview that has led him to prolong it in a form of everyday therapy consisting mainly of 'doing things you like to do'.

> Actually, in therapy, it's the exercises, it's understanding how we operate, how... what we feel about what happens to us... and exercises to erase it all [...]. It could be music, doing things you like to do. I love walking my dog – bizarre, not many people [like that], but I take my dog out and when I come back, I've forgotten everything that's happened, everything that happened that day. I listen to music I like - not the music they play on the radio, [music] I like – in a neutral, relaxing room, everything goes well. I wake up, it's like I'm just getting up.

His therapy ultimately encouraged him to adopt a hedonistic posture, conceived as an avoidance of suffering and a methodical search for pleasure. For all that, when he puts this injunction to hedonism into action, Philippe reactivates his disposition to asceticism, in the sense of a discipline of the body and mind, that he had already demonstrated earlier in life, particularly when studying for his degrees. He says he regularly does 'exercises' to know how to enjoy himself, has thought and worked on himself a great deal thanks to this therapy, and tries hard to lead a 'healthy' life (going to bed early, not 'partying') so as not to endanger the mental balance he has developed as a result.

As he describes it, the primary objective of the introspective work associated with the therapy is to arrive at a mastery of one's emotions in order to cancel, reduce, or control negative emotions and replace them with positive ones. It is a matter of learning to 'think positive' and 'be well'. To do so he must above all prioritise activities that he 'enjoys' in his free time: walking his dog, listening to the music he likes. Philippe has also renewed his fondness for motor sports, one of his favourite interests (he bought a quad and is restoring an old Opel). He says he deprived himself of this pastime when he was suffering from OCD:

PHILIPPE: In fact, in the illness I used to have, I'd deprive myself of things I like doing. Weird. And so in my therapy, I discovered lots of things I liked but stopped myself from doing.

SÉVERINE: Such as?

PHILIPPE: What I really like is mechanics. Lots of things that I wanted to do and that I ... it wasn't planned, so no [I didn't do it].

One can see that Philippe attributes the renunciation of these hobbies to his 'illness', and their resumption to the therapy. And yet he further notes that he used to practice these activities when he was 'a renter' and 'had no children' and suggests that it was also – or even mainly – the intense demands of his family and professional lives in the 1990s that drove him to give up these costly hobbies because they did not include his family. One might also note that, in light of this injunction to well-being, Philippe returns to pastimes that are rather ordinary, especially in the working class, when the Chapalains had previously tried out several leisure sports associated with higher social positions (tennis and badminton for him, riding for her), but never for long. Marianne's main pastimes are watching television and shopping in clothing and home décor stores. Listening to music is Philippe's most legitimate hobby (in the sense of legitimate culture), and it mainly consists of listening to French and international variety music on the television music channel D17.

In other aspects of the couple's relationship, Philippe's cognitive behavioural therapy seems to have shaken the extreme rationalisation they previously demonstrated. Concerning domestic work, for instance, Philippe describes a major relaxing of an 'extremely polished' system: their schedule is less rigid, they lowered their standards, and they now allow themselves to be spontaneous.

> And then sometimes, if it doesn't get done, it's fine! Sometimes [Marianne] might say, 'Yeah, the cleaning isn't done, I can't…' OK, it's fine, you can do your cleaning tomorrow. As much as before I could be really organised, my illness told me 'gotta do it this way', as much… Before, it was 'whatever is planned was planned, it absolutely has to be done'. Now, no. If my daughter calls, 'Hey, come out to eat tonight?' - it's unplanned, it's my wife who's thrown into a tailspin, and me, I'm already on my way! It was unthinkable [before].

As this quote suggests, Marianne's psychotherapy, which was more recent and for other reasons, does not seem to have produced a similar transformation. As a result, there are several discernible differences between them. For example, Philippe is more an advocate of a parental style based on listening and building confidence than Marianne, who leaves him to handle their troubles with their younger daughter; they agreed that they should to take her to a social and psychological centre for help.

Financially, Philippe's constant concern with anticipating and calculating has been partially challenged by this order to enjoy the present. Although he still plans ahead and stresses his propensity for saving ('It's a personal management style – there's some who say, "I got a bonus, I'm gonna spend it", while I'm more, "I got a bonus, I'll save it"') and his strict management of accounts ('It's squared away', 'We aren't going to spend wildly'), these elements are in tension with a will to 'not deprive ourselves' that surges forth from time to time, like 'a day when we're working like mad and then we say, "Alright, that's enough, let's indulge ourselves"'. However, the injunction to enjoy the present and 'think positive' that he got from his behavioural therapy flies in the face of his justifiably worrisome economic situation at work since 2008, which fuels his well-developed inclination to save money. The Chapalains are thus characterised by a relationship with consumption that is split between the spending they allow to 'indulge themselves', which are mostly small leisure expenses (movies, restaurant), and material investment expenses (house, cars, equipment) for which they have now to 'make do with what [they] have' and refrain from making plans.

In the end, Philippe's psychotherapy led to a conversion to hedonism that modified, or rather strengthened in another form, the ascetic dispositions that were partially behind the couple's ascendant careers. This paradoxical form of hedonism resulting from vigorous self-improvement work is indeed a characteristic Philippe acquired while in care for his OCD, along with the reflexive and discursive dispositions that it activated or honed: as he sums it up, 'I learned to know how to indulge myself, too'.

The psychologisation of the working world, or the need to 'adapt'

There is another facet to the psychologisation of the experiences recounted by the couple. When speaking of their work, both Philippe and Marianne describe a recurring opposition between 'Us' and 'Them', understood from the perspective of the psychological ideas that each developed while following their therapeutic path. 'Them' is hierarchical superiors, obsessed with profit, personnel management, and figures, who are 'in their own world' far from reality 'on the ground'; 'Us' is rank-and-file employees, the 'humans' in which higher-ups lose interest, who are subjugated, suffer, and demand to be 'heard' more than anything else. This especially is one of the points they raise again and again to emphasise how similar their respective employment situations are, despite working in different sectors.

Their interviews are filled with various formulations concerning listening, social issues, humanity, communication, and the psyche: taking time to 'listen' to those that 'need to talk' is indispensable to letting them be 'at peace with themselves', but you cannot count on your superiors when you are 'depressed', 'demoralised', or have 'reached your saturation point'.

While Philippe repeatedly reproaches his superiors for not being able to fill this role of listener, he relates many instances at work where he practically presents himself as a lay psychologist to his colleagues, which he says allows him to perform his duties in the best way possible. In his accounts of these scenes, he details how he reactivates knowledge and postures he learned during psychotherapy: playing the role of confidant and letting people talk, leading them to think positively and never putting them down. Speaking of a co-worker who changed work teams so she could carpool but struggles to get used to her new position, Philippe explained:

> I manage to figure people out better than before, and actually I… there are things that I understand now that I didn't understand [before therapy]. And so, it really bothered her to leave, she was good [here], and when she went there… So I said, 'Good or not good, discuss it with someone, talk about it. Just because you left…' And so she came to see me, she cried, 'I don't know if I'll manage, I have a ton of things to memorise'. And then, so, simply talking about it… […] There some things that are worse, others that are better, and I said, 'Hold on to the good things during the bad times'. […] With that person, I brought some positivity and she's managing to cheer up. Whereas otherwise she'll be stuck in negative thoughts and she's someone who'd take a break [on sick leave]. Whereas with us, she never took a leave. Whereas I learned that in the position she had before, she was often on sick leave for depression.

For all that, the Chapalain's recurrent virulent discourse on company executives – how they do not listen, their inhumanity, their obsession with financial matters – is coupled with a form of resignation regarding their own professional situations. Philippe's understanding of the world through a psychological lens has led him to analyse Marianne's work problems from a particular angle. In one interview, as they each tried to identify the causes behind her suicide attempt, she mentioned a fundamental shift arising from inadequate funding on the part of the Regional Health Agency (Agence Régionale de Santé) that resulted in budget cuts that degraded the working conditions of all auxiliary nurses: 'They increasingly put pressure on business owners, of course, but [also] on institutions. Gotta operate, but with less and less every year'. But Philippe raised the figure of the manager several times in the discussion, making her directly responsible for Marianne's act: 'They are the perverse ones', he finally shot back, this layman's diagnosis being based on his recent reading of a general-readership book about 'malignant narcissists'. Throughout the interviews, his focus on the manager's personality and use of an essentially psychological template for analysing situations prevented him from thinking more deeply about the structural causes of her malaise, of which he nonetheless seems to be aware and which are the factors Marianne herself stresses.

Furthermore, in his work, Philippe's insistence on listening and good relations is entirely compatible with contemporary supervisory norms (Illouz 2007): he subscribes to such expectations from his superiors, despite the fact that many of his co-workers widely disparage the figure of the 'social worker' supervisor (Misset 2009).

Lastly, Philippe's reception of the injunction to 'think positive' strongly orients how he handles adversity at work and paradoxically makes him speak highly of his professional situation, despite its constraints, his disillusionment, and his strongly critical commentary.

> Today I think I'm good the way I am, because I'm used to it. You need that. Actually, today, you've gotta adapt. Today you can't think… I mean, today, you can no longer say 'I want to develop, I want to get training' […] Before you could say, 'If I want to, I can', like I did, I went knocking on the door to say 'I'm going for it' […]. Today, you've got a job, be happy, you've got a job. Be happy with your wages.

Although he regularly portrays himself as particularly determined, able to 'win' the 'fight' (against his illness, for instance, or his younger daughter's troubles at school), throughout the interviews he constantly brought up the need 'to adapt' to anything that happens, whatever the cost in terms of 'effort'. 'The watchword today is "adapt". "Adapt", it's really strong, adapt to everything, all proposals, everything. Whether you want to or not, you've got to adapt'. Philippe instead tries to fight by adopting an obstinate attitude (*Eigen-sinn*; Lüdtke 1995, 19) that combines docility and distance: he refuses to let the stress get to him and 'put pressure' on the Operators, holds to a form of 'straight-talk' when addressing his superiors, and insists on listening and mutual help when dealing with Operators. Practices of this kind, protecting from the intrusion of work into the private sphere and/or its impact on physical or mental health, give him the feeling of going counter to the tendencies that he endlessly criticises. Indeed, Philippe presents not 'putting pressure on' himself, and not passing it along to his subordinates, as an imperative necessity for mental well-being and an integral part of his therapy.

> I hate running around. Before it was the opposite. But then… I'm not the kind to say "I'm not going to do anything today," it's not that. I go to work, but I don't want to see anyone running around, I don't want to see anyone stressing out because he doesn't want to stop the line. That's what I don't want to see anymore.

As he indicates here, this desire to not put pressure on himself or others contrasts with his previous behaviour. It should be noted that the obsessional problems for which he was treated had heavy repercussions on his private life, which is what drove him to seek help. But it seems they had no negative impact in the professional sphere, where Philippe was seen as 'someone who's organised, thorough, serious' – in short, a perfectionist, which was held in rather high esteem by his superiors. Today, this concern with 'taking his time', not 'running around' – even during break-downs when pressure is especially intense and managers rush to the shop only minutes after the shut-down – goes counter to the demands of high productivity in a lean manufacturing industry where stopping the line should be avoided at all costs. As a result, Philippe now gets warnings. For example, after his supervisor rushed to the scene of an automation breakdown, he heard it said that he ought to be more 'reactive' and reconsider an earlier suggestion (made in jest) that he buy roller skates so he could intervene more rapidly.

> I left to do my job, I analysed the thing, what he'd said, and the next day, I told him what I had to say. [...] So I said, "You'll never see me run, I have no use for your pressure, and I don't want to work like that".

Despite his ways of keeping his distance, Philippe contributes to maintaining order in the factory. In professional elections, he votes for a union that makes few demands (whereas Marianne chose to 'defend' herself by recently joining the CFDT [French Democratic Confederation of Labour], which is more assertive). He is hostile to strikes and having a confrontational relationship with the boss, and usually ends up assiduously applying the guidelines that he had previously denounced. Philippe's psychotherapy thus led to specific but ambivalent consequences in the professional sphere, fluctuating between denunciation of managerial behaviour and/or injunctions, self-examination, and forms of docility when faced with other demands.

This portrait of Philippe and Marianne Chapalain serves as a reminder of one of the conditions for the penetration of mass psychological culture into the working class: like the bus drivers studied by Olivier Schwartz (2011), the characteristics of their jobs (mostly managerial for him, in a medical setting for her, both under considerable pressure) facilitate the appropriation of a template that tends to psychologise and individualise their experiences. This appropriation, which also owes much to the specificities of their professional and personal trajectories, has paradoxical effects in every sphere of their life as a couple. It reshapes their earlier ascetic dispositions and produces a critical but partially disarmed approach for protesting the domination to which they are subjected in the professional sphere.

Notes

1 For an explanation of the French educational system, see the Appendix.
2 An offshoot of behavioural psychology, cognitive behavioural therapy consists of modifying unsuitable behaviours through gradual repeated exposure to situations that trigger obsessions while resisting resorting to compulsive rituals thanks to alternative techniques for calming the resultant anxiety (the behavioural aspect), while simultaneously working on intrusive thoughts by deeply modifying the systems of reasoning activated in such thinking (the cognitive aspect).

References

Bury, Michael. 1982. 'Chronic illness as biographical disruption.' *Sociology of Health and Illness* 4, no. 2: 167–182.

Castel, Pierre-Henri. 2012. *La Fin des coupables. Obsessions et contrainte intérieure de la psychanalyse aux neurosciences*. Paris: Les Editions d'Ithaque.

Illouz, Eva. 2007. *Cold Intimacies: The Making of Emotional Capitalism*. Hoboken, NJ: Wiley.

Lüdtke, Alf. 1995. *The History of Everyday Life: Reconstructing Historical Experiences and Ways of Life*. Princeton, NJ: Princeton University Press.

Misset, Séverine. 2009. 'Proximité professionnelle et distance scolaire: les jeunes ouvriers qualifiés et leurs trajectoires.' *Revue française de pédagogie* 167: 59–71.

Morgiève, Margot, and Xavier Briffault. 2014. 'La fabrique du TOC moderne: une analyse ethnographique de la cérébralisation de la névrose obsessionnelle dans un laboratoire de neurosciences cliniques.' *Socio-logos* 9. http://journals.openedition.org/socio-logos/2882.

Morgiève, Margot, and Antoine Pelissolo. 2016. *TOC: la maladie de l'hyper-contrôle*. Paris: Le cavalier bleu.

Schwartz, Olivier. 2011. 'La pénétration de la "culture psychologique de masse" dans un groupe populaire: paroles de conducteurs de bus.' *Sociologie* 2, no. 4: 345–361.

Wolff, Loup. 2005. 'Monitorat, maîtrise, administration et direction. Quatre formes du travail d'encadrement dans l'industrie.' *Réseaux* 134: 123–155.

27

CONCLUSION: GOODWILL AS NECESSITY

Aspirations of the middle fraction of the working classes and how they relate to norms

Marie-Hélène Lechien and Olivier Masclet

The portraits at the heart of this volume highlight the splintering of situations and lifestyles of the stable-modest fractions of the working classes.[1] As one of the research programme's aims was to comprehend the working-class condition through household rather than individual experience, this conclusion explores the lessons these household portraits have to teach us. The selection of household case studies as research method (detailed in Chapter 2) led us to interview both members of couples, and sometimes children, on their private and occupational practices, allowing us to interconnect men's and women's social scenes and perspectives. The notion of goodwill emerged in several portraits as a descriptor of how these households relate to the world, most strikingly in the third section focused on how the interviewed people relate to institutions and other social groups; if they rarely express 'cultural goodwill', they do show goodwill towards education, health and hygiene, professional investment, and/or egalitarianism in conjugal and familial relations. Recall that in *Distinction* (1984), Pierre Bourdieu titled the chapter devoted to the petite bourgeoisie 'Cultural Goodwill', and the chapter devoted to the working classes 'The Choice of the Necessary'. We propose a contracted formulation – 'goodwill as necessity' – because we think it encapsulates the most important characteristics to emerge from the studied households: assignation to a dominated position in the social space, more visibility of women's imprints with the inclusion of basic employees in the definition of the working classes, and several forms of goodwill paired with a disposition to play by the social rules without entirely subscribing to them.

DOI: 10.4324/9781003330073-30

'Impoverished' middle classes, 'respectable' working classes?

This volume has retained the notion of 'the working classes', although the choice was debated among the sociologists in our programme. It indicates an affiliation with a sociological tradition focused on the study of power relations and lifestyles among social classes. It makes sense given the social properties of the households of labourers and basic employees that we got to know: most of them are from working-class families and possess low educational attainments. They have subaltern jobs and their children often have trouble at school. They have neither the material or cultural resources nor the protections of the middle classes. To put a finer line on it, one could even say that, in their everyday lives, they are subject to potential disqualification by members of the middle and upper classes, who are in a position to evaluate their educational practices, health-related behaviours, or professional efforts. Management can refuse them promotions, teachers may deplore how slow or undisciplined their children are, doctors and nurses disapprove of their dietary practices. Consequently, the notion of the 'impoverished middle classes' is not helpful for comprehending the condition of these households, because it is implicitly based on the postulates that French society is moving to the middle, that inequalities are disappearing, or that social classes don't even exist, said to belong to a bygone age and contradict the democratic ideal. But as the first two chapters laid out in detail, statistical objectification in study after study demonstrates that these disparities are maintained or shift between social groups, in terms of access to promotions at work, consistent working hours, or advanced educations.

For all that, the interviewed households were chosen for their relative stability: most of them were 'more or less getting by' and had little to no contact with the social, police, judicial, or penitentiary institutions that the unstable fractions of the working classes have to deal with more frequently. That being the case, why not describe them as belonging to the 'respectable' working classes? To us, this notion seems to refer to the old state of moral power relations between social groups, the one described by Richard Hoggart in *The Uses of Literacy* (1957). In the English working classes of the 1930s–1950s, women mainly took care of the home, which counted more children than today; sexuality, whose norms and controls were obviously not the same as they are today, figured large in the view dominant groups held of labour families; they lived in a tightly localised in-group setting; and lastly, the youngest generations, born in the 1930s, had 'gone into their own worlds, supported now by a greater body of entertaining and flattering provisions than their parents knew' (76). But 60 years later, the portraits in this book show that the working-class households they represent do not close in on themselves or avoid other social groups: the tertiarisation of the job market means that they have more regular contact with the middle and upper classes, both as their clients (as with doctors) or as their employees (as is the case for childminders working for parents in better-paying jobs requiring higher educations). The stability of the households we met, linked to resources accumulated through two jobs, does not produce a 'respectable' lifestyle closed in on itself. The studied households are far from the familialism and localism of labouring men and housewives favouring a dense social life in the fold of family, neighbourhood, and workplace and seem closer to the lifestyles of other social groups, even aspiring 'to be like everyone else'.[2]

Households and individuals: understanding a social condition through the couple

As we have said, one of the research objectives was to comprehend the working-class condition through the household. In line with the work of Michel Verret, we mainly sought to analyse the tangle of the ethos of basic employees and women, of labourers and men, and the lifestyles and meanings attributed to the social position they occupy as a result.[3] It proved difficult to approach the interpenetration of professional cultures – meaning the sense of skills, values, and knowledge acquired in the practice of an occupation – through interviews. While domestic partners in all socio-professional categories talk to each other about work much more than they used to (Bozon 2009), interviews do not always provide traces of these conversations. Research participants hold subaltern jobs, in many cases gendered, and they do not seem inclined to talk about their partners' jobs: at first glance, women do not take much interest in men's rather technical occupations (automotive industry, mechanic, transportation, plumbing) and men are not particularly interested in the more relational work of women (sales, health, early childhood, elder care).[4] Since the case studies cover a variety of themes – work as well as private practices like taking time for oneself and health issues – it is no stretch to imagine that couples do, in fact, regularly compare their professional situations: women in sheltered basic-employee office jobs versus men in labourer jobs exposed to noise and dangerous machinery, women whose job puts them at the service of clients versus men sheltered by more solitary technical work, the poor ambiance of working in a supermarket versus the camaraderie of the factory. Comparisons of the physical and psychological hardship of the tasks they perform may lead to recognition of the merit of a partner who is seen as putting up with more burdensome working conditions.[5] As a result, equality between partners is not merely measured by the sharing of domestic and parental labour; it is also indexed on this comparison of working conditions.

It is evident that several couples in this study talk frequently about work. Every evening Cécile and Jean-Marc Pilier give a 'little report' on their days to 'unwind' (she is a hairdresser, he a security officer)[6]; Marianne and Philippe Chapalain liken their working conditions to decry the same degradation and contempt for 'the human' from the hierarchy (she is an auxiliary nurse in geriatrics, he a skilled labourer in the automobile industry).[7] Cécilia and Éric

Dufar also talk about work often, and Eric makes a significant contribution to housework so that Cécilia can rest after her work as a cashier in a supermarket ('She gets it full-on all day long'), which she describes in the language of contamination and wear: some unpleasant interactions with customers, a hierarchy that mocks cashiers who dress in slim trousers tucked into boots ('Where's your horse?' one of her supervisors asks her regularly, preferring cashiers wear skirts and heels), controlled bathroom breaks, and sexual jokes from male co-workers.[8]

So people talk about work, be it peacefully or with vitriol. Such two-person reflexivity is also manifest in the construction of a common or very similar discourse on the social position they hold, relative to other social groups and their own sibling groups. For instance, Marianne and Philippe Chapalain both express a humanist vision of the world and a moral definition of relationships of domination at work, based on a rather striking familiarity with the psychological register ('We're not in their world – for them, it's profit. [...] You get the impression that they would only understand if it was done to them – would they accept it?', wondered Philippe). Other couples stand for a hedonistic worldview that they compare to the lifestyles of their siblings, who they describe as being socially successful but austere, calculating, or arrogant. Mireille and Roger Monteil, who come from farming families and went to the city, speak at length of the tensions between them over consumption and 'modernity'. As Henri Eckert shows, as the only child of well-off farmers but without any educational attainments, Mireille's residential and professional trajectory (housecleaner, printing worker, secretary in a marriage agency, agent at the unemployment office) is characterised by her struggle to avoid social downclassing. They both say that she has imposed a few changes of residence and distinctive consumption on Roger, a skilled worker with a higher income, because of 'her money', inherited from her parents. They describe their power relations, such as they are, with humour ('"You, you're really Mrs More!"; "OK," she replies, "well, you're Mister Less!"'). But a common discourse emerges when they are asked about their relations with the extended family. Roger is the youngest of three sons of parents who were poor farmers, although their situation has since improved; he describes his brothers as 'tough farmers'. Mireille jumped in to say there is a 'wall' between them: 'We're the exception, we're not like them'. 'Yes, that's it,' Roger responded, 'they're bosses, we're labourers'.[9]

A working-class feminism?

The household case studies, especially those in the second section of this volume, expose another dimension of life as a couple: the norms of paternal involvement and the sharing of domestic work. Some men take responsibility for domestic and family tasks, but many others do very little.[10] In this way the case studies reveal the tensions and conflicts elicited by the feeling among women that domestic work is unfairly distributed. But even in this case, a certain egalitarian goodwill appears among men and women alike: men's involvement in housework proves to be 'both less demeaning and less optional' than it used to be. The 'masculine exemption' is declining in discourse as well as practice (Cartier, Letrait, and Sorin 2018, 68). In interviews women and men justify this exemption (because of night hours or a job that takes them away from home, like driving a tourist coach); in practice, men may periodically perform household and parental tasks, but only ones requiring minimal skills, which they say they never observed in their fathers. Some of the interviewed women claim to enjoy domestic work but describe it as a trap or even an addiction, something like a sense of practice that they would like to purge from their bodies. Seeing their mothers as 'maniacal housekeepers', more concerned with cleanliness and tidying their home than with their children, they are trying to find their own path.

This goodwill relates to a series of previously described factors: women's attachment to paid employment and more continuous careers that limit their presence in the home; irregular hours becoming commonplace for basic employees and labourers and thus favouring arrangements and turn-taking in the couple; longer educations; the women's and feminist movements and their coverage in the media; the building of a 'State feminism' (public policy for professional and wage equality between men and women)[11]; the development of sport and leisure activities stemming from greater attention to health and the spread of 'mass psychological culture' (Castel and Le Cerf 1980) – all processes that call for the assertion of independence and looking after oneself. Another factor is the injunction to be a 'good parent' (Martin 2014), which encourages parents to show more affection for their children, and fathers to spend more time with them. This goodwill can be found with Valentin Dufour and Laeticia Kergal, when he encourages her to 'take some time for herself' and 'go out' (but then he calls her to ask when she'll be back, or where she is, or where to find something he needs for their eight-month-old daughter) while she is pursuing strategies to find a job and end this interval of unequally shared domestic work.[12]

It is difficult to describe this egalitarian goodwill without being class-centric.[13] Is it feminism? If it is, is it a specifically working-class version of feminism? As we have said elsewhere, the women participating in this study manifested something of an inclination for maternal and domestic tasks; women and men tend to naturalise the division of work (women inside, men outside, in a complementarity of roles). Practices and above all words are thus rather far from expressing equality as it is defined by the cultural fractions of the middle and upper classes to which sociologists belong, where equality often implicitly means the complete interchangeability of roles between men and women, thought to be the sole way to end gendered assignations and the unequal value of 'male' and 'female' domains. This leads to the question of how to analyse interviews in a way that avoids applying an interpretative framework comparing the differences in definitions of equality and ultimately assigning 'bad feminist points' to research participants when, for example, they are inattentive to commonplace vocabulary naturalising masculine and feminine tastes. Inversely, how to avoid assigning interviewees 'good points' on the assumption that they are feminists 'without knowing it', and are only put off by the term because it is socially and politically discredited (Gasquet 2015)? Warning of these pitfalls of using the category 'feminist', Béatrice de Gasquet has suggested the alternative notion of 'gender reflexivity', which aptly applies to how several study participants refer to it when speaking of themselves or in recounting discussions with their partner, friends, co-workers, and family.

We should be cautious in assuming that the hypothesis of egalitarian goodwill can be generalised, however. First of all, it does not cover all current practices, nor the meanings the studied households give them. It is not to be confused with other ways of defining equality or equity between members of a couple – as we saw in the discussion of couples' comparisons of the difficulty of their working conditions – or with forms of protest that are more expressions of how fed up some interviewed women are with the accumulated exhaustion of paid work and housework than they are expressions of 'gender reflexivity'. It is absent in the functioning of some couples who are unfamiliar or even hostile to the egalitarian norm, such as some young couples in Benoît Coquard's research (2019).[14] Likewise, it is unlikely that most research participants, men or women, would call themselves feminists if asked to state their position. The women in our study who work in labour or basic-employee positions who most decry their domestic burden and their partners' 'passivity' are not necessarily trying to change anything, or feel they have no power to do so, unlike the middle-class women they may meet in places like the school parents' association, whose propensity to argue with school reforms and 'remake the world' annoys them.

Statistical research on the distribution of domestic work demonstrates that the lack of egalitarian goodwill is, in fact, found across the social space, and the differences between socio-professional categories are minor. The same can be said for the discrediting of feminism as a political or moral category and also found in every social group and highest in the 'upper right' of the social space.[15] The egalitarian norm is no more at work in the practices of middle- and upper-class households than in those in the working classes. On the other hand, it is a strategy of distinction in the cultural middle and upper classes, which generally consider themselves ahead of the curve on this point. But even – or perhaps mainly – in these social categories, women are charged with 'maternal availability' and thus subject to a distinct division of family work resulting from several social processes, including the success of Françoise Dolto's 'children's cause' (Garcia 2011) and the promotion of demedicalised childbirth, breastfeeding, and, most recently, 'positive parenting'. With the growing role of school, middle- and upper-class women are as responsible for social reproduction as they ever were, if not more so (Garcia 2018). The educational role of the 'occupation of mother' (Gojard 2010) is even more prominent, and those with the necessary economic capital can delegate the most physical aspects of this work to employees (childminders, babysitters, housecleaners). This does not set them significantly apart from the women we met who work as basic employees or labourers, whose educational goodwill emerged from the case studies: these working-class women are also engaged in education, even if their involvement in their children's schooling proves to be less socially effective.[16]

For all these reasons, we cannot say that egalitarian goodwill is a generalisable finding for the research presented in this volume: its presence is as variable in the working classes as it is in the middle and upper classes. There are other arguments for taking it into account, however. For one, when the interviewed women speak of domestic and familial work, in one single interview they may naturalise the fact that it is their responsibility and contradict this logic by describing this division of labour as 'force of habit', meaning it is more due to socialisation than any intrinsic complementarity of roles ('we're used to it that way', 'we were brought up that way'). Secondly, the women we interviewed do not necessarily run up against the same expressions of masculine domination as women in the middle and upper classes. Indeed, historically and socially the figure of the 'head of the household' has taken different forms and obviously should not be ranked according to how violent they are thought to be. To take the example of who keeps the household accounts in the labouring world, women have long controlled this aspect of family governance (Schwartz 1990).

The households in this study are no exception. More often than not, the women controlled the budgets, which is a burden: several of them mentioned the stress they felt in anticipation of budgeting work and the constant calculations that colonised their minds, their need to unplug by watching television – in other words, to take a break from thinking, their domestic and budgetary worries, their concern for their children's educations, or their projections of their working situations (when they are considering a career change, for example).[17] This burden is also a power, however, of which middle- and upper-class women are often deprived, since accounts and income tax declarations are still somewhat men's business in these social groups (Spire 2018).[18] As a result, egalitarian goodwill cannot be described in the same form in the working-class and other social milieus because the dispossession of women in the family does not play out in the same way, especially when where the distribution of power over finances is concerned.

Lastly, as Marie Cartier shows using the example of Régine Leblanc, even an occupation as gendered and socially devalued as childminder helps to spread a certain egalitarian goodwill. Although it consigns her to the house and tends to accentuate the unequal division of domestic and parental work in the couple, it may favour 'gender reflexivity' and the search for physical and temporal autonomy through practice of a leisure pursuit that releases her from the bounds of the home, due to her training and familiarity with labour law, interactions with the more highly educated women supervising her work, and personal discussions with other childminders comparing their professional and private experiences and thus de-singularising and denaturalising their situations.[19]

Goodwill as necessity: consequences of including basic employees in the working classes

Egalitarian goodwill is thus related to new gender relations in the working classes that research in the 1960s–1970s was unable to anticipate, as women are now more highly educated and more invested in paid employment. In *Distinction*, 'the choice of the necessary' characterising the working-class lifestyle was based largely on the practices of male labourers and farmers; certain descriptions lead one to think that they are a cultural isolate, although women are repeatedly mentioned for being more open to legitimate cultural practices. But once sociologists began to agree on counting basic employees amongst the working classes, some of the dispositions of the office and retail workers that Pierre Bourdieu had categorised as the executant petite bourgeoisie switched their position to the new category of 'new executant wage-earners', to use Michel Verret's term. If researchers in our programme used the notion of goodwill, it is due to both of these shifts – women into paid employment and basic employees into the working classes. The notion of 'tertiary-sector working classes', developed in the study of auxiliary nurses (Arborio 2012), and the expression 'another working-class world' for speaking of home care service providers (Avril 2014) were calls to pay heed to these shifts and their consequences: the working-class condition is no longer mainly that of male labourers and peasants and their 'non-working' wives.

One might object that the women in our study hold the most-dominated positions of the 'basic-employee' category. Indeed, many of them are workers in major chain stores (cashiers), personal services (childminders, home care service providers, housecleaners), or at the lowest levels of education, health, and social work (teaching assistant, auxiliary nurse, foster carer). With modest wages, part-time jobs, often irregular, variable, or unusual working hours, and lack of recognition of seniority or experience, they are all jobs designated as low skill. All these occupational traits socially distance them from the lifestyles of office and retail workers assigned to the petite bourgeoisie in *Distinction*. And indeed, the goodwill that we encountered in these households was rarely of the same ilk as that of the petite bourgeoisie: the ascetic logic of cultural and/or economic capital accumulation is rarely found in our interviewees' practices or how they relate to the world, if only because of their limited cultural resources and tenuous economic resources. Although many aspire to a professional promotion or to not merely work for the sake of working and paying the bills, and although many hope that their children pursue post-secondary education and get work in more legitimate occupations than theirs, they are not organising their lives around the quest for social ascension that Pierre Bourdieu described as typical of the petite bourgeoisie, people 'of the deferred pleasure, the deferred present'.[20]

This is another form of goodwill, which breaks down into educational, health and hygienic, professional, economic, and institutional goodwill. By institutional goodwill we mean the narrow sense of the work of conforming to the expectations of social institutions, as illustrated in the attitude of Sylvie Barderon, former hairstylist trying to find a 'normal life' by seeking help from social workers and psychologists after a series of challenges.[21] We also mean institutional goodwill in a broader sense, a disposition to play by the rules (we will return to this in a moment), expressed by voting regularly, which is related to the action of norm-producing institutions to which the interviewed households are exposed.[22] The women in basic-employee jobs presented in the portraits do hold subaltern positions, but in institutions or fields that contribute to the extension of the ever-present realms of the common, judgement, and aspirations that were analysed in the introduction of this book. They are both objects and agents of the diffusion of institutional behavioural rationalisation processes in the private as well as the professional sphere, which emerges clearly through the case-study approach. Jointly or apart from their partners, a majority demonstrate economic goodwill by saving money to buy a home and invest in interior decoration, educational goodwill by helping their children with schoolwork and participating in parents' association activities, and joint health and educational goodwill by enrolling them in sport clubs.[23] All these transformations attest to their work 'to be like everyone else', a modification of behaviours and aspirations borne by institutions of education, medicine, and other domains such as the cultural industry for early childhood development (Montmasson-Michel 2018) or credit institutions, with resulting changes in sensibilities.

Auxiliary nurses and early childhood care workers thus internalise health and hygiene and child-rearing norms over the course of training and professional experience to which they can 'convert' patients, parents of young children, and their friends and families. The occupation of childminder is an apt illustration of such dominated participation in the logic of a field, applied to the space of early childhood. Since the 1970s, it has gradually come in line with common labour law and developed professional norms: in 1977, 'nannies' and 'sitters' became 'childminders', granted a formal status. They came to be licenced by public authorities at the level of the administrative department, based on evaluation by early childhood educators working for Mother and Child Protection Services (Protection Maternelle et Infantile; PMI); 60 hours of optional training was also available. In 1992, departments were required to offer this now-mandatory training to provide 'knowledge on the development, pace, and needs of the child'. Legal oversight of the occupation deepened, with a new collective agreement in 2005 that doubled the hours of training required and strengthened 'educational aptitude' requirements. The jobs of childminder and foster-care provider (full-time care of children who have been taken into care by children's services) were separated and became specialised. In 2006, access to continuing education was facilitated, and childminders henceforth have the right to individual training.[24]

If this occupation still lacks prestige, it refracts tensions in the space of institutions for early childhood and the constant raising of professional norms with competition over the legitimate definition of childcare between medically oriented actors (hygiene and safety norms, knowledge of childhood illnesses, and treatment techniques) and actors with a psychological approach (developmental norms and norms for the respect of children's integrity, sometimes opposing certain acts that have gradually come to be defined as too intrusive). Increasingly supervised by institutions like the RAM (*Relais Assistantes Maternelles*, centres providing support for childminders that are often headed by early childhood educators), these subaltern early childhood workers develop interactional skills by minding children of a variety of social backgrounds and becoming proficient in certain childcare norms.

So rather than social ascension, we use the notion of goodwill to highlight efforts in the 'conquest of norms' (Verret 1979) in some areas (but not others) under the influence of specific institutional processes. This makes it possible to understand the queried households' adoption of legitimate practices in a given sphere of family life, such as rejecting corporeal punishment in child discipline, but not in others, such as strict control over screen time. Along the same lines, the studied households manifest goodwill towards health and hygiene by watching their weight and seeking leisure-time activities for themselves and their children that are both fun and considered to be healthy, such as a regular sport (basketball, gymnastics, and judo are the most common among our interviewees).[25] This health and hygienic goodwill has developed counter to previous generations, which are seen as having worn their bodies out on 'maniacal' housework and overwork in physically demanding jobs. It has also developed counter to the most insecure: the stigmatisation of so-called non-workers indissociably targets the physical and moral postures of those who let themselves go, gain weight, spend their days slumped in front of the television, live off welfare, and do not get involved in their children's education.

These demarcations, which allowed the people we met to keep themselves at arms' length from the legacy of past generations and the allegedly 'bad poor', come with other practices. Some try to reform loved ones' relationship to their bodies, for example. A childminder who does Zumba to keep her weight in check, Véronique Delage is conscious of her mother's excess weight, so she pressed her to take up water aerobics (even signing up to go with her), and now her mother is comfortable swimming in front of others.[26] Reforming a social condition from the inside means adjusting to certain legitimate norms.[27] It also means adjusting the loved ones to whom interviewees feel indebted or responsible.[28]

Playing by the rules of a social order that belittles you

One expression crops up in several interviews: 'to have a clear conscience'. For instance, Véronique Delage used it when talking about wanting to sit for an employment qualification examination, even if she doesn't think she will pass ('I'll do it, then I've got a clear conscience, that way I know that I did it, gotta do it'). More than a strategy, here again, the demarcation with the working classes receiving social assistance is an expression of a relationship to the social order and the future: several basic employees and labourers are trying to improve their position, playing by the rules and exposing themselves to social sanctions – trying for a qualifying certificate in early childhood development after a sharp break with school lasting several years, sitting multiple times for the classroom assistant examination, accepting paths to promotion proposed by one's superiors, and ending up in class with young people rebellious against the scholastic order ('I'm not the sort to say no. I'm more the sort to say, "OK, I'll try!",' says Philippe Chapalain, an unskilled labourer who went on the become a systems operator). Women also play the education game: several come face to face with the reactivation of their difficulties or disillusions with school when they become mothers. They get involved in school trips in elementary school and participate in school parents' associations, often holding dominated positions in a division of voluntary labour allotting them material and periodic tasks (they give their time and labour into manning stands at fairs, preparing prizes in assembly lines, and chaperoning school trips, ceding leadership to teachers and specialists). They are present, however: as Olivier Masclet and Gérard Mauger note in speaking of Myriam Sanatanazefi, the simple fact of being a school parent authorises people to go places that are seen as socially neutral. These attitudes towards work and school could be interpreted as a way of bringing oneself in line with the rules, believing at least a little bit in the social promotion game.

Our younger interviewees expressed a stronger aspiration to improve their social condition. The portraits suggest that young women are the most subjected to belittling. Forced to adapt on the job market, they are up against their low educational attainments and misleading promotions. Working strings of insecure employment contracts and irregular hours, they and their partners have no choice but to favour the most stable job in the couple, as seen in the string of failures that ended up trapping Laeticia Kergal at home, seen in the portrait by Angel Baraud. Laeticia repeatedly says she is 'mad' – at politicians, who are clientelistic and 'paid too much' when they only 'go visit farms'; at 'Arabs, their council flat rent and luxury cars' while her household gets no help with the rent; at 'medical care for the rich' in the United States; and so on. This reactivity to everything could be explained by her dissatisfaction with the poor outcome of all her efforts to play by the rules:

> It makes me mad, actually. Because I want to make something of my life and now I'll end up … I mean, I'm not saying that it's pejorative to work

> in a factory [...] because so long as you pay your bills... [...] But... I don't wanna end up like that. It's not what I wanna do [...]. That's what makes me mad [...]. All our money, actually we work to pay our bills, so you think, [*speaks ironically*] 'Your life's great. You've got 100 euros left for fun. Woohoo!' That's when you're at the bottom of the ladder.

This young woman, an unemployed labourer, sums up many interviewees' moral indignation towards 'benefits scroungers' and politicians who are seen as favouring the poor and ignoring those at the bottom of the ladder, just above the cut-off for public assistance. The households we met are obviously not the only ones to reject both politicians and people receiving benefits, as it is also common in the middle and upper classes, in the form of a critique of taxation or an increase in votes for the former Front National (the far-right party renamed Rassemblement National in 2018) among the professions and small business owners. Among interviewees, this moral indignation does not mean they are not open to others, as they may assert the value of less-valued occupations that 'everyone needs' and/or devote time to community groups.[29]

Goodwill does not capture the sense of all of the practices of all of the basic employees and labourers whose lifestyles and living conditions are described in this book. Some of them keep their distance from other people's norms and are attached to the cultural norms described in *The Uses of Literacy*, including staying within the in-group, politeness, and respect for others as values to be passed along to children, and a preference for vocational over academic training. Others conform to some norms to respond to employers' or institutional expectations.[30] Goodwill can also fail, and with it the disposition to play by the rules when the social order repeatedly subjects a household to the ordeal of being belittled at work or school.[31] The aspiration to be like everyone else thus varies in meaning, depending on social experience and contexts of politicisation. It may mean having a goodwill supported by institutions producing legitimate norms, notably those where basic employees work (in health, early childhood, or social work). But being like everyone else can also mean being in the majority, in opposition to the dominant fractions of the upper classes who are described as elites 'a world apart', 'in their own world', or at least far indeed from the common world, and in opposition to people who 'don't work', who are not even seen as being at the bottom of the ladder, but completely off the scale.

Notes

1 We wholeheartedly thank Stéphane Beaud, Gérard Mauger, and Olivier Schwartz for their work on this conclusion, which is based on the research programme's collective findings and analyses.

2 In other words, they are living in the cultural porosity that has emerged since the 1950s and 1960s. Indeed, historical research suggests that there were several interacting forms of cultural desegregation throughout the nineteenth century, with the

generalisation of primary school, the medicalisation of childhood, and newspapers allowing great numbers of people to read the news.

3 'Basic employees used to be set apart from the common people. But now, due to their backgrounds, their remuneration (the median wage of a basic employee is the same as the median wage of a labourer), basic employees are getting closer. Isn't there a new common people in the making, composed of executant workers? [...] We may be witnessing a reconfigured People that could lead to reconfigured cultures. Research on the world of women's work has developed because, if this reconfiguration is taking place, and this is something decisive, it occurs with equality between the sexes [...]. It would be a culture marked by the feminine as much as the masculine' (Interview with Michel Verret, *Les Inrockuptibles*, 2002).

4 The gendered division of work is tied to the opposition between the 'world of human things' and the 'world of material things' (Mauger and Poliak 1998). It tends to obfuscate the physical and technical dimensions of 'feminine' occupations that have been put in the spotlight by work on auxiliary nurses (Arborio 2012) and home care service providers (Avril 2006), just like it obscured the relational dimension of 'masculine' occupations such as bus (Schwartz 2011) and tourist coach drivers, labourers promoted to supervisory positions (as Séverine Misset highlights for Philippe Chapalain in this volume), and security guards and caretakers, just to name a few of our interviewees' occupations. For more on this, see Benelli, Le Feuvre, and Rey (2012).

5 On the stakes of getting recognition for gendered aspects of strenuousness at work and the porosity of private and professional spheres, see Avril and Marichalar (2016).

6 See 'A business that works: Breaking away from the family model, relying on family help' by Violaine Girard and Maulde Urbain-Mathis.

7 See '"I've had two lives": Self-improvement work and the infiltration of psychological culture into working-class worlds' by Séverine Misset.

8 See 'Keeping the conjugal peace: A compensatory domestic equality' by Olivier Masclet.

9 Developing this example lets us stress the similarity of two processes: the one that is the focus of this book (providing an account of basic employees' and labourers' aspiration to 'be like everyone else') and the transformation of the condition of farmers since the 1960s. With the building of the European Union and the French planned economy, 'modernisation' policy consigned 'old peasants' to the past (Champagne 1979) and encountered the aspirations of younger generations who 'went to the city' (like the Monteils) or who fought to speed up farm transmission. To describe this process to which they were witness, some sociologists use the term 'parity', as Rose-Marie Lagrave shows in her tribute to Placide Rambaud, 'Filiations intellectuelles et espérance sociale'. Rambaud was part of the rural sociology wave of the 1960s–1980s, son of mountain farmers and a former priest with the Mission de France. His work was always guided 'by his disposition to rehabilitate farmers, give them a central role in the production of societies' and give 'credit to public authorities who, through the dispositions of laws for orienting agriculture in the 1960s, intended to guarantee parity between farmers and other social classes. [...] He did not see the equal integration of farmers into French society, which nonetheless presupposed excluded and favoured members, as the planned disappearance of the small peasantry, but, on the contrary, as a sign of the end of "the agricultural exception"' (Lagrave 2009, 56, 58).

10 Vanessa Stettinger analysed the same households and found that mothers spent much more time taking care of children than fathers (2018).

11 On 'State feminism' see the work of Anne Revillard (2016).

12 See 'Being a mother and unemployed: Resisting being stuck at home' by Angel Baraud.

13 This is a widely addressed issue, and our discussion relies particularly on work by Skeggs (1997), Clair (2011), Pochic (2014), Jacquemart, Albenga, and Bereni (2015), Pouly (2015), Amossé and Cartier (2018), Cartier, Letrait, and Sorin (2018), Thin (2018), as well as the introduction to this second section of this book.

14 We cannot expand on it here, but we join several other publications in calling for a more systematic comparison of the two studied populations focusing on the role played by the position in the life cycle and locally available possibilities – the training and employment market for men and women, the childcare supply, the leisure activities on offer, interactions between social groups, and how they shape experiences of the social world (Mischi and Renahy 2008, Lemêtre and Orange 2016, Beaud and Mauger 2017, Bruneau et al. 2018).

15 This is a reference to the title of a special issue of *Politix*, 'En bas à droite' (Beaumont, Challier, and Lejeune 2018).

16 In an analysis based on the same group of households, Tristan Poullaouec has emphasised the 'educational voluntarism' (2019).

17 Olivier Schwartz demonstrates this, based on the same households (2018).

18 That being said, with the steep decline in the number of full-time housewives, men's responsibility for household accounting no longer follows the ritual once standard to certain families of the petite and moyenne bourgeoisie through the 1970s, wherein the 'head of the household' verified every expenditure using receipts presented to him by his wife. Work in history, sociology, and literature describe conjugal relations under the sway of the 'head of the household', notably Christophe Granger (2003) on family vacations in the 1950–1975, and Annie Ernaux's *A Frozen Woman* ([1981] 1995), which gives an accurate portrayal of one model of gender relations in the upper classes through the example of her in-laws: 'A charming couple. The man of the house […] a constant flow of witty remarks and spoonerisms of all kinds as his indulgent wife looks on, beaming. But watch out, no fool he, behind all the jests there's authority in his voice and eye, in the way he calls for the menu in restaurants, makes pronouncements on the subject of wine or the tactics of bridge. Always perky, his lady wife, never still for a moment, she drags me away, let's leave the men to their talking, we'll go fix the dinner, no no no son, we'll take care of everything, you'd just be in the way! […] "Coffee!" bellows the lord and master. "Coming, coming!" chirps his bustling spouse. "Oh, don't pay any attention, pet, it's a game they play, he hollers and she jumps, but they adore each other"' (142–144). It is a family model that the son ends up reproducing, minus the authoritative tone, when he goes into management after university. Ernaux writes, 'A [child's] life completely and absolutely in my care. I have the burden, but not the responsibility! I'm raising kiddo alone, but under supervision. What did the doctor say, his nails are too long, you should cut them, what's that on his knee, did he fall, where were you? Accounts to render, constantly, but the tone is normal, soft-spoken, not tyrannical. In the evening, when he picks up a beaming Kiddo – washed, fed, and freshly diapered for the night – it's as though I've lived the entire day for these ten minutes: the presentation of the child to his father' (169–170).

19 As Olivier Masclet emphasises in his analysis of 'time for oneself' among the same interviewees (2018).

20 'Because he is committed to strategies extending over several generations, he is the man of the deferred pleasure, the deferred present that will be taken later, "when there is time", "when we've paid off the mortgage", "when the children are older" of "when we've retired", in other words, very often when it is too late, when, having given credit on his life, he has no time to collect his "due" and must "cut his coat according to his cloth." There is no compensation for a lost present' (Bourdieu 1984, 353).

21 See 'Getting back to a "normal life": Biographical disruptions and "institutional goodwill"' by Vanessa Stettinger.

22 It is difficult to situate households in the 'bottom right' of the social space (Beaumont, Challier, and Lejeune 2018), perhaps because the research focused on couples, not individuals, in an effort to understand their practices both public (work, community engagements, how they relate to politics and institutions) and private (domestic economy, health, individual sports). It is difficult to decide whether a household in the 'lower' levels of the social space is oriented more toward the economic or more toward culture – thus situating it politically – and the main forms of goodwill are professional, educational, and health-related. Somewhat like Gérard Mauger (1991) did with the young working-class men, distinguishing the specific axis of 'gangs' of mates alongside the 'working-class bohemian' axis (culturally leaning) and the 'middle' axis (economically inclined), there is a need to pursue the analysis of resources and forms of wellbeing that, if they are not particular to the working classes, are at least more frequent among them. Finally, one notes that the people featured in this book manifest a 'triangular social consciousness' (Collovald and Schwartz 2006) whereas the working-class activists for the political right studied by Raphaël Challier demonstrated 'subjective proximity to the upper classes' and a 'legitimist social consciousness' (Challier 2018, 122). For more on these issues, see Collovald (2004) and Mauger and Pelletier (2016).

23 This economic goodwill is based on ascetic dispositions and 'consumption work' (Amossé and Cartier 2019). Several of the studied households devote notable time to interior decoration (see the portraits of Laurent Douillard and Thomas Guillet, Laeticia Kergal and Valentin Dufour, Marianne and Philippe Chapalain), so it is no longer solely an interest of women in the petite and moyenne bourgeoisie, as it was in *Distinction* (Bourdieu 1984).

24 We drew on the work of Catherine Bouve and Catherine Sellenet (2011) for this outline of the history of the occupation of childminder.

25 This has been analysed among the same group of interviewees by Anne-Marie Arborio and Marie-Hélène Lechien (2019).

26 See 'Holding on: Sparing no effort to stabilise an unstable position' by Marie-Hélène Lechien and Marie-Pierre Pouly.

27 See Arborio and Lechien (2019). The notion of 'reform from the inside' was developed to describe one of the ways in which interviewees relate to their social condition. It is inspired by the work of Yasmine Siblot (2018), which reveals another way. Using the notion of a 'mobilised relationship to one's condition', she shows how unionised hospital laundry workers, all immigrants or from French overseas departments, work to 'defend the values of female labourers while staying in [their] place', far from aspirations to the cultural middle-class lifestyle. In his research on union engagement in a railway repair shop located in a rural region with a significant labouring population, Julian Mischi has shown that unionised workers in the shop have tense relations with fellow union members who are teachers or social workers, who they meet at local and department-level union assemblies. Although unionised railway labourers do acquire activist cultural capital, they do not necessarily manifest other cultural aspirations and they find union members from the cultural petite bourgeoisie too 'intellectual' and 'individualistic' (Mischi 2013).

28 This adjustment to legitimate norms is more than a mere response to injunctions from the upper reaches of the social space. The rejection of corporal punishment, for example, can also be explained by the harshness of quick-handed parents that interviewees did not want to reproduce when they became parents. Softer child-rearing norms may lend legitimacy and clout to these child-rearing principles, asserted in interviews, that emerged in reaction to experience.

29 On the first point, Éric Dufar (formerly a labourer doing temporary work, now library caretaker) has alternated his vote between the Front National and the Socialist Party list in his town. He stands up for the 'services rendered' by poorly remunerated occupations that harm the health of those practicing them: 'The plumber who works all day twisting his pipes and all, he renders a service to people; when they take a shower, they're happy to have water. They're people who do something for other people, people can do their shopping. [...] Them who've got the butcher shop there, they're in the cold all day long, always bending over to pick up hams and stuff... There's one of them, her back's a right mess [...] she's 50 years old, she's got arthritis all over, her work's done her in. [...] They're occupations that should pay a lot better than that. It's not right!' The second point has been argued by Séverine Misset and Yasmine Siblot based on the same group of households (2019).

30 Once again, the example of childminder attests to this. Some conform to exterior prescriptions – child-rearing norms they may think arbitrary or ridiculous but that reassure parents and early childhood development educators – and some manifest a 'desire to learn' and 'improve' by using the internet (Havard Duclos 2018, 48–49). Furthermore, these scenarios are not mutually exclusive; a childminder may go from one to the other over her career, or may manifest both at the same time concerning prescriptions on different topics.

31 This is increasingly true as early as nursery school (Millet and Croizet 2016).

References

Amossé, Thomas, and Marie Cartier, eds. 2018. 'Ménages populaires.' Special issue, *Travail, genre et sociétés* 39.

Amossé, Thomas, and Marie Cartier. 2019. '"*Si je travaille, c'est pas pour acheter du premier prix.*" Modes de consommation des classes populaires depuis leurs ménages stabilisés.' *Sociétés contemporaines* 114, no. 2: 89–122.

Arborio, Anne-Marie. (2001) 2012. *Un Personnel invisible. Les aides-soignantes à l'hôpital.* Paris: Economica.

Arborio, Anne-Marie, and Marie-Hélène Lechien. 2019. 'Que font les usages "psy" aux classes populaires?' Paper presented at the seminar 'Une société d'individus, c'est-à-dire?,' CERLIS, 16–18 January.

Avril, Christelle. 2006. 'Le travail des aides à domicile pour personnes âgées : contraintes et savoir-faire.' *Le Mouvement Social* 216: 87–99.

Avril, Christelle. 2014. *Les Aides à domicile : un autre monde populaire.* Paris: La Dispute.

Avril, Christelle, and Pascal Marichalar. 2016. 'Quand la pénibilité du travail s'invite à la maison. Perspectives féministes en santé au travail.' *Travail et emploi* 147, no. 3: 5–26.

Beaud, Stéphane, and Gérard Mauger. 2017. *Une Génération sacrifiée? Jeunes des classes populaires dans la France désindustrialisée.* Paris: Rue d'Ulm.

Beaumont, Amélie, Raphaël Challier, and Guillaume Lejeune. 2018. 'En bas à droite. Travail, visions du monde et prises de position politiques dans le quart en bas à droite de l'espace social.' *Politix* 122: 9–31.

Benelli, Nathalie, Nicky Le Feuvre, and Séverine Rey, eds. 2012. 'Métiers de service.' Special issue, *Nouvelles questions féministes* 31, no. 2.

Bourdieu, Pierre. (1979) 1984. *Distinction: A Social Critique of the Judgment of Taste.* Translated by Richard Nice. Cambridge, MA: Harvard University Press.

Bouve, Catherine, and Catherine Sellenet. 2011. *Confier son enfant. L'univers des assistantes maternelles.* Paris: Editions Autrement.

Bozon, Michel. 2009. 'Comment le travail empiète et la famille déborde : différences sociales dans l'arrangement des sexes.' In *Entre famille et travail. Des arrangements de couple aux pratiques des employeurs,* edited by Ariane Pailhé, 29–54. Paris: La Découverte.

Bruneau, Ivan, Gilles Laferté, Julian Mischi, and Nicolas Renahy, eds. 2018. *Mondes ruraux et classes sociales.* Paris: Editions EHESS.

Cartier, Marie, Muriel Letrait, and Matéo Sorin. 2018. 'Travail domestique : des classes populaires conservatrices?' *Travail, genre et sociétés* 39: 63–81.

Castel, Robert, and Jean-François Le Cerf. 1980. 'Le phénomène "psy" et la société française. Vers une nouvelle culture psychologique.' *Le Débat* 1: 32–45.

Challier, Raphaël. 2018. 'S'engager "du côté des gens bien." La conscience sociale légitimiste des soutiens populaires de l'UMP en banlieue parisienne.' *Politix* 122: 33–56.

Champagne, Patrick. 1979. 'Jeunes agriculteurs et vieux paysans. Crise de la succession et apparition du "troisième âge".' *Actes de la recherche en sciences sociales* 26–27: 83–107.

Clair, Isabelle. 2011. 'La découverte de l'ennui conjugal. Les manifestations contrariées de l'idéal conjugal et de l'ethos égalitaire dans la vie quotidienne de jeunes de milieux populaires.' *Sociétés contemporaines* 83: 59–81.

Collovald, Annie. 2004. *Le 'Populisme du FN,' un dangereux contresens.* Paris: Le Croquant.

Collovald, Annie, and Olivier Schwartz. 2006. 'Haut, bas, fragile : sociologies du populaire.' *Vacarme* 37: 50–55.

Coquard, Benoît. 2019. *Ceux qui restent. Faire sa vie dans les campagnes en déclin.* Paris: La Découverte.

Ernaux, Annie. (1981) 1995. *A Frozen Woman.* Translated by Linda Coverdale. London, New York: Four Walls Eight Windows.

Garcia, Sandrine. 2011. *Mères sous influence. De la cause des femmes à la cause des enfants.* Paris: La Découverte.

Garcia, Sandrine. 2018. *Le Goût de l'effort. La construction familiale des dispositions scolaires.* Paris: Presses Universitaires de France.

Gasquet, Béatrice de. 2015. 'Que fait le féminisme au regard de l'ethnographe? La réflexivité sur le genre comme connaissance située.' *SociologieS* (online). http://journals.openedition.org/sociologies/5081

Gojard, Séverine. 2010. *Le Métier de mère.* Paris: La Dispute.

Granger, Christophe. 2003. 'Le genre prend-il des vacances? Visions et divisions sexuelles face aux mutations du temps libre (1950–1975).' In *Le genre face aux mutations. Masculin et féminin du Moyen Âge à nos jours,* edited by Luc Capdevila, Sophie Cassagnes, Martine Cocaud, Dominique Godineau, François Rouquert, and Jaqueline Sainclivier, 361–370. Rennes: Presses Universitaires de Rennes.

Havard Duclos, Bénédicte. 2018. 'L'Internet des assistantes maternelles: Un outil pour faire vivre le métier.' *Réseaux* 208–209: 28–61.

Hoggart, Richard. 1957. *The Uses of Literacy: Aspects of Working Class Life.* London: Chatto and Windus.

Jacquemart, Alban, Viviane Albenga, and Laure Bereni, eds. 2015. 'Appropriations ordinaires des idées féministes.' Special issue, *Politix* 109.

Lagrave, Rose-Marie. 2009. 'Filiations intellectuelles et espérance sociale. Figure et œuvre de Placide Rambaud.' *Etudes rurales* 183: 51–66.

Lemêtre, Claire, and Sophie Orange, eds. 2016. 'Jeunesses rurales – jeunesses ordinaires.' *Savoir/Agir* 37: 9–13.

Martin, Claude, ed. 2014. *'Être un bon parent.' Une injonction contemporaine.* Rennes: Presses de l'EHESP.

Masclet, Olivier. 2018. '"C'est mon moment". Le temps pour soi des ouvrières et des employées.' *Travail, genre et sociétés* 39: 101–119.
Mauger, Gérard. 1991. 'Enquêter en milieu populaire.' *Genèses* 6: 125–143.
Mauger, Gérard, and Willy Pelletier, eds. 2016. *Les Classes populaires et le FN.* Vullaines sur Seine: Edition du Croquant.
Mauger, Gérard, and Claude Poliak. 1998. 'Les usages sociaux de la lecture.' *Actes de la recherche en sciences sociales* 128: 3–24.
Millet, Mathias, and Jean-Claude Croizet. 2016. *L'École des incapables? La maternelle, un apprentissage de la domination.* Paris: La Dispute.
Mischi, Julian. 2013. 'Savoirs militants et rapports aux intellectuels dans un syndicat cheminot.' *Actes de la recherche en sciences sociales* 196–197: 132–151.
Mischi, Julian, and Nicolas Renahy. 2008. 'Pour une sociologie politique des mondes ruraux.' *Politix* 83: 9–21.
Misset, Séverine, and Yasmine Siblot. 2019. '"Donner de son temps" pour ne pas être des "assistés." Bénévolat associatif et rapports à la politique au sein de ménages stables des classes populaires.' *Sociologie* 10, no. 1: 73–89.
Montmasson-Michel, Fabienne. 2018. 'Enfances du langage et langages de l'enfance. Socialisation plurielle et différenciation sociale de la petite enfance scolarisée.' PhD dissertation, Université de Poitiers.
Pochic, Sophie. 2014. 'Femmes responsables syndicales en Angleterre et identification féministe : neutraliser leur genre pour mieux représenter leur classe?' *Sociologie* 5, no. 4: 369–386.
Poullaouec, Tristan. 2019. 'Regrets d'école. Le report des aspirations scolaires dans les familles populaires.' *Sociétés contemporaines* 114: 123–150.
Pouly, Marie-Pierre. 2015. 'Domination culturelle et respectabilité,' afterword to *Des femmes respectables. Classe et genre en milieu populaire*, by Beverly Skeggs, 359–389. Translated by Marie-Pierre Pouly. Paris: Agone.
Revillard, Anne. 2016. *La Cause des femmes dans l'État. Une comparaison France-Québec.* Grenoble: Presses Universitaires de Grenoble.
Schwartz, Olivier. 1990. *Le Monde privé des ouvriers. Hommes et femmes du Nord.* Paris: Presses Universitaires de France.
Schwartz, Olivier. 2011. 'La pénétration de la "culture psychologique de masse" dans un groupe populaire : paroles de conducteurs de bus.' *Sociologie* 2, no. 4: 345–361.
Schwartz, Olivier. 2018. 'Les femmes dans les classes populaires, entre permanence et rupture.' *Travail, genre et sociétés* 39: 121–138.
Siblot, Yasmine. 2018. 'Entretenir un rapport mobilisé à sa condition sociale en milieu populaire. Engagement syndical et sociabilité parmi des ouvrières de blanchisserie.' *Sociétés contemporaines* 109: 65–92.
Skeggs, Beverley. 1997. *Formations of Class & Gender: Becoming Respectable.* Thousand Oaks, CA: Sage.
Spire, Alexis. 2018. *Résistances à l'impôt, attachement à l'Etat. Enquête sur les contribuables français.* Paris: Seuil.
Stettinger, Vanessa. 2018. 'Mère "je fais tout". Des pratiques éducatives populaires en tension.' *Travail, genre et sociétés* 39: 83–99.
Thin, Daniel. 2018. '"Les plus hauts ils aiment bien que le peuple… reste aveugle". Groupes de femmes de quartiers populaires et socialisation politique.' *Sociétés contemporaines* 112: 23–44.
Verret, Michel. 1979. *L'Espace ouvrier.* Paris: Armand Colin.

APPENDIX A
SOCIO-PROFESSIONAL CATEGORIES

The French statistical institute INSEE (Institut National de la Statistique et des Etudes Economiques; National Institute of Statistics and Economic Studies) uses a socioeconomic classification nomenclature called the PCS (Professions et Catégories Socioprofessionnelles; Professions and Socio-professional Categories). It consists of eight major employment categories, which we have translated as follows:

1 *Agriculteur exploitant*: Farm operator.
2 *Artisan, Commerçant, chef d'entreprise*: Tradesperson, shopkeeper, company head.
3 *Cadre, profession intellectuelle supérieure*: *Cadre*, higher intellectual profession.
4 *Profession intermédiaire*: Intermediary profession.
5 *Employé*: Basic employee.
6 *Ouvrier*: Labourer.
7 *Retraité*: Retired.
8 *Autre sans activité professionelle*: Other without paid employment.

Four of these categories are mentioned frequently in this book and do not correspond perfectly to categories used in other countries, so an explanation is warranted. For a detailed description of the categories and their history, see the definitive reference on the topic, *Les Catégories Socio-professionelles* (Desrosières and Thévenot 2002).

***Cadre* and higher intellectual profession**: This category clusters different kinds of work that generally have high educational prerequisites and remuneration. There is no simple translation for *cadre*; following the choice made in the translation of the definitive work on the subject *The Making of a Class: Cadres in French Society* (Boltanski 1987), we have thus chosen to keep it in French and describe its meaning. *Cadres* are employees that have specialised skillsets and positions of administrative, decision-making, and/or managerial responsibility (without being at the top) in businesses, banks, organisations, and the civil service, and they enjoy the benefits and security that come with such positions. 'Higher intellectual professions' include scientists, professors, journalists, artists, librarians, and engineers as well as occupations in the professions (including doctors, dentists, solicitors, and architects), most of whom are self-employed.

Intermediate profession: A category defined more by its neighbours than by its own merits, people in 'intermediary professions' are neither *cadres* with significant responsibilities nor executant workers performing routine tasks. They include foremen and supervisors, skilled technicians, skilled specialised office workers, schoolteachers, social workers, and nurses.

Basic employee: INSEE's website admits that this category is 'quite varied and often poorly defined'. Its occupations are executant jobs (doing what one is told rather than having responsibilities), for the most part requiring few to no formal educational prerequisites. They are generally low-level 'white-collar' or 'pink-collar' jobs, although the blurring boundary with 'labourer' occupations means there are many more manual exceptions. The classic 'basic employee' occupations were secretaries and office clerks, and now they include salespeople, business administrative workers, hospital workers, firefighters, police officers, military, low-level civil servants, and a whole array of domestic and care workers. Three out of four 'basic employees' are women, and younger workers are overrepresented.

Labourer: A category whose definition is rooted in the post-World War II collective 'Parodi' conventions, it was originally conceived as 'blue collar' manual industrial workers but has gradually broadened to include occupations that could almost be 'basic employee' jobs. Today's 'labourers' are predominantly male, and in addition to factories, they work in small businesses in the trades, construction, and the food industry, as maintenance and cleaning workers, as farm labour, drivers, and cooks.

References

Boltanski, Luc. (1982) 1987. *The Making of a Class: Cadres in French Society.* Translated by Arthur Goldhammer. Cambridge, UK: Cambridge University Press.

Desrosières, Alain, and Laurent Thévenot. 2002. *Les Catégories Socio-professionelles.* Paris: La Découverte.

APPENDIX B

EQUIVALENCY CHART OF THE PRIMARY AND SECONDARY EDUCATIONAL SYSTEMS IN FRANCE, THE UK, AND THE US

France		*(avg age)*	*US*	*UK*
Lycée			**High school**	
(a.k.a. *second cycle*)	*Classe Terminale*	17–18	12th grade	*(Post-secondary)*
	Première	16–17	11th grade	Sixth form (A-levels)
Lycées are specialised according to category of bac	*Seconde*	15–16	10th grade	Sixth form (A-levels)
Collège			**Middle school**[b]	
(a.k.a. *premier cycle*)	*3ème*[a]	14–15	9th grade	Year 10
	4ème	13–14	8th grade	Year 9
	5ème	12–13	7th grade	Year 8
			Elementary school	
	6ème	11–12	6th grade	Year 7
École primaire				**Primary school**
	CM2	10–11	5th grade	Year 6
	CM1 (Cours Moyen)	9–10	4th grade	Year 5
	CE2	8–9	3rd grade	Year 4
	CE1 (Cours Elémentaire)	7–8	2nd grade	Year 3
	CP (Cours Préparatoire)	6–7	1st grade	Year 2

(*Continued*)

France	*(avg age)*	*US*	*UK*
Maternelle	3–6	Kindergarten (age 5) Nursery school/ Preschool (age 3–5)	Year 1 (age 5) Reception (age 4) Nursery (age 3)

[a]*In 3ème, students are oriented towards the academic or vocational track that will determine their future educational and career possibilities.*

[b]*This breakdown varies between school districts in the United States, where sixth grade and/or ninth grade may be included in middle school or may be put into high school (9th grade) or elementary school (6th).*

APPENDIX C

EDUCATIONAL QUALIFICATIONS

The French school system begins tracking children in early secondary school, based on whether teachers and guidance staff think they are more suited to manual or intellectual work. There is a vast array of certificates and degrees awarded for each level of each track of education, vocational or academic. These qualifications have changed over time. For one thing, the system has been modified – for example, the old primary school certificate has vanished as secondary education has become compulsory, and reconfigurations of the educational system have led to changes in the names of equivalent degrees and the disappearance of others. Just as importantly, however, is the fact that there has been considerable effort invested in prolonging the education of as many young French people as possible, resulting in a rapid rate of degree inflation. This has significant repercussions for sociological comparisons of people's educational capitals across generations, since the very low (by today's standards) diploma held by a retired person may have been rather advanced when he or she was starting his or her career.

Primary school

CEP: certificat d'études primaires (Primary studies certificate): Last awarded in 1989, the CEP was a certificate marking the end of primary school. Not every child went that far, so possessing one was already a sign of a modest accomplishment, especially in the working classes.

Secondary school

***Collège*-level (lower secondary school):**

Brevet des collèges (Middle-school certificate): Diploma awarded upon successful completion of *collège*, the early part of secondary school.

At the end of collège*, children are oriented to more specialised tracks and institutions: 'General', 'Technical', or 'Vocational'* lycées *preparing them for a* baccalauréat *(or a lower-level degree in Technical and Vocational* lycées*) or trade schools for lower-level qualifications.*

***Lycée*-level (higher secondary school), called level 3:**

Vocational track:

CAP: Certificat d'aptitude Professionnelle (Professional aptitude certificate): A diploma for mastery of a particular vocational skillset. It can be earned by examination or validation of on-the-job experience, based on classroom or apprenticeship learning or a combination thereof.

BEP: brevet d'études professionnelles (Professional Studies Certificate): From 1967 to 2009, the BEP was a prerequisite diploma for taking a 2-year programme preparing to sit for a vocational *baccalauréat* exam. Since then, it is earned while studying for a vocational *baccalauréat.*

Academic track: None before the *baccalauréat.*

Diplomas concluding secondary studies (level 4):

Brevet Professionel: A vocational qualification obtained through work-study or as a continuing education programme for people already practising an occupation.

The *baccalauréat* (commonly called 'the *bac*'): This competitive nationwide examination caps the end of secondary education. It was once quite rare, but there has been a strong push since the late 1960s to bring a strong majority of young people that far. Formerly largely reserved for elites continuing on to university, the *baccalauréat* system has now been broken out into three main categories and numerous sub-categories of '*bac*' preparing young people for different career types.

The 'General' *baccalauréat*: Academic track, leading to university. Its sub-specialisations are Literary, Economic and Social, and Scientific.

The 'Technological' *baccalauréat* ('*bac technologique*'): Prepares for shorter post-secondary studies or university in technical fields. Specialisations include Industrial Sciences and Technologies, Design, Laboratory Sciences, Health and Social Work, Agronomy, Management, Performing arts, and Hospitality.

The 'Vocational' *baccalauréat* (nicknamed the '*bac pro*'): Since 1985, there has been a series of *baccalauréat* exams for manual occupations.

It follows a BEP or CAP and is not intended to lead to further post-secondary studies. There are currently 128 specialised vocational *bacs*, ranging from home care work to airplane mechanics, masonry to logistics.

Post-Secondary degrees (only degrees mentioned in this book are discussed)

Diplôme Universitaire (DU):

A university degree offered by a specific university to train people for a particular field in response to local employment needs; they thus tend to be more vocational than academically oriented. While other university degrees are granted under the authority of the national ministry of education, DUs are under the authority of the specific university where they are offered.

Vocational:

BTS: Brevet de Technicien Supérieur (Higher Technician Certificate): Since 1959, a state-recognised degree earned by examination following a two-year programme for students already possessing a *baccalauréat.*

Academic:

DEUG (Diplôme d'Etudes Universitaires Générales): A two-year university degree, now largely obsolete, intended to provide a general education in one of six thematic fields.

Licence: A three-year entry-level state-recognised university degree, equivalent to a bachelor's degree in the US.

***Master* (1, 2)**: Master's degrees are broken into two one-year parts, 1 and 2. The prerequisite is a *licence*. It is to allow students to deepen and specialise their knowledge.

INDEX

Note: **Bold** page numbers refer to tables; *italic* page numbers refer to figures and page numbers followed by "n" denote endnotes.

For Product Safety Concerns and Information please contact our EU representative GPSR@taylorandfrancis.com
Taylor & Francis Verlag GmbH, Kaufingerstraße 24, 80331 München, Germany

www.ingramcontent.com/pod-product-compliance
Ingram Content Group UK Ltd.
Pitfield, Milton Keynes, MK11 3LW, UK
UKHW020132200926
475702UK00005B/711
* 9 7 8 1 0 3 2 3 6 0 5 6 0 *